Richard

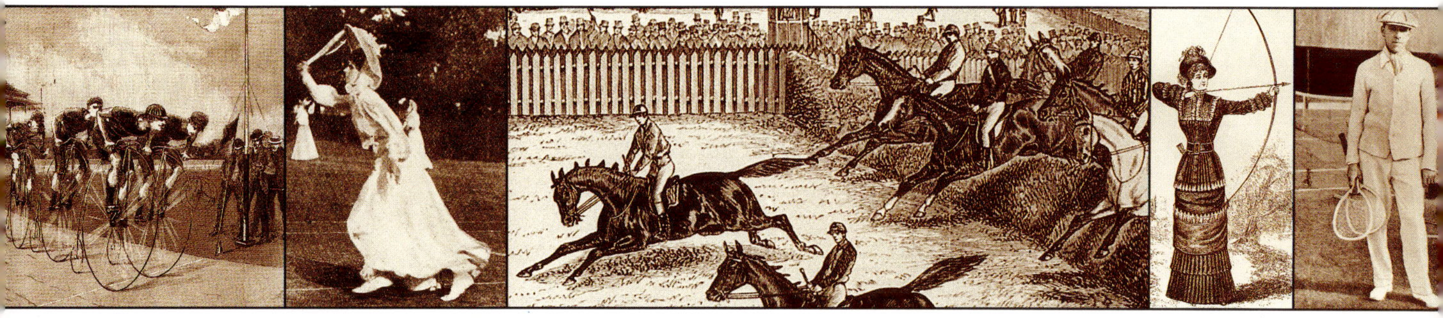

BLOOD SWEAT & TEARS

AUSTRALIANS AND SPORT

BLOOD SWEAT & TEARS

AUSTRALIANS AND SPORT

Neil Cadigan Don Hogg
Brian Mossop Venetia Nelson
Richard Sleeman Jim Webster
Phil Wilkins

LOTHIAN PUBLISHING COMPANY PTY LTD
Melbourne · Sydney · Auckland

A Lothian Book
Lothian Publishing Company Pty Ltd
11 Munro Street, Port Melbourne, Victoria 3207

Copyright © State Bank Victoria 1989
First published 1989

National Library of Australia
Cataloguing-in-Publication data:

Blood, sweat and tears: Australians and sport

   Includes index.
   ISBN 0 85091 313 6.

   1. Sports — Australia — History.
   I. Cadigan, Neil.

796'.0994

Design Tom Kurema
Jacket design David Constable
Typeset in Cheltenham light by Bookset Pty Ltd
Production by Island Graphics
Printed in Australia by Impact Printing

Contents

Acknowledgements		ix
CHAPTER 1	Obsession, *Brian Mossop*	1
CHAPTER 2	Blood and Guts, *Phil Wilkins*	24
CHAPTER 3	Punters and Wowsers, *Venetia Nelson*	56
CHAPTER 4	Silvertails and Yobbos, *Don Hogg*	85
CHAPTER 5	Kill the Bastards, *Neil Cadigan*	104
CHAPTER 6	Black Diamonds, *Neil Cadigan*	131
CHAPTER 7	Beauty and the Beast, *Jim Webster*	157
CHAPTER 8	Image Makers, *Richard Sleeman*	179
CHAPTER 9	Bought Sport, *Richard Sleeman*	200
CHAPTER 10	Winners and Losers, *Brian Mossop*	224
CHAPTER 11	You've Got to Have Heart, *Don Hogg*	244
CHAPTER 12	Political Football, *Brian Mossop*	266
CHAPTER 13	Wearing the Green and Gold, *Jim Webster*	291
Index		320

Acknowledgements

The concept for the television series 'Blood, Sweat and Tears, Australians and Sport' and this book was developed by Frank Seres of Frank Seres Productions Pty Ltd. To him go the authors' and publishers' thanks and their grateful acknowledgement of his contribution. Thanks are also due to him for material from the television series used in this book.

Our thanks, too, are due to the many people who were interviewed for the series: Geoff Ashton, Ron Barassi, John Bay, John Bertrand, Bob Bottom, Rocky Bradley, John Brown, Ron Casey, Dr Richard Cashman, Graham Cassidy, Evonne Cawley, Ian Chappell, Phil Coles, Jim Collins, Margaret Court, Lorraine Crapp, Keith Dunstan, Mark Ella, the Ella family, Herb Elliott, Chris Evert-Lloyd, Peter Falconer, Bruce Fletcher, Dawn Fraser, Carole Grahame, Tony Greig, Graham Hannan, Ian Hanson, Roy Higgins, Sinclair Hill, Lew Hoad, Marjorie Jackson, John Landy, Rod Laver, Heather McKay, Alan McGilvray, Louise MacKinley, Ian Meckiff, Bill Moyes, Fred Nile, Bill O'Reilly, Bill Palmer, Neville Penton, Charles Perkins, John Quayle, Johnny Raper, Des Renford, Lou Richards, Ken Rosewall, Bob Rowland-Smith, Anne Sargeant, Richard Sibthorpe, Dr Brian Stoddart, Professor Colin Tatz, Jeff Thomson, Tracey Wickham, Richard Winten and Jack Woodward. Their particular contributions are acknowledged with each chapter.

The authors and publishers also acknowledge and thank the following for their help in reviewing the draft chapters for historical accuracy, interpretation and appropriateness of source material: Dr Richard Cashman of the History Department in the University of New South Wales, Dr John O'Hara of the History Department in the Macarthur Institute of Higher Education, Dr Brian Stoddart of the Department of Sports Studies in the Canberra College of Advanced Education, Professor Colin Tatz of the Department of History, Philosophy and Politics in Macquarie University, and Dr Wray Vamplew of the School of Social Science in Flinders University.

For help with picture research we thank the staff of the Mitchell Library, State Library of New South Wales, for their skilled and always pleasant assistance, Vedat Acikalin of Live Action, Neil Cadigan, Debbie Cramer, the always helpful Don Richards and Daryl Richardson of the Herald and Weekly Times, Simon Townley, and staff of John Fairfax & Sons Ltd, News Limited, the Battye Library in Western Australia and the National Library of Australia. All photographs from the television series 'Blood, Sweat and Tears' are by courtesy of photographer Paul Tatz. It is not possible to list everyone who contributed photographs and information at very short notice, but we record our thanks. Sources for all the photographs are included with the captions.

Every effort has been made to trace copyright holders of historical material, and the publishers would be grateful to have any information about these illustrations.

Our thanks also go to Venetia Nelson who edited the book, as well as contributing a chapter, and to John Ross for writing the captions.

CHAPTER 1

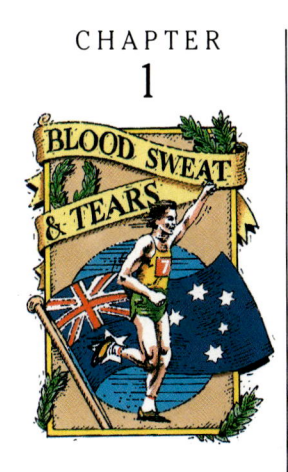

OBSESSION
Brian Mossop

The Pan-Am jet touched down at Sydney's Kingsford-Smith Airport and the American pilot, no doubt confident of *Liberty*'s ability — she did, after all, hold a good lead over *Australia II* rounding the fourth mark — switched the race commentary through to the passengers on the 747's public address system. Twenty minutes later only a trickle of passengers had left their seats. The response to the pilot's request to quit the aircraft was reluctant at best.

The terminal was packed with early morning arrivals, but rarely had it hosted so many with thoughts focused as singlemindedly — on the *America*'s Cup and its outcome. At least one of the arriving passengers had a radio, and when the cheer nearly raised the roof of the immigration and customs hall, everyone knew which of the 12-metre yachts had crossed the line first. *Australia II* had done the impossible, coming from 1–3 down in the best of seven series to break a 132-year domination of the event by the United States.

No one working in the terminal building on that September morning in 1983 had heard the like of the roar accompanying *Australia II*'s win. Outside, all over Sydney and throughout Australia, car horns blew, people waved from their windows, strangers smiled at each other. For the moment, indeed for a while after the gun signalled victory, Australians were arguably the most united race on earth — exuberant, ecstatic, basking. The sense of national pride was at the same time wonderful and almost overwhelming.

There was a certain irony in it all. To most Australians 12-metre yacht racing was a silvertail pastime available only to the very rich and far removed from everyday sporting pursuits like running, football and cricket. What everyone was so keyed up about was winning. The *America*'s Cup itself was far less important than the fact that a team of Australians had wrested from a dominant nation a trophy which had seemed inviolate.

While sport may appear to have been the obsession, winning was: the winning of anything in the name of Australia. There are those who feel it is a sign of our immaturity as a nation that we take such great pride in the achievements of our sportsmen and women. But it is more likely that our obsession with winning manifests itself more keenly in sport because it is a pursuit with which all of us can identify. We may have the best brass band in the world, the finest harpists, the most astute bridge players — but they don't capture the collective imagination. Sporting figures do, winning sporting figures especially so.

Blood, Sweat and Tears

Australians are imbued with a mania for sport; in Melbourne particularly, the feeling for Australian Rules football is almost tangible. Even the summer months see vast columns of newspaper space devoted to the off-season movement of players between clubs, to new signings, to the likelihood of a certain player's availability for the early matches following an operation, to the analysis of the season past and to the prognostications for the season ahead. Not even cricket, which evokes interest in the most remote corners of the country, can sustain as much out-of-season comment as its winter companion. Not unless Australia happens to be involved in an Ashes tour.

Australia's greatest moment in yachting: Australia II wins a tacking duel to lead on the last leg of the deciding heat in the America's Cup
Roger Gould

Melbourne has long been considered the Australian sporting Mecca, the one city capable of drawing a crowd no matter what the event. It is also Melbourne which boasts probably the major sporting cathedral in Australia — the Melbourne Cricket Ground. There is much tradition at the Sydney Cricket Ground, but the MCG assumed added importance in our sporting credo after the 1956 Olympic Games. There is a mystique about an Olympic venue. As Australia has no Twickenham, no Yankee Stadium, no Lord's — devoted as they are to specific sports — the MCG has assumed an aura all its own.

Melbourne has also assumed the role of headquarters for Australian tennis. There was a time when the Australian championships were played at different venues each year. That changed soon after the advent of Open tennis in 1968. White City, in Sydney, was a world famous venue — as was Kooyong in Melbourne. A Davis Cup record crowd of 25 578 — a record which still stands — packed White City for the Challenge Round against the United States in 1954, but by the early 1970s Kooyong had become the permanent site for the Australian Open. The Open switched in 1988 from the grass of Kooyong to the synthetic surface of a grand new National Tennis Centre in Melbourne at Flinders Park — a name which in time will become as well known as Wimbledon in England, Stade Roland Garros in Paris and Flushing Meadow in New York.

If the Australian penchant for sport is all-embracing, the obsession — and it is undeniably present — has to be seen in its proper context. We are obsessed in the broadest sense, but can be grouped as devotees, fanatics, zealots and, in some cases, even worshippers at a religious altar called sport. We also have a collective pride in the success of both sporting individuals and teams which sets us apart, if not from every other nation, at least from a good many. Nations use sport for different reasons: ideologically, as a means of distraction, as a showcase for their progress. But it is often argued that Australia has no sporting philosophy other than a desire to succeed — whether pitted against a country our own population size or against the giants such as China, the Soviet Union or the United States.

We love to bathe in the reflected glory of an Olympic gold medal, a Bledisloe Cup or an Ashes victory, but not to be too concerned about the resources for enabling our athletes to reach the point where they can succeed — at least not until relatively recent times when Federal government support for sport emerged from the Dark Ages with the establishment of the Australian Institute of Sport and its ancillary components. Even so, we tend to expect a wholly professional attitude and approach from our sporting personalities when, for the most part, sport is but a diversion rather than a career in itself.

Strangely, many of our legends are about losers — Ned Kelly, Burke and Wills, Eureka Stockade and Gallipoli — and yet as a nation our history is overwhelmingly dedicated to the victor. Perhaps inevitably so. Our first winners were sportsmen; it was sport which gave us the antidote to a toxic criminal and colonial beginning. A convict ancestry has only been fashionable in recent years. If we were to become obsessed with anything, it had to be with what made us winners: sport.

The European annexation of Australia was, in itself, a bit of a game. Exploration and the winning of an Empire was something European nations did — a little after the manner in which countries today compete in the Olympic Games. Laying claim to Australia was a race between England and France. Had La Perouse sailed into Botany Bay eleven days earlier than he did, our obsessions, and our language, may have been very different. But the English won, and we inherited English sports and English attitudes to them. And, to some degree, those attitudes included, among our early colonial leaders, a proclaimed indifference to winning. It may have been a fiction, but there was a school of thought which advocated that the game was the thing, not the outcome.

There are those who still subscribe to that school. But it is difficult to pretend that, overall, Australians are happy just to have played the game. They may not have

Blood, Sweat and Tears

A visit by an all England Eleven to Australia in 1862 certainly drew the crowds to this match in Sydney and presaged the intense rivalry that exists in England–Australia Test series. The 1861–2 tour was the first by an English team
Mitchell Library

expected Pat Cash to win the Wimbledon title in 1987, and they all walked tall when he did. But when he failed in his defence of the title in 1988, the indifference was such as to suggest no one expected him to win anyway. No one expected Evonne Goolagong to beat Margaret Court in the all-Australian Wimbledon final of 1971, and most nodded matter-of-factly when Goolagong lost the final the following year to America's Billie Jean King. But in each instance the expectation was high — as it always is on the part of an Australian public which perhaps little realises the pressure under which it places its sporting stars. Goolagong was one of the few true champions who could honestly say she played tennis for the sheer enjoyment of it, that whether she won or lost was really secondary. It was a philosophy which made her no less a champion.

Again in 1988, much was made of the Australian Rugby League team's superiority over England, the traditional opponent. The crowds which attended the matches were disappointing to say the least, and after Australia had duly clinched the Ashes by winning the first two Tests, even fewer bothered to turn up for the third in which England staged a form reversal to win the match handsomely. Therein lies a contradiction peculiar to Australian sports followers.

In its days as an international rugby power, South Africa went into national mourning at almost every Test loss; the better soccer-playing nations of South America do the same at most international losses — specifically Argentina which in 1988 saw its image as the World Cup champion dented by Australia in Sydney. And while Australians generally tend to disregard soccer as a sport of substance — in spite of the fact that it is the most international of all the football codes — they puffed their collective chests when the home team startled the world with its win.

Cricket is one of the nation's passions; cricket and tennis's Davis Cup. Cricket was a sport given by England to its colonies: Australia, New Zealand, India, Pakistan, Sri Lanka, the West Indies, South Africa. Tennis too was English in its origins and, like cricket, a sport which in Australia knows no parochial boundaries — at least not in its play or its following. They are sports climatically suited to Australia, and sports in which Australians have enjoyed a considerable success at international level.

There is nothing quite like the satisfaction of beating the English at their own game. The taste of success came early for Australians. Although H. H. Stephenson's Englishmen won most of the matches on their visit in 1861–2 — the first by a touring side from England — a Castlemaine XXII beat the visitors to become the first Australian winners. The passion for beating English cricket teams had begun. So had the start of sporting sponsorship, the Englishmen having been brought to Australia by the Melbourne catering firm of Spiers and Pond.

Eleven years later Dr W. G. Grace, described by the Sydney correspondent of the *Australasian* after one match as a 'bumptious and overbearing captain', asked for and received £1500 to lead an English side on another visit to Australia.

It was not until 1877 at the Melbourne Cricket Ground that Australia and England played what was to become known as the first official Test match — won by the Australians. The stage was set for an international event which, five years later, saw the birth of the Ashes — a small urn containing what is purported to be the burnt remains of a bail symbolising the death of English cricket — and which has been keenly contested over the years. Anglo–Australian cricket has been not just a game, but a balm to soothe the agonies of the Depression and of world wars — an escape from the harsh reality of life.

The game has also been taken beyond the field of play to bring bitter exchanges between the administrative bodies of both Australia and England — none more so than during the 1932–3 tour of Australia, the tour which went down in history as the infamous Bodyline series. That will be dealt with elsewhere in these pages, but it was a tour which roused the ire of both the players and the public. The depth of feeling about English tactics which were, in a technical, if not truly sportsmanlike, sense, legal, was perhaps unlike anything seen or felt before. It simply wasn't cricket.

Cricket outlawed Bodyline by altering the rules to restrict the number of fieldsmen permitted on the legside. But the 1974–5 series against England saw Dennis Lillee and Jeff Thomson create just as much havoc as Harold Larwood and Bill Voce had forty-two years earlier. It was acceptable enough to us because Lillee and Thomson were Australians. It is another of our quirks which allows that, if we are being given a hard time, the opposition becomes the transgressor, but if we are dishing out the troubles, it is the other fellow's bad luck. Australians collectively are able to rationalise to suit the situation — acceptable if we are doing it, unacceptable if we're not. There are occasions, however, when that is not quite the case.

One such occasion, and another indication of the passionate feelings aroused by cricket, came at the Melbourne Cricket Ground in the closing stages of the 1980–1 season. Tired, and determined not to have to play a third match in a series of finals, Australian captain Greg Chappell ordered his brother, Trevor, to bowl the last ball of the match against New Zealand underarm. The result was that Australia won the match and the limited overs series — but at a cost. Chappell was condemned on both sides of the Tasman, from prime ministers down to former players and the person in the street.

The incident was not without mild irony. A year before the underarm delivery the New Zealand Rugby Union team, the All Blacks, were playing Wales in Cardiff and were trailing with only minutes left. As the ball was thrown in to what loomed as possibly the last lineout, New Zealand number eight, Andy Haden, threw himself out of the line. Television replays showed that not a Welsh hand had been laid on him, but the referee awarded a penalty to the All Blacks. It was as underhand as underarm. The All Black fullback kicked the penalty and New Zealand won the game. And the man who kicked it was Brian McKechnie — the same man Trevor Chappell delivered the underarm ball to the following year.

While cricketers and tennis players — especially those tennis players who left the brand 'Australian Made' imprinted all over the world — were, and still are, national figures, the achievers in many other sports often have to battle for recognition. Parochialism is rife in Australia, and splintered affiliations, particularly in football, keep reputations confined to sections of the country. That very fact sometimes makes for inflated reputations and for hero worship above and beyond the usual. Nowhere is that more evident than in Victoria where 'footie fever' turns the better Rules footballers into veritable gods to be worshipped fervently during the winter months and only a little less so in the others. If ever a sport could be classified as religion, it is Australian Rules football. Its adherents not only follow the fortunes of their star players, but become quite blinded in their loyalty, though professionalism has tended to erode this.

Impressions too can build keen support and provide a rallying point for a club team. An example is the Sydney Rugby League side Western Suburbs, labelled a bunch of working-class battlers. It instilled in the players the feeling that it was 'us against the world', a feeling which often managed to inspire them to deeds greater than even they might have considered possible. Northern beaches club Manly–Warringah on the other hand was regarded as the 'silvertail' of the competition, evoking a genuine 'them and us' feeling whenever Wests clashed with them. It was a psychological ploy designed to draw the most from the players, but it engendered feeling which probably carried over into the supporters of both clubs.

Television has also helped to shape the average Australian's perception of sport, as it has altered the coverage of everything from darts to football. It has also perhaps lifted what veil of mystery may once have cloaked many of our great sporting figures. It is interesting to speculate on whether Don Bradman would have become the larger than life figure he did had he been a daily loungeroom visitor courtesy of the television screen. What thrill there once was in watching an Ashes series or those entertainers from the Caribbean has been largely dissipated by constant exposure — through newspapers, radio, television and frequency of tours.

The public once could only read about the deeds of their sporting heroes. Radio gave them an added dimension, and newsreel film gave glimpses of the action which merely served to whet the reading appetite. Television rounded the picture, and forced newspapers, once a matter of record, to broaden the horizons of their coverage; to look more closely behind the scenes and to rely more heavily on the interview; to expect from the sportswriter a critical analysis rather than a colourful match report. The irony is that sports figures are undoubtedly less revered than they were earlier in the twentieth century when communications were more primitive.

Television is able to offer viewers pictures which no one present at an event is able to get. They can follow the flight of a golf ball, watch the shot played from behind, head-on, side-on. Cricket coverage places umpires under pressure because of the ability of the camera to stop-frame in the case of a close runout decision or a catch taken at bootlace level. Cameras are able to isolate almost every incident. Newspapers as a result have to come up with something different. That leads to sensationalism, to blowing up what may once have been regarded as trivia, and to overworked clichés. Even so, sports reporting in Australia maintains a high standard, as does our presentation of sport on both television and radio.

The danger is saturation. Australians in the 1980s have far more options when it comes to their leisure time, and television coverage is such that large crowds are becoming harder to attract. That at least is true of Sydney, which is perhaps one of the most spoilt cities in terms of what is available to the viewer. In many ways, the sporting obsession is disappearing. We don't give ourselves to it as persistently as we used to but there is no denying it flares on special occasions. The Melbourne Cup is a horse race which stops the nation for several minutes in each November. It is debatable whether that is because the interest is overwhelming or whether it has become traditional to drop everything and listen to the race.

Sport is different things to different people: besetting addiction to some participants, a method of relaxation to some, to others a job of work. But there are few Australians who remain untouched by sport, whether they play it or not. It offers an escape from the daily grind for the many who prefer either to watch or to read about what is happening in sport. Parents have a direct involvement, even if in no way other than having to get their offspring to training or to one kind of game or another. Sport plays a more than useful part in the development of children, teaching them the value of teamwork, the value of striving for a goal (in the broadest sense), and the character-building quality of winning with grace and accepting defeat with a measure of equanimity — each without diminishing the competitive nature of the individual.

An entire industry has grown up around sport, an industry catering to the requirements of the games and the people who play them. It is an industry heavily involved in economic standards and principles; an industry providing employment in equipment manufacture, wholesale and retail outlets; a subsidiary industry concerned with such accoutrements as footwear, clothing and the many commercial items which hang on its coattails; a sub-industry concerned with the health of a nation. Sports clothing has moved into the realm of fashion; joggers who once wore an ordinary sandshoe now have a range of specially designed footwear to choose from; comfortable casual dress spawned by the designers of sportswear is acceptable almost everywhere.

Sport itself has succumbed to the 'designer label'. White or cream clothing was once the only acceptable dress for cricketers and tennis players. That has changed. White or cream still holds for most regular cricket matches, but the birth of World Series Cricket in 1977–8 brought with it coloured clothing — a fashion trend continued in one-day cricket in Australia after the unification of the game in 1979–80. White or pastel shades still predominate in tennis, but colour is far more evident on the world's courts than it was before the introduction of professional Team Tennis in the 1960s.

Sports sponsorship can be counted in millions of dollars as sport has grown into the vehicle through which to sell everything from cornflakes to motor cars, from chewing gum to beer. And around the growth of sponsorship is the sports management industry, which looks after the contracts of clients, attracts sponsorship and advertising deals, and cares for their general welfare. In the economic sense, sport is big and getting bigger all the time. Thousands of jobs depend on it, and for many professional sportsmen it is sport which has offered them a way of life they might otherwise never have been able to look forward to.

Sportsmen have also assumed, or have had themselves thrust into, the role of opinion-shaper. This is not unique to Australia. Although most are reluctant to ally themselves publicly, elections see some of them lending their support to one political party or another. Sport also offers itself as a launch pad for the few sportsmen and women who decide to enter politics — cyclist Sir Hubert Opperman, hockey's Ric Charlesworth, athlete Michael Cleary and swimmer Dawn Fraser to name just a handful. It has been the base upon which others such as Sir Donald Bradman, Bob Cowper and Greg Chappell have succeeded in building outstanding careers in the commercial world. Cricketers, like Rugby Union players, seem to make contacts which stand them in good stead both as players and when their playing days are over.

There are spin-offs for the players who loom larger than life in the eyes of the public. They become the sporting goods experts, the radio and television commentators able to offer first-hand opinions. Even before their careers are over they are snapped up by newspapers to write columns (usually ghosted) in the belief that readers want to read what their heroes think of a particular player, match or incident. It is that very high profile which in turn can determine worth in the market place, be it in negotiating a new playing contract or a new advertising and management contract.

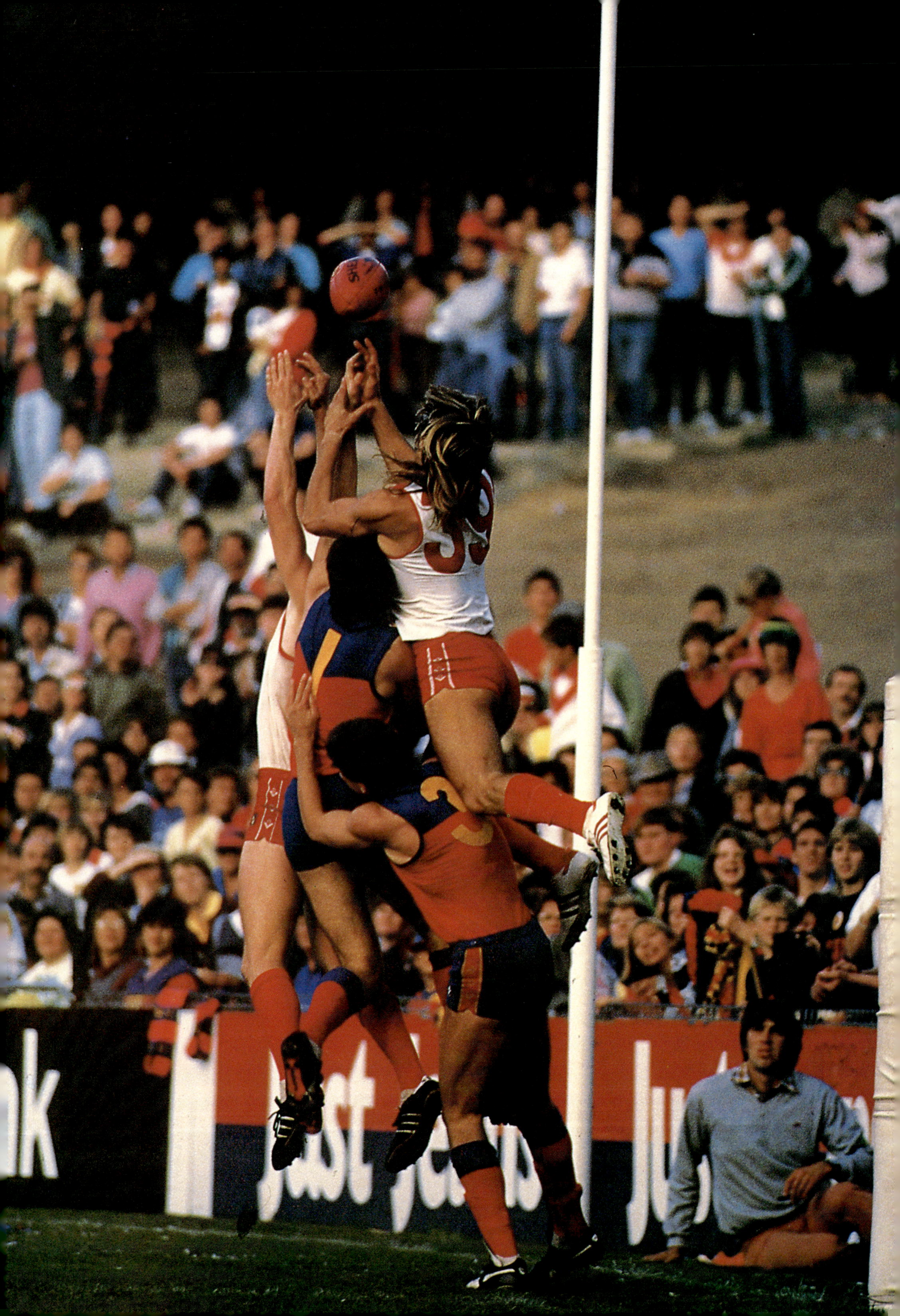

just jeans

Obsession

Right:
The supreme attraction of Australian Rules is the long, accurate kicking and high marking. Fitzroy full back Gary Pert splits the pack to take a superb mark against Carlton
Live Action: Michael Rayner

Opposite:
The sensational Sydney Swans full forward Warwick Capper (who has since transferred to the Brisbane Bears) flies high in the goal square. Capper's flowing blond hair, tight shorts and fantastic high marks drew the Sydney crowds like a magnet and were a big factor in establishing the Swans in Sydney
Live Action: Tony Nolan

With the profile, however, goes added responsibility. As with anyone else in the public eye, misdemeanours which may otherwise have gone unnoticed and unreported become headline news; public appearances require a curbing of what may be natural exuberance; behaviour becomes all-important; a photograph of a sporting hero having a quiet cigarette becomes a subject for debate about the dangers of smoking.

There are few sports about which we are as fanatical as Australian Rules football, the game invented in order to keep cricketers fit throughout the winter months. Those who follow it do so with a zealousness approaching religious fervour — in spite of the fact that as no other nation plays it we can never really test ourselves at international level, and that, while it may have been conceived by a New South Welshman, it is basically a Victorian game. The Victorian Football League, or the VFL, is not merely a body or the competition itself — it is another term for Australian Rules.

Blood, Sweat and Tears

Footy fever as adoring spectators and jubilant players share the excitement of Hawthorn's fourth championship victory this decade.
Live Action

Co-winner of the 1986 Brownlow Medal, Robert DiPierdominico parades the VFL Premiership Cup following Hawthorn's triumphant win against Melbourne in the 1988 VFL Grand Final.
Live Action

It is played in Perth, Adelaide and Hobart, and there are Sydney and Brisbane teams in the competition. But Melbourne is where it was born; where it means the most; where the best players end up; where summer is an irritating interval between football seasons. Such are the extremes of the game in Melbourne that writer and journalist Keith Dunstan has all but made a career out of commenting on, cataloguing and satirising them. Founder of the Anti-Football League, he is none the less an affectionate chronicler of the VFL's fanaticism and foibles.

Some of the stories he recalls are in fact universal. Many countries and sports have their own version of the question: 'If God came to Melbourne what would you do?' The Hawthorn answer was: 'Move Peter Hudson to centre-half forward'. In giving the Ron Barassi Memorial Lecture at Monash University, Professor Ian Turner said that in telling that story outside Hawthorn people asked, 'Who's Peter Hudson?' In Hawthorn they asked, 'Who's God?' The fact that such a universal tale is re-told as original and unique to VFL is, in itself, one measure of Melbourne's obsession with the game. That one of its universities actually has something called the Ron Barassi Memorial Lecture is another.

How much Barassi was revered as a player was best measured by the hatred his move from Melbourne to Carlton in 1965 engendered — at least among Melbourne club supporters. His acceptance of the player-coach job with Carlton was one of the great running stories of the decade. He gave Carlton two premierships before, in 1973, taking over as the coach of North Melbourne which, two years later, he took to its first Grand Final victory. He returned 'home' to coach his old club, Melbourne, in 1981.

Australian Rules football was designed as a game in which the players would not get hurt — at least not to the extent they did in Rugby Union. But they do get hurt and, as in all physical sports, there is an enduring hypocrisy concerning on-field violence. It is decried and officially dealt with, but it is part of the reason we watch. The tough stuff, the biff, is an element of the football legend. The 1945 Grand Final between Carlton and South Melbourne was more like an extension of World War II. In all, ten players were reported, including one who wasn't even playing. Freddie Fitzgibbon was sitting in the stand, already under suspension. But when things got tough on the field, he ran in and joined the fracas.

The biggest football crowds of all watch Australian Rules, and particularly the Victorian Football League. A vital home-and-away game can attract 60 000 plus, while the Grand Final at the Melbourne Cricket Ground draws crowds approaching 100 000. The record crowd, before bookings were instituted, was 121 696 for the 1970 Grand Final

Roger Gould

In 1987 the VFL, in an attempt to spread the gospel, took teams to Canada and England. In Vancouver the marketers of the game promoted it as violent. Players tearing into raw steak was one of the images used to support the toughness. Both in Vancouver and at the Oval in London the teams lived up to the pre-match publicity and got stuck into one another. While the VFL reprimanded its marketers for going over the top, it was hard not to be cynical. Spectators interviewed after the game in London admitted to enjoying the violence. If there seems to be a contradiction in promoting the tribal warfare that is Australian Rules — or any other code of football for that matter — while appearing shocked at the punch-ups, it is no more than Australians expect. It seems that's what spectators the world over enjoy.

Any doubts that both Australian Rules and Rugby League are obsessions can be laid to rest on that spring weekend each year on which League Grand Final is played in Sydney and the VFL Grand Final is played in Melbourne. By a quirk of uncharacteristic co-operation between the two cities, one is played on Saturday, the other on Sunday. Prime Minister Bob Hawke turned out for both matches in 1987, and was booed at the end of each game — the price he had to pay for having publicly announced his pre-match support for the subsequent losers. Where else but Australia would a politician, let alone a prime minister, feel compelled to commit himself so totally in the knowledge that he is bound to incur the wrath of around half the people at the game. Then again, refusal to takes sides would show a lack of judgement and be equally unpopular.

Perhaps only on the Indian sub-continent do politicians involve themselves in sport to a greater extent. Sir Robert Menzies, a former Australian prime minister, revelled in being Carlton's number one ticket holder. He invariably managed to have pressing business in London at the same time as Australian cricket teams toured England. Bob Hawke's golf swing was often ridiculed; he was hit in the face by a cricket ball while playing in a match against the Canberra Press Gallery; he revived the Prime Minister's XI match against each summer's visiting internationals.

A former prime minister, Harold Holt, disappeared while swimming alone in the ocean.

Not even Holt's disappearance, and presumed death, touched the nation with the impact of the fatal poisoning of a racehorse in 1932. The death of Phar Lap in the United States aroused some paranoia in us. We accused the Americans — and some still do — of deliberately poisoning the big red gelding. They would do anything to stop the heroic horse from sweeping all before him. The anti-American feeling was not new. Fifteen years earlier we had felt the same way when boxer Les Darcy collapsed and died in the United States.

After Phar Lap's death, we brought him home — and shared the bits around. His skeleton is in Wellington, New Zealand, where, like so many of the best Australian horses, he had been born and bred; his heart is in the Science Museum in Canberra; his stuffed hide is in Melbourne in a class case. After all these years, Phar Lap's story still has magic. A skinny animal standing over seventeen hands, Phar Lap numbered the AJC Derby and the Melbourne Cup among his 37 wins from 51 starts.

The death of Phar Lap in America threw Australia into mourning. The Referee newspaper ran his complete performance and stake winnings in its coverage of the wonder horse's death by poisoning in its 13 April 1932 issue

Like many of our obsessions with great horses, the adulation of Phar Lap was coloured by money. He was winning in the dark days of the Depression. A little each way on the Red Terror meant, for many, that as long as he won they went a little less hungry. A feature film about Phar Lap may have helped to keep the legend alive, but the fact that the horse remains one of Australia's folk heroes may well have something to do with that love of winners. His agonising death also helps.

As Tommy Woodcock, one-time jockey and Phar Lap's strapper and then trainer, recalled it: the American vet told him to keep him moving until he returned with help and not to let him stop. 'But when Phar Lap had swollen to half his size again and was groaning in pain, I took him to the barn. He whinnied, he groaned dementedly. I rushed about to make him more comfortable. Coming toward me he nosed affectionately under my arm. Then something inside him burst; he drenched me in blood and fell dead at my feet.'

Woodcock's graphic description of the great horse's death still hurts. Australia was stunned by the news. The horse had gone off to America to begin a new career, and had made a sensational start by winning the $50 000 Agua Caliente Handicap in Mexico. Rumour had it that Phar Lap had been poisoned; news of his death saw flags flying at half-mast. Phar Lap has never been forgotten; nor have we ever quite forgiven the Americans, even if they did not really poison him.

The feelings of Australians about a racehorse are a little more understandable in the light of what happens to the country on the first Tuesday of every November. There are few races in the world, if any, which can match the Melbourne Cup. It stops the nation at 2.40 p.m.; Melbourne itself seems to lead up to the moment with a week-long holiday. The prize-money mounts each year courtesy of Carlton Brewery, and in 1985 the race became the Foster's Melbourne Cup. As a handicap rather than a weight-for-age race, it is not Australia's classiest. But because some donkey from the bush has a chance of winning, it is closest to our hearts. Favourites seldom win. Every runner is in there with a chance.

Australian racing is in trouble. Not financially — the TABs see to that — but as something people go to watch. The rails bookmakers are a declining if not dying breed and, while few tears will be shed for them, their decline is the decline of racing. In 1988 Sky Channel and its extensive coverage of racing was installed in TABs as well as hotels and clubs. Fewer will be those who venture to the track. History suggests that only great horses — the Phar Laps and the Carbines — are capable of bringing crowds back to racing. Attempts to make heroes out of the Bonecrushers and the Beau Zams have not quite worked. As for the long-standing debate about whether racing is really a sport, in Australia it seems to be.

The fact that no history of Australian sport can ignore racing says that we at least have decided what it is. When Kensai and Larry Olsen won the Melbourne Cup in 1987 we all rejoiced. A little Aussie battler — albeit a Kiwi one in the case of Kensai — had beaten the Sheiks and the Sangsters, the Packers and the Willesees. Australian sport has long needed to believe that anything is possible. Kensai had been bought for $15 000 as a yearling, almost a song in an era of million-dollar horses. Trainer Les Bridge was not exactly the highest flier in his profession, and Olsen appeared to be finished as a jockey, beaten by a weight problem. He had announced his retirement five times, but was back for just one more riding tilt. He fought back from 72 kilos, and there he was, booting home the winner in the Melbourne Cup. The Aussie battler lived.

They are around, the battlers of sport. In 1983 one of them almost unbelievably won the inaugural Sydney to Melbourne ultra marathon. He was Cliff Young, a 61-year-old potato farmer from Victoria, and the nation warmed to him. An unlikely sporting figure, he appeared as if in a time warp to take us back to the days before sport was a multi-national industry, before there was something called the Australian Institute of Sport helping Kelloggs sell breakfast cereals, to a time when the underdog could still get lucky. Australians have a soft spot for their regular athletic champions, but they love nothing better than to see an unlikely hero emerge from the ranks. And if ever there was an unlikely hero, it was Cliff Young.

Swimmer Dawn Fraser also captured the imagination of her compatriots, as much through her highly publicised brushes with officialdom as through her extraordinary ability in the water. Part of her problem was that she came from Balmain, in the 1950s still a tough, working-class suburb. The girl who was to become the greatest swimmer of all time, and one of the greats of Australian sport, never swam in the easy lane.

She won Olympic gold medals at Melbourne in 1956, Rome in 1960 and Tokyo in 1964 — despite constant warring with officials. Sheer courage took her to Tokyo following a motorcar accident in which her mother was killed, and when she was involved in a souveniring raid which netted a Japanese flag from the Imperial Palace, swimming officialdom took the opportunity to rid itself of what it saw as a gigantic headache. For her part in an escapade which would once have made Australians heroes, Fraser was banned from swimming for ten years.

The Australian Swimming Union ban was lifted after four years, but too late to allow Fraser to swim in the Mexico Olympics where the winning time for the 100 metres was half a second slower than her Tokyo time. In 1967 she was awarded the MBE. Fraser's story gives us both sides of the sporting coin. In spite of the training discipline required, sporting genius is still genius. It has its temperament and its flaws. Fraser was not the first nor will she be the last champion to fall foul of sporting administrators — and Australians have almost always backed the champion, the underdog, in any altercation with officialdom. Dawn Fraser, ever the underdog, was ever loved, and in 1988 Balmain, for all its newfound trendiness, gave her its State election preferences to make her its Independent Member of Parliament.

How much Dawn Fraser suffered because she was a woman is open to conjecture. But fast bowler Dennis Lillee was banned for no more than a few one-day matches after taking a kick at Pakistan batsman Javed Miandad during a cricket Test in Perth. The same Lillee was brazen enough to ask the Queen for an autograph when introduced during the Centenary Test in Melbourne in 1977. He did not get it then, but later received a signed photograph of Her Majesty. And it was Lillee and his wicketkeeping partner Rod Marsh who bet on an English Test victory at Headingley when such an outcome seemed impossible. Apart from being found out, the most embarrassing thing was that England, against all the odds, won.

Sculler Stuart Mackenzie first won the Diamond Sculls at Henley in 1957, and then every year for the next five. And he delighted in opposing the stuffiness of the Henley Royal Regatta. He splashed, abused or showed a few fingers to any who jeered him, and his arrogance was such that he would sometimes pause in mid-race to raise his hat to the crowd, or row back to console a well beaten opponent. English rowing officials may have wanted to hang him, but he was never even banned.

If the demand is for winners — and Australians demand them at every outing — there seems little point in complaining when they become bad losers. There is a certain sanctimonious self-righteousness when some of our sporting heroes behave badly. Once sportsmen and women are paid like movie stars and are generally treated like movie stars, they tend to act accordingly. If they sometimes behave like spoiled brats, it is perhaps our own fault. Ours and our money.

Amateurism, and the period of shamateurism, are all but over. In less than a generation tennis champions, particularly, have advanced from four guineas a day Davis Cup expenses to millionaire circuit players. And Australian tennis players did Australia proud, particularly in our see-sawing battles with the Americans for what was virtually supremacy of the tennis world in the 1950s and 1960s. Athletics, once filled with the hypocrisy of under-the-table payments to lure the leading track and field stars to meets, tried to move with the times by permitting payment into a trust fund from the 1980s. It did not stop bargaining by athletes and officials over appearance money, but it was a step in the right direction. And cricketers, once the poor relations of big sport in Australia, had the arrival of World Series Cricket in 1977 to thank for subsequent fatter pay packets. We are quick to criticise the highly paid sporting personalities when they fail to produce the goods.

Australia's sporting heritage, and perhaps our attitudes towards sport and sportsmen and women, can be traced back to the arrival of the First Fleet in Sydney Cove. Boomerang throwing, swimming and a form of netball may have been the extent of the sporting pursuits of the Aborigines, but the arrival of the white man brought with it traditional English games such as boxing, wrestling and running, games which themselves could be traced back to the ancient Greeks and Romans. Equipment was virtually non-existent, and the harshness of life such that there really was little time for the frivolity of games, other than as a diversion. The first priority was ensuring there was enough to eat in a land where the quality of food, much of it brought from the Mother Country, was either appalling or rotten.

When fights took place they were invariably drink-induced and, while the first known duel took place in August of 1788, duelling was not exactly a pastime of the convicts who made up a sizeable proportion of the settlement of New South Wales. Where there were differences of opinion they were settled with bare knuckles, a method traditionally effective in Ireland from which many of the new settlers came, along with English, Scots and Welsh. While there may always have been time for a fight, there was not a lot of it left for hunting and fishing. These were the days before the forty-hour week, and most energy was expended at work rather than play.

Not that the convicts would have had much success had they spent longer hours chasing game and fish. Most hailed from the cities of England and Ireland, areas not conducive to learning the finer points of catching one's fare. Picking a pocket or two may have been more in their line, but it was of little help in the day-to-day business of survival in a foreign land. Strength and energy were needed for living, never mind the pursuits of pleasure — although somehow there was always room for such diversions.

There came a time when the hunting of animals for food went beyond the bounds of necessity, a killing time which threatened the very existence of species, as the English military and gentry sought and destroyed koalas, kangaroos, ducks, wild geese and even lyre birds. Aborigines too lived in fear of their lives, as 'sport' took up a sinister pen to write a dark chapter in our history — the indiscriminate slaughter of the indigenous people was in fact regarded by some as sport.

Cock-fighting was popular until well into the nineteenth century. A recreation which allowed gambling, it was patronised by the officers and the commercial gentry as well as by the convicts; it allowed its followers to let off steam in a bloody sport in which the birds, fitted with razor-sharp spurs, fought to the death. For a while, too, there was strong support for ratting in which bets were made on how many rodents could be killed by a terrier in a given time.

Horse-racing, which was to blossom into the huge industry it is today, had its beginnings in the mid-1790s. Few of the First Fleet cargo of seven stallions and mares survived the arduous trip, but those which did apparently flourished, their numbers swelled by further imports over the next dozen or so years. Privately owned for the most part, they were put to the test in match races for stakes as high as £50.

Although few, if any, of the new settlers knew how to swim — and the currents and dashing waves made the beaches too dangerous anyway — much of Sydney's relaxation revolved around the waters of the harbour. Rowing was popular, and regattas afforded the populace not only a break from the mundane, but also an avenue for betting. Gig racing was another outlet but, as with rowing, was not a sport in which the convicts were able to indulge.

Rowing was a very popular sport in the 19th century, and the inter-state rivalry which has fuelled crowd excitement at many Australian sporting contests was in evidence on Sydney Harbour as Victoria and New South Wales battled out a fours race in an 1883 regatta. From the crowd reaction we must assume New South Wales is in front
Mitchell Library

Cricket almost certainly had been played by the turn of the century, although the first formally organised game is recognised as having taken place in Hyde Park in December 1803. The organisation of the hunting and shooting crowd was such that a yearning for the sports of the old country led to the importation of deer, foxes, partridge, pheasants and what were in later years to become such a problem for Australian farmers — rabbits and hares.

Most of these activities were male-oriented, the women of the time being expected by their men to remain in the background and take care of house and children. By the early 1800s there were reports in the *Sydney Gazette* of females having taken part in running races. It would take a long time, but sport for women was gradually becoming acknowledged.

Leisure and pleasure were still strongholds of the gentry, who played billiards and croquet, rode in point-to-point steeplechases and went hunting and shooting. Yachting was for those who could afford life's luxuries, leaving the pubs and taverns as the centres for the entertainment of the common man and woman.

If sport in Australia began a rapid development with the arrival of the horses and men of the First Fleet, the next two hundred years of migration, especially the influx of Europeans which followed World War II, added greatly to the country's sporting dimensions. From the Americans who came in the gold-rush days of the 1850s there was baseball and, later, basketball; there was soccer from England, with European flair added much later; the Scots brought the Caledonian Games, the miners of Devon and Cornwall their wrestling matches, the Chinese their penchant for gambling games such as fan-tan.

Greeks, Yugoslavs, Hungarians, Italians and Spaniards, steeped in the traditions of soccer and basketball, and the Turks and Asians, with their emphasis on the martial arts, all contributed enormously to the development of sport in a land which even in the nineteenth century prompted some visitors to proclaim that the influence of sport was such as to be unhealthy: there was far too much emphasis on, and importance attached to, sport, and at the cost of more meaningful pursuits.

Obsession

There are, of course, those who today say nothing has changed. Sport is an intrinsic part of Australian life. It offers personal challenge and enjoyment for most of its participants, and goals such as international competition and national representation for others. For the majority, participation implies a concern with a healthy lifestyle, a concern exemplified by the growth of health and fitness centres and aerobics classes later in our century. In the main, however, sporting interest is determined by social environment, at home, at school and in the workplace.

Cricket, which along with tennis has developed into one of Australia's few truly national sports, not defined by State boundaries, was being played in the early 1800s. Clubs and organised matches were around by the 1820s, in Tasmania as well as in New South Wales, and had taken root in Victoria by 1838. By 1853 the Melbourne Cricket Ground was headquarters for the Melbourne Cricket Club, and it was there, in 1877, that the first 'Test' was played between a team of Australians, led by big Dave Gregory, and an English side led by James Lillywhite.

The MCG was also the venue for the first match played against H. H. Stephenson's visiting side from England. The English XI then proved much too strong for a Melbourne and Districts XVIII. Their tour took them to Victoria, New South Wales and Tasmania. On their return to England, Roger Idison went down on record as the first player to venture an opinion on the Australian as a cricketer, maintaining, 'Well, o'i doant think mooch of their play, but they are a wonderful lot of drinking men'.

Ironically, it was the search for something to keep cricketers fit in the winter which led to the development of Australian Rules football. Tom Wills, a versatile

In this early cricket match between Sydney and Melbourne in 1855, the fieldsman seems in danger of getting mixed up with the crowd who seem oblivious to the on-field action. The match was played at Yarra Park, Richmond, where the MCG now stands
Mitchell Library

Blood, Sweat and Tears

The all England Eleven who toured Australia in 1862 took on a twenty-two of Ballarat and won. It is hard to see how they could score many runs against the packed field but, as one Englishman said they were not very good cricketers but 'they were fine drinking men!'
La Trobe Collection, State Library of Victoria

sportsman who had played both cricket and football at Rugby school in England, was the catalyst for the new game, along with his cousin, Henry Harrison. The first rules were drawn up in 1859, but a game which seemed to be a combination of Gaelic football, rugby and soccer was played a year earlier between Melbourne Church of England Grammar School and Scotch College.

By then rugby had been played in New South Wales for about thirty years, although the exact date of the game's official beginnings in the colony is unknown. Today a sport of the GPS schools, it was not introduced to that area until late in the century. But scratch teams made up of members of the military appear to have played in the 1840s.

If a parliamentary plea by Elmer Harmer is any criterion, rugby had more than a little difficulty gaining acceptance. Harmer in 1864 described rugby to the House in eloquent terms as 'vicious displays of brutish fist-fighting' which had been taking place for thirty-five years. While there was a good deal of truth in Harmer's viewpoint, his plea to have the game banned fell on deaf ears.

Brutality was a problem facing rugby around the 1870s, so much so that a number of clubs switched to playing Australian Rules football, then known as Victorian Rules. Games were becoming farcical, with referees having little or no control and many games being played without a referee. Rules differed virtually from suburb to suburb, and by 1874 it was necessary to call a conference of delegates to determine rules.

The first overseas tour came in 1882 when a team representing New South Wales played in New Zealand, and two years later the New Zealanders returned for a full tour. The international era had begun.

Obsession

By 1894 a number of teams in England had opted for professional rugby — the compensation of players for lost wages and travelling expenses — and by 1898 full professionalism had touched the game. When Sydney forward Alec Burdon broke his arm and was denied compensation for the time he spent off work, thoughts of professionalism were translated into action. That was in 1907. The New South Wales Rugby League was off and running. What assured the new game of success was the fact that the great rugby player of the era, Dally Messenger, was persuaded by J. J. Giltinan, one of the founders of Rugby League, to join the breakaway. Three matches arranged against a New Zealand team, the All Golds, which was on its way to England, proved popular with the public.

At the end of the first season in 1908 Giltinan, not one to waste an opportunity, took thirty-four players on a tour of England. His timing was bad. The English economy was going through a rough patch, and the tour failed to make money. It left both Giltinan and the game struggling to make ends meet. Rugby League was saved later in 1909 when a number of rugby internationals were persuaded to play against their League counterparts for payment. They joined the professional ranks and the game of Rugby League never looked back.

'The Master' Dally Messenger, considered Australia's greatest Rugby League player. The Australian captain's unpredictable running baffled the English, so much so that he once scored a try from behind his own goal line. He refused offers to join English soccer clubs, and returned to Australia to help create Rugby League as the 'big time' sport it is today
Rugby League Week

Blood, Sweat and Tears

Opposite, top:
Everything Ray Price did for Parramatta had his Rugby League fans screaming with delight, and a touchdown was the tough guy's ultimate gift to the crowd
Rugby League Week

Right:
Canterbury captain and front rower Peter Tunks shows his determination to keep possession. Plagued by ankle and groin injuries in 1988 and unable to join routine practices, Tunks refused to let this prevent him from match play
Rugby League Week

Opposite, far left:
One of Australia's and Queensland's toughest and most formidable players, Greg Dowling is scarcely stopped by this unorthodox tackle. In 1988 he joined the Brisbane Broncos in their first year
News Limited

Opposite, right:
John Sattler, who captained Souths during their halcyon days in the late 1960s, discusses a finer point of play with the referee in a game against Newtown. Sattler was a very tough and courageous player, once playing a whole game with a broken jaw
John Fairfax & Sons Pty Ltd; Ted Golding

Australian soccer player Craig Johnston made a successful transition to the English professional arena, where he played for the highly successful club Liverpool. He is pictured here with the 1987 FA Cup. Johnston represented success and fair play in a sport that has often been marred by poor crowd behaviour
Live Action: Acikalin

While kicking a ball had probably been a pastime indulged in by First Fleeters and the early troops, it was not until 1880, just seventeen years after the formation of the Football Association in England, the birthplace of soccer, that the game as we know it began appearing in the public schools in Sydney.

If soccer began in the public schools, as it did in England, it was quickly taken up as a sport for the people. Clubs were formed, visiting ships' companies played matches against the locals, and interstate contests developed. Popular on the coalfields of Newcastle and the New South Wales south coast, soccer in Australia went international with a visit by a New Zealand team in 1904.

The 1950s provided a real impetus for the game with the arrival of migrants from Britain and Europe, tours by teams from those same areas, and the Olympic Games

Blood, Sweat and Tears

in Melbourne. By 1965 Australia had entered the World Cup, and by 1974 had made its first appearance among the sixteen at the World Cup finals in West Germany. Unfortunately, the game still seems to be regarded as foreign, and while the country's appearance in West Germany was looked on with pride by the nation, soccer lost what impetus it should have gained once the team returned home.

New games such as bocce, handball, Olympic wrestling and many more arrived with the influx of migrants after World War II. Swimming, in which Australians excelled, developed from paddling on the beach to the point where the first Australian championships were staged in 1894, the first for women having to wait until 1930. Tennis, introduced from England in the 1870s, was another sport for which Australians seemed to have an aptitude, and while it was not until 1905 that the first national titles were played, it would be only another two years before an Australian, Sir Norman Brookes, won a Wimbledon title for the first time.

Although a young country, Australia lays claim to the oldest professional foot

The premier professional footrunning race in Australia is the Stawell Gift, conducted annually at the small Victorian town since 1878. The race, over 110 metres, is held with heats and finals over the Easter weekend. The 1986 winner was Glenn Chapman
Herald & Weekly Times

Dennis Lillee kept his fitness and his great bowling skill long enough to take the record for most Test wickets (since surpassed by England's Ian Botham and New Zealand's Richard Hadlee). Lillee was Australia's bowling mainstay in the 1970s. He retired in 1984
Photobank/All Sport

race in the world, the Stawell Gift. Instituted in 1878 and run as a handicap over 130 yards in the small Victorian town of Stawell, it is an annual event which attracts athletes from far and wide. Athletics — running, putting the shot, high jumping and hurdling — had been engaged in from the outset of colonisation, but it was at the first modern Olympics in Athens in 1896 that Australia made the rest of the world sit up and take notice. Australia's Edwin Flack won gold medals over 800 and 1500 metres, retired after 37 kilometres of the marathon, while leading, and played tennis in which he lost in the first round of both the singles and doubles.

It was, however, the start of a tradition which has seen Australia represented at every Olympic Games, and a continuation of what had already become an Australian sporting obsession.

Sources and references

This chapter draws on the author's own observations and research, and was assisted by contributions from Keith Aberdein. The following books were consulted:

Keith Dunstan, *Sports* (Sun Books, 1981); Keith Dunstan, *The Paddock that Grew: The Story of the Melbourne Cricket Club* (Cassell, 1962, rev. edn 1974); David Frith, *Pageant of Cricket* (Macmillan, 1987); R. and M. Howell, *A History of Australian Sport* (Shakespeare Head, 1987); Neville Penton, *A Racing Heart: The Story of the Australian Turf* (Collins, 1987); Brian Stoddart, *Saturday Afternoon Fever* (Angus & Robertson, 1986); *The Wide World of Sports*; *Sporting Hall of Fame* (Angus & Robertson, 1984). The reference to W. G. Grace is in Dunstan, *Paddock That Grew*, p.40; the Tommy Woodcock quotation is in Dunstan, *Sports*, p.60.

CHAPTER 2

BLOOD AND GUTS

Phil Wilkins

Australia's boxing history embraces its most famous bushranger Ned Kelly. This photograph was taken to commemorate his epic bare knuckle victory over 'Wild' Wright in a 20-rounder that gave him the title of Champion of North-Eastern Victoria

An inborn impulse caused primitive man to play games, even though it might be only hitting a stone with a branch. After all, to hit an object was so much better than to hit a friend (Rabbi Brasch).

Legend from before the birth and death of Christ claims bloodshed brought about the Olympic Games in ancient Greece. Hercules promised to muck out, in one day, the vast stables of Augeas, King of Elis, owner of some 3000 head of oxen. It was a feat he achieved by diverting the rivers Alpheus and Peneus through the stables in the region now known as Olympia. Upon completion of his task, Hercules was incensed to learn the king intended forsaking his promise to repay him with a tenth of the herd. Hercules killed Augeas and his family and confiscated all the cattle and horses of the kingdom. To celebrate his newly-acquired wealth, he consecrated a grove of trees on the site of Olympia and introduced a sporting festival on the small plain, an athletic carnival which became known as the Olympic Games.

Myth it may be, but athletics and sporting competition were part of everyday Greek life, and the Games became the most important of festivities. Originally, the Games lasted just one day, the single event being a sprint of approximately 200 metres, the length of the stadium. Ultimately, the festival was enlarged to five days, containing a variety of sports including four running events: the length of the stadium sprint, a race over two lengths of the stadium, a distance event of about 4.25 kilometres, and a race in armour. Combat sports included boxing and what seemed to be a free-for-all brawl called the pankration in which apparently any violence was accepted except eye-gouging and biting. Four-horse chariot races and a pentathlon were introduced and the highest level of sportsmanship was demanded of competitors. Ultimately, the corruption of politics ruined the Games. The Roman emperor Nero entered the chariot race and was permitted a rails run to claim the crown of wild olives in A.D. 66. The Olympic Games were abolished by decree of the conquering Romans in A.D. 393 as 'pagan idolatry' and the sacred site of the temple of Zeus was razed. It was another 1500 years before the modern Olympics were instituted in Athens in 1896.

Boxing and hand-to-hand combat are as old as life itself, dating back to prehistoric man. With the most basic of weapons, rock and club, cave dwellers fought against predators, and only the fittest and fastest survived. From the running and hunting of ancient times, for existence itself, athletics and sport have become pedestals for

The fight taking place in McLaren's boxing saloon at Ballarat in 1864 may have been to settle a bet or a personal argument, as the small crowd in such a bustling place as the Victorian goldfields suggests that it was not an advertised fight. Our money is on the man on the left, as knee-high boots are not likely to help the mobility of his opponent
Mitchell Library

personal glory and public worship. In the process, blood became the universally accepted badge of honour, in glory and defeat, in winning and losing.

When the First Fleet arrived in Botany Bay, it brought with it England's ultimate gift to Australia — men and women. Humanity, as free settlers, soldiers or convicts, struggled and survived in the harsh, strange environment. The convict hulks and bestial penal servitude accompanying them, the brutality of whip and chain, provoked inhumane behaviour. The people adapted and changed, and if many hated the new existence, they lived and overcame their primitive facilities, and their numbers grew.

Sport was also a gift from England. Boxing and wrestling in the most basic form and the simplest, most rudimentary games of folk football and cricket accompanied the fleet. Sport was an essential diversion from everyday drudgery and privation. In the colony's atmosphere of anger and antipathy, it was inevitable that wherever men met, hostility and resentment simmered near the surface. Violence was easily provoked. Brawling and blood sports were commonplace.

Bush drives for kangaroo and wallaby shooting were for gentlemen and the militia. Fighting was for the man in the muddy street. The spectacle of strength and supremacy in raw, bare-knuckle fights was relished, not least among the volatile Irish, free men or otherwise. Fighting was as essential as bread and water to live on and black wattle and daub huts to live in. Grass fights, as they became known, were as inevitable as life and death. It was not until almost a century after first settlement that a fatality in the Sydney sandhills of Kensington brought about the banning of bare-knuckle fighting. As a concession, lightweight, fingerless gloves were introduced and, later, the heavier, padded gloves. Boxing was originally an entertainment in Australia and, for all its rubbing on modern nerves, 200 years later it remains an attraction to many.

Fox-hunting in England became kangaroo-hunting in Australia for the landed gentry. From this blood sport it was a short step to coursing or greyhound racing by the 1870s with rabbits and wallabies as bait before the introduction of the artificial

A kangaroo drive with horses and hounds, depicted here in the Australian Sketcher *of 1874, provided the squatters and selectors with sport, but also with meat, furs and the removal of a pasture eating rival for their sheep and cattle*

lure — the tin hare — in 1927. Staffordshire bull terriers from England, originally bred for bull and bear baiting, were sent to Australia and matched in battles to the death, the struggles continuing for up to two hours as the dogs sought to gain a stranglehold. Around the Hawkesbury area special pits were constructed for cock fighting; finger-long razor-sharp steel spurs were attached to the birds' legs to inflict mortal wounds and provide a bloody spectacle.

Many convicts transported to Australia were guilty of poaching offences. They continued trapping game in the colony, more for food than sport. The gentry chased kangaroos, wallabies and emus on horseback and with hounds. More traditional game was introduced by a Victorian named Thomas Austin who imported deer, pheasant and rabbits. On a visit from England, Prince Albert is claimed to have killed 416 rabbits in a single hunt and 68 in ten minutes, leaving his fingers blistered from the heat of his gun. Deer and pheasant never bred in numbers and remained rare game.

Shooting koalas became a popular and lucrative pastime. Helpless in the trees in daylight hours, they fell in thousands. Their fur was much sought after and the sport highly profitable. In one year it was claimed three million koala pelts were listed for sale in America. The Queensland government declared an open season on koalas in 1927 and the animal is scarce there to this day though it remains the emblem of the State.

Blood and Guts

Right:
A rabbit hunt at Barwon Park, Western Victoria, took on the methodology of grouse hunting, when Prince Alfred, the Duke of Edinburgh, hunted there in 1867. The hapless bunnies were driven by beaters on to the waiting guns of the shooters
National Library of Australia

Below:
The colonial artist S. G. Gill's drawing of emu hunting in South Australia in the 1850s. The hunters are seen stalking the emus, but the more common practice was to pursue them with hounds on a wild horseback chase
National Library of Australia

One of the early and popular blood sports, the shooting of koalas, was not outlawed in Queensland until the 1930s, by which time the koala population of that State had been almost wiped out. An open letter from Archbishop Sharp, published in the Brisbane Courier Mail, *protests against a government declaration of an open-season on koalas in 1927*

SLAUGHTER OF BEARS.

ARCHBISHOP SHARP URGES PROTESTS.

His Grace Archbishop Sharp writes :—I think that if the Acting Premier realises how very deep an offence the permission to destroy native bears has given to a vast number of quiet, peaceable, decent-minded people, the permission would be withdrawn. I write in all seriousness when I say that our feelings ought not to be so wounded. Your newspaper penetrates into every part of the State: so may I use it as a medium for suggesting that during the fortnight that intervenes between now and August 1, protests in large numbers, from individuals, and, still better, from groups or meetings or associations of people living in the country (for country dwellers probably are more grieved even than town dwellers), should be sent to the Acting Premier in order to bring home to him how strong and real is our feeling about this.

Greyhound racing had its beginnings in Australia among the squattocracy of the Victorian Western District. The first recognised meeting was conducted by the Victorian Coursing Club in 1874. Coursing consisted of the match racing between two greyhounds, which were released to pursue a live quarry. A most important man was the 'slipper' who was trusted to give the hounds an equal start. R. G. 'Dick' Banner was a highly regarded 'slipper' of Victoria
Mitchell Library

Blood and Guts

Above:
A group of countrymen ready for a day's coursing in New South Wales. Coursing, with a live quarry, began as an elite sport in Victoria, but became popular with country people across Australia
Mitchell Library

Australasian Coursing Club

AT MASCOT

TO-MORROW NIGHT, THURSDAY, AND
EVERY TUESDAY AND SATURDAY
NIGHT AT 8

RANDWICK OF THE DOGS

The Most Up-to-Date Coursing Track in N.S.W.

Hurdle Racing and Best Dogs Engaged

TAKE BAY ST., BOTANY, OR DACEY-VILLE TRAMS.

NOTE THE PRICES.

Leger 2/-
Paddock 4/6
Ladies, Paddock, and Leger, 2/-
Res. Grandstand, Gents 7/-
Ladies 3/-

We pay tax.

Greyhound racing, behind a mechanical lure or 'tin hare', had settled down to become the sport of the working man when this advertisement for a meeting at Randwick, Sydney, appeared in the Referee *in December 1927*

While gentlemen raced and hunted, bare-knuckle fighting was the sport of the convict and the common man in the earliest days of British settlement in Australia. The organised fights went for a limitless number of Rounds, until one man was unable to continue. Dog fighting and cock fighting were also popular and, along with bare-knuckle fighting, have long since been outlawed. A re-enactment from the television series 'Blood, Sweat and Tears'

Paul Tatz

For years in the colony nothing surpassed bare-knuckle fighting for popularity, even when it was outlawed. Sometimes the fighters, mauling, wrestling, tearing at each other's eyes, went on for hours, each knock-down or fall-down marking the end of a round. The fighter then had thirty seconds to 'come up to scratch' or reach the line drawn across the centre of the ring or lose the bout. Betting was enormous. In early times, fighters were often pushed back into the ring helpless, often almost unconscious, by their handlers. When Jim Kelly fought Jonathan Smith in 1854, the fight lasted six hours. Eventually, the influence of humanity led to the introduction of a rule stipulating that a man must return to centre ring voluntarily, so reducing the number of fighters savagely beaten and injured.

In 1847, Bill Sparkes sailed to England to fight the pride of Britain, Nat Langham. Sparkes was beaten in the sixty-seventh round when the referee intervened although it was said the Australian showed pluck. He fought five rounds with his arm broken in two places.

Ned Kelly was a bare-knuckle man of some distinction. Upon his release after a three-year gaol term, he challenged the man who put him behind bars, 'Wild' Wright, and proceeded to beat Wright, 'a six foot, two inch thrashing machine', over twenty rounds to become heavyweight champion of north-eastern Victoria.

Albert Griffiths was the offspring of a tough environment. He was named 'Young Griffo' to differentiate between himself and his wharf-labouring father. Only in recent years has he gained acceptance from America as Australia's first genuine international boxing champion. Griffo was from the Sydney Rocks area, a man with

Blood and Guts

as much natural boxing genius as mad eccentricity. He trained on alcohol and was often restrained in gaol to restrict his access to liquor and to prepare him for fights. He fought inside and outside the ring, he brawled in the streets, he boozed and caroused, and kept on winning. The best featherweight in the world failed to stop Griffo nor did the disease of alcoholism.

Born in 1871, Griffo soon learned to defend himself as a newspaper boy in the harsh Sydney waterside area. Illiterate and unable to write his name, he became the street-fighting hero of a gang known as the Rocks Push, a mob which prowled the waterfront for victims. For all his behaviour and refusal to undergo the fighting man's usual Spartan existence, nothing stopped Griffo. He gained a win over the New Zealander, 'Torpedo' Billy Murphy, then considered world featherweight title holder, following Murphy's knockout of Ike Weir in 1890. Griffo was dropped twice in the early rounds, but then he began to master Murphy and by the fifteenth round the New Zealander was so badly cut and bloodied he dragged off his gloves and forfeited the fight. Americans discredited the win, claiming Murphy had relinquished the world title by leaving America.

To gain recognition, Griffo decided to venture to America. Upon his farewell, he immediately became so homesick that he plunged from the side of the boat into Sydney Harbour and was dragged by cheering admirers as he was taken back to the wharf. When he eventually reached America, he had several fights before challenging the man recognised as world champion, Jack McAuliffe, a title fight which many observers believed Griffo won. The referee Maxie Moore was apparently a friend of the champion. McAuliffe retained his title.

Griffo fought and won against boxers far heavier than himself, up to the welter division, despite his infamous training programme of saloon-crawling between which he had sparring sessions with policemen on the beat. He fought a draw with

Australian boxer Bill Sparkes and Englishman Nat Langham depicted during their epic bare-knuckle fight at Woking, England in 1847. Langham won in the 67th round, after the Australian had fought five rounds with a broken arm. From Australian Ring *magazine*

Blood, Sweat and Tears

the world lightweight champion, Kid Lavigne, and again observers considered he won though he consumed four bottles of beer during the fight, in the process making Lavigne appear a novice with the brilliance of his ringcraft.

With the retirement of McAuliffe, the world title was claimed by George Dixon and although Griffo fought the Black American three times, three draws resulted, many again believing Griffo won the bouts. Decline into alcoholism was inevitable. Convicted of assaulting a policeman, Griffo spent a year in prison and shortly after his release was found by a New York patrol in a drunken stupor on the footpath. Charged with drunkenness, he challenged everyone in court to a fight, attempted to assault the judge and was committed to an insane asylum for three years; he emerged a bloated wreck of a man although apparently cured of alcoholism. Funds were raised for his return to Australia, but Young Griffo stayed in New York, never returning to Australia before his death at 56 in 1927.

At Griffo's funeral, James J. Corbett said of him: 'There he is, boys, the ring zephyr of all time. The only one who ever hit him was the grim reaper'.

The battle which became the hallmark of ferocity in Australian boxing history and a legend in sporting folklore was a fight which involved two North Americans. The venue was Sydney Stadium, then an open-air arena on an old Chinese market garden at Rushcutters Bay. The date was Boxing Day 1908, and the bout was for the heavyweight title of the world, the only occasion the crown has ever been fought for in Australia.

A huge all-male crowd (there were a few women in disguise) gathered at Rushcutters Bay, NSW, for the now legendary fight between French-Canadian Tommy Burns and Jack Johnson in 1908. Stung by the pre-fight insults of the smaller Burns, the huge black American battered his opponent unmercifully for fourteen rounds, although he could have ended the fight at any time after the seventh round
Mitchell Library

Tommy Burns was the champion, a white French-Canadian, and Jack Johnson was his Negro challenger. Before the fight, Burns antagonised Johnson by caustically saying: 'Me fight Johnson? Who'd pay to see me give a nigger a boxing lesson? We could hold the fight in a water closet for all the crowd we'd get. Most of these niggers are yellow rather than black'.

Johnson, massive and shaven-headed, came to Australia to fight Burns only to be rebuffed. It was only the immense purse of £6000 which induced Burns to defend his crown upon the return of Johnson to Australia from England. Burns's comments belittling the challenger inflamed Johnson and, when a late dispute about the referee threatened the bout, Johnson told the promoter, Hugh D. McIntosh: 'Ah'm a nigger. Ah'm used to having to score two points to get one. You've played straight with me. Ah trust you. You referee this contest yourself'.

A crowd of 20 000 saw the fight in sweltering heat. Women were barred although several watched in various male disguises; another 20 000 people remained outside. The fight proved a mismatch, marred throughout by Johnson's jibes at Burns, the shortest of all heavyweight champions. The man known as the 'Black Colossus' rained blows on Burns's swollen and suspected broken jaw, hammering him mercilessly with his great hands and 17-inch upper arms. Johnson could have knocked out Burns at any stage after the seventh round, but he continued to slash and taunt the champion until the fourteenth round when he attacked furiously until he felled Burns for a count of eight. The police superintendent at ringside leapt to his feet, lifted his riding crop and Hugh McIntosh ended the fight, crowning Johnson the first black heavyweight champion of the world.

The story of our most tragic boxer Les Darcy will be told elsewhere.

Jack Hassen never knew his parents. Born in Cloncurry, Queensland, in 1925, he was orphaned at two and brought up on Palm Island mission station off Townsville. He worked as a stockman in north Queensland and at 18 went to the Charters Towers rodeo to 'earn a quid'. It was Christmas eve 1945, and in the main street the young Aboriginal was jostled and challenged to a fight by a stranger. Hassen threw one punch and felled his assailant, whereupon a group of locals, with the promise of £5 a fight, asked Hassen to join the local boxing troupe which was about to engage in a night of fights against the local RAAF base.

Hassen was matched over six rounds against the RAAF's main fighter, a former Melbourne main-event professional named Ernie Hammond, and Hassen won convincingly. Because of heavy wagering on Hammond, a number of angered RAAF men leapt into the ring, knocking the referee to the canvas. When law and order prevailed, Hassen returned to knock out two more opponents. Hassen received £15 and the prize-money tempted him to join the troupe of the well-known travelling boxing promoter Jimmy Sharman.

Hassen was required to mingle with the crowd and volunteer to fight one of the boxers Sharman paraded outside his tent before each programme. Fighting took Hassen south to the bright lights of Brisbane where he fought Ernie McQuillan's experienced Les Fuller. After four rounds Fuller, bleeding freely, gasped: 'That kid's fists are like hammers. He's going to kill me'.

Hassen went to Sydney as the new member of McQuillan's stable and quickly established himself as the most exciting boxer in Australia, outpointing the American Negro Tommy Stenhouse and stopping world-rated Frenchmen Pierre Montane and André Famechon.

But on the night of 19 September 1949, the spectre of death hovered over Sydney Stadium. Hassen met the Victorian Archie Kemp for the Australian lightweight title which had been vacant since the retirement of Vic Patrick. A clever boxer without Hassen's strength, Kemp outpointed the Aboriginal for the first eight rounds after which Hassen's power began to overwhelm him. Three energy-sapping stomach blows made Kemp sag visibly and Hassen stopped fighting. Hassen looked to referee Joe Wallis who issued the fateful instruction: 'Keep fighting!' Hassen unleashed another barrage which dropped Kemp. With blood oozing from his mouth, the unconscious Kemp was rushed to hospital where he died the following day from a brain haemorrhage.

The title of Australian champion meant nothing to Hassen. He was never the same fighter again and although he continued in the profession after an eight-month rest, his decline was rapid. In his first fight he walked into his dressing room and found a newspaper clipping of his fight with Kemp lying on a table. Hassen fought as if in a trance and was decisively outpointed by the highly rated Mexican, Baby Ortiz.

'Every time I threw a punch, I could see Archie Kemp's face — and the blood', Hassen said.

Freddie Dawson and Joe Brown, later to become world champion, both stopped Hassen. The end was near for the champion and although he knocked out Ken Bailey, Hassen lost twice to national welterweight champion, Mickey Tollis. In 1951 Frank Flannery stopped Hassen in the ninth round for the Australian title and he did not fight again although he continued giving exhibitions in Jimmy Sharman's tent for two years after retirement.

Time after time Australia's supreme sportsmen have emerged from poverty. Repeatedly, the words of the Prussian general of last century, Karl von Clausewitz, the commander who revolutionised the theory of war, ring true: 'Sport is the continuation of war by other means'.

Hector Thompson was born and bred in the Kempsey area, the birthplace of the mighty middleweight, Dave Sands. An Aborigine who lost his mother several months after birth, he was reared in a boys' home and married at 17 years of age. In 1970 Thompson fought and knocked out Rocco Spanja, a young Melbourne boxer, who died from the encounter. A troubled and caring man, Thompson said later: 'I know it wasn't my fault. But I felt pretty bad about it. I finally came to grips with it and realised it was something that happens'. Thompson discussed the matter with his wife and returned to the fight game although the tragedy weighed heavily on his mind, causing him to lose two fights. Thompson went on to claim the Australian junior welterweight, lightweight and welterweight titles as well as the British Commonwealth junior welter title. He fought his way into world rankings and challenged the great Panamanian champion Roberto Duran for the world lightweight title in Panama City in 1973, a fight the Australian lost by a technical knockout in the eighth round. Two years later, Thompson also lost a light welterweight world title fight in the seventh round with a badly cut eye to the Columbian, Antonio Cervantes.

Following the Rocco Spanja tragedy, Thompson invariably uttered a brief prayer before his fights: 'Please, God, don't let me kill anyone'. But fate was to deal him another terrible blow in 1976. Fighting at the Blacktown RSL club, Thompson trailed on points before stopping a 22-year-old American, Chuck Wilburn, in the tenth round. Wilburn was carried from the ring on a stretcher. He suffered a brain haemorrhage and died in a coma eight days later.

'I am not a cruel or hateful person', Thompson said after the second fatality, 'I'm sorry that it happened. But I also realise it could have been me. I fight to win. I'm a married man with a family to support, and this is my living. I'm a full-time professional fighter working to win a world title. I don't go out to kill people. I go out to win like a sportsman'.

Thompson said of campaigners striving to have boxing outlawed: 'I think boxing and other contact sports are important to the public. If they couldn't watch these contests, what would they do? They would probably be out in the streets fighting each other'.

Jeff Fenech was a street larrikin who became Australia's first triple world boxing champion. The son of Maltese migrants, born in the inner-Sydney industrial suburb of Pyrmont, Fenech spent his childhood in the working-class suburbs of Newtown and Marrickville and lived in Five Dock, yet he grew up to drive a red Ferrari and become a national celebrity. He might well have turned to crime instead of fighting as an Olympian had it not been for a providential act by the Australian representative Rugby League forward, Pat Jarvis.

At 12, Fenech spent seven weeks in a boys' home following an assault charge.

Blood and Guts

Fenech accidentally struck another boy with his bat in a cricket match and the casualty's family responded by kicking in the doors of the Fenech family's newly acquired Holden car. Jeff broke into the family's house and wrecked its interior. Pat Jarvis talked to Fenech and persuaded him to go to the local Newtown Police Boys' Club where he would have an outlet for his larrikinism and energy in the ring.

Fenech came from a poor but thrifty family. A heart problem had prevented Fenech's father, a forklift driver, from working and forced him to take an invalid pension for a number of years. His mother supported six children and worked as a factory cleaner to pay their mortgage. From this destitution, Fenech went to the 1984 Los Angeles Olympics where he was favoured to win a gold medal only to lose a disputed decision to the Yugoslav fighter, Redzep Redzepovski. He turned professional and within four years the 'Marrickville Mauler' had won three world titles.

In his own words, Fenech was 'the smallest, skinniest, scrawniest little bastard. That's why I went to the gym, to punch the bag and build up. I started boxing because I wanted to play Rugby League. When I was at school, if two kids had a fight in the playground, the whole school was there to watch in an instant. It carries on — everyone loves a good fight'.

When Fenech met Johnny Lewis, the man who became his friend and trainer, Lewis remarked: 'He was a little time bomb who could explode at any moment. I knew that to teach him self-discipline, someone had to become his boss. And I asked myself if I could do it'. Fenech recalled: 'When I get into the ring to do my job, I hate the other guy. I have to hate him. It's no use going out there liking someone if you're going to punch his head in. In boxing, you've got to knock him out before he knocks you out. It's as simple as that'.

The speed and fury of Jeff Fenech's punches not only won him this World Super-Bantamweight title fight against Samart Payakarun, but sent the Thai retreating to a Buddhist monastery to escape the wrath of disappointed Thai fans
Live Action: Acikalin

Into the square sunshine of boxing, a world of speed and power, of épée and sledgehammer, celebrities and obscurities intermingle, from prime minister to proletarian. Before Fenech's fight for the World Boxing Council world super-bantamweight title with the Thai, Samart Payakarun, Prime Minister Bob Hawke rang to wish him success. Café society beckons but Fenech prefers the company of associates of his youth and upbringing.

Fenech has been described as a throwback to another, more violent age, a man haunted by the thought of defeat. His attitude is one of 'kill or be killed'. But boxing has an appeal beyond the spectacle of blood and brutality. There is a beauty in its electrifying swiftness and movement, its technique and decisiveness.

For all boxing's ruthlessness, for all Fenech's aggression, he went to the corner of rival featherweight Tony Miller after an early title fight, still sweating from the bout, his hands bruised from the hiding he had given Miller. 'I kept thinking why doesn't his trainer or the referee stop the fight?' Fenech said. 'They should have stopped it seven rounds earlier. I said to his trainer: "Jeez, how cruel are you? Don't you care about him?"' Yet of himself, of the heaviest punches he has taken, Fenech says: 'Pain is mental. I tell myself to feel none, so I have none'. Fenech's promoter, Bill Mordey, said of him: 'Ninety per cent of him is lovely kid, and the other 10 per cent . . . well, if he didn't have that 10 per cent, he would not be a champion'.

Fenech is a man of tremendous energy and emotions, whose loyalty and friendship are as important as his titles. He reflects on his career with simultaneous pride and misgiving: 'I've loved [fighting] the last couple of years. But what I've done has been more than hard — it's been torture. I just couldn't tell anyone to do it, and there's no way in the world I'd want my children to do it'.

When Clive Churchill played his first game of Rugby League, he was told to play in the back line at centre. He ran on the field and put his head into the forward scrum. Initially, he played without boots and kicked goals with his bare feet. When chosen for his school's over-weight team, he was instructed to buy boots. He received twelve shillings and sixpence from his mother and bought his first pair of boots at a Newcastle store.

He became the 'Little Master', the most fiery fullback of all Rugby League's champions although less than 12 stone in weight. Brilliant, sometimes abrasive, possessing a baffling swerve and superb, low tackle, he played in thirty-four Tests, captained Australia and eventually coached the Kangaroos. Born at Merewether opposite South Newcastle's Rugby League ground at Mitchell Park in 1927, he came to Sydney and joined South Sydney (nicknamed the 'Rabbitohs'). In the Rabbitohs' first game against Newtown, the formidable Frank 'Bumper' Farrell marked Churchill as he played the ball. 'Hello, son!' Bumper said, and almost wrenched the youngster's head off, leaving him with a cauliflower ear, prompting a long-running feud between the pair.

So quickly did Churchill sweep on the scene and so much of a stranger was he that he was referred to in a newspaper as 'Charlie' Churchill when selected for the Kangaroo team to tour England in 1948. Against Huddersfield, Australia's savage tackling and the ferocity of the game angered the crowd which threatened to storm on the ground after Johnny Hunter, the Australian fullback with Huddersfield, swerved inside Johnny 'Whacker' Graves only to be knocked unconscious when Graves struck Hunter across the face. Hunter was carried off and when the full-time whistle blew, the crowd surged over the fence in pursuit of Graves. The local band burst into the National Anthem, the crowd stopped as one man and Graves, who had a sprained ankle, hobbled into the security of the pavilion.

In Wellington, New Zealand, Churchill was accidentally kneed in the face and his nose shattered across his face. He returned to the field, his face masked in blood. An operation was necessary, but he played in the next game with a special

Blood and Guts

'The Little Master', Clive Churchill has been described as 'the greatest all-round champion the Rugby League code has ever known'. He played in thirty-four Tests and was captain and then coach of Australia. In one club game he played with a broken wrist, which was splinted at half-time, and converted after the final bell for victory
Rugby League Week

noseguard, whereupon a rival seized the protection, pulled it to the extent of the elastic and fired it like a catapult against his broken nose.

In 1951, France's fabulous pair of second rowers Elie Brousse and Edouard Ponsinet combined to crash-tackle Churchill in the Brisbane Test as retribution for an earlier late tackle by Churchill, and the little fullback was carried off unconscious. He stumbled back on several minutes later, grinning, and said to the Frenchmen: 'That makes us quits!' and dropped a field goal from 50 metres out.

In 1955, Churchill's left wrist was broken in the first five minutes of South's game against Manly at Redfern Oval. The wrist was placed in a splint of cardboard at half-time and Churchill was given a pain-killing injection. In agony, he returned to the field. Just before full-time, Chick Cowie, the Australian lock, scored in the corner to level the scores, 7-all. South's captain Jack Rayner called out: 'Clive, you're taking the kick . . . it's your day!' The full-time bell sounded as Churchill placed the ball on the sideline, his wrist hanging by his side, and he drove the ball through the posts for victory, 9–7. It was the inspiration the Rabbitohs needed and they went on to claim the premiership.

Churchill was described by Harry 'Jersey' Flegg as 'the greatest all-round champion the Rugby League code has known'. But for all his honours and triumphs, Churchill's proudest moment came as South's coach in the 1970 grand final when the Rabbitohs' captain John Sattler walked off the Sydney Cricket Ground as the premiership skipper, his jaw shattered. Ten minutes after the kick-off, Sattler was punched from behind, the blow breaking his jaw. The prop played on and even at half-time Churchill did not suspect the extent of the injury although he questioned Sattler about his gaping jaw. Sattler mumbled 'I'm okay' and left the room. As international second rower Bob McCarthy rose to return to the ground, he told Churchill, 'Satts shouldn't be going back . . . he's broken his jaw'. Churchill rushed from the room to recall his captain, but Sattler was already out on the Sydney Cricket Ground. Churchill recalled: 'The way Satts played that second half you could not believe a man could go through so much pain. It's the bravest thing I have ever seen in all my years of football. When I walked out to greet the players after our win, tears came to my eyes.

'Just to see and know what this man had been through . . . you just can't measure that sort of courage. Satts's face was covered with blood, but he didn't complain once.'

Johnny Raper was lock forward during St George Rugby League club's greatest reign in Sydney in the 1960s. He trialled as a 17-year-old for Newtown in 1957, showing uncanny positional sense, good hands and, above all, proving a fierce tackler, transferring to Saints in 1959 without a penny changing hands before the transfer system was introduced. Raper helped Saints win eight premierships in the club's golden era 1956–66. Raper played in thirty-three Tests, had three Kangaroo tours and was involved in the World Cups of 1960 and 1968, captaining Australia to cup triumph in 1968.

He was one of nine children of a battling Catholic family from Newtown. His mother managed to save five shillings, or about 50 cents, for a second-hand pair of boots and he played in League competitions; each child was rewarded with a bottle of milk. Johnny played morning and afternoon to earn two bottles of milk, one to drink at lunch and the second 'for Mum'. When he played for Camperdown Junior C grade team, his pay was three bottles of beer. He did his best to play all three grades to receive twenty-one bottles as his payment.

'Rugby League is a love affair with me', Johnny said once. 'Luckily, I'm married to a girl who will allow me an outside romance. If Caryl didn't understand the thing I have for the game and wasn't able to make allowances for me, it would have been impossible.

'Rugby League is a man's game. It is not a thug's game as many knockers like to claim. To me the game has always been a business. You have to use tact, be forceful, alert, thinking all the time and able to show initiative. Once these qualities are developed, you are on the way to becoming a champion. But they have to be backed up by physical toughness, determination and the will to win. I was never really happy until the time came to run on the field for a big game, and the bigger the game the better I liked it.'

Friends joked about Raper's passion for the game and of his being buried on a Rugby League field. 'That's carrying things a bit far', he said, 'but if it happens, make sure it's over the other team's try line'.

Raper was incomparable. Fred Jones, Manly-Warringah's captain, said to Raper after Manly's elimination of Saints in the 1969 semi-final with the lock standing nearby, blood trickling from his right eye down his face: 'We have beaten St George today, but we did not beat you'.

Blood and Guts

Lock forward John Raper helped St George win eight Premierships in the club's golden era from 1956 to 1966. Raper played in thirty-three Tests, had three Kangaroo Tours and captained Australia to a World Cup triumph in 1968
John Fairfax & Sons Ltd

Raper fractured his left ankle on his first Kangaroo tour in 1958–9, which forced him to miss the first two Tests, but he played in the third as five-eighth and scored a try. It was on his return to England in 1963 that he proved his greatness. When the English winger Mike Sullivan flattened Raper with a head-high tackle in the sleet and snow of the second Test at Swinton, Raper peered up through blood-glazed eyes and said, 'That's one you missed!' as Peter Dimond, the Australian winger he had slipped the ball to, dashed over for the try, 50 metres away. 'I don't miss many, lad!' Sullivan snarled. Australia won by a record 50–12, and Raper was in practically every move. It was probably his finest Test.

Nearing 39 and considering a comeback for his original club, the Newtown Jets, Raper headed off for a run on Cronulla beach, pumping legs in thigh-deep surf and through the sandhills. 'It's bloody hard', he said. 'Dedication . . . it's a word often abused, attributed too easily. But you don't know what a ferocious thing it can be, especially when you've always expected one hell of a lot from yourself'.

Towards the end of his career, Raper said: 'It's a hard game to quit. But it's harder to come back. Everyone's born with some natural talent. Then it's dedication and time spent on practice that brings out the best. I've found gifted players largely to be lazy trainers, tending to rely too heavily on natural ability. This either shortens their career or leaves them sitting on the sidelines. I can't tolerate a month-by-month player. I demand a man totally committed to the task. It's got to be that way now. The rules of the game and the techniques of training have changed. The workload has increased and will get heavier. Media exposure of the game has made spectators more demanding of players. I did well out of football, but I've never gone on to the field because of the money'.

When it was all over, he said: 'Rugby League has been my life, my heart and soul. I would be nothing without it. I thought I would rather face an English Test team on my own at the SCG than face this decision. I've made the decision and the way I feel, I could beat those thirteen Poms'.

Barry Muir was a fearless firebrand of a Rugby League half from the far north coast of New South Wales at Tweed Heads. His father had deserted the family when Barry was three years old. Just before Muir was to run on to Brisbane's Lang Park for his first Test against New Zealand in 1959 a man approached him and asked, 'Do you know me?'. Barry shook the outstretched hand and said: 'How do you do, Mr Muir?' and turned and walked away with tears of anger in his eyes. It was typical of Muir that after the initial meeting and bitterness, he saw his father again on several occasions before his father's death in 1970. The Kangaroo half of twenty-six Tests and World Cup games had the harshest of childhoods, made the more tragic by the loss of his mother in 1967 when she received fatal burns after her nightdress caught fire. Barry had to identify his mother.

He developed a long pass by aiming at a goal post. He was tough and tackled the biggest players, yet the same man hid beneath his bed in England to avoid a run across the moors on the 1963 Kangaroo tour. Early in his career, he was dropped from the Toowoomba team after one game when legendary coach Duncan Thompson told him: 'You'll have to stop all this tackling if you want to make the grade. You're only wearing yourself out'.

His tenacity and willingness to mete out punishment became legendary. 'People don't go to the cricket to watch Dennis Lillee bowl off breaks . . . and they don't go to Rugby League matches to see powder puff stuff', he said. 'Yeah, sure I put the biff on early in a match. When I played it was accepted that the first ten minutes were the softening-up period.

'Players sorted each other out. The referees knew it and accepted it. But they always clamped down on spiteful play. It was simply put the stick on your opponent and see if he could cop it. If he couldn't, you knew you would be on top all day.'

There were few more brilliant half-backs in Rugby League than Great Britain's Alex Murphy, but Muir invariably unsettled him early on by clipping him on the chin. 'There was only one way to handle Alex and that was to put it on him from the start', Muir explained. 'You know, a belt over the ear or an elbow in the ribs, and he couldn't concentrate on his game any more'.

Muir rose from a Coolangatta High schoolboy to a Kangaroo half on the tour of England in 1959–60. Australia lost the Tests, 2–1, and won all three in France, but by the end of the tour, he was the man the English forwards resented and disliked the most. Reg Gasnier and Harry Wells were backs in the team and Brian Hambly

Reg Gasnier, one of the greatest Rugby League centres ever, was appointed Australia's youngest-ever Test captain in 1962 for the series against England
Rugby League Week

one of the outstanding forwards, but an English forward said: 'Nay, it weren't Wells or Gasnier or Hambly what did damage, it was that bloody little half-back'.

Tom Raudonikis was Rugby League's favourite larrikin, and 'the roughest, meanest half in the world'. Born in a migrant camp at Bathurst, his father was a Lithuanian who had escaped from a German prisoner-of-war camp, and his mother was Swiss. He grew up accustomed to fighting and claimed 'you felt better next day'.

Tom Terrific (as he was known) was puzzled by the source of his aggression. 'In football I wasn't a great natural player. I was always a good player, but I had to work my arse off to be tops. I didn't get a bad time because I had migrant parents. I was just a scrapper'. Margrit, his mother, said: 'At school his team was unbeaten for nine years . . . he doesn't like losing, you know'.

Raudonikis always played for battlers' clubs: Western Suburbs and Newtown. He wept when he was made a life member of Wests and after his 200th first grade game in which Wests beat Manly, the Sydney silvertails. Tom says: 'People say they are louts at Wests. They are good people. As for Manly . . . we all have a drink after the game, but on the field I hate them to pieces. Whatever a coach can use to gee you up is fine. If he tells you they're all lying on the beach while you're working . . . anyway, we've given them some bloody good hidings'. In fourteen seasons and twenty-one Tests, Tommy had his cheekbone, arm, nose, ribs and fingers all broken, and teeth knocked out. His rewards were two Kangaroo tours and four tours in all to England, the Order of Australia medal and Test captaincy.

When Wests' forwards were beaten to a frazzle in one game, coach Roy Masters remembered Raudonikis taking on the entire Manly pack after breaking his right thumb early in the game. He had begun the game with two broken bones in his left hand.

'It hasn't all been roses', he says. 'But football introduced me to ambition. When I came to Sydney at 18 in 1969, I had two goals — get out of the air force and make a career. I accomplished both'. In his time with Wests, he became as permanent as

Blood, Sweat and Tears

Lidcombe railway station. 'I come from a battling family, I've always been a battler, I like being with battlers. And I don't care what happens during a game as long as my team wins'. On the field friendship flew out the window. 'I hate them', he said, 'Later, we'll all have a beer together and be friends again'. When recalled to first grade after a period in reserve grade, he said: 'I'll be getting a few whacks in the mouth and it'll be beautiful'.

Newtown was an inner-city club which became an island fortress surrounded by factories in a basically non-League area due to the migrant population. Frank Farrington, former New South Wales light-heavyweight boxing champion and Newtown secretary, said: 'As a fighter, Tommy would have finished a human wreck. He's too courageous for his own good . . . too much heart. He can't take a backward step. It's not in his blood'.

Graeme Langlands was a fullback or centre of true greatness. During the 1971 tour of New Zealand, he was hit in the ribs and began spitting blood. He insisted on carrying on. An opposition second rower was heading for the try line when Langlands hit him with a tackle which took them both into the safety fence. New Zealand were well ahead, but Langlands could not countenance defeat. Langlands finished the game in great pain, and later it was established that his rib had punctured his lung.

The star of Queensland Rugby League football, Wally Lewis, in action in an Australian representative match.
Rugby League Week

There has been many a stoush in Australian Rules football, a fast-paced, high contact sport invented in Victoria and the main code of four southern States. These players, from Collingwood and the Sydney Swans, seem a little tentative, but the Swans (then South Melbourne) were involved in the roughest game of all — the 1945 'Blood Bath' Grand Final against Carlton. Ten players were reported and seven were suspended for periods ranging from eight to twelve weeks.
Live Action: Michael Rayner

The stories are legion of courage beyond the call of duty. In 1932 in what is known as the 'Battle of Brisbane', the Ipswich forward Dan Dempsey broke his arm, only to return to the field after his arm was set, pulling off the bandages and saying he would at least get in the way of the Great Britain players.

Jack Dyer, or 'Captain Blood' as he was known when captain-coach of Richmond Australian Rules Football club in Melbourne, was introduced at the University of Melbourne in 1948 as the 'most famous Australian since Ned Kelly'. He was the iron man of the Victorian Football League, a ruckman who played for more than nineteen years and in 311 games, a player hated, feared, worshipped.

When he began League football in 1931, Jack earned £3 a game, almost as much as the basic wage. 'You either played hard or not at all', he said. He had huge hands. In one season, he broke five players' collarbones. He was sometimes described as Australia's best footballer, but he never won the VFL's Brownlow Medal, the award for the best and fairest.

In one VFL game between Richmond and Footscray, Jack knocked a newcomer flat. Dyer grinned and turned away and the youngster got up, pursued him and dropped him with a smashing right to the chin. When he got to his knees, Captain Blood said: 'You nearly killed me'. 'Kill you?' came the reply, 'Couldn't kill you with a bloody axe'. Dyer pleaded for the Footscray player at the hearing and he received a one-week suspension. 'He should have got a VC', was one secretary's opinion.

Jack Dyer played his way out of the poverty of the Depression years. He said: 'If you're born in Richmond, you have to do two things: vote Labor and barrack for the Tigers. You've got to remember that Richmond was like a little island in those days. We had Victoria Street to the north. That was the front line with Collingwood. To the west we had Punt Road, which cut us off from Melbourne, and we had the Yarra River at our backs'. Dyer's father was an engine driver. Jack began playing at Yarra Junction at seven when 'football boots were like gold'. He painted a seven-room house in school holidays to buy a pair of football boots. Richmond in 1928 was about to plunge into the Depression. The area was mainly Irish, Catholic and poor. People were close and shared food if anything was left over. The religion of the unemployed was fighting, football and politics, and gangs roamed the streets.

Jack grew to be a big man, a fine mark and strong kick. And he was fast. He had the football brain of a champion. At 12 he played in the Upper Yarra Valley senior competition, barefoot, among men. It drew criticism and he was told he could not play until he obtained boots.

Brother Peter of St Ignatius' School in Melbourne, a former Rugby player, had the attitude: 'I don't care how you win, just so long as you win'. After Dyer broke an opponent's collarbone, his coach excused it by saying: 'He should have got out of your way'. 'After that', Jack said, 'I never worried about knocking opponents down. If it was all right with a Christian Brother, it was all right with me'.

He went to Richmond to train in 1931, and at 17 played for the Tigers. He said: 'My dad taught me long ago to strive to be the top dog. He used to say: "They only pay out on winners". A good punch-up never really worried me, but it frightened the hell out of some of my opponents'. One club official said of Dyer: 'I hate him. But I wish we had him on our side'.

In 1948, Melbourne ruckman Frank Hanna played all over Captain Blood until Hanna went down with a broken collarbone. The next year, back from the injury, Hanna again outplayed Dyer, and again he went down with a broken collarbone. Dyer stood over him and said: 'Many happy returns, Frank'. In one game, a Footscray fan called out: 'You rotten mug, Dyer. You'll get yours, you big gorilla'. Dyer's mother was seated nearby, and said, 'You wouldn't say that if his father was here'. The spectator responded: 'I wouldn't think he'd have a father, lady'.

Cricket came with the First Fleet and was played socially through the late eighteenth century. The match generally accepted as the first officially recorded in Australia was between officers and crew of HMS *Calcutta* in 1803. In 1877 the first Test match took place between Australia and England at the Melbourne Cricket Ground with the Australian opener, Charles Bannerman, registering the game's initial Test century. His retirement for 165 occurred only when Bannerman split a finger. Australia won the game by 45 runs. Coincidentally, Australia won the Test match 100 years later at the Melbourne Cricket Ground by precisely the same margin. In the Centenary Test, Australia's opening batsman Rick McCosker returned to the wicket with his jaw broken, his face swathed in bandages, after being struck by a rising delivery from England fast bowler, Bob Willis. McCosker's courageous stand enabled Australia to win one of the greatest games in history.

The South Australian fast bowler Ernie 'Jonah' Jones provided a forewarning of the intimidation of batsmen to come with a ball which whistled through the beard of England's champion batsman, Dr William G. Grace, on the 1896 tour of England. The Doctor came down the wicket and demanded: 'Where the hell are you bowling, Jonah?' to which Jones replied: 'Sorry, doctor, she slipped'.

The incident served to unsheath the raw edge which soon cut through the Test series between England and the colonials, an inevitable competitiveness and rivalry flaring between wealthy amateurs and working professionals.

In an attempt to master Australia's prodigious run-scorer, England's captain, Douglas Jardine, instructed his fast bowlers, Harold Larwood, Bill Voce, Bill Bowes and 'Gubby' Allen, to bowl short-pitched deliveries at the bodies of Bradman and the Australians, placing an arc of five or six fieldsmen close in on the leg side. Without field placing restrictions as they are now enforced, the Englishmen brought a physical peril to batsmen which had never previously existed. The series reached crisis point in the Adelaide Test when Bill Woodfull was hit over the heart and wicketkeeper Bert Oldfield was struck on the head.

Sir Donald Bradman said: 'It was perfectly obvious to me, from the first time I saw it, that this was a canker which, if it developed, would ruin the game'. For all the

Blood and Guts

attention he received, Don Bradman was struck only once by Harold Larwood and the great Australian finished his four Tests of the series with an average of 56.57, a marked reduction on his Test career average of 99.94. England won the series, 4–1, and the Ashes.

The advent of Kerry Packer's World Series Cricket organisation in 1977 brought a new climate of professionalism to cricket. It ushered in a new era of cricket with expensive, high-powered floodlighting installed at the Victorian Football League Park at Waverley in outer Melbourne, and led to floodlighting of the Sydney and Melbourne Cricket Grounds for day-night limited-over internationals. The promise of an immediate result, the atmosphere and high-profile nature of the evening games led to a more youthful, more demanding, more spirited following of the game. Loutish behaviour on the Sydney Hill caused officials to prevent spectators bringing alcohol to games and ended the sale of beer in cans, which had been used as missiles.

Aggression was unmasked off the cricket field and on it. The *Australian* newspaper spoke of 'barely controlled violence in the four-pronged West Indies pace attack in the 1970s and 80s, but it is within the rules of the game'. During the Test captaincy era of Ian Chappell from 1971 — Australia's most successful cricket period since Don Bradman's 1948 Invincibles' tour of England when the fast-bowling combination of Ray Lindwall, Keith Miller and Bill Johnston was at its peak — the speed attack of Jeff Thomson, Dennis Lillee, Gary Gilmour and Max Walker often brought spectators to fever pitch. Crowds in Australia soared with the number of England and West Indian batsmen struck and injured by the fast bowlers in the 1974–6 seasons. The thunder of the crowds was enormous.

A fearsome sight for English batsmen in the 1970s — the great fast bowling duo of Dennis Lillee (left) and Jeff Thomson at the point of delivery. Later in his career Thomson's form was somewhat affected by a shoulder injury he sustained in a fielding collision
Photobank/All Sport

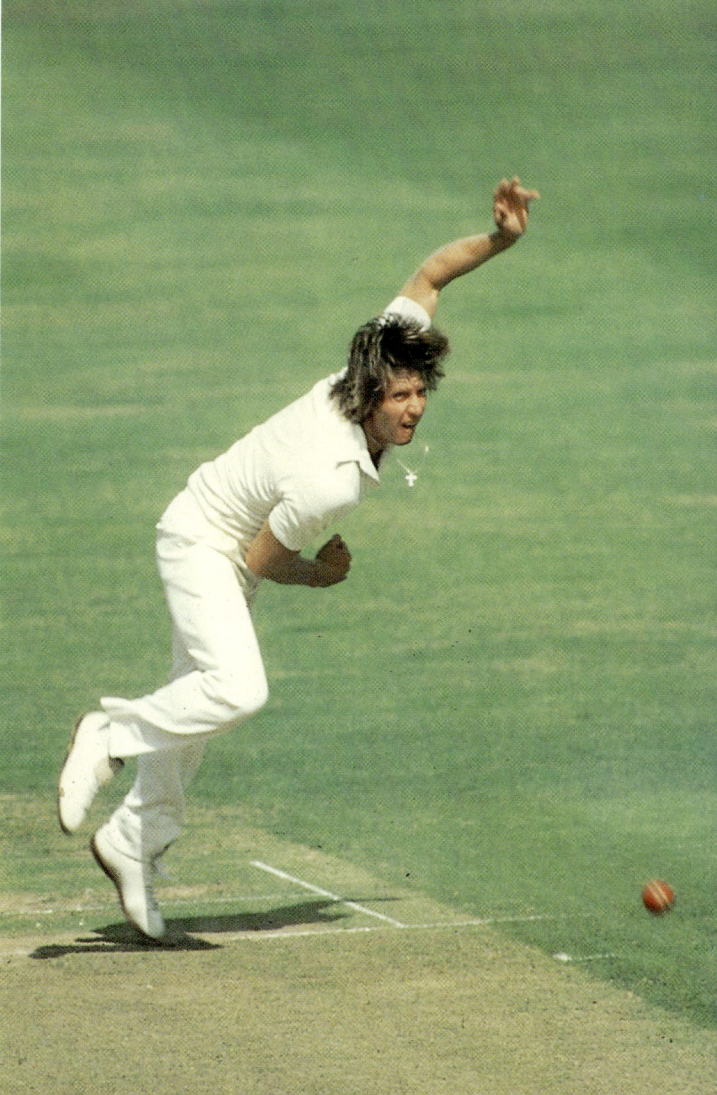

The great players for Australia, Rod Marsh, Greg Chappell and Dennis Lillee retired together in 1984, and left a huge gap in Australia's Test capabilities. Chappell had surpassed Don Bradman's record of Test runs (although in many more matches), Lillee had a record total of Test wickets and Rod Marsh had 355 Test dismissals
Photobank/All Sport

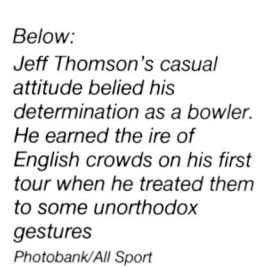

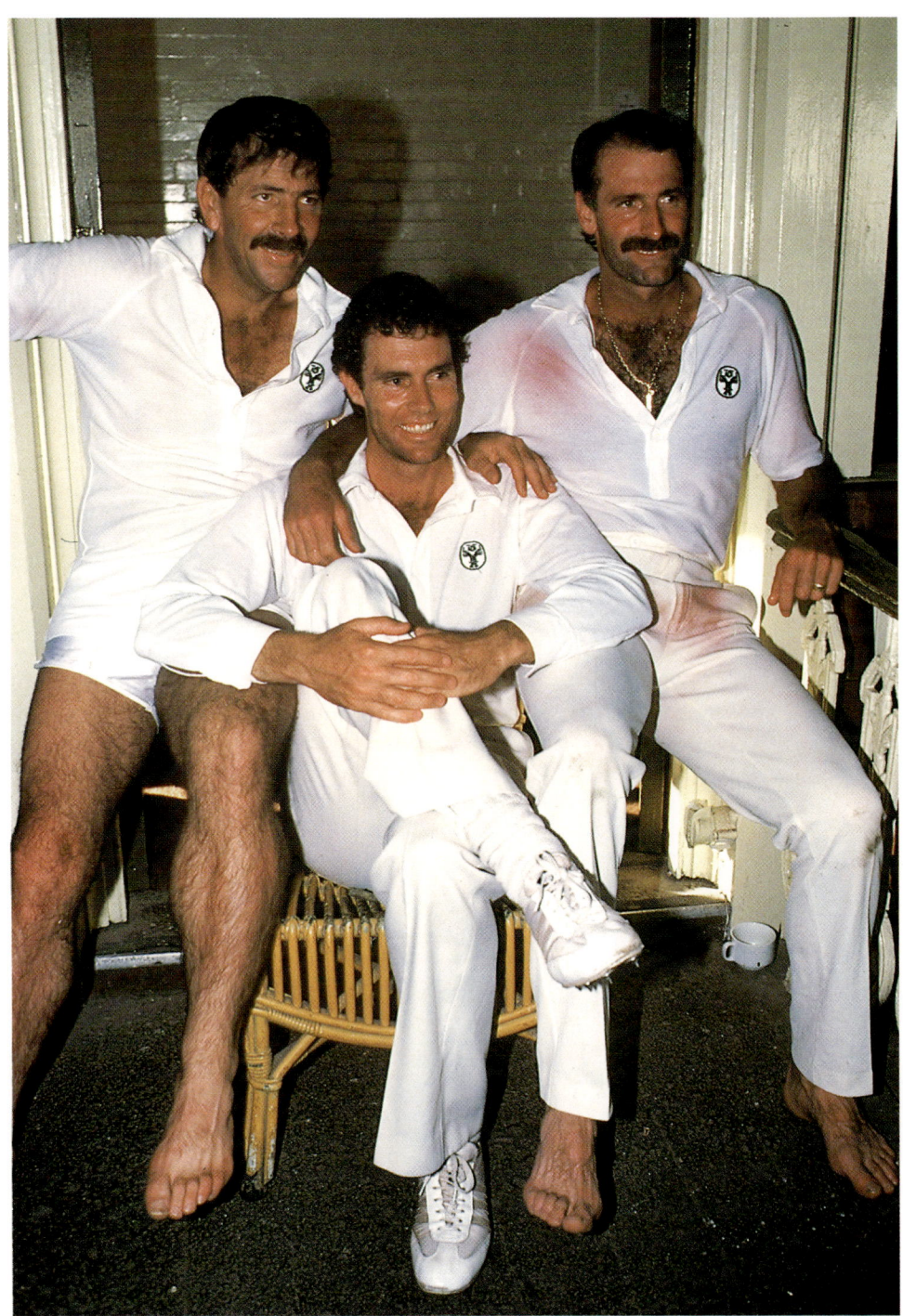

*Below:
Jeff Thomson's casual attitude belied his determination as a bowler. He earned the ire of English crowds on his first tour when he treated them to some unorthodox gestures*
Photobank/All Sport

Lillee said of the Melbourne crowds which boomed and bellowed their support: 'I love 'em all. They have meant more to me than they could imagine. They've been a constant source of inspiration and strength throughout my long, love-hate relationship with that strip of unyielding, unforgiving turf out in the middle of that great cricket arena. As I push off from my mark 30 metres away, the waves of sound push me faster, harder and stronger until there's a great crescendo at delivery stride. It's as though they are trying to offer me their own strength and muscle power. And when there's something there to be lifted, I'm lifted.'

Blood and Guts

As a young man in Sydney, Jeff Thomson, the 200-Test wicket-taker, spoke with relish of striking batsmen with deliveries with his javelin thrower's action, balls which reared from the pitch, shoulder and head-high. He admitted enjoying seeing batsmen bleeding and writhing on the ground, the thud of ball on bone, an attitude which modified as the Test speedster became a much-loved figure of the game.

Thomson's new-ball partner, Lillee, carried on a feud with champion Pakistani batsman, Javed Miandad, which brought Lillee to blood-boiling point in Perth in 1981, an encounter which saw Lillee stab-kick Miandad in the calf as the Pakistani played a ball into the deep and took a leisurely run. The startled batsman responded by waving his bat back over his shoulder, threatening to strike Lillee while umpire Tony Crafter sprang between the pair. The Australian team accused Miandad of causing the trouble and Lillee claimed he was provoked when struck in the rib cage by Miandad's bat, but the Australian Cricket Board was satisfied that Lillee had been the aggressor and suspended the fast bowler for two limited-over games.

Sports psychologists claim some sports with a degree of high risk become addictive, particularly for people with monotonous work or tedious lifestyles. Stepping off a cliff with a cord as thick as a thumb providing life's only security is the excitement of abseiling. For all people involved in sports with the high-pitched ecstasy of the ultimate risk of death, the thrill outweighs the danger.

An Australian Parachuting Association member said: 'The sport attracts people who enjoy an element of danger and who enjoy a challenge. This is the ultimate challenge. There is a terrific adrenalin rush, one of the few sports with such an adrenalin rush. It's very short and very intense, and it all happens in a few minutes'. About 9000 people make initial parachute jumps annually, but of these only about 300 become regular members.

The Australian Hang-gliding Association has 17 000 members. Hang-gliding is a sport which defies death constantly yet, because of the enhanced quality of instructors and equipment, the number of hang-gliding fatalities and serious accidents has declined dramatically in the decade from 1978. Attracted by the spectacle of tiny humans hanging below wheeling, coloured kites in the thermals over cliff tops, people have turned to hang-gliding, not for its perils but for its supreme spectacle and solitude.

As Australian hang-gliding champion Bill Moyes said: 'When I got hold of a hang glider it just fulfilled that dream'. Six weeks after his first flight he had set a new world altitude record. Moyes, like the enthusiast in the picture, is prepared to dare all for the thrill of soaring in space
Photobank/All Sport

Australia, with its comparatively calm weather and flat terrain is ideal for hot air ballooning. The 'Coca-Cola' balloon was up in the early morning at Canowindra, New South Wales
Bay Picture Library

Four people died while hang-gliding in 1978 and four perished parachuting the same year; as well, nine people were seriously injured and fifteen suffered minor injuries in hang-gliding, and there were three serious injuries in parachuting. But by 1987, not a single fatality or injury was recorded in hang-gliding despite four fatalities and one serious injury in parachute jumping. One Hang-gliding Association advocate said: 'It's a safe sport on which a lot of money has been spent on the best equipment and instructors. Most people get satisfaction out of it just because they want to fly like a bird'.

Safety precautions in such sports can only go so far. One hang-glider pilot hung for two hours over a 65-metre drop on the Mount Blackheath escarpment in the Blue Mountains, his glider wedged in rocks, after he was blown into the cliff wall. A police rescue team saved the man and he escaped with abrasions.

Jousting with nature must bring casualties and fatalities. Body contact sports like football also provide a sad toll. The refined technology of scrummaging in Rugby Union and the pressure involved in sixteen tightly bound forwards driving against each other has caused a spate of injuries, some leading to paraplegia and quadriplegia, from players being forced down suddenly on their heads. Troubled by the injuries, the International Rugby Board has modified scrummaging laws, particularly for under-19 teams, with a marked reduction in mishaps.

In the eleven years to 30 June 1987, twenty-two Rugby League players died in New South Wales and fourteen in Rugby Union, whereas Australian Football had just one fatality. The scrum and tackle provide the body contact which makes the two rugby codes so appealing to so many while giving the games inherent dangers. In the same eleven-year period in New South Wales, six cyclists died and one squash player, one diver, one hockey player, one spear fisherman, one soccer player, two canoeists and two horse-race riders.

In 1987, 21-year-old high diver Nathan Meade, of the Australian Institute of Sport, performed a handstand on the 10-metre board in Brisbane and, attempting a reverse two-and-a-half somersault, struck his head on the board, fatally injuring himself.

Sue Howland, the world-ranked Australian javelin thrower, who won the 1982 Brisbane Commonwealth Games gold medal, endured a series of injuries which made her athletic life a torment. For eighteen months before the Games she dislocated her right shoulder almost every time she threw the javelin. She required reconstructive surgery to her shoulder and six months later had her left knee reconstructed, after which her right elbow needed surgery and then her left knee again.

Questioned about the demands made on sportsmen and women, Australian Olympic Federation official Phil Coles said: 'The only pressure we apply involves our standards in that we believe the athletes should make the Olympic semi-finals. Athletes apply pressure to themselves — that's what makes them champions'.

Peril and death ride side-saddle in many sports, not least of all in the Sport of Kings. Neville Sellwood came to Sydney from Brisbane after World War II with two other outstanding jockeys, George Moore and Noel McGrowdie. McGrowdie died prematurely, killed in a car accident in Malaya, while Sellwood suffered fatal internal injuries when the filly Lucky Seven crossed her legs in slippery conditions and fell in France, rolling on him at Maisons Laffitte near Paris in 1962. Sellwood had been deliberating whether to return to ride in the Melbourne Cup or attempt to retain his lead in the French riding premiership. His decision to stay cost him his life. Sellwood's nearest rival was his close friend, Yves St Martin, who eventually finished the season level on 102 wins, and who, as a gesture, presented to Sellwood's widow the prized Golden Whip, France's award to the premier jockey. Sellwood won Melbourne Cups on Delta in 1951 and on Toparoa in 1955 and rode Tulloch to a win in the 1957 Caulfield Cup. He also won the initial Golden Slipper on the flying Todman in 1957 and the English Derby on Larkspur in 1961.

For some years the belief was widely held that watching violent sport reduced the emotional level of aggression in spectators. The theory has lost favour in recent times. Freud suggested sport offered a safety valve for people. Rather than an outlet for tension, it is now considered a source of building and unleashing aggression. Research indicates that to reduce violence, fiercely combative sports should be eliminated. Psychologists have established that people imitate their sporting idols, and if they are aggressive on the field then so, too, are spectators off it. The world's most popular sport — soccer — is a reliable gauge of social behaviour. Violence has become a way of life for some in the game. While vigorous, hard play is enjoyed and welcomed, violence is increasingly abhorred. Declining crowds in Australian and English soccer indicate that followers of the code, particularly families, have turned away from the fighting on the terraces.

There is little argument that the more aggressive the sport and its sportsmen, the more hostile are its spectators. In Hobart in 1987, a sociologist at the Institute of Criminology's seminar on 'Crime in the Future' warned that increasing commercialisation of sport and enlarged television coverage threatened more violence in sport. Television's central requirement was action, he said, and violence assured good action. Violence-related excitement attracted certain people, and sport was frequently a lure. One stratagem used to promote Rugby League in California was to publish a poster graphically showing a spear tackle. The fact that the spear tackle had been barred in Rugby League in Australia was ignored. The sociologist, Dr Stephen Mugford, said that Australia lacked Britain's tradition of male working-class violence and considered it unlikely that gangs of hoodlums would form to follow football clubs such as Parramatta and Penrith in Sydney or Collingwood and Carlton in Melbourne as gangs followed clubs in Europe. 'If this prediction is correct, the main driving forces will not have been the disreputable elements, the mindless violence — a quite incorrect description — of the working class', Dr Mugford said. 'Rather, we shall see that the motivating factor has been the search for greater profits and larger ratings by "respectable" business. In the Australian context, it is these forces rather than any tradition of violence that are developing new aspects of the violence–excitement connection today.'

Professor Leon Mann, of Adelaide's Flinders University, says the violence of soccer crowds often stems from spectators' social background rather than from the sport itself. Because of the deprivations of people following a team, the side's losses were often reflected in supporters' behaviour. Frustration accumulated because of poverty and feelings of helplessness. Defeats only aggravated the fans' frame of mind. 'One of the few satisfactions in their lives is identification with the success of their teams', Professor Mann said. 'If they win, they are elated and if they lose, they suffer a further loss in their lives. If you have virtually no opportunity for succeeding in life, you are stuck with poverty and lack of recognition. The only avenue for recognition is the success of your local team. If your team wins, you share in the recognition. When you lose, you feel you have been robbed of the recognition you deserve. This can lead to aggression.'

Professor Mann said that because Australia does not have the same degrading levels of despair as in regions of Latin America, Europe and Britain, Australia will not experience similar spectator hostility. Despite this reassurance, soccer has been Australia's most vexatious sport because of its mosaic of temperament and cosmopolitan make-up. The National Soccer League executive fined Sydney Olympic club $10 000 and applied a $20 000 good-behaviour bond after a crowd riot led to the abandonment of a game against Sydney City in 1985 when some 500 spectators invaded Pratten Park. Sydney City players and the referee were attacked after Olympic striker Marshall Soper was ordered off, an outbreak of spectator violence not uncommon among the basically nationalistic groups which formed many of Australia's more dynamic and progressive clubs.

Australian soccer's breakaway from the Fédération Internationale de Football Association, the world governing body of soccer, in 1957 saw a marked upsurge in

Green and gold plays Green in this 1981 soccer match between Australia and Northern Ireland at the Sydney Cricket Ground. Eddie Krncevic shows the style that has made him Australia's highest paid soccer player
Martin King Sportpix

Blood and Guts 51

the game's crowd appeal as high-quality players were poached illegally and introduced without the legal restriction of transfer fees. Nationalistic fervour ran high with the formation of clubs such as Prague, Sydney Austral, Pan-Hellenic, Apia-Leichhardt, Croatia, Yugal and Polonia-North Side. The soccer was of a high standard, but police intervention became commonplace as referees and players were attacked and spectators fought. The return to the international fold saw a decline in the game's popularity and a comparable quietening of passions.

Soccer was not alone in experiencing on-field mayhem. In 1987, 28-year-old Campbelltown defender Peter Betros provided an astonishing performance in a New South Wales State Rugby League grand final when he conducted a one-man war against St George at Erskineville Oval. Betros ran from player to player, punching players. Ultimately he was suspended for forty-eight weeks on charges of striking four rivals.

David Campese moves across to support Harthill and block Joe Stanley (New Zealand) in the first 1988 Test. In close support for Australia are Steve Ella and Andrew Leeds who is going wide to take the pass.
Live Action: Acikalin

Below:
Australian Socceroo captain Charlie Yankos admires the Trans-Tasman Cup after Australia's win against New Zealand in 1987
Martin King Sportpix

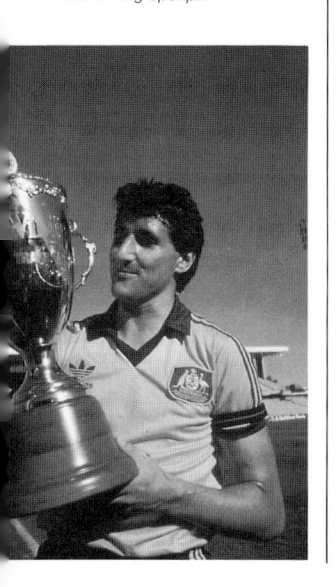

A glib adage with little truth runs: Rugby League is a gentleman's game played by thugs, and Rugby Union is a thugs' game played by gentlemen. Former Sydney League coach, Roy Masters, found winning had become so important that he wrote 'players are cannibalising each other. Never in the code's history are players so intent on destroying each other'. Masters quoted St George club's captain and former Test prop, Craig Young, a veteran of eleven years of Sydney football, in which he said: 'If a bloke hit you illegally in 1977, your first thought was to get to your feet and show it didn't hurt. Your second thought was to get square. Now, you've got blokes rolling around in mock agony and his team-mates screaming like vultures at the referee to send him off.'

The legal aspects of entertainment which becomes violent sport are under close scrutiny in Australia, with civil action and compensation within law courts increasingly frequent. Police are often uncertain whether to intervene during wild, on-field mêlées although most would prefer no involvement. Investigations into an incident concerning champion Australian Rules Hawthorn ruck-rover and captain Leigh Matthews and Geelong rover Neville Bruns, whose jaw was broken, caused widespread argument. Matthews was charged and found guilty of assault occasioning actual bodily harm, and was fined $1000, a conviction reduced to a twelve-month good-behaviour bond. Matthews was idolised by thousands of children and a host of football followers. No man played the game harder. His durability was legendary. On one occasion he cannoned into a goalpost, breaking it. He was Hawthorn's best and fairest player a record eight times, yet he became one of the first prominent sportsmen in Australia to face a criminal charge for an on-field action.

The Australian Rugby League prop Greg Dowling and his New Zealand counterpart Kevin Tamati were suspended for eight days after being ordered to the 'sin-bin' late in a Test at Brisbane's Lang Park in 1985 and then continuing their fighting as they walked towards the tunnel beneath the grandstand, a feud which inflamed spectators and led to vicious brawling in the grandstand and on the sideline. The suspension was subsequently described as 'a thrashing with a feather'.

In 1954, referee Aub Oxford told the New South Wales Rugby League that practically from the start of the game against New South Wales, the England team 'were not interested in playing football' at the Sydney Cricket Ground. Punching, stiff-arm tackles, kicking and threats by the Englishmen to put some of the New South Wales players out of action caused Oxford to abandon the game after an all-in brawl sixteen minutes into the second half. The English five-eighth Ray Price was sent off and given a five-game suspension while English lock Ken Traill, half-back Alf Burnell and New South Wales centre Harry Wells were cited and severely cautioned.

Steve Finnane is a quiet, withdrawn Sydney barrister whose football career made him one of the most controversial personalities in Australian Rugby Union history. The first significant event of his career occurred during Sydney's game against the Englishmen in 1975 when three touring forwards, Mike Burton, Bill Beaumont and Steve Callum, were felled at the Sydney Sports Ground. So began the legend of the 'Phantom Puncher'.

As a 22-year-old law student, Finnane formed a front row with hooker Peter Horton and prop Stuart Macdougall which refused to be cowed. The trio was an essential part of coach David Brockhoff's 'step forward policy', a simple but courageous statement requiring Australian forwards to stand up against the massive packs of the game from New Zealand and South Africa, packs of forwards which had previously ridden roughshod over Australia. 'Flare-ups are inevitable in football', Finnane said. 'It's a body contact sport. By nature I don't like being pushed around at any time. If someone punches you in the face, you hit him back. It's the law of survival'.

Finnane was a survivor. The Welsh and British Lions prop Graham Price and New South Wales country prop John Dawson sustained broken jaws playing against him. Finnane had no regrets throwing the punch against Price. 'I only wish it had done no more than I intended it to do — to show Price and the other Welshmen that Australians would not bow to standover tactics. He simply lost out in the ritual intimidation and counter-intimidation that has become part of modern international rugby.'

The uproar which followed Finnane's action against Price eventually caused him to withdraw from the 1978 tour of New Zealand and his desire to attract no more publicity because of his legal profession soon led to his retirement.

Several years before Finnane's stand against intimidation, the New Zealand second row giant Colin 'Pinetree' Meads ended the career of possibly the greatest Rugby Union player in Australia, the half-back, Ken Catchpole. The tiny genius was trapped in a ruck when Meads seized his leg, wrenching it so viciously that he tore ligaments and caused massive groin damage. Although Catchpole played club football again, the injury effectively ended his Test career.

One Sydney university professor claims some people find a greater attraction in football's violence than in its brilliant play. 'We are all a bit primitive', he said, 'We are not that far from the jungle.'

Blood and Guts

Parramatta skipper Ray Price retired in 1986 with the club record of two hundred and fifty-eight firsts games. Price revelled in the hard going and sustained many injuries. He played eight Rugby Union and twenty-two Rugby League tests for Australia
Rugby League Week

When the former Australian Rugby League forward Les Boyd was outed for fifteen months for gouging the face of hooker Billy Johnstone, the Kangaroo prop of yesteryear, John Sattler, remarked: 'You only get five years for murder now'. Boyd's suspension equalled the record sentence on Sydney Western Suburbs forward Bob Cooper in 1982.

Boyd was always one of the game's fiercest players. He gained notoriety when television showed him elbowing rival forward Darryl Brohman in a State-of-Origin game at Lang Park in 1983. Brohman suffered a broken jaw and Boyd received a twelve-month suspension.

Sydney sports psychologist John Bay, a former New South Wales representative Rugby Union half-back from Gordon club, says: 'The enjoyment of body contact in sport, of the collision of flesh and blood and bone, for both competitors and spectators, derives from origins far beyond the brief historical span of Australia's two centuries.

'But why the blood lust? Ask Adam. Obviously it dates back to Zeus and beyond, way back to the Java man. Man has always wanted physical contact. It is a mixture of emotions, of pride, of wanting to prove physical force. It's an instinct he has had for ages.'

Environment and economy have always been recognised as key factors in the

No names here, but an example of the fierceness of Rugby League
Rugby League Week

development of outstanding sportsmen. Bay says: 'The fastest people in the world are black Americans, and the fastest long distance runners are black Africans. Environment has much to do with it because of the need for these people to improve their standing and enhance their pride and self-esteem. If you live in the gutter and all you see around you is garbage, any person with natural talent wants to escape.

'It is a great motivating force for many of our champions. There is a little thing tapping away in their heads saying: "Hey, I want to show the world I can do better than this!"

'Built-in desire becomes a habit. Sportsmen from harsh, deprived circumstances make the commitment to training a habit much faster than someone who has been spoon-fed. It always comes back to the people who are hungriest and what is the influence on that hunger. So often blacks from ghettos simply want to improve their lot.'

John Bay referred to world champion boxer, Jeff Fenech. 'Obviously, Jeff is a very proud person. Every punch he throws is saying, "I'm showing you! I'm showing you! I'm better!" It's the same with the South Sydney Rugby League captain, Mario Fenech [no relation], playing with his heart on his sleeve. He's so emotional, so fierce. It's a pride factor.

'Every day that goes by is one less you live, so you get the best out of it. Certain priorities took control. I tried to get the most out of the eighty minutes of each football game.

'But there were other options in life for me. Jeff Fenech had to kick his goal through boxing. That's his bread and butter. He had to think of his whole future, either making it live or making it die.

'Australia can provide many examples of people rising from obscurity to become world champions, winning the *America*'s Cup, and so on. At the same time, I think we're torn between whether we're easy-going and whether we're fiercely competitive. I often wonder whether we want to present that abrasive Australian sporting image to the world or whether we range between she'll-be-right-mate to the Alan Bond-type, who is so intense about winning.

'We are a competitive nation, but when you look at the sporting sphere, New Zealand eats us for breakfast. In terms of performance, New Zealand won double the number of gold medals at the Los Angeles Olympics. They beat us at Rugby Union and Rugby League and soccer, they beat us at 12-metre sailing, the Admiral's Cup. You name the sport and they have beaten us, even cricket, with a population of 3½ million, one fifth of ours. Look what they have done on the world sporting map. To me they are far more competitive than Australians.

'We were on top in the 1950s and '60s. Australian sport was an important part of our culture. When you look at the Australia of the 1980s and consider the attitude of athletes coming through you wonder whether that hunger is there in many of them, I don't know.'

John Bay sees the attitude of modern parents as basically sound. 'Some over-obsessive parents try to live their sporting stardom through their children, getting them to train too hard, too early. We live in a country where parents are going to support and provide every opportunity for their children. Then at 17 the kids make up their own minds whether they want to make it to the big time in sport or turn to other challenges. We have so many opportunities. If you have above average intelligence, there are so many things you can do in Australia in terms of career to steer you away from the discipline and commitment of being a sporting champion.'

> *We'll make the tyrants feel the sting,*
> *O' those that they would throttle;*
> *They needn't say the fault is ours*
> *If blood should stain the wattle.*

— 'Freedom on the Wallaby' by Henry Lawson

Sources and references

The material in this chapter is the result of the author's research into newspaper files; information has also been gained from the *Daily Mirror*'s Historical Feature section. The material on Jeff Fenech is indebted to an article by Suzanne Monks in *New Idea*, 1986; *Time* Magazine, 11 May 1987; and articles by Grantlee Kieza in the *Daily Telegraph* 1986–8. Steve Finnane, *The Game they Play in Heaven* (McGraw-Hill, 1979) has been consulted for Finnane. The quotation is at p.2–3. The quotations from Stephen Mugford and Leon Mann are from newspaper files; those from John Bay from an interview conducted by the author. The quotation from Phil Coles is from the interview transcript for the television series 'Blood, Sweat and Tears'.

CHAPTER 3

PUNTERS AND WOWSERS

Venetia Nelson

There is one day in the year when Australia downs tools, takes a half-hour off work to give eyes and ears to a great Australian institution: the Melbourne Cup. Even if you never gamble on anything else, you can hardly avoid getting placed in an office sweepstake on the Cup; it is the non-punter's betting day, and for punters, an annual moment of glory. In this handicap race, where any horse has a chance of beating the champions, Australians feel that their love of racing, their devotion to gambling and their sense of fair go all find expression.

The Cup has long been famous. Mark Twain remarked of it in 1895: 'Nowhere in my travels have I encountered such a festival of the people that has such magnetic appeal for a whole nation. The Cup astonished me'.

In August 1984, in a race at Eagle Farm in Brisbane, the winner was Fine Cotton, a horse backed from 50–1 to even money. But when stewards examined the horse before declaring 'correct weight' they found it to be a ring-in: the horse racing as 'Fine Cotton' was in fact a much better-performing sprinter named Bold Personality. The horse's trainer, Haydon Haitana, maintained that he'd been forced into the ring-in by threats to his life and that of his family. Criminal charges followed, and some who had placed big bets on the ring-in were expelled for life by the New South Wales branch of the Australian Jockey Club.

Two sides of Australian gambling: an innocent bet on the races, and corruption and conspiracy. Australians have in the past argued passionately for and against gambling. Are we really a gambling people, as the myth goes, and has the gambling scene changed: is the Fine Cotton conspiracy a sign that something has gone wrong?

We are, so we have always believed, a nation of gamblers. Russel Ward in *The Australian Legend* gives a characteristic quotation from early Sydney:

> To such excesses was the pursuit of gambling carried among the convicts that some have been known, after losing money, provisions, and all their cloathing, to have staked their cloaths upon their wretched backs, standing in the midst of their associates naked, and as indifferent about it as the unconscious natives of the country. They have been seen playing at their favourite games of cribbage and all-fours, for six, eight, and ten dollars each game; and those who are not expert at these, instead of pence tossed up for dollars. (p. 32)

Commissioner Bigge, reporting in 1822 on the state of the colony, told his superiors in England that gambling started on board the convict ships: 'The practices of thieving from each other, quarrelling and gambling for their allowances of wine and lime-juice, are the common offences that occur during the voyage'. And once in Sydney, on being let out of barracks for Saturday work — a privilege — 'they resort to a particular part of the town called the Rocks, a place distinguished . . . for the practice of every debauchery and villainy, or loiter about the streets to the great annoyance of the inhabitants, and pass their time in gambling and riot'.

The phrase 'gambling and riot' is significant, for one of the chief objections to gambling was that it was part of a scenario of disorder that was the opposite of the orderly conduct of the respectable. It was inseparably connected with drinking, time-wasting and generally obstructing the progress of society. This was clearly the view of Samuel Marsden, the chaplain of early Sydney notorious for his harsh discipline. In a letter that forms part of the evidence presented to Bigge, he mentioned the convicts disembarking at Sydney:

> Very few of these Labouring Classes should be allowed to remain in Sydney, where they will entirely lose their former Habits of Industry, and be more corrupted in their morals than they were before by mixing in new Scenes of Vice, such as drunkenness, gaming and debaucheries, as so many opportunities abound on every side for them to indulge their evil propensities . . .

The Quaker James Backhouse, travelling through the Hunter region in the 1840s, found that men would go to any lengths to equip themselves for gambling. He describes the miserable huts of a party of bridge-builders:

> No religious instruction was provided for these men, nor any suitable occupation for the first day of the week. Bibles were distributed among them about three years ago, but none are now to be found. Men in such situations often take to card-playing, or other demoralizing occupation, to fill up vacant time. In some places in these Colonies, they have been known to convert the leaves of their Bibles into cards, and to mark the figures upon them with blood and soot!

Not only was gambling the antithesis of respectability, it was against religion. In Australia's history it was to be the churches that objected most strenuously to gambling: above all it was found to be contrary to Christian behaviour. In fact Backhouse mentions gambling only twice in his long narrative, but both times his words are significant. After dinner one evening at Government House, he found himself invited to join in cards. No, he said, he could not. Quakers objected in principle to the practice 'on account of its dissipating effect upon the mind, and its tendency to draw into an immoral risking of property'.

> Where money is risked in gaming, to take it one from another on such a ground, seems to me, not only objectionable for the reasons already stated, but as a breach of that consideration one for another, which is an essential ingredient in true politeness. And I have remarked, that the inconsistency of the characteristics of card-playing, forces itself so quickly upon the minds of persons, on their coming decidedly under religious conviction, that they soon discontinue the practice.

Backhouse's words are mild compared with the torrent of criticism that poured from the churchmen in the later crusade for reform. The scene is interesting in that here we find the gentry and the authorities indulging in the unholy vice; it was not only the lower orders, then, who were given over to dissipation. In fact, says academic John O'Hara, 'such gaming for nominal stakes at cards was legitimised in polite society, not only by the practices at government house, but also by the institutionalisation of the practice through the establishment of gentlemen's clubs in the major centres in the late 1830s and early 1840s' (pp. 31–2). The ambivalent attitude to gambling that has allowed it to flourish was already apparent.

The 'Habits of Industry' Marsden hoped to preserve were those required by the new industrial capitalism of England. The Industrial Revolution and the rise of capitalism, with its clear demarcation of the new labouring classes as those who worked the machines which made the profit, had inevitably changed the way leisure was seen. In the rural economy of pre-industrial England, according to O'Hara, the dominant classes viewed popular recreation

> as a useful means of social control. It was capable of channelling hostilities into isolated, manageable conflicts. It gave the workers something to look forward to as well as something to reminisce about . . . Recreation . . . promoted the happiness and well-being of the workers. A century later the dominant culture's view had changed. Society was then concerned with progress, and progress could be achieved only by industry. In this new industrial society there was no time for the lower classes to waste in idleness. If recreation had to exist at all then it should be rational, and should be designed to prepare both the mind and the body for work. (pp. 2–3)

Much of the energy of Australia's early rulers was given over to trying to teach a shiftless, rebellious populace the industrious habits demanded by progress and 'respectability' — the two cannot easily be disentangled. The free, unburdened life of the Aborigines seemed to these people the ultimate in laziness and fecklessness, and missionaries combined the forces of religion and industry to try to change them; for religion, especially in the form of the Protestant work ethic, had been allied to industry. The early comments we find on the dissolute manners of the convicts have this alliance behind them.

At the same time those Australians who saw themselves as 'gentry' had brought with them a tradition of English leisured classes who accepted as a right the frequent recourse to sports such as hunting, shooting and racing, and who gambled large sums at the racecourse and in private clubs. John O'Hara makes the point that in England the involvement of the gentry — of both sexes — in gambling had the effect of protecting the pastimes of the lower classes from the evangelical reform that gathered momentum from the eighteenth century on. It was the new middle class, the owners of factories and mills, who demanded industry from the masses and who were supported by the proponents of moral reform of the individual. He argues that in Australia this patronage of gambling by the gentry persisted enough to allow it to flourish in spite of the opposition of churchmen.

Another result of this was that the forms of gambling espoused by the gentry, especially horse-racing, were seen as acceptable while pastimes specifically of the people, such as two-up, were not. The ambivalence we saw in Backhouse's encounter at Government House eventually produced the long-running battle between the punter and the wowser: gambling was intrinsically bad both for the soul and for progress, but the high-ups insisted on it as their right and the lower orders refused to stop it no matter how much they were bullied.

An obsession with gambling? J. H. Plumb, writing on Georgian England, informs us that the obsession came from Mother England:

> Raindrops running down a window pane, the fertility of a dean's wife, steeple-chasing by moonlight, anything and everything were grounds for a bet. Amongst the rich stakes ran high — Fox lost two fortunes before middle age; Georgiana Duchess of Devonshire ruined her marriage and herself through her incapacity to restrain her feckless itch to gamble. Craftsmen and shopkeepers were often no more thrifty and reduced their families to penury through a passion for cock-fighting or cricket.

For people with such a compulsion, dumped on the shores of an inhospitable land, everything must have seemed a gamble: would the pioneering traveller find land or food or would he get lost and starve? Would the pastoralist venturing into the

Punters and Wowsers

interior make a living or would he be defeated and forced back to the cities? Would the digger make his fortune in gold or would he toil for years with no result but penury?

In the miserable conditions of early Sydney Town risk may not have seemed such a bad thing, since there was so little to lose. Certainly misery would have driven people to seek relief in the recreations they knew. Neville Penton, former jockey and author of *A Racing Heart*, believes this was the stimulus for the organisation of horse-racing: 'Such pathetic morale was a key factor in the unfolding story of the turf in the Great Brown Land, and indeed the wretched social climate for both higher and lower orders directly provoked the birth of organised horse-racing' (p. 10).

There were horses in the colony from the earliest times, and in the second decade sires like Northumberland and the Arab Hector had been imported to improve the breeding stock. Match-races had been held on the colony's roads from about 1804. But racing as an organised sport had to wait till 1810.

S. A. Lindsey's painting captures the excitement of a bush race meeting on the Darling Downs in Queensland, probably in the 1890s. The race is obviously along a farm track, and the stern property owner has been given the task of judging the event
National Library of Australia

At the end of 1809 the 73rd Regiment arrived in Macquarie's Sydney from India. The purpose of bringing them was to restore order and organise a firm government after the Rum Rebellion and the Bligh mutiny. The officers wanted to establish some of the sports they had enjoyed in India, such as match-races between their horses. The commanding officer, Colonel Maurice O'Connell, organised the first racetrack in what was to become Hyde Park, and worked for several months to prepare a three-day racing programme to be held in October. His organising found a ready response among the public: the horses were there and the people were thirsty for entertainment. Penton recreates the scene:

> Rumours flashed around the colony concerning the training and ability of various horses, and this is probably when touting began in Australia. The working class became no less intrigued than their superiors and chose their

> favourite horses from those being galloped nearest their homes . . . In time there was earnest debate in taverns and on street corners regarding the merits and/or fitness of the likely competitors, and thus the great Australian punting fraternity — lifeblood of the turf — was born. (p. 11)

Governor Macquarie gave the workers a holiday to celebrate the occasion:

> the Government Labourers shall be excused from Work on Monday, Wednesday, and Friday next, being the three Days fixed for the ensuing Races, in order to give them an opportunity of partaking of that amusement; and His Excellency trusts that they will not make a bad use of this indulgence, but on the contrary, that they will conduct themselves in a sober, discreet and orderly manner.

To prevent the holiday being an occasion for 'riot' and to ensure that the evil propensities of the lower orders were discouraged, alcohol was forbidden. But the name of the winner of the first prize at this meeting was Chance. Nothing could have been a better omen for the progress of betting in this country.

As well as amusing the workers and entertaining the gentry, the purpose of the races was to encourage horsebreeding, in particular for military reasons. The *Sydney Gazette* expressed 'its hope that the races . . . would promote "the most important advantage of amending the breed of the most useful and most noble animal that nature has bestowed on man"'

This purpose combined with the admiration that the horse has always aroused to give us a long string of heroes. 'Since the days of Northumberland', says Cumes, 'great horses had become famous colonial personalities and were remembered long after they had ceased to race and had gone to their equine heaven' (p. 135). Perhaps that is why horse-racing is the favourite sport for betting: it depends on the physical splendour of the animals. It is true that more money has been spent on off-course betting and on other forms of gambling such as poker machines, but nothing else can explain the affection and adulation given to horses like Junius, Jorrocks, Carbine and the hero of heroes Phar Lap. An unpromising, ugly colt with Carbine's blood somewhere in his veins, Phar Lap showed his breeding on the track, and became one of Australia's legends.

John Dunmore Lang's rather sour comments attest to the ubiquity of racing and the social prestige it gained from the earliest times. Describing the amenities of Melbourne in the mid-nineteenth century, he remarks: 'There is a Queen's Theatre also for those who frequent such places of amusement, and a Jockey Club, with a Race-course, that never-failing accompaniment of Australian civilization, in the vicinity'. And again, describing Albury:

> Although there is as yet no police establishment and no place of worship of any denomination in the neighbourhood of Albury, there are 'The Albury Races;' and regularly as the proper season returns, —
> *Quadrupedante putrem sonitu quatit ungula campum.*
> 'There is racing and chasing o'er Albury lea.'
> . . . There was, of course, much betting and much drinking on the occasion.

Lang refers with disgust to the 'rum in bucket-fulls' that the innkeeper at Albury was obliged to serve out to 'his lawless customers on the race-ground'. At Geelong the racecourse is again 'this universal accompaniment of Australian civilization'.

Like horse-racing, most sports were inseparably connected with betting. The point of a cockfight, besides sheer bloodlust, was to bet on the outcome; in the same way the brutality of bare-knuckle boxing — the form prizefighting took in the colony's early days — satisfied the spirit of competitiveness-plus-violence and made an ideal opportunity for a wager.

Dog fights and cockfights were a carryover from violent times when people went to see public hangings and tortured bears and bulls for the sake of amusement. Cockfighting was illegal in Australia, but as with many illegal pursuits, police

Punters and Wowsers

The old English card game of cribbage is keeping these two bushmen occupied in this somewhat romanticised view of an afternoon in a country pub. From the Australasian Sketcher, *27 July 1886*
National Library of Australia

looked the other way. Cumes cites the challenge of Richard Puckeridge, in July 1846, to

> anyone in New South Wales to fight a main of cocks, either 7 or 11 for £50, and no less than £25. He said that his money was ready at the Old Struggler [hotel] in Parramatta Street. In that same month, it was publicly announced that a main of five cocks would be fought at the sign of the Old Struggler on Monday 27 July for £10 a side and £2 a battle. (p. 289)

Prizefighting was also illegal, in Britain on the grounds that it threatened the public peace. As Peter Corris remarks, 'it was a time when nervous landholders and mill owners feared for their wealth and property' (p. 4). In Australia the constant fear of revolt by the convicts made the establishment uneasy. Violent fighting was a potential cause of sedition, and the betting that inevitably accompanied it an occasion of disorder and wasted time. The organisation of prizefighting, unlike horse-racing, was slow because 'there were few men in the colony', says Corris, 'with the time, money or inclination for patronizing a rough and tumble sport intimately associated with the convict class' (p. 6).

The first fight recorded in Australia was between John Parton, alias John Bellinger, and Charles Sefton. They fought 'more than fifty rounds for something over two hours'. Corris says: 'We can assume that money changed hands in the form of a side-bet and that other bets were laid because this was no quickly got-up affair. The fight was arranged at least one day before it took place giving people plenty of time to get their money on' (p. 1). In fact prizefighting depended on such backing, and to the end of the bare-knuckle era in 1884 gambling was its *raison d'être*. Cumes says that its disreputable nature caused it to be 'mainly an underground, outlaw type of sport [which], unlike racing, cricket and other more acceptable sports, contributed little to the development of a free, plural society. Its being technically at least "underground" tended to cause its brutality and its lack of organisation to persist longer than they otherwise would' (p. 61).

Another recorded fight was between an emancipist's son, Young John Kable, from Windsor, and 'Big' Dan Chalker. Kable was a local hero, and had given the colonials a sense of patriotic pride when he beat an English fighter Sam Clark in 1824. But he lost the fight with Chalker.

It was not only the prestigious sports of horse-racing or cricket or the brutal underground ones of prizefighting and cockfighting that attracted bets. Cumes cites some of the oddities on which people wagered: competitive dancing, a match of quoits, and the strange challenge of Joseph Hilton, alias Joe the Basket Maker: 'I hereby challenge to fight any man in the country of 44 years of age, and 12 st.; and my wife shall fight any woman in the country, bar none; and my dog shall fight any dog in the country 48 lbs; and my cock shall fight any cock in the country of any weight; each battle shall be for £5 a-side'. There was even a grinning match for a stake of £10.

'Pedestrianism', which came to be known as athletics, took various and marvellous forms. One performer of prodigious feats of walking was William Francis King, known as the 'Flying Pieman'. His exploits were performed as a pastime in between serving behind the bar at the Hope and Anchor, at the corner of Pitt and King Streets in Sydney. Before this he had been clerk, schoolteacher and tutor to children. Cumes recounts some of his feats, in which he showed an extraordinary strength and endurance:

> On one occasion he walked 1 634 miles (2 614 km) in thirty-nine days only nine of which were reported to have offered fair weather. He carried a 70-lb (32-kg) dog in walking from Campbelltown to Sydney in just over 8½ hours and a 92-lb (41.7-kg) live goat, plus a deadweight of 12 lbs (5.4 kg) in walking from Brickfield Hill, Sydney, to Parramatta in 6 hours 48 minutes. He beat the coach from Windsor to Sydney by seven minutes and walked from Sydney to Parramatta and back twice a day for six consecutive days. (pp. 286–7)

Another marathon walk was so strenuous that his friends and backers became alarmed for his survival. 'For £30 a side, he undertook to walk 360 miles (579 km) in seventy-two hours . . . Quite a crowd accompanied him to and from Black Watch Swamp, most of them in gigs or on horseback.'

Cricket, football, boxing, pedestrianism, sculling, yachting, cycling, swimming: anything and everything was fair game for a wager. A cricket match played at Hyde

A wood engraving of the 'Flying Pieman'. His walking feats were performed as a bet-winning pastime when he was off duty from his job as a barman at the Anchor and Hope tavern in Sydney
National Library of Australia

'Pedestrianism', a forerunner to athletics in Australia, brought prodigious feats of endurance, particularly from William King, the 'Flying Pieman'. In one effort he carried a live goat and a deadweight of 5.4 kg in walking from Brickfield Hill, Sydney to Parramatta in 6 hours 48 minutes. A re-enactment from the television series, 'Blood, Sweat and Tears'

Paul Tatz

Park in 1830 between the military and Australian-born youths was accompanied by heavy betting, according to Cumes, 'in both cash and kind, with some punters wagering such items as sawn timber, dripstones, fat pigs, maize, butter, salted fish and snake-skin shoes' (p. 288).

By the late nineteenth century betting on sport was still the accepted thing. Sport was increasingly a source of national pride, and its efficient organisation and constant reporting in the press made it more and more prominent. Since gambling was tied to sport, the one abetted the other, and the chances of suppressing gambling became more and more remote.

Racing has given us some of our national legends, but a game more exclusively Australian is two-up. It is the simplest of games, and according to many, the fairest. Its paraphernalia is nothing but a few coins, a piece of wood to toss them with, and a bit of floor somewhere to stand around. It was played in the trenches in Turkey in World War I, and today the authorities turn a blind eye when old-timers play it on

Anzac Day. It is illegal in most of Australia, and yet it has been played with fervour from our earliest days and refuses to die.

Because of its survival, its simplicity and its ability to dodge the police, two-up partakes of that part of the national legend which celebrates a rough honesty and an implacable resistance to oppressive authority. Thommo's famous two-up game survived for decades in inner Sydney, evading the police by floating from one venue to another. Its heyday was in the 1940s, but it began in 1908 and survived till the 1970s — a venerable history for an enterprise that has lived so much on its wits.

Lionel Dunn described it in a memorable article in the *Bulletin*.

> It was not easy to gain entrance. Newcomers, like regulars, were required to identify themselves at the sanctum sanctorum — 'The Office' . . . The successful customer would be sent 'Down the lane'.
>
> It was a walk of about 20 yards down a gloomy dark alleyway to be greeted by a sepulchral, whisky-throated voice from the shadows 'Turn right near the post, cocko!' Further on, a sombre figure would appear from the blackness. 'The second door, 20 yards on the right, mate.'
>
> Upon crossing the entrance into the cement floor of a huge defunct warehouse, one was deafened by the roar of voices of varied pitches and accents shouting bets at each other. Naked light bulbs dimly lit an enormous room smelling of cigarette smoke and dank cordage. The centre was covered by a large green coir mat. Around it, set in a square, were long stools. Seated on the stools were at least 100 men . . . Rows of players, two deep, stood around the stools.

Men of all classes sat together without distinction. Alcohol and drunks were banned.

> A seat on a stool qualified one for a spin, which was optional. It came in rotation and one could spin for any amount. The money was placed in the centre of the mat and other players would bet to it. Once the centre was set, players bet among themselves as to whether the pennies would fall with both heads, or tails, facing upwards . . . Single bets ranged from one pound to 5000 pounds on one spin of the coins.
>
> 'Heads . . . Heads . . . I'll back the head . . . Two quid he heads 'em!' 'Right, Snow, yer set. There's my two on the tail!' 'Tails . . . Tails . . . I'll back the tail . . . Anything you like on the tail. A fiver, Smiler? Right. You're set. Any more want to back a head? There's plenty of money here to say a tail will fall.'

The man who ran this splendid set-up was Joe Thomas, a vibrant, powerful human being, but softly spoken and generous in the extreme to down-and-outs and the battlers. His combination of benevolence, power and charisma was the stuff legends are made of.

Two-up was legalised in 1985 in the Western Australian mining town of Kalgoorlie, as a tourist attraction. The committee of inquiry that investigated the game there came up with five points in its favour. The community supported it because of

> i) the history and tradition attached to it.
> ii) the fairness of it and the evenness of the odds for the punter.
> iii) its popularity as an enjoyable pastime.
> iv) the fact that it can be played by all levels of society with equal opportunity to win; and
> v) the fact that it can be played both in the open or indoors, day or night.

Most other states have followed with legalisation in casinos.

'Nappy' Ollington was until a few years ago the owner of Nappy's Two-Up Game in Melbourne. He has played two-up since he was a boy of ten, and has been involved in two-up schools for twenty-five years.

Two-up, a uniquely Australian game, is illegal throughout Australia, except in casinos and in the mining town of Kalgoorlie, where it is a tourist attraction. The game has been played with a fervour from our earliest days and refused to die. It was a particular favourite with troops in both world wars. A re-creation of Thommo's famous two-up school, from the television series, 'Blood, Sweat and Tears'

Paul Tatz

He feels strongly that two-up should be legalised. No other gambling game in the world, he says, has been so harassed, but it refuses to die. He speaks passionately of its fairness and its enormous appeal. He says most games of skill, such as those played in casinos, are legal; it is the games of chance like two-up that are banned. He suspects it has something to do with the way the power goes: two-up is a game of the ordinary person. In the casinos the novice, confronted with roulette or blackjack, has little chance of winning because he doesn't have the skill. With two-up he has as much chance as anyone else.

For twenty years Ollington has campaigned vigorously for two-up's legalisation, in the press and on radio and TV. He remarks that never during this campaign did any political or church group voice objections to two-up, when they had the chance. He does not understand why it is still illegal. He has campaigned against a casino as a tourist attraction for Melbourne because casinos are boring — once you've seen one you've seen the lot; casinos won't bring tourists but two-up will.

The game is also known as swy, from the German *zwei* meaning 'two'. According to Ollington the ancient Greeks in 500 BC played a form of it with stones which had sides coloured black and white. The *Sydney Gazette*'s reference in 1804 to 'the little chuck-farthing mob that generally assembles at the Quay in the afternoon' is clearly a reference to a form of two-up. At some stage the coins were tossed against a wall, but this seems to have been abandoned by the time the game reached Australia. Two-up boomed in the gold rushes. Danny Sheehan remarks: 'Two-up . . . became very popular with Eastern States diggers overburdened with gold. They had few pleasures to count, so two-up became their recreational outlet' (p. 2).

Sheehan has some very interesting observations about the game in Kalgoorlie. Several national groups play it there without racial tension, possibly because its simplicity means there are few language problems. He also says there is 'expectation as to what a "good bloke" is regardless of race or creed. Essentially, he does not try to "put it over" another fellow or try to deceive him' (p. 150) — a noteworthy comment on the Australian character.

The same reputation for fair dealing has attached itself to another famous Australian gambling venture: George Adams's Tattersall's lottery. Adams came of poor farming people who emigrated from England in 1855 after the discovery of gold had made the colony suddenly attractive. George was then 16. He worked at various trades in New South Wales: a Cobb & Co. driver, farmhand, butcher. During the 1860s he bought the Steam Packet Hotel at Kiama, and part-owned a sheepstation. His visits to Sydney for the races and agricultural shows brought him in contact with Tattersall's betting club, operating in a small inn in Pitt Street. It was called after the famous Tattersall's club in London. In 1878, in a strange beginning to a business venture, three of Adams's friends bought the licence of the pub for him, and Adams's long-lasting gambling enterprise was born.

The draw for a £2000 sweep for the Melbourne Cup is conducted at Tattersall's betting club in Sydney in 1877. George Adams took over the Tattersall's operation in 1878 and changed the sweepstake to a lottery, removing the need for knowledge and skill and giving the operation a deserved image of honesty. It has grown into a booming, government-owned lottery operation
Australasian Sketcher

The difference between Tattersall's and an ordinary lottery — which had been banned in 1844 — was that a lottery based on the results of a horse-race combined sheer chance with the skill and knowledge that race betting involved; sweepstakes, then, were a matter of part chance, part skill, and thus were not strictly covered by the 1844 legislation. Adams's sweeps did so well that he was soon able to pay back his friends for the hotel. 'The secret of Tattersall's success', says John O'Hara, 'was the promotional flair of George Adams, who built an image of honesty and respectability by deducting only 10 per cent from the total pool and by having the draws done by prominent citizens in public, with the press in attendance' (p. 99). During the 1880s he spent some of his huge profits, £30 000 in fact, in building the Marble Bar (which can still be seen in Sydney's Hilton Hotel). It was one of Sydney's masterpieces. Imported marble, in various colours, combined with wall panels painted by the Sydney artist Julian Ashton to create a sumptuous interior unique in Australia. Trevor Wilson, who tells Adams's story in *The Luck of the Draw*, says that it was patronised by rich and poor (p. 33) which made it markedly different from later sumptuous casinos that only the rich could afford.

Tattersall's was eventually driven from Sydney by pressure from the churches to close the apparent loophole by which it operated. Adams set up business in Brisbane, but after only two years he was forced to leave there also. Tattersall's found refuge in Tasmania. The Van Diemen's Land Bank, along with others, had collapsed in the 1890s depression. A legal solution had been found to such a disastrous financial situation in the organisation of lotteries to sell off banks' properties. Adams was invited to organise a lottery to save the VDL bank; in return, he asked if he could organise his sweepstakes legally in Tasmania. Legalisation came in 1897, while other forms of gambling were forbidden. This time Adams won over the strenuous objections of the churches and dozens of petitions, which cited the previous outlawing of his sweeps by the governments of Queensland and New South Wales.

Tattersall's stayed in Tasmania for fifty-eight years, during which Adams turned to building and property development and helped by his enterprises to bring Tasmania out of the depression. Wilson observes:

> During this time Tattersall's became a household word in Australia and New Zealand. They laid the foundations for their success by the integrity and honesty with which the sweeps were conducted. Other states followed the example and state lotteries were set up eventually in New South Wales, Queensland, South Australia and Western Australia. Today, Tattersall's operates legally in Victoria, Tasmania and the Australian Capital Territory. (p. 103)

In 1972 Tattslotto, a variation on the sweeps, gave Australians yet another way to pursue their love of gambling.

In the mid-nineteenth century many thousands of Chinese were among the goldseekers on the Australian fields. They came in increasing numbers, attracted by tales of fortunes that could be made. By 1857, according to historian Manning Clark, there were 25 424 in Victoria alone. Their strange habits and their industry in extracting a profit from working the poorer claims quickly drew resentment from the Europeans. They were periodically driven off their claims by parties of Europeans who would 'form up' on horseback, and who might return from the chase with bunches of severed pigtails.

On the fields and in the cities the Chinese were devotees of various kinds of gambling games: dominoes, fan-tan, which was a coin game, and the numbers game pak-a-pu. They also smoked opium. It was the opium more than anything else that provided the focus for a xenophobic hatred that has made a shameful episode in our history. As usual, there was a sexual edge to the xenophobia: white women could be degraded in Chinese opium dens. It was the same hysteria that has been applied to blacks, Germans, Asians, communists at various times in our history.

Though some on the goldfields fraternised with them and enjoyed their food, the Chinese were in general regarded as an inferior kind of human being intrinsically given over to vice, namely gambling and opium, but at the same time a terrifying menace to Australians and their way of life. Manning Clark records that Caroline Chisholm spoke against the humiliation of the Chinese.

By association with Chinese 'immorality', gambling acquired a considerable taint of disrepute which persisted for decades after the gold rushes.

No one is quite sure of the origin of the word 'wowser'. Dictionaries suggest an English dialect word *wow*, to 'whine' or 'complain', but the word is popularly supposed to be an acronym for 'We Only Want Social Evils Remedied', a slogan of John Norton expressing a dig at the pious moralising of the evangelicals. Norton was the editor of the notorious newspaper *Truth* in the late nineteenth century. Whether true or not, he claimed the invention of the word and used it proudly to express his exuberant contempt for the whingeing killjoys.

The 'wowsers' and the law are out in force trying to capture and subdue the gambling spirit in Australia. The artist Norman Lindsay leaves no doubt where his allegiances lie in the 1905 Bulletin *cartoon*
© Janet Glad

This was how artist Norman Lindsay saw them too. At the *Bulletin*, as cartoonist and reviewer, he satirised everything to do with wowserism: pious earnestness, sentimentality, prudery, moral and social restraints. He stood for beauty, passion, vitality, sexuality and courage, and attacked the wowsers with as much vehemence as they attacked drink and gambling.

The battlelines, of course, were not as simple as this. Lindsay is possibly as guilty of oversimplification as his opponents, who might with some justification have accused his attitudes of irresponsible male hedonism. The result of this campaign was that the anti-wowser platform achieved a degree of popular orthodoxy in which an irresponsible larrikinism was equated with a genuine resistance to unjust restraint.

Keith Dunstan, in his *Wowsers*, quotes a passage from the Methodist *Spectator* of 1906 that expresses various aspects of the reformers' position on gambling:

> The harm of gambling and betting: It seeks another's gold without an equivalent. The better seeks to have without earning or paying for his gain. True Christianity is unselfish, and regards such a method as unmanly and unfair. It is unmanly to get for nothing what another has won by work . . . The bookmaker or totalisator manager renders no service of any value whatever . . . Who has not seen the ruined home, the heart-broken wife, the ragged children, whose condition is due to gambling by the head of the house? (p. 212)

A number of ideas are present here: the biblical injunction in *Genesis* to earn one's bread by the sweat of one's brow, the Protestant work ethic, various social notions of what manliness is. The appeal to the broken family might be dismissed as sentimental, but the reality it pointed to surely could not. Gambling — and drink — did do these things.

The opposing positions were complicated by getting tangled up in sectarianism. Australia was not all Protestant: a minority of its people, but a large and noisy one, were Roman Catholics, most of them Irish. The Englishman's and Scotsman's detestation of the Irish, the Protestant's and Catholic's hatred for each other, the ruling class's determination to control the workers and the workers' resistance to being controlled — all this was touched on in the wowser battles.

John Dunmore Lang was the most vociferous and articulate of the Protestant churchmen. He was a Presbyterian; W. H. Judkin, famed for his battles with Collingwood's tote boss John Wren, was a Methodist. It was the evangelical religious tradition that attacked drink and gambling, more than the Church of England. The Catholic Church, to the intense disapproval of the evangelicals, scarcely seemed to worry about gambling at all. And this was part of the trouble: popery, as well as being from the point of view of men like Lang intolerable in every way, took a patently immoral stand on gambling. Irish Catholicism in Australia funded its enormous building programme partly by gambling, and Catholic finances have always included bazaars, raffles, bingo and so on. None of these was admissible to the Protestants; even the Sydney Anglicans outlawed them in 1884.

Lang in fact did not attack gambling in particular, but he did attack Catholicism — or popery, as the language of sectarian hatred called it. A fascinating spectacle is his strenuous objections to Caroline Chisholm, a convert to Catholicism who is herself, rather unfairly, characterised as a wowser. Both Chisholm and Lang argued passionately for increased emigration to Australia to populate its hinterland and get its economy going, but Lang wanted no Irish Catholics, and was convinced Chisholm wanted to flood the country with papists. These two famous Australians, both concerned with the welfare of young Australia, both appalled at the social degradation they saw here, both concerned with the moral well-being of the individual, fought long and energetically for their causes but on separate tracks.

In 1847, in her open letter to Earl Grey pleading for family emigration, Caroline

In Melbourne Punch's *campaign against gambling it displayed its low opinion of bookmakers in this cartoon, 'A Model of Young Australia'. Dr L. L. Smith MLA at left is lampooned for his stated view that he 'did not see that the bookmaker's profession should not be as honourable as any other'*

This picture in the Bulletin *magazine depicts some desperate characters in a gambling den in King Street, Sydney, in 1880. Gambling clubs remain illegal in Australia; a citizen's urge to gamble is well catered for in other ways, but illegal gambling is still seen as an 'unstoppable vice'*
National Library of Australia

Chisholm makes a very significant point about Australian society as it was then: there were very few women. She saw the degradation of the male population as partly a consequence of this. She wrote:

> If Her Majesty's Government be really desirous of seeing a well-conducted community spring up in these Colonies, the social wants of the people must be considered. If the paternal Government wish to entitle itself to that honoured appellation, it must look to the materials it may send as a nucleus for the formation of a good and great people. For all the clergy you can despatch, all the schoolmasters you can appoint, all the churches you can build, and all the books you can export, will never do much good without what a gentleman in that Colony very appropriately called 'God's police' — wives and little children

— good and virtuous women. Oh! it is frightful to look upon the monster evil which our penal policy has entailed upon that country, and which the Emigration Rules have in some degree cherished.

She was also concerned about the immorality (that is, prostitution) that the women in the colony tended to fall into, and did notable social reform work in this area.

J. W. C. Cumes has remarked on the maleness of early Australian pastimes:

> Many of those activities were for men living alone — or living without women. They were activities suited to immature boys in a segregated public school or to men in the army or convicts in a segregated gaol. Often, therefore, they were activities which placed their greatest emphasis on physical endeavour, on athleticism, on male forms of competition, on the rougher, more obvious manifestations of art forms, on booze and the general ... male recklessness of gambling everything because everything consisted of nothing but a footloose bachelor's own. (p. 86)

He qualifies this by saying that of course there were women in early Australia who were 'certainly robust drinkers and might well have been pretty good gamblers'. But they were women who had abandoned the role of 'God's police'. The dichotomy between virtuous and immoral women, of course, is much deeper than any distinction set up between good and bad men, because it reflects a very old ambivalence about women.

Certainly the fact that drinking and gambling were bachelor male activities and could rarely be accommodated to family life was one of the reasons the religious reformers attacked them, for wholesome family life, presided over by a virtuous woman (who, however, oddly enough, was not head of the household) was the recipe for the social stability desired by religion, by middle-class respectability, and by industrial capitalism. Catholicism also subscribed to some of these values, but the Irish working-class nature of the Australian Catholic population gave them a different slant. And Catholics were, by virtue of being Irish and working-class, inveterate gamblers.

A frozen moment in the dull life of the Australian bushmen, as seen in the Australasian Sketcher *of 1891*
National Library of Australia

The Melbourne Cup had achieved its eminence as a horse race across the country by the mid-19th century. Here the Australasian Sketcher depicts the arrival of the news of the Cup winner at Billybung in 1884. The sweep notice is on the wall and celebrations seem about to begin.
National Library of Australia

Carbine wins the Melbourne Cup by three lengths in 1890. Carbine was sold to the Duke of Portland and became a sire in England, where three generations of his stock won English Derbies.
News Limited

The Melbourne Cup of 1890 was won by the great horse Carbine. Two men responded to it in very different ways. Henry Varley, an English evangelist prominent in the Anti-Gambling Association, railed against it bitterly, pouring contempt on the adulation of the people for the horse and its owner. John Wren backed Carbine and won £180. With the winnings he started the Collingwood Tote, an illegal off-course betting shop that was throughout its long history the target of police raids. The Collingwood Tote is the most famous (or notorious) of Australia's illegal betting shops. It was in operation from 1893 to 1906, when it was suppressed by legislation. Somehow, the authorities managed to turn a blind eye to it and to its enormous clientele.

A crowd of 160 000 was estimated to have attended the Flemington Racecourse on Melbourne Cup Day in 1927, but a great number of them watched from surrounding hills around the course. Spearfelt won the Cup and the £10 000 prize-money

Right:
A bookmaker and his penciller hard at work during a Victorian Racing Club spring meeting at Flemington in 1891. As legal race betting was only available on course there was much more incentive for punters to attend the races. Their only recourse otherwise was the illegal SP (starting price) bookmaker
National Library of Australia

Like Thommo's two-up school and Adams's Tattersall's, Wren's tote had a reputation for fairness and straight dealing, and indeed Wren, like most gambling entrepreneurs, was a superb businessman. His shop prospered during the 1890s depression when those on hard times could make a shilling bet and for this small outlay get some enjoyment and maybe some profit. The working class revered Adams for his fairness; his own working-class background and Catholic connections ensured hostility from the Protestant reformers.

William Henry Judkins was a Methodist preacher in Melbourne in the early twentieth century. He had regular Sunday sessions at his church which were known as Pleasant Sunday Afternoons. These were the scene of his famous diatribes against gambling and other evils and against John Wren in particular. Keith Dunstan quotes some of the diverse opinions about these antagonists: John Norton of *Truth*, a man given to the tongue-tripping verbosities of the *Magic Pudding* era, called Judkins

> either a holy, howling humbug or a Bible-banging, pulpit-pounding, penny-pinching, 'trey-bit'-trapping pharisaical parasite.
>
> Then, *Review of Reviews*, on behalf of the Wowser push, had this to say of John Wren: 'Wren produces nothing, manufactures nothing, does no useful work; he is merely a parasite who thrives on the monumental folly of the community'.

The wowser view here is noticeably similar to one of the points made in the *Spectator* quotation above: the gambler is bad for society because he is not *producing* goods. It was the age of produce, and progress, the age of industrial capitalism.

Wren fought back, writing an open letter in September 1906 in which he accused Judkins of being a sensation-monger and a humbug. At the end of it he said:

> The one crime of which I am accused is that I am a gambler. Well, I am a gambler, and I will remain one as long as I live, and when I look at those non-betters who are opposed to me, analyse their actions, weigh their words [Wren obviously was also given to alliteration], and see them stripped of their robes of mock sanctity I feel inclined to be thankful that I am a gambler, rather than a wanton libeller should be applied to me.

Judkins also delivered himself of a much-quoted piece of invective against Tattersall's when it finally found refuge in Tasmania:

> Kicked out of Australia like a diseased dog is kicked out into the street, the institution known all over Australia as Tattersall's found a welcome and a kennel in Tasmania. It was too bad to be received anywhere else, but it shivered at Tasmania's door and offered to pay for board and lodging. It was evident that its presence would spell corruption, for itself was corrupt; but what mattered that?

It was precisely because gambling ventures could pay for board and lodging, and governments needed that board, that the wowsers finally lost the fight. Gambling could get money out of people's pocket as nothing else could, and no government could afford to ignore this.

The last two decades of the nineteenth century saw mounting pressure from the churches to have gambling, as one of several social evils, controlled by legislation. John O'Hara quotes a Methodist minister, P. J. Stephen, as advocating pressure on the legislature: 'every voter . . . should bring pressure . . . to bear upon the legislature, that machinery of the State may be set in motion to suppress this vice. The aristocratic clubs must be dealt with as well as the "two-up schools" and the chinese dens' (p. 92)

The chief opponents of the reformers were neither the gentry who patronised the 'aristocratic clubs' nor the working classes who would have been the main clients of the two-up schools. O'Hara sees the conflict of this time as being

> between rival middle-class values. On the one hand the values promoted by the Protestant churches sought to prohibit gaming and betting, or at least to protect the working classes from themselves. On the other hand gambling entrepreneurs, protected by the lingering gentry values, sought to reconcile the working-class value system, which saw gaming and betting as a possible means of escape, with the middle-class concept of commercial profit. (p. 94)

The reformers wished to stop working people gambling, for the good of their souls, their families and productivity; the entrepreneurs exploited their need for entertainment and made money out of them. Class alignments, of course, are somewhat fluid here: Adams and Wren came from the working class, but their success and prosperity put them squarely in the middle class — upward social mobility is not a recent phenomenon; Adams in particular became a pillar of society and a figure of great respectability.

The legislature had been plagued by the existence of off-course betting since horse racing began in the colonies. Even on course, the bookmaker was seen as a scourge. The totalisator, or *pari-mutuel*, invented by Frenchman Pierre Oller in 1872, was an attempt to provide a fair system of racecourse betting. It was simply a calculating machine which totalled the bets made on a horse and distributed an equal amount to those who had won on it; later it became a much more sophisticated electronic gadget. The tote was known on Australian racecourses by the end of the same decade, but its presence did not bring consensus: on the one hand, would its very fairness not cause more people to bet? On the other, would not the disreputable bookmaker disappear if it were adopted? The legislators scratched their heads. The bookmakers feared the machine as a rival and, ironically, found themselves in the company of the churches, who opposed it for quite other reasons: it would be tantamount to state sanction of vice, since the tote was to be taxed.

The reformers did manage to get sweepstakes outlawed in every State except Tasmania, where the government's pressing need to shore up the State bank overcame scruples and objections; but the parliaments of Tasmania, Queensland and South Australia legalised the tote, while those of New South Wales and Victoria did not. All other gaming and betting, in streets, shops or private houses, was prohibited in a series of bills enacted between 1876 and 1897. The aim of all colonial legislatures, says John O'Hara, was similar. 'They wanted to remove gaming and betting from the public eye, to permit them only in prescribed places such as racecourses, where they could be controlled and regulated' (p. 115). The police, however, were not given enough powers of search and entry to carry out these laws.

In the new century evangelical Protestantism mustered its forces for a renewed attack on gambling. It tried to impose on the population a puritan morality which frowned on idleness and amusements as occasions of temptation to sin. The Reverend Dill Macky's Australian Protestant Defence Association and the Carruthers Liberal and Reform Association government, elected in 1904, presented a formidable alliance against intemperance, gambling and an increasingly militant Catholicism under Sydney's Cardinal Moran.

In 1906 the reformers won victory in the passage of two significant Bills, the New South Wales Gaming and Betting Act and the Victorian Lotteries, Gaming and Betting Act. These had much more clout than previous legislation, even the 1905 Vagrancy Act which had banned two-up and the Chinese games of fan-tan and pak-a-pu. Wren's Collingwood Tote closed within a week, though his racehorses and pony-racing track at Richmond enabled him to survive, and he turned his energies towards reviving the ailing sport of trotting. In New South Wales, the Labor Party attacked the Gaming and Betting Act as discriminatory, since it acted against the gambling dens and betting shops frequented by the lower orders while leaving

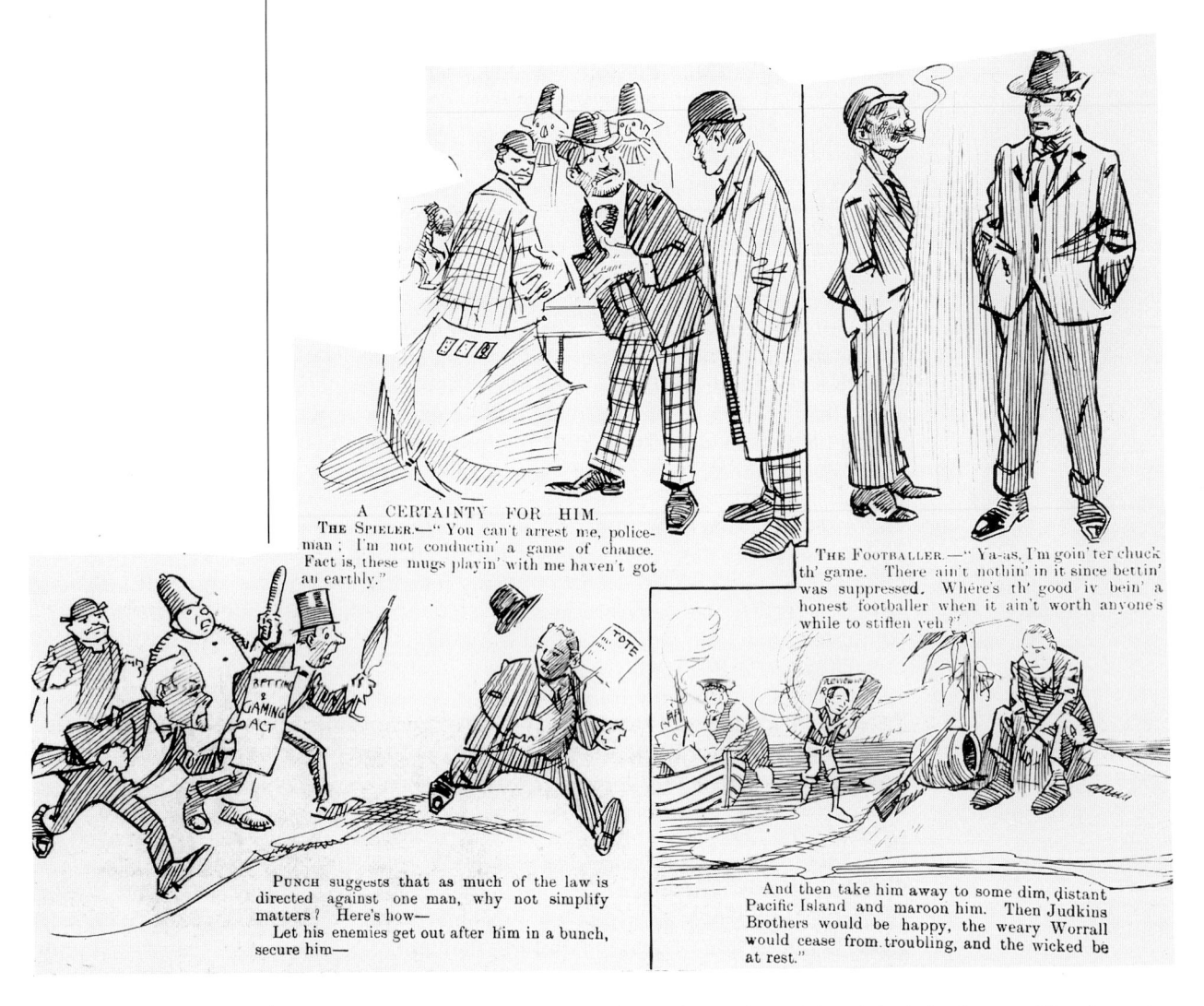

A CERTAINTY FOR HIM.
THE SPIELER.—"You can't arrest me, policeman; I'm not conductin' a game of chance. Fact is, these mugs playin' with me haven't got an earthly."

THE FOOTBALLER.—"Ya-as, I'm goin' ter chuck th' game. There ain't nothin' in it since bettin' was suppressed. Where's th' good iv bein' a honest footballer when it ain't worth anyone's while to stiffen yeh?"

PUNCH suggests that as much of the law is directed against one man, why not simplify matters? Here's how—
Let his enemies get out after him in a bunch, secure him—

And then take him away to some dim, distant Pacific Island and maroon him. Then Judkins Brothers would be happy, the weary Worrall would cease from troubling, and the wicked be at rest."

The passing of the Victorian Lotteries, Gaming and Betting Act brought this triumphant reaction from Melbourne Punch *in 1906. The legislation was the culmination of a long campaign by the 'wowsers' led by Methodist preacher W. H. Judkins*

prestigious race meetings and gentlemen's residential clubs intact. The force behind the Victorian Act had been W. H. Judkins's mobilisation of public opinion.

While racing prospered, and became an important source of employment, one effect of the 1906 Acts was to drive the various forms of illegal betting underground. People gambled on card games, two-up or sweepstakes and frequented the off-course betting shops as much as ever, and neither public opinion nor police action could stop it.

Alfred McCoy, in his book on organised crime, *Drug Traffic*, quotes a State Labor member arguing against further legislation:

> There is a strong propensity in human nature to gamble in some form or another. I have a right to risk a shilling or two if I have it to spare, just as much as a man who goes down to the Stock Exchange and gambles in mining scrip. That is a form of gambling that is infinitely worse than gambling on a racecourse. (p. 149)

The question of legalising the tote persisted. A royal commission in 1912 found enormous support for legalisation, among which was the significant point that gambling was a rich potential source of revenue for the state. During World War I this pot of gold could not be ignored, and the tote was made legal in New South Wales in 1916. The victory so recently won had been partly overturned.

After the war, the story of gambling in Australia is one of increasing liberalisation.

Punters and Wowsers

In the same year that the tote was legalised, Queensland introduced the Golden Casket lottery, at first to finance patriotic enterprises and then to fund its hospital system. New South Wales followed with the first state lottery in 1931. The government-run lotteries that helped to fund the Sydney Opera House in the 1950s are well remembered. The present situation was well under way: governments have become big-time gamblers because there is money in it.

The Totalisator Agency Board (TAB) came to be recognised during the 1960s as the sensible solution to the problem of off-course betting. The evangelical campaign to force a certain kind of Christian morality on to people was discredited; it was generally acknowledged that laws which did not have public support and could not be enforced simply brought the law into disrepute. The TAB was introduced successively into all States, starting with Victoria in 1960. TAB shops are now a familiar sight in suburban shopping centres.

O'Hara sees the introduction of the TAB as one of a number of examples of liberalisation that represent a victory for the working-class gambler over the ideals of middle-class respectability, hard work and clean living. Betting on the TAB is also much cheaper than going to the racecourse, and so more people can afford it. Greyhound racing, which to Premier Jack Lang at the start of the 1930s was the 'people's sport', is, similarly, more available to ordinary people, because of its relative cheapness, and it does not have the upper-class associations of thorough-bred-horse-racing.

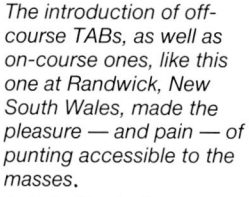

The introduction of off-course TABs, as well as on-course ones, like this one at Randwick, New South Wales, made the pleasure — and pain — of punting accessible to the masses.
Australian Broadcasting Corporation

Lotteries and the numbers games of bingo (housie-housie) and lotto — and its later form Tattslotto — are also games of the masses. Bingo in particular is played very much by women, and the traditional male associations of gambling are absent. It is widely used for fund-raising, particularly in Catholic circles.

The 'pokies', on the other hand, are a phenomenon on their own. The poker machine arrived here from America in the 1920s. Very quickly the 'one-armed bandit', as it came to be known, was surrounded by controversy. The ease with which it could swallow a family's pay packet alarmed many, and it was banned from hotels, where it was regarded as too easily available, and restricted to licensed clubs. Several times poker machines were withdrawn from clubs, but finally their use by clubs was authorised in 1956. McCoy has this comment on licensed clubs.

> New South Wales' licensed clubs are a social phenomenon without equal in Australia and without parallel anywhere else in the world. Sydney's clubs are a unique marriage of Australian working-class culture — embodied in mateship, sport, patriotism and beer drinking — and the poker machine . . . Poker machine gambling became something of a mania among segments of Sydney working-class communities. (pp. 213, 215)

The figures on them are extraordinary. To quote O'Hara: 'By 1980 [New South Wales'] 48 000 registered poker machines outnumbered those of Las Vegas by more than two to one and the annual turnover figure of $4000 million represented a figure of $2000 per club member' (p. 199).

A movement of protest about the amount of money they were swallowing started in the 1960s. The churches, Catholic and Protestant, joined ranks in a bid to have them made illegal. McCoy quotes one man's rejoinder. George Wintle, 'Mr Poker Machines', secretary-manager of South Sydney Union League Club, one of the biggest, wrote, somewhat illogically, in their defence:

> Sure, some people may do their weekly wages. Sure, some people may be compulsive gamblers . . . But we also have people with a mental obsession to religion, we also have people who are compulsive church-attenders, compulsive Bible-readers, compulsive attenders at rallies. The Catholic Church . . . has received millions from housie-housie, raffles, silver circles, etc. The Church of England is a big absentee landlord and in Sydney has the best land and is getting the best rents. (p. 217)

Enter corruption, and at its heels organised crime. Corruption, like human nature, has always been with us. There have always been jockeys who will pull up a horse, policemen who will take a bribe to look the other way; politicians have always been tempted to desert their principles and their constituents in the cause of expediency. But in 1988, Australia's bicentennial year, the Fitzgerald Inquiry in Queensland, constantly in the press, was threatening to uncover a hornets' nest of police, lawyers, criminals and politicians, all with their hands in each other's pockets or at each other's throats; New South Wales saw endless scandals and allegations of corruption; and the Costigan Royal Commission in Victoria, though politicians forgot about it with indecent haste, still stood in public memory as having suggested links between the underworld and society's VIPs that were terrifying in their implications. It was the Moffitt Royal Commission in 1973 that first brought these matters to public awareness.

One of the rackets that was a focus of charges of corruption, and provided much of the finance for the growth of organised crime, was SP betting. Alfred McCoy shows how intimately SP betting has been bound up with the organised crime that at the present time distributes narcotics to Australia's youth. With sly grog, prostitution, and the early cocaine traffic — stopped in 1929 — it was at the centre of the Australian underworld. Since the sly grog trade finished in the 1950s SP betting remained, in company with prostitution, illegal casinos and the new and powerful drug trade, an unstoppable vice. McCoy says that it came to be seen 'by police and the N.S.W. Labor Party as a constant Australian vice which . . . was utterly beyond the influence of law enforcement' (p. 147).

There were blitzes on SP betting in 1929–31 and again in 1938, but each time the law tried to close the shops they simply adjusted to changed circumstances and went on as before; when they were forced out of hotels they resorted to the ever-expanding telephone system, which was even harder to police. McCoy quotes a sinister prediction in the *Daily Telegraph* of 1938:

> The harder the police drive, the deeper into the underworld the bookmakers will go. The Government will have accomplished precisely the opposite of what it set out to accomplish. SP will be so closely wedded to crime, that it will be almost impossible to clean up the mess. (p. 150)

Of Western attempts at suppressing vice in general, McCoy says: 'The effective "de-legalization" of these vices has not abolished them, but transferred them to the province of vice entrepreneurs, a change which has been instrumental in the rise of organized crime' (p. 28). The reformers' push for clean streets and well-swept hearts by legislation must, in this argument, bear some of the blame. An inversion of the argument is heard nowadays about narcotics: legalise them and criminal involvement will lessen as the prices fall.

Illegal casinos were another of the scandals that plagued State governments. They were started long ago by Henry Stokes, one of the big three of Melbourne's criminal world after World War I; the other two were 'Squizzy' Taylor and 'Long Harry' Slater. Stokes and Taylor had a famous fight, which sent Stokes wounded into exile in Tasmania, but when Taylor died violently in 1927 Stokes returned to Melbourne and set up business. 'An intelligent and methodical businessman,' says McCoy, 'Stokes protected his two-up casinos with payments to the police and an elaborate security system' (p. 110). He launched a sumptuous floating casino on a boat, and when this was seized by police, turned to baccarat schools.

It was Sydney, however, sinful Sydney, that was our crime capital. McCoy has a theory about the reasons for this:

> Sydney is the birthplace of organized crime in Australia. It has had all the requisite elements in the formation of a professional *milieu*: a colonial legacy of strong anti-police sentiment, a weak port economy producing prolonged periods of insufficient employment, impoverished slum dwellers for whom crime was an economic necessity, and a police force often incapable and sometimes unwilling to check the growth of organized crime. (p. 112)

The State Labor machine in New South Wales had associations of violence and corruption that it appeared unable to shake off; the very solidarity that Australians express as mateship and loyalty led, some say, to a Labor tendency to 'jobs for the boys'. And yet it was the Askin Liberal–Country Party government, in power from 1965 to 1976, that many blamed for the real emergence of organised crime in New South Wales and thence in Australia as a whole. McCoy again:

> [In] the decade following the 1967–8 gang wars . . . Sydney became the last of the big, bad cities. Under the tolerant gaze of a *laissez-faire* State government, Sydney was the centre for all the major vice trades and her syndicate leaders prospered as never before . . . No city in the world could rival Sydney's tolerance for organized crime. (p. 199)

The succeeding Labor government under Neville Wran banned the casinos when public controversy became too great, but Wran himself was the subject of a royal commission into allegations of corruption and, though he was cleared, a smell of corruption lingered in the public mind about both parties in New South Wales. The

National Party in Queensland seemed to smell even worse with the Fitzgerald Inquiry turning up evidence that linked Queensland political figures with corrupt police in prostitution, drugs and SP betting.

There are now legal casinos in Australia. Hobart's Wrest Point was the first. Set in beautiful scenery, it became a major tourist attraction, and when it opened in 1973 it held the promise of excitement and glamour for a country too long seen as narrowly provincial in entertainment. Others followed at Launceston, Darwin, Alice Springs, Perth, Adelaide, Townsville and the Gold Coast. The Wran government's attempt to build a casino at Darling Harbour in the heart of Sydney was continually fouled with suspicions about the reputation of those that tendered for it. A change of government in 1988 put an end to these plans. The Cain Labor government in Victoria likewise said no casinos.

In an interview, Bob Bottom spoke of the changes in the casino scene. 'There were people like Joe Taylor, the old gentleman gamblers who ran the back street baccarat and the like. What changed it in the mid-1960s is that people from overseas, as well as up-and-coming hard-line criminals, moved in and created shopfront casinos as against the back street ones. In that period some of the people mixed up with the casinos were not only running protection rackets but ultimately branched out into syndicated SP bookmaking and ultimately entered the drug trade, and the whole scene changed. So the days of the so-called friendly Joe Taylors were over . . . In a real sense by the late 1960s the shopfront casinos had all the appointments you'd find in a Las Vegas casino, with the poker machines, glamorous women, free drinks, and some of them were better appointed than the one legal casino at Wrest Point. Sydney ended up with thirteen major illegal casinos, the 33 Club, Forbes Club and the like.

'These casinos were truly palatial. The Forbes Club, for instance, in Forbes Street, East Sydney, was housed in a three-storey terraced house, and furnished Vogue-style. The doorman needed to recognise your face all right, but there was never really what you'd call an elaborate security system. The ground floor was taken up with baccarat, and an intimate coffee lounge at the back. In the middle floor was the roulette table, overseen on a high chair by well-known figures . . . Adjacent to the roulette was a blackjack table where some of Sydney's best-known names and faces gambled until dawn. On the top floor was the craps table. Everywhere people gambled and gorged themselves on complimentary food and drink. If a punter lost everything, he could even scrounge a $50 present from the overseer. At the very least, he would be given a taxi-fare home. On one memorable occasion, a group of gamblers lost heavily at the night greyhounds, went to the Forbes Club to plead bankruptcy and get the $50 gift, then went back to the greyhounds for the last couple of races and managed to turn the $50 into several thousand dollars.'

About corruption on the racecourse, Bottom said that racing was the real Mecca for criminals. 'Randwick is the meeting place between the so-called underworld and Sydney's upper world, and that's where you'll get the business people and the bankers mixing with the crims. And all — doesn't matter who people are, a bank manager or a director of a company — they like to win when they bet. They as much as the crims have been involved in setting up race fixes . . . One major racing identity there would have had quite a proportion of Australia's major jockeys in his payroll over the years. Originally he was the leader in fixing trotting races. There was a separate group got in and started fixing the greyhounds; some of that still goes on. In the horse racing field it got so bad at one stage . . . you wouldn't even put a bet on. It's far better now but nevertheless it's a pretty sinister old scene . . . Millions upon millions invest in horseflesh, and to have it all negated by a few crooks . . . is pretty scandalous.'

Bob Bottom was the investigative journalist whose work precipitated some of the startling facts about organised crime into the public arena. In 1983 Bottom was privy to tapes recording a massive telephone-bugging operation carried out by a

Punters and Wowsers

There are always many punters who enjoy watching the odds rise and fall from one bookmaker to the next, and 'plunge' when the price is right
Australian Broadcasting Corporation

special unit of the New South Wales police between 1976 and 1983. The telephone taps had been set up to bust some of the organised criminal network, and had had some success there. What they revealed was so staggering that Bottom, after using some of the material in the *Bulletin* and in his book *The Godfather in Australia*, presented them to the Stewart Royal Commission set up after the criminal Robert Trimbole had fled Australia.

Strangely, Bottom's tapes were ignored, but when it appeared that he might reveal them elsewhere, the laws were changed to prevent him doing so, and at the last minute, before senior police came to fetch him, he flew to Melbourne to the *Age*, one of the few newspapers in Australia that had a high reputation for freedom of opinion.

Publication of the transcripts began in the *Age* on 2 February 1984. The revelations involved illegal gambling and race-fixing (Trimbole's speciality) among other things. In *Without Fear or Favour*, published in the same year, Bottom says that they confirmed 'many of the findings of the Costigan Commission which exposed connections between criminals involved in drug trafficking, prostitution, tax frauds and extortion with politicians, lawyers, businessmen and corrupt police officers' (p. 136).

Two of his comments in this book are sobering:

> The authority of the law has been so eroded in Australian society that the 'scales of justice' now weigh very heavily in favour of criminals rather than victims of crime . . . It is not without significance that with the whittling down of police authority over the past decade, organised criminals have graduated from the old-style racketeering to sophisticated, syndicated organised crime. (p. 156)

As Bob Bottom said in an interview, 'Some of the available phone-tap records show that, in one race alone, Bob Trimbole was able actually to pay twelve jockeys . . . That only left one honest jockey, whom they allowed to win. People would be shattered to see who among the top trainers of Australia and who among the household-name jockeys are liaising every day with the people who run the drugs and organised crime of Australia. It's a great conspiracy. By and large, there's pretty regular race-fixing.'

There's a seamy, sinister side to gambling in Australia now, Bottom said. 'In the twenty years since the criminal element took over the casinos, SP betting and the like, we've developed a horrifying drug problem which amounts to a turnover of $2000 million a year. There are many, many deaths. The fact is that some of the people who have been stripped of their money in casinos and while having a bit of a fling with an SP bookmaker have been indirectly funding the drug trade.'

One of the results of the *Age* tapes was the Fitzgerald Inquiry in Queensland.

The debate between punters and wowsers goes on.

Rev. Fred Nile of the Festival of Light has gambling in his family background. He is a man who for many typifies the wowser of our times. From similar religious premises as his forebears Judkin *et al.*, he is opposed to alcohol, gambling, prostitution and drugs because of the social damage they do, and opposes further legalisation because he thinks it will make things worse. He is regularly caught up in fierce debate about people's freedom to do what they like, prostitution as not socially harmful, the legalisation of hard drugs etc. Some see him as a dreadful puritan, others as someone genuinely concerned about the social ills of our day and a voice of sanity in troubled times.

'Our home', he said, 'was one where there was a lot of emphasis on horse-racing and dog-racing and lottery tickets and so on. My father was a very keen gambler; he always had that dream he was going to win. Of course he was one of those who never won . . .

'Sometimes I smile when people say to me, "Fred Nile has these narrow-minded views because he doesn't know the other side". I knew the other side because I really got hooked on gambling myself. Every bit of pocket money I had went on dog-racing or horse-racing . . . My father was very much involved in SP betting and I used to become a little SP bookie runner as a boy.

'You often hear that remark that Australians would bet on two flies crawling up a wall . . . It's probably true. That's why I think in our society we should do more to discourage gambling and to help reduce the temptation at the moment'. He is appalled that governments can exploit people's legitimate dreams by offering a house as prize in a lottery.

Fred Nile rejected the view that it was these campaigns that drove gambling, etc. into the arms of the gangsters. 'That's the only strong argument they've really got. They use it against me, on almost every issue, whether it's X-rated videos, gambling, drugs . . . They say if we legalise heroin and marijuana we'd get rid of organised crime. I say they'll still run it . . . The sort of men who will run the casino will still be, I believe, a front for organised crime in general . . . Decriminalise marijuana and some people think it means get rid of the criminals. I say no, it means get rid of the police . . . When you legalise casinos etc. you . . . give organised crime a free hand to organise another department for their activities.'

Why do people gamble? For the same reason, presumably, as people do anything else that is wonderful some of the time and painful the rest. John O'Hara argues in *A Mug's Game* that the aristocracy needed to display their wealth, and losing large sums was as much part of this as winning. Working people, on the other hand, would, by risking a small sum, be continually tempted to make the sort of money they normally never got.

Fred Nile argued that gambling is a form of greed. In his submission to the Wran government against a casino he pointed out that the Labor Party is 'supposed to care for the working man and is supposed to be against greed in the sense of capitalist greed, materialism. I said, wouldn't you say a casino represents that at its worst?'

The Australian poet Vincent Buckley described himself as a long-time bettor but not a gambler. He didn't see the ordinary racegoer as a gambler. He said the people who bet fortunes on the races were few. He had in mind a certain well-known figure who had his own string of horses and could end up two or three hundred thousand the richer at the end of a day's betting on them. It's obvious, he said, that the general intention of such a man was to gamble. But at the same time he chose optimum conditions: he knew his horses and their jockeys and trainers, so his risk was minimised. He was not betting blind, but was gambling in the sense that he was putting money on a series of contingencies: by the time he got to the fourth or fifth race on an all-up bet he was risking a lot of money he'd already won.

The average punter, Buckley said, was not prepared to risk a great deal of his own money: it's common to hear people saying, 'I never take more than $100 to the races' or 'I never borrow money to bet with'. He pointed out the calculation involved in a punt. The demeanour of racegoers was in his experience thoughtful and equable rather than excitable. Going to the races was a meditative act — you got a chance to think at the races. This was a far cry from the hectic, turbulent scenes of violence and 'riot' described in some of the early references to gambling.

Immoral, pathetic, thrilling or criminal — Australians keep on gambling, and as never before. The figures are staggering. Official statistics were leaked to the *Australian* of 11–12 June 1988 which showed that legal gambling alone would make more than $20 billion in 1988 — an annual outlay of more than $1200 for every person in the country. Gambling turnover in the financial year 1986–7 was $18 627.756 million; losses stood at $3 040.169 million. In all the figures New South Wales led the field, telling us that Sydney was as sinful as ever.

Two-thirds of the losses were in non-racing gambling, that is, lotteries, casinos, poker machines, bingo, etc., a change which has come since the mid-1970s. Racing has a bigger turnover than all these, and the punter's chances on the racecourse are higher.

The *Australian* described some of the technological and entertainment breakthroughs that are changing the face of gambling:

> Computer and satellite hook-ups will provide bigger and bigger prize pools, punters will bet from home on Viatel and international race meetings will be beamed into betting parlours.
>
> Gambling has become increasingly interwoven with leisure, entertainment and tourism, and is being driven by consumer demand for windfall prizes worth millions of dollars.
>
> Governments are the real winners — and the biggest promoters of the change. They actively encourage the trend by mounting large advertising campaigns and using computer and satellite technology to boost business.

The reformers' plans for a sober, industrious Australia have in one sense been entirely frustrated, in another ironically fulfilled: Australians work very hard indeed at winning and losing and extracting money from each other. The state that was to have protected people from their greed has become the biggest entrepreneur of all.

Sources and references

Books consulted:

Peter Corris, *Lords of the Ring: A History of Prize-fighting in Australia* (Cassell Australia, 1980); J. W. C. Cumes, *Their Chastity was not too Rigid: Leisure Time in Early Australia* (Longman Cheshire/Reed, 1979); Keith Dunstan, *Wowsers: Being an Account of the Prudery Exhibited by Certain Outstanding Men and Women in such Matters as Drinking, Smoking, Prostitution, Censorship, Gambling* (Cassell Australia, 1968); Alfred W. McCoy, *Drug Traffic: Narcotics and Organized Crime in Australia* (Harper & Row, 1980); McCoy, 'Sport as Modern Mythology: SP Bookmaking in New South Wales 1920–1979' in Richard Cashman and Michael McKernan (eds), *Sport: Money, Morality and the Media* (NSW University Press, 1981);

John O'Hara, *A Mug's Game: A History of Gaming and Betting in Australia* (NSW University Press, 1988); O'Hara, 'The Australian Gambling Tradition' in Cashman and McKernan, *Sport*; Neville Penton, *A Racing Heart: The Story of the Australian Turf* (Collins, 1987); Danny Sheehan with Wayne Lamotte, *Heads and Tails: The Story of Kalgoorlie Two-Up School* (Uniquely Australian, 1985); Trevor Wilson, *The Luck of the Draw: A Centenary of Tattersall's Sweeps, 1881–1981* (T. Wilson Publishing Company, 1980)

Bob Bottom, Fred Nile: Interview transcripts from the television series 'Blood, Sweat and Tears': the interviews with Vincent Buckley and Nappy Ollington were conducted by the author.

Other sources are as follows:

The material from the Bigge Report: House of Commons, *Report of the Commission of Inquiry into the State of the Colony of New South Wales*, 19 June 1822, pp.8–9; Backhouse: James Backhouse, *A Narrative of a Visit to the Australian Colonies* (London, 1843), pp.395, 238–9; Marsden: John Ritchie, *The Evidence to the Bigge Reports: New South Wales under Governor Macquarie*, vol.2 (Heinemann, 1971), p.92; J. H. Plumb: quoted in Cumes, p.16; Governor Macquarie on the Hyde Park races: quoted in Cumes, p.55; *Sydney Gazette* quote: Cumes, p.52; J. D. Lang: *Port-Phillip: or the Colony of Victoria* (Glasgow, 1853), pp.77, 278, 116; Joe the Basket Maker: Cumes, p.285; two-up: Lionel Dunn, 'Pennies that will spin forever', *Bulletin*, 14 August 1979; points in favour of two-up in Kalgoorlie: Sheehan, p.172; *Sydney Gazette* quote on chuck-farthing mob: Sheehan p.1; the Chinese: C. M. H. Clark, *A History of Australia* (Melbourne University Press, 1978), vol.4, p.115; Caroline Chisholm's letter to Earl Grey: quoted in Mary Hoban, *51 Pieces of Wedding Cake: A Biography of Caroline Chisholm* (Lowden, 1973) p.211; John Norton quote on Judkins: quoted in Dunstan p.251; Wren quote: in Dunstan, p.257; Judkins quote on Tattersall's in Tasmania: in Dunstan p.289.

CHAPTER 4

SILVERTAILS AND YOBBOS

Don Hogg

I was taken into the Australian Swimming Union office and it was stated to me across a certain gentleman's desk that I would never ever represent Australia because I was from the wrong side of the tracks. I didn't belong in the silver-spoon sport and whatever I did I wouldn't ever be able to represent Australia.

I was a kid from Balmain — that was an industrial area when I was young. I became a world champion, an Olympic champion in a silvertail sport. I wasn't supposed to do that, and they put all the hurdles they could possibly put in front of me.

That was the experience of a 14-year-old girl from Balmain, the harbour-bound, shabby working-class inner suburb of Sydney. Her name was Dawn Fraser. Not only did she represent her country at three successive Olympics, winning gold medals at each, she became an inspiration for Australia's economically and socially under-privileged youth. In 1988 she was elected to represent her beloved Balmain in the parliament of New South Wales.

Dawn Fraser survived many brushes with the swimming establishment but, as she explained in an interview, childhood in a large family had given her broad shoulders: 'I was the youngest of eight, having two elder brothers. I had to hang around with them at school, I had to play football with them, I had to play cricket, I had to climb trees, I had to play chasings and then after we finished playing all those sports I had to pick up all the equipment. If I didn't do that I'd get a clip over the ears from my brothers. That sort of gave me an outside shell that nothing hurt. But inside it made me a loner. I used to not show my emotions very much to people on the outside, but inside I used to just ache and I think that was from my upbringing.'

Dawn Fraser's later experiences with authority, social prejudice and bigotry are, sadly, by no means unique in Australia's sporting history. The years are littered with similar accounts, though perhaps few are as graphic. From the time men and women first hit or kicked a ball, ran against each other, or competed in any way social, racial and economic divisions have been drawn.

In an interview, the sport historian Brian Stoddart poured cold water on the idea that sport is the one great classless institution of Australian life. 'Perhaps the greatest myth in Australian history has been . . . that sport has been the one social event that's been accessible to everybody. If you want to play something you can go and do it. It's simply never been true, because of very simple things, like how much

Dawn Fraser, who won gold medals for 100 metres freestyle in three successive Olympics, remained one of Australia's most popular sportswomen despite her battles with officialdom. The esteem in which she is held was illustrated when she was elected an independent member of parliament in New South Wales in 1988. She represents the people of her birth-place, Balmain, and lives close to Drummoyne baths where she began in junior competition. A still from the television series, 'Blood, Sweat and Tears'
Paul Tatz

Blood, Sweat and Tears

money you've got, what kind of social background you came from, and who your social connections were.

Stoddart points to the way sports clubs and associations became social vehicles from the earliest days in Australia: 'If you look at the racing clubs that were set up in each of the major colonies, they were the gathering place for the élite, the social, political, and the economic élite of that particular community. You could only get membership in it if you really passed all the tests about whether you had a proper social pedigree, whether you had enough money, whether other people in the club would accept you as being a fit and proper person to obtain membership. It's not simply a question of having money . . . in some cases it's about what kind of money you've got, whether it's "old" or "new" money, or money that's been earned in a respectable profession such as the law, or whether you've earned it as a publican or a labourer or a bookie's clerk.' Golf, Stoddart says, is a good example of the complexity of the social pecking order: in one sense, anyone can go and play golf on a public course, but to join a wealthy or prestigious club one may have to undergo stringent vetting.

It is clear that from the time men and women first engaged in sport in Australia, some of those sports were, and remain, the exclusive preserve of the affluent. Polo is one such activity.

The first recorded game of polo took place in Melbourne's leafy Albert Park in 1875. The event, arranged by Englishmen visiting the colony on a horse-buying expedition, attracted the Governor of the day and the landed folk of Victoria together with prominent citizens of the city. Since then the sport has continued to involve the well-to-do from the country and city alike and to provide for its participants and followers a social aura that remains a matter of mystery for those engaged in more ordinary and commonplace sporting pursuits.

In 1988 there were polo associations in five mainland States with more than 1200

The officers and gentlemen of New South Wales followed the tradition of their homeland and raced their horses on makeshift tracks around the Port Jackson colony. The formidable and unyielding obstacles made steeplechasing an even more hazardous form of racing that it is today, as can be seen in this painting of the Five Dock Steeplechase of 1844. The long stirrup 'straight back' style was in vogue until well into the 20th century
From the original by E. Winstanley in the Mitchell Library

Silvertails and Yobbos

Polo has 'a social aura that remains a matter of mystery for those engaged in more commonplace sporting pursuits'. Kerry Packer and his son Jamie, seen here practising in Centennial Park, Sydney, are devotees of the sport which, despite the status of many of its participants, is tough and demanding on both riders and horses
John Fairfax & Son Limited

active players. Matches attract not only those with a genuine love of the sport but also those who wish to have their presence noted for the added prestige they believe it delivers. Polo is not a sport that readily attracts casual spectators, who might feel embarrassed about being in such company.

Andrew McNulty, an accountant from the Sydney harbourside suburb of Kirribilli, told of an experience of watching polo. 'I took my wife and kids to a day of polo at Warwick Farm. Both my wife and I felt a bit odd about going, almost as though we were intruding on a private club, moving beyond our social station. We really enjoyed the polo, though neither of us understood it very well, but we were quite intimidated by the other people there and by their possessions . . . We'd really dressed the kids up for the day, but the other kids there made them look shabby. I think even the kids felt out of place — we certainly did. We won't go again, we were thoroughly uncomfortable.'

The most famous Australian polo player of all time is Sinclair Hill, the New South Welshman who rose in the 1970s to be among the world's finest players. He describes how he became involved in the sport: 'When I left school I was sent to England. My family originally came from England a couple of generations back and we've always maintained an English connection. So I think they thought it would be best to send me to Cirencester Agricultural College instead of Cambridge or Oxford. And there I started to play polo and bought a couple of lame horses, patched them up and started to play.'

Sinclair Hill says that most of Australia's polo players originally came from the country 'because it was easier to have four horses in the country and a truck that you drove around. Australian polo players are virtually all farmers or graziers, but there's a greater city influence today than there was in my youth. Polo is an élitist sport. You can take that any way you like, but I think it's such a magnificent sport that you're bloody lucky if you can play polo.'

Asked whether it is a rich man's sport, Sinclair Hill says yes and no: 'Yes, it costs

Blood, Sweat and Tears

Sinclair Hill, a NSW property owner and one of the world's best polo players, leans low to strike the ball during the Australian Open Polo Championships at Warwick Farm in NSW
News Limited

Polo-crosse is a more egalitarian version of the long-established game of polo, although it still requires ownership of a team of horses and is therefore most suited to owners of country properties. It is a blend of polo and lacrosse, and is thought by some to be a more spectacular game than polo. The game in progress here is being played at Sale, Victoria
Bay Picture Library

money to play polo but it's not necessarily a rich man's sport. Take the farmers that play — they have some old god-forsaken truck and they've got four horses running around the paddock with no feed and no rugs and they put one saddle on and head off towards the town on Saturday morning. Well, is that an élitist sport? Is that costly?' He sees as misconceived the notion that polo players need to be wealthy.

Another view of polo is given by Geoff Ashton of the Goulburn district of New South Wales. He put Australian polo on the world map in 1930 with a highly publicised trip with his father and three brothers to Britain and the United States. In Britain, the Ashton family, representing Australia, won two major tournaments and were narrowly beaten in the Champion Cup, Britain's most prestigious event. On a later trip in 1937, they won the Champion Cup, causing Australia to be regarded as one of the world's leading polo countries. In Australia for more than half a century since the early 1920s, the name of Ashton has been synonymous with polo.

Commenting on the popular impression that polo is a rich man's game, Geoff Ashton said: 'For the people who play in the country it hasn't been all that expensive. It's got a lot more expensive . . . with inflation, but for the city player it can be expensive because he can't make his ponies as we did. He has to buy made ponies, which may cost him quite a bit of money. And full-time grooms are not inexpensive and he's got to pay for his feed, which comes from a good way away. How it compares with owning a yacht or running racehorses I don't know. The country player will often sell a pony to help with his expenses, and he probably forgoes other things he'd like to do such as going skiing or taking a trip abroad. We really had to watch our expenditure. We lived very frugally'.

The Ashtons took twenty-five ponies by ship to England in 1930 and from there shipped the horses to the United States to play there. At Long Island they played among the millionaires, men like Averill Harriman, J. H. Whitney who became ambassador to England, and the Vanderbilts.

There was some public criticism of the Ashtons for making their overseas trip during the Depression: 'I think the criticism was not unnatural because a lot of people said this was the most extravagant sort of trip that could be made. The risk we took was whether we could sell the horses overseas to pay for our adventure. And it turned out that way. It was splashed across the *Sydney Morning Herald* "Australian Ponies Sell On Long Island for $76,000". These horses in Australia wouldn't have been worth more than $6,000. Of course our expenses had to come out of the seventy-six.' When the sale was made public much of the criticism stopped.

The Ashton family made a second trip to Britain in 1937, taking their ponies. Playing with their spare man Bob Skene replacing Phil Ashton at number 1, they won the Champion Cup and the four brothers defeated the British Army. Before leaving Gloucestershire for London they received a disposition from the polo authorities to split the team up to even up the games and this reduced their opportunities to develop team play. 'The sad thing was that at the end of the trip we had to sell the ponies, and for a few days after that we felt very down in the dumps', Ashton said.

While the Sinclair Hills and Geoff Ashtons of polo clearly made great sacrifices to pursue their sporting loves and establish Australia as a force in their field of endeavour, they were people of assets and education able to turn their pursuits into economically viable indulgences. Others of less privileged background made quite different kinds of sacrifices to rise to the top of their chosen sports.

Marjorie Jackson, the girl from the bleak coalmining town of Lithgow, who became the first Australian woman for forty years to win an Olympic gold medal for Australia in a track event says: 'I used to pay my own way to go down to Sydney to compete and we had to buy our own running shoes and starting blocks. In fact, my very first pair of running shoes my father bought second hand and they were too big but that was all we could afford. We used to stuff them with newspaper before I ran in them. There was definitely no money.'

When she went to Finland for the Olympics in 1952, of the ninety-six in the team only thirty-one had their fares paid. Jackson worked several times a week at the Harold Park greyhound races, putting sashes on the dogs and collecting money for those in the team who hadn't had their fares paid.

Marjorie Jackson's successes did not go to her head. ' I remember when I won my first race, I think I went around with my head in the air a bit, thinking I was somebody. But I had a very wise father who just took me into the lounge room and said that God gives us all a gift and that mine just happened to be running and I wasn't any better than anybody else. That was something that stayed with me all my life. That was the best advice that any parent could ever give to a child.'

Marjorie Jackson has a big break on the field as she wins the 100 metres Gold Medal at the 1952 Olympics at Helsinki. The girl from the coal mining town of Lithgow NSW became the first Australian woman for forty years to win a gold medal for Australia in a track event
News Limited

Marjorie Jackson, 'The Lithgow Flyer', began to capture world attention in 1949 when, at the age of 17, she twice beat the Olympic Champion Fanny Blankers-Koen. She went on to win four gold medals at the Auckland Empire Games and the 100 and 200 metres at the Olympic Games in Helsinki
John Fairfax & Sons Limited

Silvertails and Yobbos

It is no accident that one of the communities to which Marjorie Jackson appealed for funds was that community, or fraternity, of people who administer and support greyhound racing. Here was a case of a girl of a working-class background appealing to her peers for help, knowing they would sympathise with her cause.

In the boom days of greyhound racing in Australia a meeting could attract as many as 25 000 people. Greyhound racing, the battlers' answer to the thoroughbred and standard-bred racing industries, has suffered a checkered and controversial history.

When the sport was introduced to New South Wales in May 1927 by an *émigré* from South America, a man known as Judge Frederick Swindell, the government refused to allow betting on the races. As a result, says Jack Woodward, who attended the first meeting at the Epping course (as the Harold Park Raceway in Sydney was then called), the first few meetings were very poorly attended.

Woodward recalls: 'The government was sympathetic towards the establishment of greyhound racing. The premier, Jack Lang, considered it could be introduced as a working man's sport, so he wanted to help. Within three weeks a bill went through State Parliament legalising betting on greyhound racing. It was early June of 1927 that the first meeting with legalised betting took place. All the big bookmakers, people like Ken Matthews and Jack Shaw, came along. It gave a big lift to greyhound racing and the crowd flocked there.'

The rough and ready conditions of the 'working man's sport' of greyhound racing is graphically depicted in this photograph of a race in progress at Lithgow. The dogs are intent on running down the 'tin hare', which is dragged along a pair of rails
John Fairfax & Sons Ltd

Woodward says greyhound racing has always been a working-class sport. Asked whether conservative governments of the 1920s and 1930s had discriminated against it because its following was among working people he said, 'It could have been that, but on the other hand the motion picture industry was very powerful back in those days, and the Opposition had their support. I think it just generally didn't appeal to the Nationalist government . . . Yes, it was definitely a working man's sport and I don't really think it has changed much . . . The one thing sticks in my mind . . . I would go into a home and the wife would say, "Have a look at our lovely new refrigerator, so-and-so won the last race at Harold Park last Saturday night and that's what she won for us". The prize-money would go into the home of the working people.'

Greyhound racing has always been a family thing, Woodward says. The trainer got out very early in the morning and walked his dogs. Then with his wife's assistance, he would kennel them, give them their breakfast, and go off to work. In the evening she and the children would have all the greyhounds ready for him to take out on the road again. There was a combined family effort amongst working-class people.

Sydney greyhound trainer Bruce Fletcher says in 1988 it cost him about $40 a week to train each of his greyhounds. In Sydney at the same time racehorse owners were paying leading trainers an average of $300 a week to condition each horse.

An indication of the vastly different prize-money available in the two codes of racing came on a Saturday in June 1988, when racehorses entered at an unremarkable meeting at Randwick competed for $177 000 in prize-money while on the same night greyhounds running at Wentworth Park, Sydney, competed for a total of $19 100. On that day at Randwick the collective career prize-money already earned by the starters totalled $2 916 309, while at Wentworth Park the figure was $61 320.

The 'Dish Lickers' leap out of the boxes at a greyhound meeting in Western Australia. Owning and training costs allow the 'man in the street' to participate in the sport, but the prize-money is but a fraction of the stakes earned in the high rolling sport of horse racing
Bay Picture Library

Silvertails and Yobbos

The New Years Day meeting at Randwick in 1877. The Randwick Racecourse was cleared by convicts and the first meeting was held there in 1833. The race and the grandstand was depicted in the Australasian Sketcher
Mitchell Library

Even more astonishing was the prize-money for which the horses racing at Eagle Farm, Brisbane, were competing on the same date: a massive $725 000. The thirteen starters in just one race, the Brisbane Cup, had amassed during their collective careers a hefty $2 386 185. In the main race at Wentworth Park that night the career prize-money of the eight starters was a little over $41 000.

While Australia's premier greyhound race, the Australian Cup, run at Olympic Park in Melbourne, offered $100 000 in prize-money, the thoroughbred racing calendar boasted three races with prize-money of more than $1 million, over a dozen worth more than $500 000, and nearly a hundred of $100 000 or thereabouts.

A commonplace Saturday horse-race at Randwick in Sydney or Flemington in Melbourne was worth $13 000 to the winner, while at Wentworth Park in Sydney and Olympic Park in Melbourne the first prize-money was a more humble $1100. Australia's leading racehorses of the day — Beau Zam, Bonecrusher and Campaign King — had won between them $5.6 million and there were scores of other thoroughbreds of the same era to have bettered the $500 000 mark. The all-time stakes winning record for a greyhound was $102 000.

An interesting sidelight to greyhound racing is that each unplaced starter in a race at Wentworth Park earns $35, a sum that goes most of the way towards meeting the week's training expenses. The practice is widespread among other greyhound racing clubs around Australia, although the amounts vary. Clearly the clubs, recognising the nature of the participants in the sport, are prepared to give them a financial hand. No such practice exists in thoroughbred racing.

Certainly, if thoroughbred racing is the Sport of Kings, then greyhound racing, and to a lesser extent, standard-bred racing, or trotting, are the pursuits of their subjects. At a Melbourne Cup, New South Wales Derby, Adelaide, Perth or Brisbane Cup meeting you can expect to find society's rich, powerful and famous in attendance. Major race day appearances are, for many of these people, almost obligatory.

There can scarcely be an adult Australian who is unaware of the annual gathering of the landed, the mighty, the wealthy and the fashionable who collect among the exotic motor cars in the members' car park at Flemington racecourse on Melbourne Cup day. There they enjoy champagne and caviar, salmon and sauvignon blanc, cognac and cold collations, while the punters over the fence queue for a meat pie

The citizens of Melbourne in all their finery parade on the lawns at Flemington on Melbourne Cup Day near the turn of the century.
Herald & Weekly Times

and a beer. The newspapers are full of the antics in the members' car park. They send their social reporters with photographer in tow from as far afield as Brisbane and Perth to cover the goings-on of the rich and beautiful.

That the occasion is one of thoroughbred racing, and, in terms of the devotee, thoroughbred racing of some moment, seems to have little relevance for these once-a-year racegoers. Many of them, it is often said, do not leave the comfortable precincts of their picnic areas to watch the race.

Thoroughbred racing in Australia has always enjoyed vice-regal and political patronage and the principal turf clubs of each of the States have always been bodies of immense social and political power. In New South Wales a place on the committee of the Australian Jockey Club has always indicated social status of the loftiest order.

In the middle and late 1970s one Sydney gentleman, with what appeared to be little more than a passing interest in the administration of the sport but who enjoyed a high profile in social circles, sought elevation from the membership of the AJC to its committee. To that end he placed a number of newspaper advertisements exhorting his fellow members to vote for him in the forthcoming elections. His advertising dollars were spent in vain, but the matter did amuse those who follow such events.

The world of thoroughbred racing throws up its own class divisions. For instance, the bookmaking fraternity, around whom much racing activity revolves, and without whom much of the glamour and excitement of a race meeting would dissipate, are still required to pay their way into a racecourse. And along with other licensed persons their presence is banned from certain areas of the racecourse — the members' bars and other members' facilities. Despite their huge contribution to the development and success of the industry in Australia, the bookmakers are treated by the clubs as second-class citizens. And so also with the trainers and jockeys, whose behaviour is strictly controlled. Any licensed person who dares speak in criticism of a club does so in the sure knowledge they will be sternly

Above:
The great New Zealand sprinter Bonecrusher heads for the winning post in the 1986 W. S. Cox Plate at Moonee Valley. Bonecrusher had some sterling tussles with the best that Australia could offer.
Martin King Sportpix

Left:
The glamour horse of 1987 Vo Rogue with his part-owner and trainer Vic Rail. The big Queensland horse has sensational speed and likes to lead early and defy efforts to run him down
Martin King Sportpix

disciplined and face the prospect of being suspended or even removed completely from the means of earning their livelihood.

Then, there are the punters. No one has ever challenged the proposition that it is the punter who keeps the industry alive and well. Yet until recent times, when it began to become clear that the punters were forsaking the racecourses in their thousands, the administrators of racing had chosen largely to ignore that huge body of the public which, through its betting on racehorses, was providing most of the finance for the industry.

Since the introduction of Totalisator Agency Boards (TABs) around Australia in the late 1950s and early 1960s the betting public of Australia has poured billions of dollars into the coffers of the thoroughbred, trotting and greyhound industries. The main beneficiaries of the punters' involvement have been the breeders and owners of racehorses, whether thoroughbred or standard-bred, and greyhounds.

In the thoroughbred racing industry the prize-money offered today is huge compared with what it was before the introduction of legal off-course betting through TAB agencies. Tulloch, the champion galloper of the late 1950s and early 1960s, raced for four seasons, won thirty-six races and was placed sixteen times in Australia's premier races, to earn $220 247. The champion galloper of 1988, Beau Zam, before he had finished his second racing season, had earned more than $2 million from fewer than twenty starts. Indeed, in 1988 there were no fewer than 317 thoroughbreds racing in Australia who had earned more than the legendary Tulloch, and many of them will never rate a mention among racing enthusiasts when great performers of the Australian turf are discussed a few years hence.

The effect the huge prize-money has had is to attract already rich men and women to the industry as owners and breeders. The Federal government offers enticing tax concessions to racehorse owners, and prize earnings do not attract tax in any form. Yet the percentages of prize-money paid to trainers and jockeys is taxed. The punters themselves are, of course, heavily taxed for their support of this Sport of Kings. Each bet written in a TAB or on course attracts a minimum tax of 7.5 per cent (it varies from State to State) and some forms of multiple betting are taxed as much as 25 per cent.

Everything sold on a racecourse, from a cup of tea to a pencil, a glass of beer or a racebook, attracts a State tax, as does the price of admission, which in 1988

The mighty Tulloch storms to a win in 1960. Tulloch raced fifty-three times for thirty-six wins and sixteen placings. His only non-placed race was in the 1960 Melbourne Cup, when he had to carry the huge weight of 10st. 11 lb. He was trained by Tommy Smith and his regular jockey was George Moore
News Limited

Silvertails and Yobbos

Myocard blitzed a field of highly fancied horses to win the 1987 AJC Derby at Randwick, Sydney. A major event on the Australian racing calendar, the Derby was first run at Randwick in 1861.
Martin King Sportpix

Below:
The Foster's Melbourne Cup remains the premier sporting event in all Australia. Run on the first Tuesday in November, it creates a public holiday in its home state and 'stops the clock' nationwide at 2.40 p.m. The grey What a Nuisance is pictured winning the 1985 Cup.
Martin King Sportpix

averaged $5 on metropolitan courses. Certainly in recent years the major clubs have used the windfall the TABs provide to build more comfortable facilities for racegoers. By 1988 virtually every major racecourse in Australia had erected new, air-conditioned grandstands with carpets, smart bars and air-conditioning.

The sceptics were saying that the clubs had provided these facilities only because race attendances were falling, that the goose that laid the golden eggs must not be allowed to die. Others were arguing that what they perceived as a new-found concern for the punter in the hearts of the administrators resulted from nothing more than the insistence of State governments that part of the TAB rake-off going to the clubs should be returned to the patrons in the form of facilities.

No matter what the truth of this, the fact is that while the punter of the 1980s is much more comfortable on a racetrack than were his hardy and long-suffering forebears, he is still treated as a necessary evil by the administrators.

At the Victorian Amateur Turf Club's Caulfield racecourse a sign that existed until the middle 1960s seemed to express for many of the ordinary folk who attend race meetings just what the racing clubs of the day thought of them. Under the general heading of 'Toilets' there were two finger-posts. One, pointing in one direction, said 'Gentlemen'. The other, pointing the other way, said 'Public'.

Perhaps the most disturbing discriminatory aspect of racing administration still surviving into the late 1980s is the power of a major racing club committee to remove the licence from a licensed person without reason. The power has in the past been used sparingly and, one hopes, used with great responsibility; nevertheless the authority still exists and a licensed person's livelihood may be removed without either the accused or the public being told why.

Only in more recent times have licensed persons resorted to the courts for redress when they have felt they have been unfairly or harshly treated. And it is of recent times that some of the governing clubs have appointed tribunals to hear grievances. In the case of the governing body of New South Wales, the Australian Jockey Club, a judge has been appointed to head its independent tribunal.

As Neville Penton, Sydney journalist and writer, says: 'Without the little punter in racing there is no racing. The little punter is the life blood of the turf.'

For all the criticism that may be levelled at thoroughbred racing by those who would argue that more than any other sport in Australia it has created and entrenched socially discriminatory practices, there are many in the community who would say racing still offers the 'little' man or woman — the battler — the chance of real success or riches, or both. There's Vic Rail, they'll say, the hitherto unknown Queensland racehorse trainer who found national prominence with his wonderful, unfashionably bred racehorse, Vo Rogue, in Melbourne in 1987. And what about the group of Sydney garbage collectors who won major races with their horse Mighty Keys, back in the early 1960s? Racing history in Australia is liberally sprinkled with instances where battlers have come up trumps. Those are the occasions other battlers remember; they have an awesome capacity for overlooking the real odds.

It is true that the modern thoroughbred racing industry has embraced and nurtured a phenomenon that has made it more possible for an ordinary citizen to own, or at least part-own, a racehorse. It's called racehorse syndication and it had its origins in New South Wales in the late 1970s, a time when racing was undergoing great change.

Breeding experts, or at least people claiming to be such, would buy yearling racehorses both in Australia and New Zealand and offer shares in them for sale to all comers. Before the sale, the syndicator would often make an arrangement with a well-known trainer for the education and training of the horse and a monthly figure for the trainer's services would be agreed, so when the horse was ready for syndication the would-be part-owners were given a clear indication of what would be their ongoing costs. In this way thousands of ordinary people who had only dreamed of

Silvertails and Yobbos

racing a thoroughbred were able to gain themselves a share in one. The principal racing clubs took time to warm to the idea and sanction it, but once approved the idea gained momentum, and customers, at an astonishing rate.

In 1988 Roy Higgins, champion Victorian jockey of the 1960s and 1970s, was the manager of the syndication company, Hyperion Thoroughbreds. He explained what he described as the advantages of the system: 'We travel Australia to all the yearling sales. We purchase horses and we syndicate them out into partnerships of up to six. We then vary it into syndication of up to twenties and we stay in then and manage all these people's affairs for them. The advantage is to the little people, who not only can't afford the original cost of a horse, but the ongoing cost. It's not unusual to see $60 plus per day to have a horse just standing in the stable. Now there are not many people out today that can afford that, so through syndication they can buy a one-twentieth share in a horse and share costs and prize-money'.

Higgins said he thought that by the mid-1990s 80 per cent of thoroughbreds being raced in Australia would be owned by syndicates. This will be good for racing, for syndicate members would bring families, friends and neighbours to the racetrack.

Higgins's rags-to-riches story is one that helps keep the dream of success alive in many a mug punter's mind. He worked in a stables for two shillings a week when he was still at school. He was very small; being from a very poor family and deprived of many things stunted his growth. 'I should be thankful for that', he says, 'because when I look back on it I can say that racing's been good to me'. Roy Higgins went on to ride the winners of two Melbourne Cups in addition to winning most other horse-races on the Australian calendar.

Of course, Higgins is not the only underprivileged kid to have done well in racing and to have come to rub shoulders with the influential. Another was Darby McCarthy, perhaps the most famous of all Aboriginal jockeys.

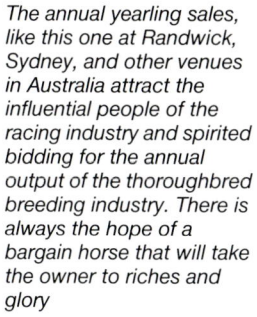

The annual yearling sales, like this one at Randwick, Sydney, and other venues in Australia attract the influential people of the racing industry and spirited bidding for the annual output of the thoroughbred breeding industry. There is always the hope of a bargain horse that will take the owner to riches and glory
Live Action: Acikalin

Blood, Sweat and Tears

The week-long Melbourne Cup Carnival at Flemington is a cause for festivity in Melbourne. It consists of the Victoria Derby meeting, the Melbourne Cup meeting, the Oaks meeting and the Final Day. One of the traditions, particularly on Derby Day, is an al fresco *lunch in the members' car park*
Martin King Sportpix

Victorian Derby Day at the Melbourne Cup Carnival is the most correct and formal day of the sometimes riotous Melbourne Cup Carnival. Morning suits and grey 'toppers' are still much in evidence in the members' enclosure
Martin King Sportpix

Richard Laurence McCarthy was born at Cunnamulla, on the Queensland side of the New South Wales border, in 1945. 'There was neither a right side nor a wrong side of the tracks in Cunnamulla. If you were born there you were born on the wrong side of the world', wrote Pat Farrell, the Sydney writer and journalist. 'It was a place with an Aboriginal slum on its edge — humpies and lean-to shacks and skinny mongrel dogs, shuffling old women and lazy men, and boggle-eyed kids running naked in the hot, red dust'. Farrell himself was born there.

McCarthy's leap from that squalor and hopelessness catapulted him to fame, success and wealth, to England's Royal Ascot wearing a top hat and morning suit, to a private box in the grandstand at Deauville, France, where he watched the races with the newly-weds Frank Sinatra and Mia Farrow. It won him the company and confidence of multimillionaires and European royalty, and it won him many of the most important horse-races in Australia.

That leap, wrote Farrell, gave Darby — the nickname he had chosen for himself because of his admiration for the legendary jockey Darby Munro — exotic cars and fine homes and suites in the best hotels, travel to all corners of the earth. It permitted him, in one burst of recklessness, to spend or give away $250 000 in five years. But it also brought him disillusionment, unhappiness, fear and undeserved social disgrace, and left him on a fast backslide to skid row, poverty and desperation.

In October 1969, within one hour, Darby McCarthy rode the winners of the AJC Derby and the Epsom Handicap, two of the most important races on the Australian thoroughbred calendar. It was a riding double rarely achieved, before or since. Those achievements brought the 24-year-old instant fame and wealth. 'People wouldn't believe me if I told them how much money I got out of those two races. It was a hell of a lot more than the $3070 that was my percentage of the prize-money. Some people would live a lifetime and never see as much money as I got in that hour. But to me it was just another tightly packed mess of coloured paper, something to be spent, something to have a wild time with.

'I didn't keep count of my money then. It didn't seem to matter. When the winnings from what I got out of the Derby and the Epsom had gone it had gone the same way as $250 000 I'd earned in the five years after I came out of my apprenticeship. Before I won those two big races at Randwick life in racing had been good to me. I'd won three Stradbroke Handicaps, a Brisbane Cup and a Doomben Ten Thousand.

'There was money galore, and nobody could spend it quite as fast or flashily as I could. A banknote was to me a symbol, a bridge over the gulf from where I'd been as a child to the kind of life I dreamed of and reckoned was my right.'

McCarthy was the eighth of twelve children and says that as a child he knew poverty as only an Aboriginal family can know it. He says that when he watched the races that day at Deauville with Sinatra and Mia Farrow he couldn't concentrate on the racing. 'I was too busy thinking what the odds must have been against me, an Aboriginal from Cunnamulla, sitting there in a private box watching the races with two of the world's most famous people. The odds had to be a million to one.'

It wasn't long after that historic day at Randwick that McCarthy suffered an accident that nearly ended his racing career. In the course of a domestic argument at his Sydney home, the jockey crashed through a plate-glass window and nearly severed an arm. From that point his career began to go downhill. The long stint out of the saddle saw his weight increase alarmingly, and it was rumoured he was drinking heavily. About a year after the accident he attempted his first comeback, but the breaks didn't seem to go his way and he vanished from the racing scene again. Then in 1972 he began his second comeback, this time riding at obscure meetings in the Northern Rivers district of New South Wales. A Sydney newspaper reported he had ridden four winners, a second and a third from his first six comeback rides. In the same article the newspaper said, 'The big question now is whether McCarthy can overcome the hoodoo that seems to haunt members of his race in sport and make a successful comeback'.

That comeback took the gifted rider to Melbourne in 1973 where he worked in a factory making shower screens to augment his income from racing. For that he was paid $50 a week. He said at the time: 'I count the money now. The $50 keeps my wife and two baby boys while, thanks to the people who still have faith in me and my gift for riding race horses that I almost destroyed, I'm trying to rebuild the ruins of a career that looked so good three and a half years ago. I'm not sure that I really deserve the chance, but the chance is there.'

McCarthy rode successfully in Melbourne until June 1976, although never with the success he had enjoyed in Queensland or New South Wales. Then, in June 1976, he was disqualified for seven years following his ride in a race at Hamilton earlier in the year. He was found guilty of conspiracy and dishonest practices. On appeal the sentence was reduced to two years, a penalty most racing reporters of the day described as 'overly harsh' and eventually, the disqualification was dropped.

He told a Melbourne interviewer, 'Soon after my disqualification I put myself in a hospital for alcoholics and drug addicts and stayed there for nine weeks to dry out. The drink helped in destroying my marriage. I lost my home, and most importantly, my two young children'. The interviewer asked what had given the jockey the will to come back on earlier occasions, to which he replied, 'It was the need to prove to my race and my family that I could be a capable, and hopefully, a responsible person'.

McCarthy did come back after that disqualification but his weight had become an increasing problem and few rides were made available to him. Slowly he drifted from the limelight again and there were whispers that the once great rider had again become a victim of alcohol.

In 1983 the newspapers announced another comeback, this time in Sydney, and the *Sun-Herald* quoted the jockey as saying he'd earned more than $2 million during his career, but none of it was left. He told how for the past eighteen months he'd been chipping weeds, picking tomatoes and trawler fishing in Queensland. 'It hasn't been easy', he said, 'That kind of work only pays $5 an hour'. But that comeback did not succeed, indeed it scarcely got off the ground. Then in 1984 the boy from Cunnamulla was back in the news again when it was announced he would be put in charge of Australia's first training school for apprentice jockeys, at Toowoomba in Queensland. The project was funded by a grant from the Department of Technical and Further Education. The grant ran out and McCarthy turned his hand to training racehorses.

The story of the great Aboriginal boxer, Lionel Rose MBE, bears a sad relationship to that of Darby McCarthy. Rose, a professional fighter by the time he was 17, was world bantamweight champion at 19 years of age. Here was only the second Australian in history to win a world boxing championship and the first Aborigine. As the new champion he stood on the steps of the Melbourne Town Hall in 1968 and cried as 250 000 people gathered to pay homage to his courage and awesome skill.

He was reported to have earned $500 000 from his short career, yet by the time he was in his middle-twenties he was broke. 'I once spent $100 000 in a single year on wine, women and song', he said, a line that was to be echoed by McCarthy just a few years later. And like McCarthy, Lionel Rose has never been slow to acknowledge that alcohol played a large part in his transition from hero to has-been.

Following one of Lionel Rose's brushes with the law the Adelaide writer Max Harris put this view:

> His fate is our guilt . . . what a fearsome burden he must have had to bear. The burden didn't arise from his pugilistic genius . . . he carried his world fame with the dignity and restraint which is inherent to his race when these qualities are permitted to surface and survive.
>
> The burden was heaped on his back after the title went, and the fame began to fade. Lionel Rose was still there as a symbol for Aboriginal people, as living proof of their potential capacity . . . pursuit of the bubble reputation has become such a common destroyer of lives in an age of public exposure, media performance and role-playing, that we take the risks for granted . . . we had a great Aboriginal in our midst and let him be savaged in the jungle of an uncaring world. Maybe his problems were too great for the caring to be extended to him. One thing is certain, and that is that we'll never know unless we care to find out.

Aboriginal apprentice Darby McCarthy scores his first race win on Kordes at Eagle Farm in December 1958. McCarthy hit the heights and earned huge prizes, but spent the money too freely and was a victim of injury, disqualification and high living
News Limited

Max Harris could have been writing of Darby McCarthy. The facts surrounding his slide from greatness were almost the same. Both were from humble beginnings, both were Aborigines, neither of them was able to handle the wealth and fame their achievements brought in their chosen pursuits. Both had tried to cross the bridge to the world of the silvertail. Both had failed.

But it would be misleading and inaccurate to suggest all great Aboriginal sportspeople have coped inadequately with fame, wealth and position. The great Australian tennis player of the late 1970s and early 1980s, Evonne Goolagong, and Doug Nicholls, the Australian Rules star who played with Fitzroy in the 1920s and 1930s, were able to make quite remarkable social transitions. Both came from humble backgrounds to achieve a new status not only through their sporting achievements, but also because of their demeanour and integrity and their ability to keep fame in its proper perspective.

There are, of course, some sports and recreational pursuits which in the public mind readily fall into social categories. Ocean-racing, for instance, is immediately perceived as the preserve of the wealthy, while dinghy-racing is seen as a form of yachting for the less privileged. Then there are the football codes. Australian Rules may seem classless, yet in the 1980s the Carlton Club was known as a club attracting so-called silvertail support while others such as Richmond and Footscray were seen to be favoured by working-class people.

Rugby Union was seen as the football code of the privileged, no doubt because of its private school origins, both in Britain and Australia, and it has remained a steadfastly amateur game. Rugby League, on the other hand, has until recently been seen in Australia as a social step down from Union. Of recent years the issue has been clouded somewhat by the shift some of Australia's greatest Union players have made to the League code in search of financial rewards.

Boxing, as always, remained a sport in which only the battlers seemed to have an interest in participating, and the history of the ring in Australia provides name after name of Aborigines and migrants.

Pigeon-racing and cycling, wrestling and dirt-track speedway, by their very mention in the Australian community have always found their own class category, as indeed have clay pigeon shooting, vintage motor racing and hunting to hounds found theirs.

Baseball, basketball, volleyball, a legion of other sports and pursuits appear to be without class or social distinction. Cricket has moved out of the realm of being for the socially successful into a sport where anyone may participate and succeed, and certainly the makeup of the personnel of Australian cricket teams over the years would support the contention that — at the player level at least — background has ceased to be an important consideration.

But it needs to be said that the classic sports (if they may be so termed), the sports which had their origins among the landed people of England — polo, rowing, thoroughbred horse-racing, rugby — are the sports most favoured by Australia's equivalent of their English landed forebears as the sports they would most like to have their sons and daughters pursue.

Sources and references

The material in this chapter is derived from the author's own research and observation, with the use of interviews and newspaper articles.

Interview transcripts of the television series 'Blood, Sweat and Tears':

Geoff Ashton, Bruce Fletcher, Dawn Fraser, Roy Higgins, Sinclair Hill, Marjorie Jackson, Neville Penton, Brian Stoddart, Jack Woodward.

Other quotations are as follows:

Doug Nicholls: obituary, *SMH*, 11 June 1988; Neil Newnham, Melbourne *Herald*, 20 August 1949; Sydney *Daily Telegraph*, 3 June 1972; Lionel Rose: Max Harris, *Australian*, 18 June 1983; Mike Rowbotham, *Sun*, 17 June 1983; Darby McCarthy: Pat Farrell, *Daily Mirror*, 11 May 1981.

CHAPTER 5

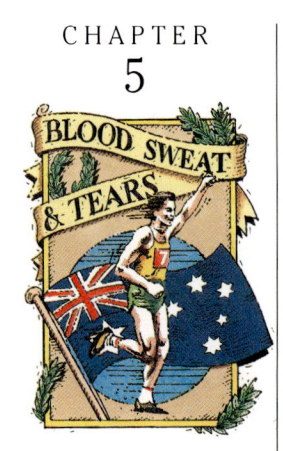

KILL THE BASTARDS

Neil Cadigan

'And which team do you follow? . . . Oh, the Tigers? . . . You poor fool, must have thought of slitting your throat at least once.' It can often be the opening line of conversation, after introductions, in any pub in Melbourne or Sydney. It explains a certain preoccupation with identifying your allegiances, a strange prerequisite for determining if you are a good bloke.

Following a football team can be serious stuff. The marketing experts of Melbourne in the 1960s saw it when they introduced gas stoves, refrigerators and even wigs in the colours of Victorian Football League clubs. Rugby League's Ray Price saw it when he found his six-year-old son hiding in a cupboard crying after arriving home from school.

Tribalism is the division of people into groups held together by strong inner loyalty and cohesiveness and a corresponding hostility to outsiders. In Australian sport it exists at three levels: our nation against another, a manifestation of nationalism; rivalry between the States, or between capital cities; and the aggressive hostility between clubs, which is at its most intense in Sydney Rugby League and in the Victorian Football League.

Australia's emphasis on sport goes back to the early days of settlement. As a convict nation we were seen as inferior to the motherland, England. As an undeveloped country we could not compete, or show equality, in industry or culture. There were frequent and painful reminders of our brashness, our crudity. We could compete in sport, the activity which depended on God-given physical gifts, human endeavour and a favourable climate where much could be done out of doors. It was in cricket, our most popular early sport, that a proud sense of patriotism was first seen. *Bell's Life* said in 1861 that our ability to compete in cricket did 'more than anything which has occurred in many years to break the Imperial assumption of colonial inferiority'. In those days it was Australia opposed to Britain. In the following decades New South Wales and Victoria developed a rivalry which was at its greatest on the cricket field.

Towards the end of the century and in the first decade of the 1900s the spreading suburbs of Sydney and Melbourne began to find one of their focal points in their local football and cricket clubs. Sporting clubs were established in virtually every town in the country, and sport for recreation became competitive sport, marked by interclub hostilities and rivalry.

Sporting tastes can bring out surprising emotion. The first spectator cricket riot took place in 1879. The Bodyline series of 1932–3 did unbelievable harm to Australian–British international relations. A crowd invasion at the Sydney Cricket Ground in 1971 saw English cricket captain Ray Illingworth lead his team off the field. These are cases where our sporting patriotism has turned into blind nationalism, where national pride over our own feats has given way to a narrow-minded anger towards opposing nations.

At State level rivalry has often been taken too far. The most petty crowd campaign in history was against Rugby League's greatest player of the 1980s, Australian captain Wally Lewis. Lewis has been subject to a distasteful 'not welcome' reception from Sydney crowds which included lewd signs and fruit-throwing. Why? Because he was an alien from Queensland, even though he was the best player in the land.

Brawls at football in Sydney (Rugby League) and Melbourne (Australian Rules) have marred our major winter sports for decades. But the ugliest scene was a soccer fracas involving hundreds of opposing (and ethnic) groups at Pratten Park in Sydney which caused the Sydney Olympic–Sydney City soccer match to be abandoned in 1983.

All these deplorable incidents were sparked by the form of life that was designed as a recreation, as an outlet. Sport.

Cricket had evolved from being merely a favourite recreation in the 1820s to an organised team sport in the 1850s and 1860s. Interclub cricket in Sydney and Melbourne at first retained its 'gentlemanly' nature, and small peaceful spectator followings. But when it came to interstate matches or games against the first three English touring sides — H. H. Stephenson's Englishmen of 1861, J. J. Lillywhite's men of 1876–7 and Lord Harris's tourists of 1878–80 — emotional rivalry grew. A certain 'hatred' of the Englishmen was shown because of the colony's inferior image in the eyes of the English: beating England was a sign of the vitality of Australian manhood and even then our top cricketers became national heroes and were idolised.

As intercolonial rivalry developed, so did crowd violence, particularly in Sydney which was notorious for its more biased sporting following. Rivalry developed between New South Wales and Victoria, or more specifically between the two larger settlements Sydney and Melbourne, and this interstate rivalry is still more prevalent between these two States more than any others. Richard Cashman's book, *'Ave a Go, Yer Mug*, describes the preposterous situation where Victorian cricketers thought it dangerous to walk the streets of Sydney after a cricket match. The comment to one player was: 'There's a Victorian cricketer, 'eave half a brick at him'. In 1861, as Cashman records, Victorian wicketkeeper Marshall unfairly ran out a New South Wales batsman's runner who walked out of his crease, and Marshall stumped a batsman after the ball was presumably thought 'dead' at the end of an over. The crowd swarmed the field and the Victorian captain was struck on the head.

Still the rivalry between Australia and England remained greater, focussing in the 1870s on the infamous Englishman W. G. Grace. Often when Grace was dismissed hats were thrown into air and there were shouts of jubilation. Already, for the English, we had earned a reputation of being 'one-eyed', unruly and treating sport more like war than recreation.

In February 1879 the first infamous crowd riot in an England–New South Wales match occurred. New South Wales batsman Murdoch was run out in a contentious decision. Then followed a delay in the appearance of a new batsman, and discussion on the field between the opposing captains, so about 2000 fans rushed the ground, jostling the English players. The mêlée lasted for half an hour.

Richard Cashman, describing the incident, noted:

> It is worth exploring some of the ingredients of this riot to establish its links with previous unrest. One continuing factor was the strong crowd identification with the home team which represented a form of nationalism or perhaps chauvinism. It was possibly fuelled by the reported comments of two English professionals, Emmett and Ulyett, who referred to the crowd as 'sons of convicts' and supposedly about the time Harris was struck.

By the first two decades of the twentieth century Australian 'inferiority' began to diminish. Australia had gained Federation and the nation was growing rapidly. We had seen World War I and fought alongside the British, establishing a legend as brave soldiers at Gallipoli. In sporting terms we could compete on any level and had had victories over the English in cricket and the two codes of rugby.

Still the rivalry with the Old Dart remained, but within Australia a new competitiveness between people and classes had developed alongside it. The Victorian Football League in Melbourne was characterised by its support from the people as the city expanded into suburbs. Territorial armies of football followers emerged. While Aussie Rules dominated public popularity in Victoria, in New South Wales the game was overshadowed by the traditional English football code of Rugby Union. But rugby soon had its own division when Rugby League was formed in 1908 after a dispute over payment of injury compensation to players. The breakaway movement agreed to pay compensation and within a few years players were being paid match fees.

So Union remained the game of the upper classes, its strength emanating from the private school system. League was the 'working man's sport'. Australia's own code, Aussie Rules, saw both as opponents; it dominated in Melbourne and had developed rapidly in South Australia, Western Australia and Tasmania, while the rugby codes were concentrated only in New South Wales and Queensland. In the same period Rugby Union had achieved a foothold in Melbourne's private schools.

Cricket was the only truly national team game. Club cricket in Sydney and Melbourne drew thousands to its weekend matches; Sheffield Shield cricket between the States had remarkable crowd and press following — much diminished today —

Kill the Bastards

The dour expression of the English Captain Douglas Jardine and his direction of Bodyline tactics stirred up great hostility from Australian crowds and the nation as a whole. The crisis on the 1932–3 tour led to the outlawing of Bodyline
Photobank/All Sport

Harold Larwood was the spearhead of the Bodyline attack, which consisted mainly of bouncers aimed at the body and head supported by a packed leg-side field, ready to accept catches as the batsman warded off the ball
John Fairfax & Sons Ltd: SMH 1935

Despite Larwood's bowling, the bluff Yorkshireman was quite popular with Australian crowds, who reserved their enmity mainly for Jardine. He waves his bat after being caught out for 98 at the Sydney Cricket Ground. Larwood eventually settled in Sydney.
National Library of Australia

and our champions were fêted as the pinnacles of society. During the Great Depression, success on the cricket field was one of the things that gave Australians on the dole queues something to smile about. Australia's team, and Australia's Don, Donald Bradman, were the best in the world . . . until an Englishman named Douglas Jardine invented 'leg theory' bowling as a counter to the genius of Bradman. He had floored the English bowling on the previous Australian tour to Britain and was seen in this country as a demigod. Crowds more than doubled on days when Bradman batted, and people drove out through the turnstiles after he was dismissed.

During the Bodyline series when Australia's hero was the victim of such unsporting tactics by Jardine and his men, the game attracted greater attention — and greater emotion against the English than ever. According to Cashman, when the Englishmen travelled to Adelaide where crowds were normally most sedate, the English captain even drew an angry crowd of thousands to a practice session where he was abused when he batted.

Cashman describes the events of the most infamous day in that Bodyline series when the popular Bert Oldfield was hit in the face by a Larwood delivery. 'When Oldfield was hit there was a tremendous "crack" — one player in the game can still "hear" the sound of the crack — and for an instant there was an absolute silence followed by an angry murmur which swept the ground. It appeared a prelude to a hostile demonstration.'

The match was being broadcast on radio. The 'gentleman's game' had created a mass anger throughout a nation, a genuine hatred not just for Jardine and Larwood but for the Mother Country they represented. For the competitive Jardine, the need to win and thus show superiority was an obsession. But the behaviour of both sides engendered a hatred that reignited old fires from colonial days.

There were several times when we heard the call that 'this is just not cricket' over the decades that followed, but there was no major confrontation in Australia until 1971 in circumstances similar to the Bodyline saga of the 1930s. This time the major players from England were stocky Yorkshireman Ray Illingworth, like Jardine renowned for his ruthlessness, and fast bowler John Snow. The 'disagreement' between the nations again was short-pitched bowling, again the crowd emotion reached fever pitch at the striking of an Australian batsman by a 'bumper'. This time though, because the laws of the game had been altered, there were no leg theory field placings.

The Australian public had grown to dislike Snow. Snow had overdone bowling short-pitched deliveries during that tour and the crowds had shown their dissatisfaction in most games. I remember, as a 15-year-old in the crowd at the Sydney Cricket Ground in February 1971, watching Australian leg spinner Terry Jenner being put on his back by a Snow 'bumper' which hit him in the head. It was a hot summer's day and many spectators around me on the hill had had their share of beer. Jenner had to be helped from the field and umpire Lou Rowan became locked in an argument with English skipper Ray Illingworth and Snow. By the time Snow walked to his fielding position near the fence in front of the hill, the 'Hillites' were hopping mad and one man jumped the fence and grabbed Snow. Snow retaliated, and then began the can-throwing from angry spectators. Illingworth, not concerned about the blow to Jenner's head, was at least worried enough about Snow's safety, and led his players off the field, bringing to boiling point the feeling between the two nations . . . again over a game of cricket.

During the English team's tour of Australia in 1982, celebrating English supporters who invaded the West Australian Cricket Association Ground in Perth caused pace bowler Terry Alderman to pursue a 19-year-old fan who struck him a blow behind the head with his hand. As Alderman tried to tackle him on the arena, the youth ducked and Alderman fell heavily to the turf, severely dislocating his shoulder and rupturing nerves in his bowling arm. Alderman, a professional cricketer, was forced out of the game for more than a year and his young assailant was fined $500 and ordered to perform 200 hours of community service on charges of disorderly conduct and assault.

Sadly this type of drunken behaviour became common a decade later as Australian cricket went commercial after the defection of Australia's top players to Kerry Packer's World Series Cricket troupe. The reunion of WSC with 'establishment' cricket saw international matches marketed by PBL (Publishing Broadcasting Ltd) Marketing. The traditional five or three day gentleman's game was replaced by a glut of one-day matches, 'sold' through modern marketing techniques to followers more interested in the entertainment value of a night out.

Sales of sunhats and cricket caps with the Australian emblem hit the roof, the jingle 'Come on, Aussies, come on, come on' became a second national anthem and PBL made millions of dollars. The extremes to which the crowd's jingoism went was evident in the summer of 1987–8 when Australia played New Zealand. New Zealand's great fast bowler Richard Hadlee was driven to complain officially to the Australian Cricket Board because the jibes from the crowd had become so personal and so unfair. Smartly worded banners around cricket grounds had become the vogue, but signs with infantile messages such as 'Hadlee is a Wanker' and 'Hadlee Sux' were far too personal. Rightly the Kiwis believed this sort of behaviour was taking things too far. Even in peaceful Hobart Hadlee became incensed with his treatment and the unsavoury comments of the crowd, some of which he said came from five and six-year-old children. Yet the more Hadlee publicly

Australian fast bowler Terry Alderman received a severe shoulder injury when spectators invaded the pitch in the First Test between England and Australia in 1982. He chased an invader, but fell awkwardly and injured his shoulder. He struggled to regain fitness and form over the ensuing seasons and his comeback reached the heights of success in the 1989 Ashes series in England when Alderman was the leading wicket-taker.
Photobank/All Sport

objected and cried 'victimisation', the more it affected his relationship with the crowd. In the end he was retaliating with gestures back to the crowds while on the field.

New Zealand manager Alby Duckmanton commented in the *Sydney Morning Herald*: 'As far as I am concerned Australian crowds are just like parrots. Somebody starts something and everyone else wants to get into the act'.

If that was a poor example of national sentiment created by international sport, the *America*'s Cup of 1983 was a stunning contrast. The yachting piece of silverware had belonged to the Americans since 1851. Nobody really cared, for yachting was the sport of presumptuous millionaires, had virtually no public or media appeal and existed only for the wealthy to show off their wealth. That was until Frank Packer became involved and launched challenges for the *America*'s Cup in the early 1970s. At least Australians then knew there was another yachting race beside the annual Sydney to Hobart. Yet in the face of any real challenge the Americans were able to hang onto the Cup, sometimes seeming to alter the racing regulations to suit themselves.

The Alan Bond–financed challenge, skippered by John Bertrand, gained attention in 1983. *Australia II* designed by the late Ben Lexcen with its revolutionary winged keel made the Americans uneasy and added a bit of mystery to the contest. *Australia II* was 3–0 down in the best-of-seven race final. Amazingly they came back to take the final four races and made the front page of every newspaper. Headlines like 'The day a nation triumphed', 'Australia Day' or simply 'We Did It' were splashed across the billboards. The Westpac Bank flew a huge banner outside its Sydney head office which said 'We undid it!!'. People danced in the street, champagne flowed in yacht clubs around the country and people packed electrical stores in the early morning to watch the final minutes of the last race. Prime minister and self-acclaimed friend of sport, Bob Hawke, announced there had been 'not a greater moment of pride in Australian history'.

Tribalism at the local level was born in interclub cricket in the nineteenth century. Australian Rules football was perhaps the twentieth-century substitute. The first Australian Rules club emerged directly from the Melbourne Cricket Club in 1858. By the time of Bodyline in the 1930s Aussie Rules had outstripped the traditional summer game in spectator appeal in Melbourne and created a character of its own, unmatched by any other Australian sport.

Melbourne was settled in 1837 and grew quickly, along with outlying Victorian towns. William Westgarth wrote in 1868: 'Every Australian township strives for certain attainments, without which it is . . . not worth living in. Thus, it must have its municipality . . . and its newspapers, and its race-course, but even more essential, to the junior world at least, is its cricket ground'. By the 1860s there were twenty cricket clubs in Melbourne.

The Melbourne Football Club, an offshoot of the cricket club which already used the wonderful MCG, was formed in 1858. In 1860 came Richmond, an offshoot from the club. The game spread quickly from a Saturday afternoon pick-up match to a weekly contest between groups of young men who not only formed themselves into clubs but were seen as representatives of the different communities of Melbourne. Club prestige, interclub competitiveness and spectator satisfaction had already become more important than the simple pleasure of the sport. In 1869 when competition was conducted under the banner of the Challenge Cup, it was noted that of the eight club presidents four were members of Parliament, two were doctors and one was a university professor. In that year the game, which had been played until one team scored two goals (there were no behinds), was changed to a fixed-time event. Clubs began to wear different-coloured shorts and caps for identification: Melbourne were the reds and Carlton the blues. As the different working-class suburbs were established: over the Yarra to South Melbourne and Port Melbourne, west to Essendon and Footscray and Williamstown, north to Brunswick, round the

Bay to Geelong, along the railway line that linked Melbourne with Ballarat, so the Victorian Football Association was born. Albert Park was formed in 1879 and then came Hotham (which changed to North Melbourne in 1888), St Kilda, Essendon in 1882, Fitzroy and Footscray in 1883, Williamstown in 1884, Richmond 1885, Port Melbourne 1886, Collingwood 1892. Melbourne, many of whose middle-class members had moved out from the inner city, was aligned to the Melbourne Cricket Club rather than to a specific district and thus had a less fanatical following. It lost players to the new clubs and found itself in financial trouble, especially after the grandstand at its ground burnt down in 1885. It was taken over by the Melbourne Cricket Club (which still controls it) and has used the cricket ground as its base since 1965.

As Melbourne's population virtually doubled from 1866 to 1896, so crowds at football games grew. Crowds of up to 10 000 were common by the 1880s. Collingwood drew 16 000 people to their first home match and in 1890 33 000 people watched South Melbourne beat Carlton in the final at the MCG. The game gave skilled working-class players the chance to escape from their class stigma; it gave committee men prestige and power and the public a sense of pride; it created community bonds and, of course, it was a spectacular form of entertainment and recreation.

By 1896 crowds had begun to diminish slightly. There was the occasional disturbance at matches highlighted by an incident in a Collingwood match when the umpire was mobbed and two people were knocked unconscious by a man allegedly wielding an iron bar concealed in brown paper. 'Touting' of players by clubs with better finances was causing concern, as was the rise in the cost of admission from two to six shillings over the years. In that climate began the Victorian Football League. The six strongest clubs financially — Collingwood, Essendon, Fitzroy, Geelong, Melbourne, South Melbourne — broke away from the VFA, inviting St Kilda and Carlton to join them. From the start the VFL attracted better crowds than the VFA. The involvement of powerful men like John Wren, a well-known gambler and businessman who aligned himself with Collingwood and who supposedly illegally paid players through his gambling money, led to full-time professionalism in 1911.

After the war came the golden heroes like South Melbourne's Roy Cazaly, Collingwood's Dick Lee and Carlton's Harry Clover, reclaiming some joy lost through a war which saw 416 809 diggers fight for their country. As the level of unemployment became critical and the Wall Street crash of 1929 plunged us into our severest depression, the Saturday footie match gave players and their supporters that chance to be on the 'winning side'. Being a member of a successful football team gave young men advantages in life — some could earn thirty shillings a match (the average wage was only five shillings) and in times of unemployment often the celebrity players could find jobs where others could not.

Cazaly was the biggest hero. He stood 5 ft 11 in. (180 cm), weighed 12½ stone (80 kg) and played until he was 48 years old. He had a huge leap which he practised daily. In a game a team-mate would yell 'Up there Cazaly!' as the ball came his way: this cry was taken by the crowds, and was well-known enough to be adopted as the war cry of infantrymen in North Africa during World War II, as well as the title of a hit record put out by Mike Brady in 1979.

The game had become so important in Geelong that when they made the 1925 Grand Final all the industries of the town worked an extra hour during the week so they could have Saturday off to get to Melbourne for the big game, which they won against Collingwood.

Australian Rules became part of the lives of virtually all Melburnians from birth, and so did the traditional rivalries between clubs. As in any sport, rivalry between two clubs is at its greatest when both are enjoying success.

Collingwood was basically a shoe factory area. Their successful football team

Kill the Bastards

Australian Rules footballer, Roy Cazaly, of the South Melbourne club, was a symbol of a united nation during World War II. As our troops went into battle, one of their rallying cries was the old barrackers' shout, 'Up There, Cazaly'. The cry has become one of the theme songs in the marketing of Australian Rules football

Herald & Weekly Times

was the working-class insignia of the inner suburbs. Melbourne was Melbourne Cricket Club which meant 'silvertail' to Collingwood. Neighbouring areas Fitzroy and Collingwood have also, for a long period, had an intense rivalry. When Collingwood played in eight Grand Finals (winning four in succession) from 1920 to 1930, the clubs combined against the Collingwood Magpies in opposition.

Richmond's favourite son Jack Dyer said of those years: 'If you were born in Richmond you have to do two things — vote Labor and barrack for the Tigers'. Collingwood's legendary player Lou Richards, current media personality, often recalls the Collingwood lifestyle. To him it was a tough area which saw its team's football feats as the finger-up gesture to the other suburbs. North Melbourne then was a close-knit, working-class area which took on the nickname of 'shin boners' because butchers would decorate their windows on Saturday mornings with the shin bones of cattle with blue and white ribbons tied around them. People lived and worked in the same area; there were not many motor cars for them to get around freely. As Melbourne's public transport system developed the crowds increased as opposing supporters began to travel to 'away' games by tram and train, and to travel in big, vocal groups. Players too represented their local clubs, most often for their whole careers.

In the 1950s Collingwood and Melbourne were arch enemies and strongest opponents. At least one of the clubs played in the Grand Final in every year from 1952 to 1960. They opposed each other in 1955, 1956 and 1960, with the Demons (until the 1930s Melbourne had been called the Fuschias) victorious each time. Crowds were at their largest during this time. Every Grand Final drew 80 000 or more, with 115 802 (then a record) packing the MCG for the 1956 decider. In 1958, 99 346 attended a competition round between the two clubs on the Queen's Birthday weekend at the MCG.

The darling of the Melbourne crowd was Ron Barassi, who wore the Demons No. 31 jumper from 1953 to 1964. He was regarded as Mr Football in Melbourne and greater than God. People taught their budgerigars to shriek such things as 'Come on, Ron' and 'Good kick, Barassi'. A shop called Poodle's Paradise made jackets for dogs in football club colours: the Melbourne No. 31 was the most saleable product. Seemingly, every kid on every corner had a jersey with No. 31.

Barassi's father, a Melbourne rover who was killed at Tobruk, had worn the number. It was reserved for his son. When he began to make his presence felt, he revolutionised the concept of the ruckman. They had always been big men, and two were needed because neither was fit enough or fast enough to do it all on his own. But Barassi was smaller and faster — and he was everywhere. The Melbourne fans loved him, and those supporters of other clubs who appreciated the finer points of the game loved him too. He became as big an institution as the game itself. And so it can be imagined what effect it had, and how the game and its loyalty factor changed for ever, when Ron Barassi announced he was leaving Melbourne to captain-coach Carlton in December 1963.

Noted Melbourne sports writer Keith Dunstan has described it as 'like Field Marshal Montgomery saying he was going to work for Marshal Rommel'. It made screaming headlines in the newspapers: people wept in the streets; radio stations, television and newspaper offices were flooded with calls of complaint. The city, except around Carlton way, was grief-stricken.

It came at a time when a whole range of goods were being manufactured in club colours, and footy giveaways meant that these product sales boomed. Businessmen were given crash courses in VFL football in order to be accepted in the corporate world, and socially. Belonging to one club — and showing that allegiance readily — was a prerequisite to a full and happy life for most Victorians.

Dunstan commented: 'I believe that was such a climactic thing at that time that it completely changed the whole football scene, not only in Melbourne but in Australia. No one after that really expected players to stay permanently with their team.

How did he get up there? Not surprisingly this photograph was an award winner! Richmond full forward Michael Roach rode the pack to take this amazing mark against Hawthorn in the 1979 season. In the following season Richmond won the Premiership and Roach was the leading goal kicker with 112 goals
Herald & Weekly Times

Blood, Sweat and Tears

It became normal for topline players to be bought and go elsewhere. And that was the sort of benchmark for the end of club loyalty. Australian football was never quite the same after that.'

Indeed the following years saw the influx of top businessmen, and financial power often decided the success of a club. Players changed teams for better financial reward and the VFL clubs had to adopt more businesslike methods to attract crowds and sponsors. Australian Rules became as much a business and entertainment as a sport and the traditional images of some clubs changed with new men at the helm, with some of Australia's highest-profile businessmen taking on senior positions.

In the mid-1960s leading businessman George Harris led what was referred to as the Progress Party to get the ailing Carlton club firing. They added entrepreneurial skills to the operation, began the licensed social club and with this new direction the Blues took the VFL title in 1968 and 1970. In the 1980s Elders IXL' boss, John Elliott, has been president of Carlton. North Melbourne had a great awakening in the 1970s when dentist Allen Aylett (president of the VFL in the 1980s) took over the reins of the club and acquired Ron Barassi as coach. A social club was opened and North lost the shin boners image, becoming the most professionally run club in the VFL. Bob Ansett took over the helm of North Melbourne in later years. And top politicians like former prime minister Malcolm Fraser, an avid follower of Carlton, have seen the need to align themselves with the sport, as if for public acceptance. Expansion of the VFL continues and now includes interstate teams.

In this period of professionalism of marketing, media coverage, swank business lunches, highly paid players and the traffic of stars between clubs, the traditionalists will claim sport has moved too far from its roots. In 1967 Keith Dunstan formed an Anti-Football League in rebellion against the 'overwhelming drenching of the Melbourne winter season by football ballyhoo'. At the time all four television stations ran Aussie Rules replays on Saturday nights; there was a total of twenty-six hours television coverage of the game a week. But the reaction to Dunstan was savage — he was accused of being a 'fairy' and a 'communist'. Nothing could show

A coach's stirring address can fire up a team when the going is tough. Hawthorn coach Alan Jeans talks to his team at three-quarter time in a match against Carlton at Princes Park
Herald & Weekly Times

'Finals Fever' hits Melbourne each September and the cheer squads reach artistic heights. Here the Hawthorn team bursts through their marvellous banner which celebrates Buckenara's winning goal, kicked after the siren, in the preliminary final against Melbourne which brought them here to the MCG for the 1987 Final against Carlton.
Roger Gould

more clearly the extent to which the brainwashing and the new commercialism had succeeded.

By the 1980s the demographic characteristics of the inner suburbs were changing. Half the population of Footscray, Fitzroy and Richmond were European migrants. In Collingwood terrace houses were replaced by freeways, high-rise flats and factories. The population halved, and 80 per cent were migrants. Fitzroy moved its headquarters to St Kilda; Richmond shared the MCG with Melbourne. Melbourne had lost its public support to the extent that by the late 1970s it had the smallest membership in the League. The traditional pockets of local support had all but disappeared. The influence of the smart businessmen was clearly what kept most clubs alive. Still the exposure supplied by well-publicised club allegiance, the prestige and the power, was what the wealthy corporate bosses received in return. When elections for the presidency of some VFL clubs are held there is fervent politicking and how-to-vote forms are handed out.

While the touch of big business has come to the VFL, there is still a need for the 'little people' to show their loyalty. Cheer squads show how strong this loyalty still is. In 1987 Carlton met Hawthorn. Carlton, with John Elliott at the helm, were seen as the 'big business' club, but they had a strong following from the lower middle class, while Hawthorn had the image of being 'toffs', middle-class and family-oriented. The Hawks derived their financial support from businesses and club members, many of them 'professional' people, rather than from the backing of a big corporation.

Cheer squads traditionally make a giant banner through which the players run as they troop onto the ground for the big match. The Carlton cheer squad leader in 1987 was 17-year-old Rocky Bradley, and its members were mostly teenagers with a few older participants. The theme of the banner for the 1987 Grand Final was to play for the two unfortunate former Carlton players Des English, who months earlier was found to have had cancer, and Peter Motley, who had become incapacitated in a

The Sydney Swans brought a new razzmatazz to the Victorian Football League competition when they began playing in Sydney. Their promotion, designed to convert Sydney-siders to the southern code and to embrace the former South Melbourne team, included the 'Swanettes' — a troupe of dancing girls who went into a routine at every home-side goal
Action Photographics

car accident. The message of the banner was to remind the fans that the pair were still part of the Carlton club.

Bradley said of his cheer squad leader role: 'The cheer squad adds some colour to the support of the side and shows the players they have got support and that we are prepared to get in, give up our time and work to get behind them'. Young Rocky has had a pie hurled in his face by opposing fans but has also been invited to be part of the official celebrations at the Southern Cross Ballroom after Grand Final victories: he is known personally to his playing heroes.

At Hawthorn the cheer squad gave the responsibility of making the banner to a group of former squad members who call themselves the Maniacs. They have professional skills in design and painting and came up with a much more professional-looking banner featuring Hawthorn Captain Michael Tuck dressed as a wizard waving a magic wand. On the reverse side was a cartoon montage of Hawthorn fans, emphasising the family theme of the club.

Kill the Bastards

These youngsters perched in the trees at Kardinia Park, the home ground of the Geelong team in the VFL, seem to have a much more comfortable and clear view of the game than the packed crowd in the outer
Herald & Weekly Times

Above:
A group of fanatical Essendon supporters cheer their team on during the 1985 VFL Grand Final against Hawthorn. The MCG is packed out for this culmination of the football year

Live Action: Michael Rayner

Everyone knows who Wally is, and the crowd enjoys taking a rise out of Queensland bogeyman Wally Lewis at this Rugby League State-of-Origin match

Rugby League Week

Sydney Rugby League developed along similar lines as the VFL. The inaugural 1908 competition consisted of clubs from the inner suburbs of South Sydney, North Sydney, Glebe, Eastern Suburbs, Newtown, Balmain, Western Suburbs who represented the sprawl to the west, Newcastle 160 km to the north, and Cumberland, an offshoot of Western Suburbs Rugby Union club (Cumberland lasted only one year). In following years Annandale, University and St George came in. The movement of population away from the city into the suburbs saw Glebe, Annandale and University die and Canterbury-Bankstown (1935), Parramatta and Manly (1947), Penrith and Cronulla (1967) come into competition. Then came the expansion scheme of the League in the 1980s, with Canberra and Illawarra (Wollongong) entering in 1982, and Brisbane, Gold Coast and Newcastle (who had retreated to their own local competition in 1910) joining in 1988.

Despite having a larger population Sydney never attracted the crowds to its major winter sport, Rugby League, as VFL did in Melbourne. Perhaps it was Sydney's more temperate winter climate; perhaps because it was a more diverse city. Rugby Union had retained a traditional following, particularly strong in the middle- and upper-class North Shore and in the eastern suburbs. But the club loyalty and community bondage through League was strong. League followers were brought up to watch and support their own team as a natural thing, but in each country town families adopted Sydney clubs and this devotion became stronger as television gave the supporters access to the stars of the sport.

There was rivalry, often between neighbouring clubs. Eastern Suburbs were seen as the more fortunate compared to the working-class South Sydney, the Collingwood of Sydney Rugby League, with similar demographic qualities and a club which had similar early success. League games were played on Saturdays until the 1950s when they were changed to Sundays except for the traditional match of the round at the Sydney Cricket Ground; this attracted big crowds from the supporters of all clubs, who made it routine to watch the best match of the weekend (and the only one on a Saturday). This continued until the early 1970s.

Because Manly and Parramatta joined the New South Wales first division in 1947 together, they became traditional rivals though Manly was a more middle-class, beachside suburb, while Parramatta and its ever-spreading near-by suburbs were predominantly Housing Department communities. While Manly had fairly rapid success (they made the Grand Final in 1951), Parramatta battled perennially until a golden stretch from 1962 to 1965 when they made the semi-finals. Manly won their first two premierships in 1972 and 1973 before Parramatta had even made a Grand Final. When the Parramatta Eels, easybeats for the early part of the 1970s, made their first Grand Final in 1976 it was against Manly — who won.

Most clubs operated on local talent brought up from their junior leagues, plus a network of country talent scouts who sent promising youngsters from the bush. A residential rule operated for several decades (until the 1960s), so, as in Melbourne, there was little movement of players, and then usually when they changed residency.

By the 1970s Manly, Eastern Suburbs, St George (who won a record eleven successive titles from 1956 to 1966) and South Sydney had established themselves as the more powerful clubs (until Souths had horrendous financial troubles and lost several established players). It took Balmain player Dennis Tutty to take the New South Wales Rugby League to the High Court to challenge the transfer system (a player could not leave unless transfer-listed by his club) to spark movement of players on the inducement of better money.

But it wasn't until Sydney's version of the Ron Barassi situation came about in 1979 that players moved freely from club to club. The spreading of Sydney's population, mostly west away from the coastline, saw a dilution of specific local support areas. South Sydney people may have moved west to St Marys but retained their support of Souths because Penrith, a young club with no tradition, would not demand following. And a club like Western Suburbs saw their catchment area carved up as the city moved out: Parramatta in 1947 and Penrith in 1967 took part of what had earlier been assigned Wests' territory.

Wests, the Magpies, retained their working-class image. In the late 1950s they had been classed the 'millionaires' temporarily when they had spent big to import some big-name players, but by the late 1970s they were comparative paupers relying on local talent of tough, working-class men and the importation of young players from country areas.

Coach Roy Masters was a schoolteacher and a master of psychology. He drummed into his men the theme that Manly, the most successful and wealthiest club of the 1970s, were the 'silvertails' who lived in comfortable brick homes near the luscious beaches, while Wests were the 'fibros'. Every time the clubs met splash headlines depicted the 'silvertails' versus the 'fibros' as grudge matches. Manly was a club with a big cheque book created from a successful leagues club operation and three recent premierships. They played a fast, stylish brand of football and were a team littered with big-name internationals. Wests were the battlers: they had few Australian players, played a rough-and-tumble, physical brand of football but were successful and attracted huge crowds to their humble Lidcombe Oval. Feeling between the clubs sank to such depths that an ugly all-in brawl followed shortly after the kick-off in a match in Melbourne in 1978 which had been organised to promote Rugby League. It did grave harm to the game's hopes of grabbing an attentive audience in Australian Rules' home base.

There was uproar, then, when three of Wests' leading players — Les Boyd, John Dorahy and Ray Brown — all of whom had been nurtured by Wests since being brought from the country districts for a crack at the big time, defected for big money to Manly. League fans saw it as an indication that money ruled both the game and players' loyalties. It was the start of a decade of intense competition for players as clubs embarked on pricing wars which almost destroyed many of them.

Local loyalty remained, though not as strong as before. And rivalry between the top clubs went to extremes. There were brawls aplenty at matches and some grounds. At Parramatta's Cumberland Oval barbed wire had to be placed around the picket fences to keep crowds off the ground and away from opposing players and referees. Parramatta finally won a first grade premiership in 1981 and continued with another two in 1982 and 1983, beating Manly in the Grand Final both times, and at last became the successful club, its arch rival still Manly. Then in the mid-1980s along came Canterbury. Until coach Warren Ryan took over in 1984 they were known as an open-style, fast and flash type of team. Ryan turned them into a more efficient, intimidating side and challenged Parramatta for success. The Bulldogs beat Parramatta in the 1984 Grand Final and knocked the Eels out in the preliminary final in 1985 before beating St George for the title. In 1986 Parramatta struck back, beating Canterbury in the Grand Final.

Parramatta's great lock forward Ray Price told of being kicked, spat on and abused by spectators when he played at Manly's Brookvale Oval during the period of their great rivalry, and Manly players spoke of similar treatment at Cumberland Oval, the home of a notoriously fanatical and one-eyed support. In his autobiography, *Perpetual Motion*, Price cited the hardship suffered by his children because he lived in the Canterbury district.

> A lot of people, even children, have been spiteful towards my family. The day my son Ben came home from school petrified and hid in the wardrobe after he had been bullied on the bus by other kids — because he was my son — will live in my memory forever.
>
> At semi-final time we couldn't let Ben travel on the school bus because of the treatment he was getting. Chris [his wife] had to drive him to and from school. When he was in first class, just six years old, a couple of second year boys

bashed him up because they hated Parramatta. Ben didn't understand. He knew I played football but had rarely been to a match and knew nothing about the rivalry between Parramatta and Canterbury.

That sort of blind devotion spread further than club Rugby League. In fact it was magnified with the introduction of State-of-Origin football in 1980. The concept had been thrust forward by Australian Rules in the late 1970s with a great degree of success. Players had come from other States (particularly Western Australia and South Australia) to join the VFL territory, making it unrealistic for the other States to compete against Victoria. The State-of-Origin idea allowed those playing in the VFL to represent their home States during the interstate carnival. Obviously all States saw the Big Brother, Victoria, as the main rival, but the 'big Vee' still dominated.

In Rugby League though, New South Wales' domination ended abruptly. They had beaten Queensland in every interstate series for twenty years and often won by big scores as the best of Queensland talent had usually been bought by the rich Sydney clubs and those players turned out for New South Wales. For the third match of the series in 1980 Queensland were allowed to have their own players back, including a Rugby League legend in Arthur Beetson, by then 35 years old and playing second grade with Parramatta. Beetson led the way with an uncompromising performance and the strong feeling was obvious from the start when Beetson belted his Parramatta team-mate Michael Cronin, regarded as the cleanest player in the game, early in the match. Queensland won the match convincingly. The underdog had conquered and all of Queensland celebrated the end of what they claimed an unfair domination by New South Wales.

The third match of the 1981 interstate series again played under State-of-Origin conditions after New South Wales had won the first two, and again Queensland was victorious. Since 1982 a fully fledged State-of-Origin three-match series has been played. It was 1985 before New South Wales won a series.

Rivalry, which many players admitted became a deep-seated hatred once they were on the field, has been incredible. New South Wales are uncomplimentarily tagged 'Cockroaches' by Queenslanders (a play on a slur used by flamboyant Queensland coach Barry Muir in the 1970s). Queenslanders are referred to as the 'Cane toads'. 'Kill a cockroach' or 'Squash a cane toad' T-shirts have been marketed. Lang Park is seen as the most parochial battlefield in the game and a show of New South Wales sympathy attracts a flurry of cans in your direction, some at least half-full. As a pre-match entertainment at one Lang Park match a man in a cockroach costume was wiped out with 'insect repellent' at the hands of an 'exterminator' — causing a roar of appreciation from the crowd. The New South Wales team is met by an avalanche of boos every time they run onto Lang Park.

While this new interstate competition had attracted a huge public following in Queensland where their team had been the underdog for decades but were now the better side, it wasn't until 1984 that the Sydney public put their weight behind State-of-Origin football, their pride by then buckled because of the Queensland domination. And a man called Wally Lewis, a target of abuse every time he sets foot on Sydney playing fields, typifies the level of spiteful rivalry between the two States — caused by State-of-Origin.

Lewis dominated man-of-the-match awards in the series, winning five out of a possible six from the last match of the 1982 series. If the game was being played in Sydney the announcement of Lewis as man of the match would be greeted by boos. By 1984 Lewis was the Australian Test captain and despite doing his country proud in that year's 3–0 series victory over Great Britain, he was booed when named man of the match in the second Test in Sydney. He was often confronted with 'Wally Sucks' chants and had fruit thrown at him during a mid-week cup match in 1985. Later, when he captained the Brisbane Broncos into the Sydney competition in 1988, he had empty drink bottles thrown at him at Orana Park, Campbelltown, and

The rising popularity of basketball in Australia is largely due to the success that the Australian team has achieved at home and overseas. Here, superplayer Andrew Gaze evades a member of the Yugoslavian team at the Seoul Olympics.
Live Action

was struck on the back of the head by a youth at Endeavour Field, home of the Cronulla Sharks. Lewis dislikes the Sydney public and the Sydney media, feeling victimised because he is a Brisbane player.

In Origin Rugby League the rules of allegiance are clear — you are either a Queenslander or a New South Welshman. It is the same as in interstate Australian Rules. In club competition the decentralisation of Sydney and Melbourne has had its effect. South Melbourne were virtually dead until their rebirth as the Sydney Swans. In the mid-1980s Brisbane (Bears) and Perth (West Coast Eagles) entered what was still referred to as the Victorian Football League. In Sydney, inner-city Newtown, with a majority of its dwindling population migrants, folded in 1983. The same fate confronted Western Suburbs, with its area containing mostly elderly residents and industry. Wests took the New South Wales Rugby League to court when the League tried to kick them out of the competition, and won their case. But their hardships continued and it was only because of their move to the satellite city Campbelltown that they were able to survive. In 1982 came the addition of Canberra and Illawarra; in 1988 Gold Coast–Tweed, the Brisbane Broncos and Newcastle. Of the sixteen teams in the 'Sydney premiership' in 1988 seven came from outside the Sydney metropolitan area (Penrith — with city status on the very edge of the Sydney sprawl, Wests, Canberra, Illawarra, Newcastle, Brisbane, Gold Coast–Tweed) and Parramatta and Cronulla both had their base more than 30 km from the city centre. It is expected that there will be mergers of the inner-city clubs and more 'out of town' clubs in the next decade because of the reliance on local lifelines of spectators and junior clubs to feed the senior club its talent.

Kill the Bastards

The first national club competitions in Australia were begun in the 1970s — in soccer and then in basketball. While soccer since had unsettled years and only limited success in crowd appeal, the National Basketball League became a modern marvel. The sport which previously attracted few big crowds outside Melbourne thrived on the one-town-one-team concept and packed stadiums with people who delighted in the atmosphere of continual action and the community strength of being part of an all-home crowd. The NBL, formed in 1979, included the Perth Wildcats (who won fourteen of sixteen home matches in 1987), Newcastle Falcons, Hobart Tassie Devils, Brisbane Bullets, Illawarra Hawks, Canberra Cannons, Geelong Supercats, Adelaide 36ers, plus four Melbourne teams (Tigers, North Melbourne Giants, Eastside Melbourne Spectres, Westside Melbourne Saints) and one from Sydney (Kings — previously they had the Bankstown Bruins and Sydney Supersonics).

The Brisbane Bullets often packed 10 000 into the Boondall Stadium. Adelaide outgrew its stadium and at their top the Canberra Cannons filled the Institute of Sport indoor venue with 5000. 'Developing parochial followings has been a key in our success', said NBL general manager Bill Palmer. 'Before 1979 the power base of basketball was definitely in Melbourne. But we have had a bleeding of talent away from Melbourne and we have had periods where Perth, Canberra and Brisbane have been most successful — with results and crowds.'

Australian soccer, with a predominantly European migrant influence, was perhaps the worst example of crowd and player parochialism. Sydney and Melbourne have been the sport's strongholds although the National Soccer League had strong clubs in Adelaide and Brisbane. Most clubs had ethnic names and strong followings from a particular group. Sydney Olympic (formerly Pan Hellenic) generated their support from the Greeks; in Melbourne Heidelberg and South Melbourne were the Greek clubs. Sydney City (formerly Hakoah) were originally Jewish-based but gradually lost that following. Because of many problems and lack of spectator support the club folded in early 1987. In the western suburbs area of Fairfield there were two very strong soccer clubs, with huge licensed premises, situated only a few kilometres apart — Sydney Croatia (Yugoslavs and Croatians) and Marconi (Italian). Apia–Leichhardt, in the inner city, also had a strong Italian club. Brunswick Juventus represented the Italian community of Melbourne while Footscray (Yugoslav) and Melbourne Croatia represented other groups. Brisbane City and Adelaide City were Italian while Brisbane Lions were predominantly Dutch. The European blood and imported bitter rivalries sparked some of the ugliest crowd violence in Australian sport.

Peter Falconer, from Newcastle in Britain and a player who played for first division Derby County, could not believe the extent of the fanaticism in Australian soccer. Falconer grew up in the tradition where every boy followed his town's soccer club. In Britain, he says, each club has its own territory at its ground, and the visitors had another. It was only when troublemakers crossed lines that hooliganism began. All British clubs were banned from competing in the European Club championships after Liverpool fans clashed with Juventus supporters in Rome, knocking down a barricade and causing several deaths in the crush.

In Australia there is a greater fear of violence, Falconer claimed. He was involved in the worst riot here, at Sydney's Pratten Park in 1985 while playing for Sydney City against Sydney Olympic. The two clubs had been arch rivals for several years and there had been some trouble at their previous match.

Australian international Marshall Soper, playing for Olympic, was sent off by referee Ken Small after 32 minutes after a second spiteful clash with City's Gerry Gomez. More than five hundred Olympic fans stormed the ground wielding fists and boots. The City players formed a circle around the referee. City coach Eddie Thompson was chased and hit by a corner post until he gained refuge in the dressing room. Thirty angry fans accosted City goalkeeper Tony Pezzano, knocking him to

Fans batter players, ref
Soccer riot madness

Mrs Pezzano, mother of goalkeeper Tony, collapsed in the crowd when her son was attacked

By JOHN TAYLOR, CHRISTOPHER HOLCROFT, ARTHUR STANLEY and GRANTLEE KIEZA

HUNDREDS of rioting soccer fans yesterday brought a National League match to a violent halt and cast a shadow over the sport in Australia.

The referee, players and officials were attacked when supporters of the Greek club, Sydney Olympic, stormed on to the field during the game against rival Jewish club, Sydney City.

In scenes reminiscent of the Liverpool-Juventus disaster in Brussels five weeks ago, fans brawled with each other on the field at Pratten Park, Ashfield.

The referee, Ken Small, and Sydney City players were attacked with anything the angry Olympic supporters could grab — flagpoles, umbrellas and a first aid case.

Players ran a gauntlet of punches, kicks and abuse as they frantically sought to escape their attackers and seek the safety of the dressing rooms.

Sydney City goalkeeper, Tony Pezzano, scampered around the field in his bid to get away.

He was grabbed several times by fist and boot-swinging attackers before wrenching himself clear and reaching safety.

His mother, watching in the stand, collapsed as she watched him being punched and kicked.

"It was lucky no one was killed," said Sydney City midfielder Alex Robertson, rubbing a large lump on the back of his head.

The Police Tactical Response Unit and another 30 uniformed police were rushed to the ground and sealed it off as a police helicopter hovered above.

There were reports of continued fighting in hotels and clubs last night.

Last night the State Sport Minister, Mr

Continued Page 2

Sydney City's goalkeeper, Tony Pezzano, is attacked by rioting fans of rival club Sydney Olympic
Pictures: NEIL DUNCAN

A police officer tries to restore order

Soccer mayhem in an inter-club match in Sydney made headlines in Sydney in 1965 and threw a shadow over the sport, which had received bad publicity for crowd misbehaviour in other countries. Supporters of the Greek Club Olympic stormed onto the field during a game with the rival Jewish Club, Sydney City, after the referee had ordered off an Olympic player. The referee was attacked, and Sydney City's goalkeeper Tony Pazzano had to run the gauntlet of attackers before reaching safety
Daily Telegraph

the ground and kicking him. Falconer received a nasty black eye from a flailing fist. 'We didn't know if we could get out of it alive', said Falconer. 'It was totally absurd and showed how much of a wank Australian soccer is'. He cited another incident when South Melbourne and Socceroo star Alan Davidson (who later played for Notts Forest in Britain) took a fit on the field and swallowed his tongue after a tackle by Sydney City's John Kosmina. Kosmina went to his help and the trainer rushed on to treat the distressed Davidson. The South Melbourne fans presumed Kosmina had done something illegal in the tackle. When City was scheduled to play South Melbourne in Melbourne later that season Kosmina and his family received death threats in the days before the match. The Sydney City players decided it was best to travel to Melbourne without Kosmina.

The sort of obsession with proving superiority against a peer group is not restricted to the working class. During the infamous days of unruly behaviour at Parramatta's Cumberland Oval in the 1960s there were several arrests after a wild crowd confrontation in 1964. Among those arrested were a dentist, a doctor, a social worker and other professional people. There is a story of a Geelong headmaster who preached discipline and restraint to his students during the week but at Kardinia Park on Saturday afternoons he turned into a screaming one-eyed Cats supporter. Was this a split personality or just the power of tribal allegiance?

Greater Public School sport in Sydney is a typical example of how society's upper class can be consumed with sporting rivalry. Rob Rowland-Smith, sports master at the Kings School, says that many parents send their children to particular schools because they are renowned for strength in a particular sport. They crave the prestige of having their children attend the most successful school, the symbol of success being the strength of the Rugby Union, cricket, athletics or rowing team. Kings won five successive Head-of-the-River rowing championships from 1980 and enrolments at the school soared. St Josephs was more renowned as a Rugby Union school and rivalry was so great that games between St Josephs and Kings attract up to 8000 spectators. The Head of the River annually attracts 20 000 people on the Nepean River. Just making the first XI cricket side or first XV Rugby Union team is one of the great honours of private school education and surprising pressure is brought to bear on students by their parents, many of whom had intense interschool rivalry implanted in them during their schooldays. This rivalry is encapsulated in a brief outburst heard by a teacher on the playing field at a GPS match. A father, after rushing around urging on his son, yelled out: 'What do you think this is? A bloody game?'

In the 1980s every bronzed Aussie who grew up near the surf aspired to be another Grant Kenny, or Guy Leech, our iron-man idols. Or if he preferred the skills of surfboard riding, Mark Warren or Tom Carroll was his idol. Surf sports were seen as a healthy recreation — the sun, the surf and the exercise derived from water sport would make us fit members of society. It wasn't long ago that the tendency to 'classify' the rivalry between the 'surfies', the 'clubbies' and the 'westies' in Sydney brought conflict in even the most natural and peaceful pastime of enjoying the sun, surf and sand.

The term 'surfie' referred to the surfboard riders. Until the mid-1970s when professional surfboard riding evolved, they were seen as the street kids of the beach, the troublemakers, the threat to society and the bane of all 'respectable' families in surfside suburbs. Their arch rivals were the 'westies', those who travelled from Sydney's western suburbs by car or by train and ferry and invaded the beaches around Manly and Cronulla. Sydney's leading swimming and surf journalist Ian Hanson, of the *Daily Mirror*, remembers well the days in the late 1960s when as a youth he would stand and watch the battles on Manly Wharf as the surfies 'welcomed' the arrival of the westies off the ferry. 'It was like open warfare', Hanson recalled. 'The surfies would form a human chain across the wharf so the westies couldn't get through. There were some huge fights.'

Blood, Sweat and Tears

The surfboard riders disliked the 'clubbies', the members of the surf lifesaving clubs, because they were seen as the 'goody two shoes' who rode with the establishment. Often surfboards were confiscated by the clubs if they were washed up in the patrolled areas between the flags. Yet the club members themselves in those early days had an image in some eyes of being beach bums who sat around a beer keg all day inside the clubhouse. Much has changed.

Most teenagers found their way into the surf clubs from the junior swimming clubs. They would be recruited as cadets of age 15 (before the younger 'nippers' movement began in the past decade) and, after obtaining the qualifying certificate and bronze medallion in lifesaving, would be taken into the senior ranks. Often three generations of a family would be actively involved in a surf club and, particularly around Sydney, surf clubs have become a big part of society along the coastline.

Hanson is a member of the Freshwater (Harbord) club which celebrated its eightieth birthday in 1988 and is famous for the big pine surfboard of the Hawaiian father of the sport, Duke Kaganamoko, which has been in the clubhouse since the Duke (100 m freestyle gold medallist at the 1912, 1920 Olympics) surfed the beach in the 1920s.

The ubiquitous Foster's accompanies Guy Leech as he powers his surf ski to the shore to win an Iron Man contest at North Bondi, Sydney
John Fairfax & Sons Ltd

Hanson says: 'Belonging to a surf club now is seen as a good means of "sorting kids out". It teaches them discipline and, naturally, physical fitness, plus lifesaving skills. And certainly being in a surf club acts as a sort of badge that says you are a good citizen. In the early days you had to wear being called a "clubbie" and a "dickhead" because of the conflict with the surfboard riders and the casual users of the beach. But since professional riding has come in and interclub competition has grown, and the iron-man event has been given such media exposure, little of that conflict now exists.

'The thing about the surf club movement is that it brings together people from all walks of life and it is such a family thing. The whole beachside community, in many ways, revolves around the surf club and its activities. For years we had the same R and R team at Freshwater, from when we were at school. As we got older we had a journalist, a policeman, a barrister, hairdresser, doctor, nightclub operator, a builder and an accountant. But every weekend we came together as a group, did our training, had a good time socially and then went our different ways during the week. And another thing is there is no age barrier. Often parents and their children are actively involved for many years. One of the Freshwater coaches, Barney Mullins, is over 80, but a favourite with everyone from the adults to the kids'.

In sport there are some who never believe that things are as good as they were in the old days. Then they loved the sport for what it was; for them loyalty was more treasured than today. Local teams were followed because it was 'natural' and changing sides or sports was never considered.

With a more nomadic population, and under the influence of the media propaganda and the smart marketers forever tapping new markets, the traditionalists are outnumbered; geographic divisions are less well defined.

Rugby League fans in Sydney have jumped behind the Sydney Swans Aussie Rules side; those who deplored five-day Test cricket now turn up in droves to watch the one-day stuff; the American hype of basketball has attracted a new family following in all States. And while some may follow Parramatta or Carlton when they are on top, they may soon switch to Manly or Richmond when they are not. It is as if the Australian sportsfan can be seduced by the 'flavour of the moment'. Nevertheless the need to conform is just the same and just as strong. Australians by their enthusiastic support — of whatever team or whatever sport — demonstrate a need to belong, to have a 'tribal' sense of identification. And, of course, there is always strength in numbers, satisfaction in sharing our elation and despair — in being seen as one of the mob.

Sources and references

The following books have been consulted:

Richard Cashman, 'Ave a Go, Yer Mug (Collins, 1984); Ray Price, with Neil Cadigan, *Perpetual Motion* (Angus & Robertson, 1986); Leonie Sandercock and Ian Turner, *Up Where Cazaly?* (Granada, 1981).

Interview transcripts from the television series 'Blood, Sweat and Tears' have also been used:

Rock Bradley, Keith Dunstan.

Interviews with Ian Hanson, Peter Falconer and Bob Rowland Smith were conducted by the author; the quotation from Bill Palmer is from an interview the author conducted for *Rugby League Week*, September 1987.

The material on early crowd unrest is derived from Cashman, pp.27–8, 30; the quotation is from Cashman, p.31. The material on Oldfield being hit comes from Cashman, p.96. The Westgarth quotation is from Sandercock and Turner, p.9; the author is indebted to Sandercock and Turner for material on VFL football.

The material otherwise derives from the author's own observation and research.

A wonderful cameo from a Hawthorn–North Melbourne match in 1982. North's full back David Dench objects forcefully to the attentions of Hawthorn's Michael Tuck.
Herald & Weekly Times

CHAPTER 6

BLACK DIAMONDS

Neil Cadigan

Evonne Goolagong stood wide-eyed as the crowd rose. There was royalty in the VIP box at Wimbledon — Princess Margaret and Princess Alexandra, who applauded enthusiastically with the crowd. Yet it was a skinny Aborigine from the dusty western New South Wales town of Barellan who was the queen — Queen of Wimbledon after her convincing final victory over Margaret Court, until then greatest Australian woman tennis player.

Evonne Goolagong was 19 and life was an adventure. She went on to become a heroine to Australians, revered as Lionel Rose had been only three years earlier when he became a world boxing champion. Rose had been met by a parade of 250 000 people in Melbourne when he returned home from beating Fighting Harada in Japan for the world bantamweight boxing championship. He, too, had been only 19 years of age.

These two scenes capture Aboriginal sporting heroes at their pinnacle, but they belie the true stories behind the triumphs of so many of our black athletes. Lionel Rose's rise and later sad demise represents the tale of so many of our Aboriginal sportsmen.

Rose came from a segregated upbringing at a place called Jackson's Track, near Drouin in the Gippsland district of Victoria. His was the blood sport of boxing. Like professional sprint running around the turn of the century and the football codes in recent times, boxing, with its quick financial rewards, could supply the way out of skid row. These sports, which were neither costly nor subject to the class distinctions that afflicted some others, were accessible to virtually all Aboriginal men. The representation of Aborigines in these sports far outweighs their involvement in others. Rose sums this up in his autobiography: 'There is an old saying that hard times breed the best fighters. Wars, depression, and under-privileged races have always produced the best boxers. Much of my success in the ring could probably be attributed to my hard early life.'

Rose enjoyed the rise to stardom and financial wellbeing. He made hundreds of thousands of dollars before his 21st birthday but squandered it all. He was declared bankrupt, returned to a street life and had several appearances in the courts. In 1987, aged 39, he suffered a serious heart attack.

Goolagong, now Evonne Cawley, will go down in sporting history as an Aboriginal contradiction. She was brought up away from Aboriginal segregation: hers was the only Aboriginal family in Barellan and she was brought to Sydney to live with her mentor Vic Edwards on the affluent North Shore. She is also the only Aboriginal star to be produced by the sport of tennis. She attained great wealth and fame — and kept it.

There are others who rose to great heights through sport and retained a new standing in society: Rugby Union's Ella brothers, versatile footballer-boxer-sprinter Pastor Doug Nichols, soccer's Charles Perkins. But many Aborigines in sport provide a story of struggle, of discrimination, of degradation and of sadness.

Aborigines are reminded of their colour. They have rarely been given outright equality. Lionel Rose described his increasing awareness of colour discrimination as he grew up:

> My colour always brought names like 'black boy', or 'sambo', and just 'abo'. But they never worried me when I was young. If the kid persisted I would punch him on the mouth and that would just about settle things . . .
>
> It wasn't until the move to Melbourne that I realised coloured people are often looked upon as lower-class individuals. It's a tormenting thing, prejudice . . . If people are prejudiced I would rather see them say so openly. Let them call a spade a spade. There is nothing worse than someone patting you on the back because you are world champion, while you know quite well if you weren't they would be calling you a 'black b——' and have nothing to do with you.

Rose was fortunate in one way: he received the public and official acceptance that many before him had not. He fought for a better life in the ring in the sport which Aborigines have excelled at in greater numbers than any other.

Professor Colin Tatz, who provides the best documentation of sporting Aborigines in his book *Aborigines in Sport*, said in an interview: 'I can honestly say that not a single Aboriginal athlete — and I've described some 250 of them in my book . . . — was born, if you like, with a silver spoon in their mouths or born with a pair of nice running shoes ready for the track. They all had to come up through adversity; they've all had to fight against obstacles; they've all had to prove themselves very often doubly good in order to rate as equals'.

From the earliest days of settlement, Australia's indigenous people were seen by most whites as uncivilised, as hardly worthy of the rights of human beings. In the century that followed, white killed black and black killed white, but the advantage always lay with the Europeans who had superior weapons, and the destruction of Aboriginal land and society was unrelenting. Not content with savage reprisals for Aboriginal attacks on Europeans and their flocks and herds, some whites saw hunting Aborigines as an exciting variation on the blood sports they had brought from England.

On the fringes of white society, some Aborigines were allowed to compete on the sporting field, or rather were exploited there for the sake of European gain. On the frontier, however, where the Aborigines' interests clashed with those of the pastoralists, they were frequently treated as vermin and exterminated by shotgun or poison. At the same time, as historian Henry Reynolds has shown, this was not the whole picture, and Reynolds and others have begun to describe Aboriginal ways of resistance.

Government bodies of the nineteenth century introduced protection and segregation rules for the Aborigines, supposedly to protect them from the cruelty and greed of the white man. These regulations seldom worked to the Aborigines' advantage. A Central Board of Protection for Aborigines was set up which saw many of them put on mission stations, often in remote areas, or used for labour on farms and grazing properties. Aborigines were virtually owned and controlled by the white man and needed government approval to leave the missions. Australia's record during this period is as racist as any other nation, with massacres of Aborigines occurring as late as the 1930s.

During the second half of the 1800s the natural sporting talents of many Aborigines were observed. The 'gentlemanly' sport of cricket was seen as a way to help 'civilise' Aborigines, who often joined in with white farmers for social games. Then professional foot-running saw many Aborigines — used more like the thoroughbred horses of today, virtual possessions of white trainers — enjoy great success. Many of the greatest Aboriginal sportsmen came from mission settlements, and had to be given permission to compete from 'big brother' in government. They had no rights other than those afforded them by whites. Even in modern times the discrimination still cuts deeply: Aborigines are still barred from some hotels and denied access to other 'premises' in some areas; the segregated communities are still many. Sport has, temporarily, throughout the last 200 years given them some grace and stature in a white world.

It was in this strict authoritarian climate that Australia's first international cricket tour took place. The proposal to tour England with an Aboriginal team met great opposition: some were concerned only because the Aborigines might be exploited purely for financial gain, but there was also the worry that the Aborigines might face horrendous problems in being exposed to the white world.

The players came from the western Victorian region of Harrow–Edenhope where Aborigines had been taught cricket, a sport still in its infancy in Australia, by the pastoralists for whom they worked. The first cricket club at Edenhope had an Aborigine in its first match. Bullocky, who took part in the tour, played for another club, Balmoral. There were matches between teams made up of Aborigines and Europeans in 1865. Bowling in those days was underarm and an Aboriginal side beat a European side at Bringalbert by an innings and 13 runs in 1866.

The story has been told many times. A local businessman in the area, William Hayman, sent pictures of the Aborigines to a catering firm who ran a refreshment tent at the Melbourne Cricket Ground and suggested a match. Another catering firm had sponsored the tour by H. H. Stephenson's English team in 1861 which met with some success, so it was decided to bring the Aboriginal team to Melbourne for a match on Boxing Day, 1886. The Aborigines, seemingly overawed by a crowd of 10 000 — more people than they had seen at one time ever before — were beaten by 9 wickets. Yet they delighted the crowd with an unusually athletic exhibition which became a hallmark of their appearances at various English cricket grounds on tour. Tarpot was an amazing attraction and it was unfortunate he could not tour Britain. On that day in Melbourne he reportedly ran 100 yards backwards in 14 seconds!

Two weeks later Bullocky and Cuzens played for a Victorian XI against a Tasmanian XVI. Mullagh, the most talented of the Edenhope Aborigines, was also invited but fell ill.

Visions of an Aboriginal tour started to surface. One of the early backers was Thomas Wentworth Wills who was born in New South Wales but had spent some time in England where he was captain of Rugby School and played cricket for Kent. Wills was, in fact, one of the founding fathers of Australian Rules football. He had sporting visions for the Aborigines, despite the fact that his father and family had been massacred by a group of Aborigines in 1861. Wills joined Hayman and they were approached by a Sydney businessman with the idea of staging an English tour by an Aboriginal team. Several matches were played in Australia but there were problems about going to England. As Colin Tatz says, 'Suggestions about a black tour to England were bedevilled by some financial skullduggery, concerns about Aborigines being in ill-health, anxiety by the Central Board for the Protection of Aborigines that they might be deserted while abroad'.

The tour aborted; the team was stranded in Sydney. Charles Lawrence, a Sydney hotelier and member of the Stephenson's Englishmen of 1861 who had remained in Australia, stepped in and arranged a match against his club, Albert, to raise money for their return to Melbourne. A match was arranged on arrival in Melbourne to meet the cost of their transport back to Edenhope. The effects of the blacks' exposure to white society and particularly to alcohol were already devastating. Four players were dead, two of them from pneumonia; two others were ill.

Lawrence still had hopes of an English tour and went to Edenhope to recruit players. There was opposition from local police, the government and those who saw him as an opportunist wanting only financial gain. But Lawrence was not to be stopped. Under the guise of going on a fishing holiday, he and his team left Queenscliff in Victoria and set sail for England.

They arrived on 13 May 1868 and in four months played forty-seven matches in forty areas, winning 14, losing 14, and drawing 19. Many matches were hampered by bad weather but they still managed to attract a good following, including 7000 at the Oval in London and about 5000 at Sheffield in Yorkshire and Hove in Sussex.

The attraction for the English was not just the cricket. They flocked to see this strange race from the remote colonies, and they were excited by the spectacular athletic exhibitions which accompanied play on each day. These comprised 100-yard (91.4 m) sprints (forward and backwards), high jumps, vaulting, and throwing of cricket balls, boomerangs and spears. The Aborigines could throw spears with such accuracy over a distance of 80 to 90 yards (73–82 m) that their human targets would have been struck if they had not moved. Dick-a-Dick was an expert dodger of cricket balls, often thrown three at a time. Not once was he hit. Another player, Lawrence, had his own exhibition which involved a cricket ball being thrown from some distance: he caught and balanced the ball on the blade of his bat.

The Aboriginal cricket team which toured England in 1868. They played forty-seven matches and drew big crowds who were intrigued by this strange race from the remote colonies, and marvelled at their displays of boomerang and spear throwing
Mitchell Library

The thirteen members of the team (the undignified nicknames were given because their tribal names were said to be too long and awkward to pronounce) were: Dick-a-Dick, Mullagh, Peter, Bullocky, Cuzens, Sundown, King Cole, Tiger, Red Cap, Jim Crow, Mosquito, Twopenny and Charlie Dumas. Charles Lawrence was usually captain while W. Shepherd accompanied the side as umpire but was called in to play some matches because of illness of the Aborigines. Sundown and Jim Crow returned to Australia in August because of sickness while King Cole died of tuberculosis in a London hospital. The schedule was impossibly demanding and for most of the trip the team suffered from exhaustion. The exploitation, the sickness and the pathetic nicknames are a sad accompaniment to the white curiosity aroused by the athletic skills of the Aborigines.

On the cricket field Mullagh, Cuzens and Charles Lawrence were the most skilled. Between them they took more than 600 wickets and scored more than 4000 runs. Mullagh's effort of 1679 runs at 22.51 (including a century) and 237 wickets for the cost of 2128 runs was quite outstanding considering the pitches and standard of the game at the time. Cuzens scored more than 50 nine times and took 113 wickets.

The team returned to Australia on 4 February 1869. They were scheduled to play a match on the Albert ground in Sydney but it was washed out. In mid-February they played against the Melbourne Cricket Club and drew much favourable comment from their former critics. From there the historic team dispersed. Early death took many of them, and others drifted into the obscurity that has often marked the end of Aboriginal sportsmen.

Mullagh was the prince of the group. According to Tatz, he remained a regular cricketer for the Harrow Club where he played in the Murray Cup competition until 1890. He played for Victoria, making 36 against Lord Harris's touring English team in 1879. Tatz writes of him: 'Sensitive to racial slurs, Mullagh stood up to indignity, on one occasion spending the night in the open rather than accepting a room across the yard next to the stables which the inn-keeper judged good enough for the "nigger"'. He died in 1891 and his grave, a memorial, and the oval named Mullagh Oval can be seen in the Edenhope area.

It is ironic that, though the Aboriginal people can boast Australia's first international cricket team in 1868, in the 120 years that followed they have not produced a Test player, and only a few first-class cricketers. Of recent years there have been Queensland Sheffield Shield fast bowlers, Ian King and Michael Maynard, who were involved in a 're-enactment' Aboriginal tour in 1988 which retraced the steps of the trailblazers of the previous century.

In Australia's earlier cricketing years, there was a notable trio of controversial and tragic Aboriginal figures, all fast bowlers, and all in some way victims of discrimination. It was felt that any one of them could have represented Australia. Their names were Albert 'Alec' Henry (1880–1909), Jack Marsh (1874–1916) and Eddie Gilbert (1908–78).

Henry was first to hit the cricketing scene with some magnificent performances in Brisbane club cricket. Tatz writes:

> The Englishmen who faced him during the 1903–04 tour thought him just about the fastest bowler they had ever seen . . . though his action was 'not above suspicion' . . . Involved in cricket and running, like so many, he was also, like so many, enmeshed in the rigid authoritarianism of the protection era. He was removed to Barambah . . . and imprisoned for a month 'for loafing, malingering and defying authority'. From there he was isolated further afield, to inaccessible Yarrabah, to die of tuberculosis at 29 — defiant at the system, yet certain victim of it.

Jack Marsh was a controversial player. His clean-bowling of Victor Trumper for 1 in 1900 led to the threat of being no-balled. He offered to have his bowling arm put in a splint to prove it did not bend on delivery, but this was not accepted by the umpire and Marsh did not continue. In Sydney, Marsh's action was rarely challenged, but interstate umpires often victimised him. His repertoire was uncanny for a bowler of the time. He could swing and cut the ball and had a 'peculiar dropping ball'. Tatz quotes an admiring journalist in the *Referee* in June 1916 who said Marsh 'could make the ball do stranger things in the air than any other bowler I ever saw'.

Marsh was killed after being kicked in the head during a wild brawl in Orange in 1916. His assailants were charged only with manslaughter and acquitted without the jury leaving the box. An assessment by Davis in the *Referee*, quoted by Tatz, states plainly that his Aboriginality was held against him: 'Jack Marsh would have been one of the world's greatest bowlers if he had been a white man . . . his bowling would have established a fresh standard of hard-wicket excellence and created a new type, differing altogether from anything ever known before'.

The most celebrated Aboriginal fast bowler was Gilbert, if only for being one of fifteen who conquered the great Sir Donald Bradman for no score. He was the man responsible for the 'Don's' most sensational 'duck' outside Test cricket.

Gilbert was 23 and was playing his seventh match, the first of his second season for Queensland against New South Wales. With his first ball he had New South Wales opener Wendell Hill caught behind. Bradman entered and Gilbert's first offering was a rearing delivery which took Bradman's cap on the peak, knocked it back metres and knocked Bradman off his feet. Another ball sailed over the wicketkeeper and went one bounce into the fence. Another knocked the bat out of Bradman's hands. Bradman tried to hook his sixth ball but edged the ball to the hands of wicketkeeper Waterman. In seven balls Gilbert had 2 for 7. Bradman later commented: 'Luckiest duck I ever made'. Gilbert bowled at that terrifying pace from only four paces. Bradman also claimed: 'I unhesitatingly class his short burst as faster than anything seen from Larwood or anyone else . . . The players all thought his action decidedly suspect'.

Gilbert was born on the Cherbourg Aboriginal settlement. From there he represented Queensland. So dangerous was he deemed on concrete wickets in his home district for the Barambah club that the local association tried to ban him from bowling. Later they tried to compromise, requesting a promise from Gilbert that he would bowl at only half pace.

For the sake of his career it was decided Gilbert should move from the Barambah settlement to Brisbane, but the Protector of Aborigines would not agree to the move unless he had a proper job. Gilbert had to solve the problem by sleeping in a tent in the Queensland Cricket Association secretary's backyard while he was playing first-class matches in Brisbane.

Not long after the Bradman duck, a Melbourne umpire, Andrew Barlow, tried to no-ball Gilbert out of the match against Victoria. Like Henry and Marsh before him, Gilbert's action was usually deemed fair on his home turf but questioned on foreign fields. In twenty-two first-class matches he took 89 wickets at 31 apiece.

Gilbert also retreated into oblivion. For a long time it was believed that he had suffered an early death, but the journalist David Frith found him at Goodna Psychiatric Hospital; he had been admitted at the age of 41. He was there for twenty-three years before dying in 1978 and for most of that time was incapable of speech. One of his few visitors was an old antagonist Bill Hunt, who found Gilbert remembered nothing and gave no reaction when a cricket ball was placed in his hand.

The doyen of Australian cricket commentators, Alan McGilvray, a former New South Wales captain, had vivid, if not fond, memories of Gilbert. 'He used to come in from 3 yards and he threw everything. He got me out one day after I'd got about 60. He bowled a ball which hit the pitch and came up in my face. I just had time to move the bat up to protect my face. The ball took the shoulder of my bat and flew right down to third man on the fence.' The fieldsman later told McGilvray the ball would have cleared the fence, emphasising the pace of the delivery.

The pace of pumping Aboriginal legs also has a significant — and somewhat controversial — chapter in our history books. The sport of professional sprinting, particularly in the late 1880s and the first twenty years of the new century, was an incredibly big money-making, high-profile and often corrupt Australian sport. Professional sprinting was virtually banned in England because of its reputed links with gambling and corruption, but it began to flourish in Australia. Many Aborigines were naturally gifted runners and were among the fastest men of the time in a period where they were still regarded as second-class citizens by white society. For the promoters and con-men of the day, the quick blacks, often uneducated and with little knowledge of money matters, became means to great fortune. Of course, the Aborigines themselves, in some cases, found their way off the missions and into some sort of affluence. But the promoters and managers generally made many more pounds and the great black 'peds' found their way back into the segregated communities.

During the heady days, Australia's most prestigious professional sprint race, the Stawell Gift (launched in 1878 in the Victorian country township of Stawell) and other professional handicap race meetings offered substantial prize-money, while gambling windfalls could amount to tens of thousands of pounds.

'Pedestrian' running, as professional athletics was then called, was seen as a form of vice and there was great exploitation of black athletes by trainers and backers. Running 'stiff' (that is, not running up at top capabilities, so that better odds could be acquired in a later event) became an artform. At the turn of the century there were some wild and wonderful schemes to have Aborigines banned from the track. The Queensland Amateur Athletics Association tried to bar all Aborigines because their 'inferior intelligence' made them easy pickings for the vice bosses; in 1903 all Aborigines were deemed professionals.

The first Aboriginal sprint star was Manuello, who upset a big betting plunge when he beat Tom McLeod, the fastest white man in Australia, over 100 yards on 14 February 1851. McLeod won a rematch over 150 yards but later Manuello beat New South Wales champion Freddie Furnell over 100 yards and then over 150 yards.

Bobby Kinnear won the Stawell Gift in 1883, the first Aborigine to do so. Another Aborigine, J. Dancey, won the Stawell in 1910.

In 1887 Bobby McDonald crouched in a squatting position for the start of a race at Carrington, leapt out in front and won his heat. He was banned from using the squatting position in the final because it was claimed he had an unfair advantage. McDonald virtually invented the crouch starting position which became the norm in sprinting, although Lew Hope is generally accredited with introducing the style many years later.

Aborigines had a marvellous record in the early decades of professional sprinting. Percy Mason, in his book *Professional Athletics in Australia*, comments: 'With their natural athletic ability and quick reflexes developed over the years of nomadic wandering and hunting for food, Aborigines seemed to have the ability to sprint without any proper technique or training. However, they never produced a distance runner'. This natural speed of the Aborigines was pounced on by many athletic trainers and by betting men; and black athletes were attracted with promises of money and travel — and the opportunity to break away from the stations and government settlements.

Charlie Samuels, a stockman from a station near Dalby in Queensland, hardly trained, smoked a pipe and drank a great deal of sherry. Yet he was unbeatable in his prime and was hailed by many as the best sprinter in the world. He raced in the late 1870s and 1880s and is best remembered for his wins over English champion Harry Hutchens and Irish champion Tom Malone. His most famous single victory was over Ted Lazarus in the 1887 Botany Handicap. Lazarus was backed to win £90 000 but Samuels won easily, winning thousands of pounds for his handlers; yet all he received was the prize-money of a few hundred pounds. Samuels could reportedly run better than even time — 100 yards in 10 seconds — up to 300 yards.

Samuels was something of a tragic figure. He was often unfairly handicapped, was handled by 'dubious' managers, and was classed as vocal and intelligent in a time when Aborigines were allowed to be seen but not heard. According to Tatz, he suffered a characteristic end: 'After a comeback he went to live at La Perouse in Sydney. Somewhat predictably he was seen as a "troublemaker" and sent by the police to Callan Park Lunatic Asylum for "intemperance to drink"'. Tatz quotes a sad tribute from the *Referee*: 'Poor old Charlie was one of the most marvellous sprint runners the world has ever seen, and his name will go down to posterity as the Deerfoot of Australia. He made fortunes . . . but he is likely to die in the gunyahs of his own people, dependent on the protection of charity of the Queensland Government . . .' He did in fact die in what Tatz calls 'one of those abysmal penal-type government settlements', at Barambah.

A Stawell Gift winner and fascinating Aboriginal figure in the late 1920s was Lynch Cooper whose father Bill Cooper was a well-known sprinter and hurdler. Cooper, born near Tocumwal in southern New South Wales and a fisherman on the Murray River, won the Stawell at his third attempt in 1928. He won nineteen of his twenty-three races and was backed to win £3000 in the 1926 Stawell Gift only to be forced out in the heats. He sold his fishing boat and after winning the Warracknabeal Gift in 1926 concentrated on the Stawell again in 1927, but again with no success. Unemployed and with little money left, he risked all he had in backing himself at 60–1 in 1928 and the money he won on that one day saw him and his family through the Depression.

In a series of races for the world sprint championship against the legendary Austin Robertson and Tom Miles in 1929, Cooper was awarded the championship on aggregate points after races over 75 yards, 100 yards, 130 yards and 220 yards. There were other fine Aboriginal runners: Little Willie, Fred Kingsmill, Larry and Jack Marsh (the cricketer) and the amazing diminutive athlete Doug Nicholls who won the Warracknabeal and Greensborough Gifts in 1929.

The late Sir Douglas Nicholls demands a special place in Aboriginal sporting history. He was a fine professional sprinter and boxer and a legend as a Melbourne footballer in the Victorian Football Association and Victorian Football League in the 1930s. He went on to become a Church of Christ minister, was involved in Aboriginal rights campaigns in the 1960s, was 1962 Father of the Year, was awarded an MBE and OBE and, in 1976, became the first Aboriginal governor when he was appointed by South Australian premier, Don Dunstan, as governor of South Australia.

All this for the man who was only 157 cm tall and was born on a mission station, Cumeroogunga, on the northern bank of the Murray River. Incredibly the station produced fourteen 'gift' race winners including Bobby McDonald, Lynch Cooper, Peter Dunolly, Billy and Jim Charles, Selwyn and Eddie Briggs and the Nicholls boys — Doug, Dowie (Herbert) and Wally.

Doug Nicholls's story was told in the 1960s by Mavis Thorpe Clark. At the outset Clark makes the point that sport was the catalyst in Nicholls's life:

> He was born . . . into a 'protected' society. The police represented expulsion orders and gaol. The station manager — whose personal character worked to the residents' good or ill — was the arbiter of everything but birth and death. Prescribed education was to third grade — the standard of the white eight-year-old. Doug escaped from this environment because he could run, jump and fight better than most whites. Without these gifts, it is likely that he too would have become a fringe-dweller in a humpy. Instead, sport projected him into public prominence.

Black Diamonds

Doug Nicholls, the shy Aboriginal from the Riverina region who became a sprinter, boxer and VFL footballer, led his people as Pastor Doug Nicholls, was knighted and became Governor of South Australia
Herald & Weekly Times

In 1925 Doug Nicholls received an offer to play for Tongala and a job was found for him with the Water Commission although he still lived with his family at Cumeroogunga, 42 km from Tongala. In 1927, with little money and nowhere to stay, young Doug hitched a ride on a cattle truck to Melbourne in search of an Australian Rules Football career. He slept under a trestle table in a market the first night in the city and next day found work doing odd jobs around the markets, although he was made very aware of his Aboriginality. A few weeks later, spurred on by the comments of a Carlton talent scout who once told him the club would give him a chance if he ever ventured to Melbourne, he asked for a try-out with the 'Blues' in the Victorian Football League. He was given a chance but was cut from the final playing lists after trials. Nicholls was told he was too small. The real reason was that his team-mates had not made him welcome; no one was willing to give him a pre-match rubdown such as the white players received, and there were complaints that he 'smelled'.

By this time he had found lodgings with Thomas James at North Fitzroy and the James family suggested he try Northcote in the Victorian Football Association competition. The club reluctantly gave him a trial — but only in the 'juniors'. After two matches he was put up to the senior team. The Northcote coach, however, had to address the team and tell them to ignore Nicholls's colour and 'kick to the guernsey'.

Nicholls had five years with Northcote, twice being chosen as their season's best player, and his spectacular, scrupulously fair style of play made him a great crowd favourite. Ironically, when Carlton realised his great talent they tried to steal him from Northcote into the VFL.

During the football off-season Nicholls competed in sprint races, a sport which had become something of an industry for young unemployed men desperate for money during the Depression. He won the 1929 Nyah and Warracknabeal Gifts and became such a drawcard in this second sport that he received £10 appearance money, board and expenses. He suffered an ankle injury in a motor-bike accident and his best running days were behind him, but in 1931 he shocked the Melbourne sporting public by joining Jimmy Sharman's boxing troupe. Doug's job with Northcote Council only lasted for the football season; on people's day during the Royal Melbourne Show he accepted a challenge of £5 to step up and take on one of Sharman's fighters. He won and accepted a fight against a bigger opponent later in the day. When the news spread that the football star was fighting a second time a large crowd gathered. Nicholls won again and, seeing the little Aborigine's great drawing power, Sharman offered him a three-year contract for more money than he could ever hope to receive from football.

Life as a boxer was harder than Nicholls had thought and he received some bad knocks. Several football clubs, including Northcote, tried to get Sharman to release Nicholls back to the football field. Eventually, after agreeing to offer him a job as a curator at their ground, Fitzroy was able to entice Nicholls back to football after only seven months with Sharman.

So began a magnificent five-year stint with Fitzroy alongside players like Haydn Bunton (Brownlow Medal winner 1931–2–5, runner-up 1934), 'Chicken' Smallhorn (Brownlow winner 1933) and Dinny Ryan (the youngest Brownlow winner at 19 in 1936). The first time Nicholls entered a dressing room before a match he stripped in a corner by himself, mindful of his earlier days in the sport and the discrimination he had experienced. It was Bunton who broke the ice and who always stripped next to him after that.

In 1932 Nicholls was drawn to religion and became an active member of the Church of Christ; often when Fitzroy had country promotional matches, churches would contact Nicholls and ask him to preach at their services. The players ridiculed his religious activities at first, but later showed their loyalty to their popular team-mate by attending his services. He became widely known as 'Pastor Doug' and was well respected in public life. His fine sporting background was sometimes forgotten or unknown by some as he forged a new identity in society. Yet his education had reached only third-grade standard and, if it had not been for his sporting prowess, his life might have been one of manual labour on a Murray River mission station.

Still there was a furore when he was appointed South Australian Governor in 1976, because of his Aboriginality and his background as a church pastor and Aboriginal activist. His term as governor was only brief because of ill-health and he spent the last few years of his life in a nursing home before dying in June 1988.

Another man who will go down in Australia's political annals is Charles Perkins, a man who claims he would not have reached any reasonable status in his life if it had not been for soccer.

Perkins was born at a telegraph station near Alice Springs. He rose to national soccer stardom, became the country's first Aboriginal university arts graduate, leader of the Freedom Rides (a New South Wales political movement of the 1960s), and other active groups which pushed the Aboriginal cause. He was also vice-president of the Australian Soccer Federation and the first Aborigine to become a permanent head of a Federal government department. But Charles Perkins said: 'If it wasn't for soccer in this country and the people I met, the migrants, I would have been in jail now . . . I'm exaggerating of course, saying that I could've finished up in jail, but you never know. If you're discarded by society, for no reason apart from the fact that you're an Aboriginal, then you turn to other things, either for revenge or for satisfaction or for involvement. Soccer was my fulfilment'.

Perkins pointed to the readier acceptance of him by the migrant soccer-playing community as his salvation. For him, soccer broke down the barriers. And it was certainly an unlikely combination in those times, Aborigines and soccer. Aborigines usually hankered for acceptance in mainstream sports like Australian Rules in the southern States, Rugby League in New South Wales and Queensland, boxing and running.

Not until the 1970s was soccer regarded as a mainstream sport. Colin Tatz lists two other Aborigines who have achieved prominence in the sport. John Moriarty (cousin of Charles Perkins), also a university graduate and a senior public servant, and Harry Williams, the first Aborigine to play soccer for Australia, who worked for the Department of Foreign Affairs in Canberra.

Perkins says soccer was what enabled him to go to university. He began his career in Adelaide, then played for Sydney Olympic as captain-coach. His soccer earnings paid his university fees. 'When I kicked a goal there was bread on the table for me', he said. 'There were no Aboriginal scholarships around at that time, so I played soccer for a living and I was fair dinkum, because we had nothing else really going for us. 't paid my fees at college, and my living expenses and my rent. Soccer meant everything to me.'

After moving from Alice Springs to an Adelaide boys' home Perkins came across a group of migrant teenagers (English, Irish and Scots he recalled) playing in the street. He asked to join them; they explained the rules and he never played his former sports of Rugby League or Australian Rules again.

He began with Adelaide's Port Thistle club; by the age of 21 he was one of the State's best players and from the Budapest club won the competition's best player award. He was invited to try out for the famous English club Everton but did not land a contract. He remained in England for some months playing for an amateur club. During a match against Oxford University he first thought of obtaining tertiary education. He returned to play for Croatia in Adelaide, went on to Sydney Olympic, earned his bachelor of arts degree and became a leading citizen.

When it came to racism and prejudice, Charles Perkins found soccer kind to him. He speaks of being part of an all-Aboriginal under-18 Rugby Union side which won the South Australian titles. Not one member was picked in the State side. 'In soccer though, with all the migrants who came into the country, there were no barriers. You were either a good soccer player or a bad soccer player. You were either a good person or a bad person, and to hell with race and your background . . . That's what attracted me to soccer . . . There was no racism as there was in some of the other sports.'

Seeing Charles Perkins in Canberra it may be difficult for a visitor to understand the background he came from. Perkins speaks of leaving the boys' home and living in a boarding house full of drunks. At the boys' home there was only one meal a day. He would supplement that by what he could find in the gutter and garbage bins. Perkins tells of Aborigines having to carry special identification passes with photographs, fingerprints and statements from police and a priest that they were of good character and able to move freely in the community. 'The police could pull you up anytime and ask "where's your pass". And this was Australia not South Africa.' And it was in the 1950s.

In hotels the publican was the law of the land. 'I was always embarrassed to be in a hotel', says Perkins. 'And most publicans caused me to be embarrassed, asking me what I was doing there, would I mind leaving the premises, can they serve me outside. I wasn't a real great drinker in those days . . . and I don't drink at all now. But even if I was drinking lemonade I was always served through the window of a bar of a hotel, out on this footpath, while my team-mates were inside drinking up.'

About his difficult early days in Adelaide Perkins says: 'It was pretty hard going but it made me determined to succeed, it put fire in my belly. I think hungry sportsmen are good sportsmen and I was certainly hungry. I said "I'm going to get to the top and too bad if anything, anybody's in my way" '.

Evonne Goolagong-Cawley had none of the struggles of Perkins, Nicholls or the black sportsmen of the century's early days. Many will claim that she did not have that 'fire in the belly'. Certainly she was not politically active, nor was she an ambassador for her race as much as she was for her country. She did not seem to be subject to discrimination like others. She will be remembered as the graceful, peaceful, popular soul of the tennis world, uncomplicated but now monumentally successful in achievement and in business activities. But possibly she will remain unique as a sporting heroine.

Cawley won Wimbledon twice, was a finalist three more times, and added a Wimbledon doubles title. The $1.5 million prize-money came from victories in the French Open, Australian Open (four times), New South Wales Open (five times), Canadian Open (twice), South African and Italian Opens, as well as four losing appearances in the US Open. When she beat her idol Margaret Court in the 1971 Wimbledon final she became, at 19, Wimbledon's second youngest female winner. She astonished the world when she took her second Wimbledon crown eight years after her first, and moreover was only the second mother ever to win the title.

When Evonne Goolagong started to show extraordinary talent as a young girl, the president of the local tennis club presented her with her own racquet. She was discovered by coach Vic Edwards, her future mentor, while he was doing a circuit of country coaching clinics. A Barellan tennis official called him when he was in Leeton and said, 'Come on over, I've got someone you might be interested in'. At the age of 11, Evonne Goolagong was taken from her family and home to Sydney where the Edwards became her new family. She attended Willoughby Girls High and had little trouble adapting to middle-class Sydney society. As a junior player she was brilliant. Edwards pushed her, protected her and brought out the talent from beneath a shy exterior.

Shortly after her amazing Wimbledon triumph of 1971, Evonne met a metal broker from Kent in England called Roger Cawley and a serious romance began. They married in 1975 and Roger began to look after Evonne's affairs. Astutely he

Black Diamonds

Evonne Goolagong, the gifted girl from Barellan, New South Wales, who conquered the heights in tennis. She beat her idol Margaret Court to win Wimbledon in 1970, at the age of 19. She won Wimbledon twice, the French Open, the Australian Open four times and was runner-up four times in the US Open. She now lives with her husband Roger Cawley in the USA
Photo Library

helped her forge a small fortune and a strong corporate network. Evonne Cawley has done more than twenty commercials in Australia and the US. The Cawleys live in Florida with their two children Kelly and Morgan. They own a private club and a nightclub and receive big fees from several product endorsements.

The two great names of Australian women's tennis, Margaret Court, daughter-in-law of a State Premier, and Evonne Goolagong, daughter of a NSW shearer, share centre stage on Wimbledon. Goolagong beat Court 6–4, 6–1 to take the title, but she had a consoling arm and a smile to offer her illustrious opponent
UPI Telephoto

But the coming of Roger signalled the gradual decline of the father-protector to child-pupil relationship of Edwards and Evonne. Bitterly the partnership broke up 'because' she says, 'I think Mr Edwards was treating me still as a 20-year-old person or younger really, and he had his own family problems. It was a time when I fell in love and he didn't agree with it. He was trying to put all the attention on my side but there was never a word said in any newspaper or magazine about my side of the story.'

It all came so easily for Evonne in those days. Playing the tennis circuit was one big adventure, and to beat the woman she idolised, Margaret Court, before royalty and a huge crowd, while still a teenager, was but a dream. In 1970 Court had become the first woman to win the coveted grand slam — the Australian, French, US Open plus Wimbledon. In the same year Evonne Goolagong won the Australasian under-19s title, was blasted out of Wimbledon in the second round when she was really only there to gain experience, but partnered Court in the Federation Cup.

'I remember meeting Margaret for the first time when I was 11 years old and I still have a photo which I stuck up on my fridge at home. She's somebody I admired very much, growing up in Barellan. I was very nervous every time I played her. One of my big thrills, other than winning Wimbledon, was actually beating Margaret for the first time in Melbourne.'

The Wimbledon final was abrupt and one-sided. Mrs Court could not attend the celebrations that night because she felt ill, exhausted and disoriented after the match. It was found she was pregnant, but even this did not detract from the fairytale of a 19-year-old from Barellan taking on the world and winning.

If 1971 was like strolling in the summer breeze for Evonne Goolagong, her next Wimbledon triumph as 28-year-old Evonne Cawley, mother of one, was like climbing Everest. She'd been back to that great London arena many times since the 1971 conquest. The next year she went down to America's champion of Wimbledon Billy Jean King (five times singles winner) 6–3, 6–3. Billy Jean beat her in the 1975 final in a landslide 6–0, 6–1. Evonne gave Chris Evert (Lloyd) a tougher battle in 1976, taking her to three sets of 6–3, 4–6, 8–6.

Evonne had a break from the sport after the birth of Kelly in 1977. She returned in 1978 but made only one grand slam final, beating the moderate Helen Crawley for the Australian Open, during the next two and a half years. She confessed she was starting from scratch, and injuries had begun to dog her. As much as everyone willed her on, no one really considered she could win another Wimbledon crown at a time when Navratilova and Chris Evert-Lloyd had the top two rankings.

In 1980 it was a different Evonne Cawley. The determination that was supposed to be lacking from her character was strikingly evident. Her husband revealed her attitude in a recent interview: 'Evonne is 90 per cent of what people see in public — easy going and unflappable. But the other 10 per cent is extraordinarily determined. When she really makes up her mind that she is going to do something, she will do it'.

Evonne had made up her mind she was going to show the mothers of the world great achievements were still possible. Of 1971 and 1980 she said: 'I felt like I didn't really appreciate it enough at that stage (in 1971) and that's why it was . . . such a challenge for me to win it again in 1980, particularly after having a child'.

Before she went to Britain for Wimbledon 1980 Evonne had not played for six weeks because of a blood disorder. She played in a tournament at Chichester for much-needed practice and met Chris Evert-Lloyd in the final, going down in three sets. Yet she had this inner feeling of confidence. After a week of solid practice before Wimbledon Evonne could not wait for the show to begin. 'I hadn't had that feeling in a long time', she recalled. 'I was just so excited about being there and couldn't get out on the court quick enough . . . In the dressing room I felt very relaxed but at the same time very excited. I wanted to win that tournament really badly because I'd gone through a lot of injuries after having my daughter and I was in and out a lot. When I went out to play the final I didn't say to myself I was going to win, I kept saying to myself "I'm not going to lose".'

In the final Evonne won the first set 6–1 in twenty-three minutes. Rain caused a break in play and allowed Evert to regain her composure and Cawley to lose her momentum. The second set, although much closer, went the Australian's way in a tie-breaker 7–6. The victory had all the magical fantasy of her first nine years earlier, and it set her apart from any other woman tennis player the world has seen.

Evonne gave birth to Morgan the following year and came back to Australia for another comeback in 1982, but it was short-lived. At Wimbledon in 1982 she was easily beaten in the first round by American Zina Garrison.

Boxer Lionel Rose also tasted the height of Australian adulation. In 1968 Rose became world bantamweight champion. Like Evonne Cawley he left the scene and made a comeback, but with none of her success. The one had lasting fame, fun and fortune; the other won and spent a fortune and was left a fallen idol.

Rose was one of nine children born in Drouin, Gippsland, in 1948. His home was a tiny shack settlement called Jackson's Track. Like Goolagong, he was 10 when he first saw a city. He first visited Melbourne as part of a group of Aboriginal children treated to a day in the city by a charity group. A press photographer noticed him that day and was touched by the boy's knowledge of boxing star Dave Sands (who died tragically in his prime) and his wish one day to see a professional boxing bout. The photographer took him to see the Aboriginal boxer George Bracken, Australian lightweight champion, fight that night. From then on, whenever Bracken fought in Melbourne Rose would hitch-hike down from Drouin to watch. In 1960 Rose went to near-by Warragul to learn boxing from instructor Frank Oakes. At 14 he left school to work in a sawmill; at 15 he won the Australian amateur flyweight title. At 16 Oakes advised him to turn professional and he packed his bags for Melbourne. So began a coach–pupil relationship with his mentor Jack Rennie. Rennie recalls Rose as a 'rather wild boy who smoked like a chimney and drank like a fish'. He was weaned off the drink and made to smoke a pipe — until his fighting days finished and the tragic chapter of his life began.

Rose might have been wild in those times but his autobiography pictures the discrimination he faced and his sensitivity to white reactions:

> An ordinary, unknown Aboriginal is rarely afforded the courtesy a white man gets under similar cicumstances . . . When I first came to the city there were many doors closed to me. I couldn't get a job, and I was called names and often picked on because of my colour . . . If it hadn't been for Jack and Shirley [Rennie] I would have packed up and gone back to Drouin where I would probably have finished a knock-about nobody.
>
> When I began moving up in the boxing world things were a lot different. People started to recognise me. Doors that were originally closed in my face began to open. People who once didn't want to know me began to treat me like a long-lost friend.

Of the adulation he received after becoming champion, Rose wrote:

> Some people connected with Aboriginal affairs seem to think the adulation might come from a guilt complex many white people have about the way Aborigines have been treated over the years. Maybe; maybe not. It . . . could have something to do with being the first Aboriginal to become a world champion at anything and with my assimilation into the white community.

The complexity of becoming world champion, though, was seen in the reaction of some of his own people. Rose commented:

> I have been accused by people of my own race of trying to be a white man. I received letters from other Aborigines telling me to give up the white people and go back to the black people. One letter I received had a drawing of a bone being pointed at me . . . because I am living in a white people's world.

When Rose became world bantamweight champion in 1968 he was 19 and a national idol — while he was at the top. He twice successfully defended his crown and vowed he would not end up back in the poorhouse like so many Aboriginal boxers before him. Ironically Rose did not want to share his earnings among his numerous kin, in the customary Aboriginal manner, because this was 'one of the main reasons why Aborigines in the past have quickly lost their earnings'. In the end he could not escape the dissipation of his winnings. He was advised well by the Rennies and much of the $500 000 he made from the ring was invested in the property market, but he had a lot of free-loading friends and later admitted to spending $100 000 in a year on 'wine, women and song'. Despite his early ideals he was declared bankrupt in 1982, had court appearances for various indiscretions and moved from rented home to rented home. He was married to Frank Oakes's daughter Jenny but they divorced. He made a country-and-western record for much-needed money and it sold well, but world champ, MBE, and once Australian-of-the-Year Lionel Rose could not change his wayward lifestyle.

Boxing has produced a string of Aboriginal champions at State and national level, many of whom ended in tragedy.

The travelling boxing tents of Jimmy Sharman, the Barnum & Bailey of Australian boxing, gave many boxers, Aboriginal and white, their first chance in the blood sport. Sharman took his show nonstop from Queensland to South Australia and back for decades, offering his fighters for challenge against all comers in the city and country. He would set up tent at Sydney's Royal Easter Show each year. He

Lionel Rose, aged 19 and world bantamweight champion, greets the crowd that assembled outside the Melbourne Town Hall to salute his achievement
Age, Melbourne

Black Diamonds

The first Aborigine to win a world championship in any sport was Lionel Rose who first took the World Bantamweight boxing title in February 1968. He successfully defended the title twice before losing it in August 1969
Herald & Weekly Times

often paid big money to boxers to appear in his troupe, up to £100 a day for the best. The usual offer to challengers was £5 for anyone who could stay four rounds with one of his men. They included boxers like George Cook, Billy Grime, Frank Burns, Jackie Green and Aborigines Ron Richards and Jack Hassen. For them it was the introduction to earning the 'quick quid'.

Richards was potentially the greatest of the early scrappers. The most extraordinary was Jerome, a southpaw, who did not have his first fight until he was 33 years old. At the age of 39 in 1913 he won the Australian middleweight title. He never appeared in athletic condition, but not because of drink, which he never took. His purses did not last long and, according to Tatz , he was seen as a rebel Aborigine accused of inciting other 'natives' 'to refuse to work unless paid cash for it'. He died in 1950, aged 76, in the Cherbourg settlement in Queensland.

Richards, born in Ipswich in 1910, might have been the first Aboriginal world champion had he had better opportunity. He held the Empire middleweight title and had victories over Gus Lesnevitch, who was for eight years the world champion in the light–heavyweight division (1941–9), and twice lost on points to American Archie Moore, the light–heavyweight champ 1953–60. He fought 146 times, and his private life, as Tatz describes it, was a sad affair. His Aboriginal wife died tragically

Jim Sharman poses with three members of his famous boxing troupe, Gerry Hobbley and Wally and Max Snider. Sharman offered his fighters for challenge to all-comers at fairs and shows in the city and country. His Aboriginal boxers included Doug Nicholls, Ron Richards and Jack Hassen
John Fairfax & Sons Pty Ltd

and young; he would often be found drunk and beaten up in Darlinghurst pubs in inner Sydney; he was arrested for vagrancy and taken to the Woorabinda settlement near Rockhampton and eventually died penniless in 1967 aged only 57 years.

Tragedy also attached itself to the famous Sands brothers, the most amazing family in the history of world boxing. There were six from the family (whose real name was Ritchie), from Kempsey in northern New South Wales. Between them they had 605 professional fights, 249 won by the Sands on knock-out — an amazing 41 per cent. The brothers were: Clem (born 1919, 100 fights, 45 victories 1938–51); Ritchie (born 1922, 89 fights, 45 victories 1938–56); George (born 1924, 101 fights, 54 victories 1939–52); Dave (born 1926, 110 fights, 97 victories 1941–52); Alfie (born 1929, 148 fights, 87 victories 1944–59); and Russell (born 1937, 57 fights, 34 victories 1952–9). Alfie's son, Russell Jnr, also won an Australian welterweight title.

Dave was the best — and most tragic. He died in a truck accident at the age of 26 when he held the Australian middleweight, light–heavyweight and heavyweight titles. Many thought he was on the verge of winning the world middleweight belt. He had beaten Carl (Bobo) Olson who won the world championship from Sugar Ray Robinson in 1953 and had knocked out Dick (Randolph) Turpin in the first round. Turpin contested Robinson for the world title.

Among other Aboriginal boxers in recent years, Tony Mundine, a classy middleweight who was found vulnerable to the big punch, and lightweight Hector Thompson, contested world title bouts but lost. Thompson lost in eight rounds to Roberto Duran in Panama City in 1973 for the lightweight title and had to retire because of a cut eye when he took on Antonio Cervantes for the junior welterweight crown in the same city.

Of the many outstanding Aboriginal boxers three stand out. Rose was the best, Richards might have been and Dave Sands, according to many, would have been had it not been for his tragic death.

Black Diamonds

Dave Sands held the Australian middleweight, light–heavyweight and heavyweight titles of Australia when he was killed in a motor accident at the age of 26. He was one of six brothers from Kempsey, New South Wales, who all made names in the fight game
Sporting Life

It is no coincidence that Rugby Union, since the nation's birth more aligned to the upper-class, private school section of society, can celebrate few top Aborigines. Rugby League, with the working-class image and with the promise of great financial return at its top level, has been more attractive to Aborigines. It has always been more popular in the less affluent areas — working-class Parramatta has produced the Sydney Rugby League champions of the 1980s, while Rugby Union's strongholds have traditionally been in Sydney's North Shore and in the eastern suburbs where Randwick has reigned supreme in the past decade. In Brisbane, too, its strength comes from the private school sector and many of Australia's greatest players in recent times have been professional, tertiary-educated 'honourable' men in the amateur sport. So the emergence of the Ella brothers from poverty in La Perouse to Rugby Union stardom is a remarkable story. The best of the Ella trio, Mark, received the honour of his country's captaincy.

If the Rugby Union Ella brothers, Mark, Glen and Gary, had exceptional talents individually, together they were simply freakish. I will never forget an incident the first time I watched them as a young *Daily Mirror* reporter, at North Sydney Oval in 1978. They had only just gone from schoolboy football to first grade in the one season. The ball went from Mark to Glen back to Mark who came around the outside. Mark, without looking, then passed to his right but the ball went over the touchline. He immediately turned to the youngest, Gary, and abused him for not being there to pick up the pass. The family law was that Mark should not have had to look; Gary should have been there. It was 'Ella-mentary'. The Ellas played on instinct with a type of mental telepathy; often it was mind-boggling.

The greatest of the brothers was certainly Mark. He played the most Tests for Australia, captained the country and will go down in history as the only player to score a try in every Test on the 1984 tour which saw the Wallabies win their first 'grand slam' with victories over England, Scotland, Ireland, Wales and France.

The tale of the Ella family as a whole is an amazing one. May and Gordon Ella brought up their twelve children in La Perouse, the eastern suburb of Sydney situated just near Long Bay Gaol, and home of a large Aboriginal community. Four of their offspring represented their country: twins Mark and Glen, Gary, one year younger, in Rugby Union, and younger sister Marcia at netball. Cousin Steve, a Parramatta centre, played Rugby League for Australia while an uncle, Bruce 'Larpa' Stewart, played first-grade League for Easts.

Rugby League was the game for the Ella boys until they attended Matraville High School where teacher Geoff Mould had introduced Rugby Union a few years earlier. This was not the traditional rugby: Mould insisted on the running game. As the Ellas began to make a name for themselves in high school football, the free-flowing local club, Randwick, named the Galloping Greens because of its style of play and club colour, had had two modern super-heroes: Russel Fairfax, also a Matraville High boy, and Ken Wright. Both later bowed to the riches of Rugby League; it was surprising to many that the Ellas did not succumb to the same thing.

The Ellas first made the headlines with their selection in the 1977 Australian schoolboys' team that toured Britain under Mould. The team went through their tour unbeaten and made the front pages of newspapers at home and abroad. The Ellas were the star attraction, although the team contained such notable players as Wally Lewis, later to be Australia's Rugby League Test captain: Michael O'Connor, a Rugby Union and Rugby League international: plus rugby top-names like Tony Melrose, Chris Roche and Tony D'Arcy (all of whom incidentally also switched over to League).

With more than a decade of club League behind them the Ellas seemed to enjoy the freedom and more natural running style of rugby. They graduated to Randwick and to greatness from those humble beginnings.

A birthday cake in the Ella household was always shaped like a football. All the uncles played League in the district. After school the boys would play touch on the

Mark Ella shows his kicking style: he says the toughest test of all is playing the All Blacks
Photo Library

road outside and tackle when the game flowed to the grass. The game involved up to thirty boys, many Aborigines. The Ella parents had no car but they would often be picked up by the parents of the later Test cricketer Michael Whitney to attend their sons' junior matches. They rarely missed a match. There was always a lot of love and encouragement in the Ella family, if not much money. It would be easy to assume the footballing stars would have turned professional if given the chance.

Mark had been courted by the local Eastern Suburbs, wealthy big spenders of Rugby League, but he never sold out. Later he'd virtually decided to sign with the famous St George for a huge amount. He returned home from the St George League office one night to find his father sitting in the lounge room. Gordon Ella recalled the moment: 'Mark came home and just sat in the lounge, looked up at me and said "you wanna know what I just did?" I said what? "I never . . . I never signed". I think the reason was that the boys just played for fun, I think when you go into the professional ranks the fun goes out of it. It's hard work. Anyhow they're lazy trainers, I don't think they could have taken the League training'.

Mark said that when the brothers first decided to play senior Rugby Union, after playing most of their junior football in Rugby League, they had always anticipated turning pro. 'After the schoolboys' tour and for the first few years at Randwick the attitude was to stick with Union for a couple of years and then go for the money. But the longer we played the less interested we became in Rugby League. We had so much fun and our commitment to Rugby Union just overshadowed everything else'.

The Ellas played in several Randwick premiership teams but not once did they all play in Tests together. Glen and Gary played four each, while Mark played twenty-six (nine as captain) against New Zealand, France, Scotland, England, Fiji, Ireland, Wales, Argentina, the United States and Italy. It seemed as if his brothers had outlasted him. Mark retired, in most people's view prematurely, at 26 in 1986. Glen was still playing while Gary, who had injury worries for many years after breaking his leg during his first season for Randwick, retired in 1984 and worked for some time as an Aboriginal affairs officer in Bourke before returning to Sydney, and Rugby Union, for the 1988 season.

Mark bowed out during a controversial period where he was at loggerheads with Australian coach Alan Jones, who sacked him as captain almost immediately after he took over the national coaching spot, promoting Queensland centre Andrew

Parramatta centre, Steve Ella, a cousin of Australian Rugby Union Captain Mark Ella, is possessed of great speed and skill
Rugby League Week

Slack. The most established of the trio went into a television commentary job with the ABC after his playing days, supplementing his occupation as a sales representative. But in 1988 he returned to first grade rugby with his beloved Randwick.

Mark Ella will always be remembered as something extraordinary in Rugby Union. He played the position of five-eighth which had seen so many players adopt safety-first rugby, electing to pass to the backs when space was there, or kick, kick and kick again in a tight situation. Mark Ella loved to run, and he mesmerised opponents when he did.

Among the superlatives about him perhaps the most flattering came in 1986 from the *Sydney Morning Herald*'s Jim Webster who said of Ella in action: 'It was like watching Bradman, or Torvill and Dean. Or Carl Lewis. Or listening to Sutherland. You just know there is a greatness about them'.

While Mark Ella might have been the greatest Aboriginal in Rugby Union, he wasn't the first as some believe. That honour belonged to Queenslander Lloyd McDermott, a university law student when he played two Tests against New Zealand in 1962. He is now a barrister.

There have been many more Aborigines in the sister sport of Rugby League — with numerous players competing in Sydney's first division. In the 1987 Grand Final between Manly and Canberra there were no fewer than seven Aborigines: Manly's Dale Shearer, Paul Shaw, Cliff Lyons, Ron Gibbs and Mal Cochrane, and Canberra's Sam Backo and Mal Meninga.

The greatest the game has seen, and a man who is regarded by many as the best Australian forward ever to have played Rugby League, is Arthur Beetson. 'Big Artie' was born and raised at Roma in central Queensland, and became a legend — as a player, coach and character.

After first being found by the Brisbane club scouts and starring for Redcliffe as a centre, Beetson came to Sydney's Balmain in 1966 aged 21 years. There began an illustrious career that did not end until 1980 after 224 club matches (for Balmain,

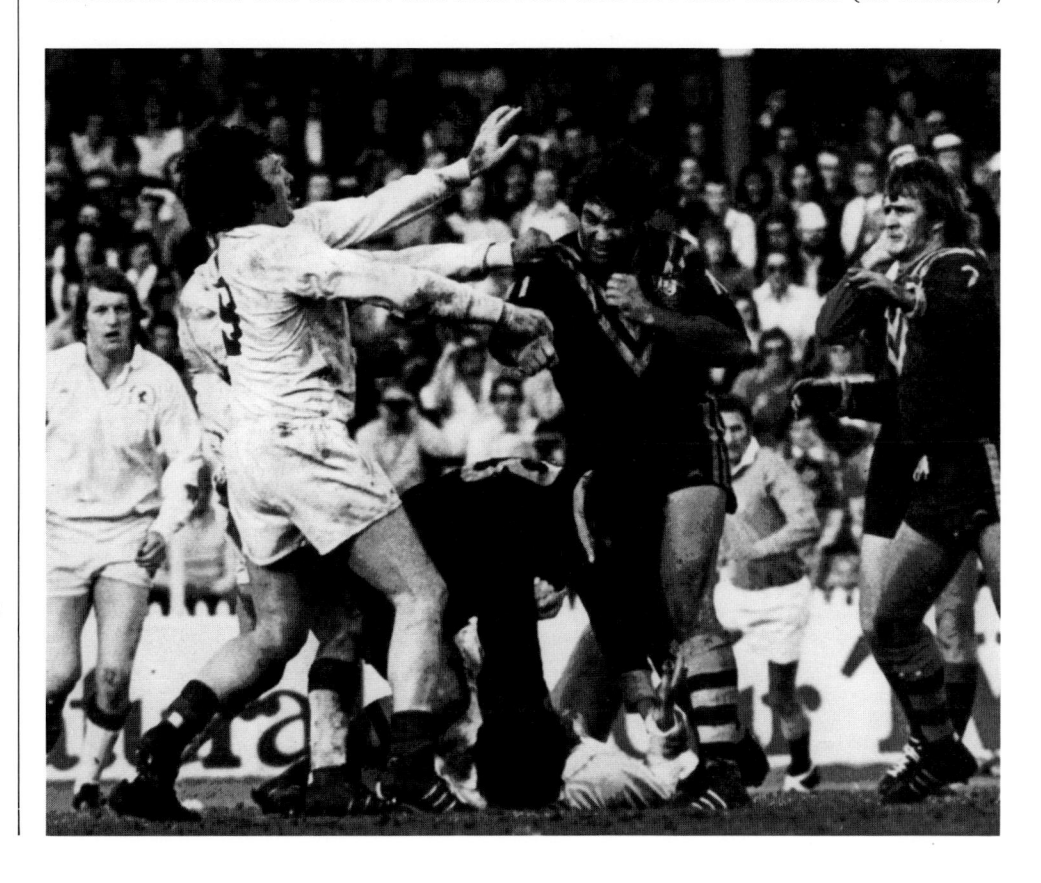

Australian Rugby League captain Arthur Beetson gets involved in a rough-house affair in a Test match against England. Beetson, regarded as the best Australian forward to have played, had a 14-year career with Balmain, Easts and Parramatta. Rugby League has seen fourteen Aboriginal internationals
Rugby League Week

Easts and Parramatta) and fourteen Tests later. In 1966 he played for Australia as a second-rower and in the many subsequent seasons amazed the fans with his ability to slip passes to his supports from seemingly impossible positions.

Rugby League has seen fourteen Aboriginal internationals: Beetson, North Sydney winger George Ambrum (who died of a heart attack in 1987), flying Balmain flanker Larry Corowa, Parramatta centre Steve Ella, three-club winger John Ferguson (while at Easts), Queensland and Canberra star centre Mal Meninga, Queenslander Lionel Morgan, Eastern Suburbs centre Ron Saddler, Queensland fullback Colin Scott, Manly's Dale Shearer, South Sydney fullback, points-scoring wizard Eric Simms, Newtown flanker Lionel Williamson, and 1988 additions Tony Currie and Sam Backo. Of those an amazing majority played in the three-quarters.

Simms played no Tests but took part in the 1970 and 1972 World Cups. He played at a time when Australia was blessed with some of the greatest fullbacks, namely Graeme Langlands, Les Johns and Ken Thornett. As a goalkicker and field goal exponent Simms was alone during his career. In 1969, the year Souths were shocked by Balmain on Grand Final day to stop what would have been five successive premierships, Simms scored 265 points from 1 try, 112 goals and 19 field goals.

The number of Aboriginal first-graders in the 1980s is unparalleled. As the most popular winter sport in New South Wales and Queensland, Rugby League is the sport which has taken over from boxing as providing a means to rise above the bread line; it is accessible to all.

In 1987, to celebrate National Aborigines Week, a New South Wales Aboriginal 'honour' side was selected from the Sydney Winfield Cup competition, and introduced to the crowd on Grand Final day. The side, which would have given most Test teams of the modern era a tough tussle, was Dale Shearer, David Liddiard, Tony Currie, Mal Meninga, John Ferguson, Steve Ella, Scott Gale, Cliff Lyons, Jeff Hardy, Ron Gibbs, Sam Backo, Mal Cochrane, Paul Roberts.

Shearer, who joined Manly from the tiny Queensland town of Sarina in 1985, may prove to be the best of the recent bunch. He played for Queensland in the State-of-Origin series in his first season for Manly, played Tests against New Zealand and toured with the Kangaroos (played in all Tests) in 1986 and was a dynamic member of the Manly side which won the title in 1987.

Ferguson, born in Grafton, will go down as the most amazing Aboriginal footballing story of the past two decades. He was over 26 years old before he joined the Sydney League scene with Newtown. With fellow Aboriginal winger Ray Blacklock, he starred as the Jets went on to make a surprise Grand Final appearance against Parramatta. Later he moved to Eastern Suburbs where he made his debut for Australia at 29, the oldest back-line player in the history of the Australian game on debut. He left for Canberra but missed almost the whole of the 1987 season because of injury. It was expected that, at the age of 33, he would retire. Instead he fought back to be a runaway leader of the tryscoring lists in the competition at the halfway mark of 1988.

The record of Aborigines in Rugby League is amazing considering their small population. Their honours list includes an Australian captain and coach in Arthur Beetson, a Rothmans Medallist (for the best and fairest player in Sydney) in Mal Cochrane and a Clive Churchill Medallist in Cliff Lyons (best player in a Grand Final). The oldest back on Test debut is John Ferguson; the man still regarded as the best postwar goalkicker is Eric Simms. Then there is Larry Corowa, MBE, who joined Balmain in 1978 from the Tweed Heads area, walked into the Australian team that year and was regarded at the time as the fastest player the game had seen for many years.

Australian Rules football, too, has seen its Aboriginal champions. None has been more popular than Graham 'Polly' Farmer. The great Geelong ruckman who was brought up in a Perth orphanage is regarded as one of the immortals of the game.

Black Diamonds

Western Australian footballer Maurice Rioli was known as 'Mr Magic' when he played for Richmond in the VFL. Rioli's superb ball getting and baulking skills took him to the forefront among VFL players, but he left the scene after a transfer dispute between Richmond and the Sydney Swans

Live Action: Michael Rayner

Farmer, born in 1935, played 255 senior games in Perth (East Perth, West Perth) before he moved into the Victorian Football League competition with Geelong in 1962. As a ruckman he was the star of their 1963 premiership victory (second in Brownlow Medal voting) and played 101 senior games in six seasons. He also captained then coached Geelong (known as the Cats), taking on the affectionate title of 'Steel Cat'. Farmer was never suspended during his long career and gained an MBE in 1971.

Tatz's book cites several other fine Aboriginal players who came from Perth to the VFL: Brian Peake who also played for Geelong, the Krakouer brothers of North Melbourne, Carlton's Syd Jackson (136 games from 1969 to 1976), Phil Narkle who joined St Kilda in 1984, Nicky Winmar who was a newcomer to the Saints in 1987, and Chris Lewis who was a local hero when the West Coast Eagles joined the VFL in 1987. Other Aborigines who have made it in the VFL competition include Les Bamblett (Footscray), Phil Egan (Richmond), Eddie Jackson (Melbourne 1947–52), Bert Johnson (North Melbourne 1965–8), Wally Lovett (Richmond), Norm McDonald (Essendon 1947–53), Doug Nicholls (Fitzroy 1932–7), Derek Peardon (Richmond 1968–71) and Elkin Reilly (South Melbourne 1962–6). Melville Islander Maurice Rioli was a notable player for the Northern Territory and Perth before he joined Richmond.

In the 1980s the Krakouer brothers of North Melbourne have delighted crowds with their sizzling style of play, yet were taunted by some spectators because of their colour, something which took time for them to come to grips with. Another man out in the middle had to put up with even worse abuse. An umpire is normally not a favourite species of sports crowds. Being an Aborigine, Glenn James was subject to some extraordinarily unsavoury barracking from VFL crowds. Yet he established himself as probably the most respected and successful umpire of the 1980s. He controlled the 1982 and 1984 Grand Finals, three night cup Grand Finals and two interstate matches.

Considering that so many Aborigines worked as stockmen for the best part of a century, it is perhaps surprising that we have not seen more Aboriginal jockeys reach prominence.

One man emerged from the outback horse-riding background to become a polished, yet enigmatic, jockey who ranked with the most gifted this country has produced. His name is Richard 'Darby' McCarthy, son of a stockman from Cunnamulla in Queensland.

McCarthy's career spanned two decades but he was at his peak in 1968–9. Who will forget the day in 1969 when he rode Broker's Tip to win the Epsom Handicap at Randwick, and then in the next race booted home Divide and Rule in the AJC Derby? He also added to his record three Stradbroke Handicaps (1963–4–6), the Brisbane Cup (1966), the Newcastle Cup (1962) and the Doomben Ten Thousand (1968) plus riding stints in France, Ireland, Germany and New Caledonia. His story has been told elsewhere in these pages.

Charles Perkins says: 'Some people say Aborigines are not disciplined or haven't got determination. But it is just that we enjoy sport more [than white people] and we believe sport should not be a drudgery. You should succeed but enjoy it while you're succeeding'.

Mark Ella talks of considering himself nothing special except that God gave him a certain gift, a gift he could enjoy using.

Chris Evert-Lloyd said of Evonne Cawley: 'Her attitude made her unique . . . she would go out like she was on a Sunday picnic. She'd stroll out there and, win or lose, she'd have the same expression on her face. She moved very, very gracefully and she had quick hands. Maybe every 25 years a talent like that will come along.'

Aboriginal poverty makes a problem of access to many sports. That may be why the boxers and footballers will always come through, and why the Ellas, Goolagongs and Perkins may remain remarkable in their sports. How many more potential super-talents are stifled by prejudice or destroyed by poverty? How many more potential super-talents would surface if Aborigines lived in a world of equality?

Aboriginal jockey Darby McCarthy, who won his first race at the age of 10. His long career was plagued by weight, suspensions and injuries and he dissipated the wealth he gained at the height of his racing fame
News Limited

Sources and references

Books consulted for this chapter were:

John Blanch, *The Ampol Australian Sporting Records* (Rigby, 1981); Mavis Thorpe Clark, *Pastor Doug* (Lansdowne Press, 1965); Percy Mason, Professional Athletics in Australia (Rigby, 1985); Ken Piesse, *The Great Australian Book of Cricket Stories* (Currey O'Neil, 1982); Jack Pollard, *Australian Cricket: the Game and the Players* (Hodder & Stoughton/ABC, 1982); Lionel Rose, *Lionel Rose, Australian* (Angus & Robertson, 1969); Colin Tatz, *Aborigines in Sport* (Australian Society for Sports History: ASSH Studies in Sport, No.3, 1987); *The Wide World of Sports: Sporting Hall of Fame* (Angus & Robertson, 1984).

The following articles have also been consulted:

Peter Owen, 'Darby McCarthy, trainer of horses and horsemen', *Racetrack*, June 1984; Ray Robinson, 'Tribute to Eddie Gilbert' in Piesse, pp.203ff.

Interview transcripts of the television series, 'Blood, Sweat and Tears':

Evonne Cawley, Mark Ella and parents, Chris Evert-Lloyd, Alan McGilvray, Charles Perkins, Colin Tatz.

The quotations from Lionel Rose are from his autobiography, pp.7, 21–22; other quotations from pp.68, 124, 147–8, 149. The story of the Aboriginal cricket team is told in Piesse, Pollard and Tatz; the account here draws mostly on Piesse. The material on Albert Henry and Jack Marsh is derived from Tatz, pp.29–31. The material on Aboriginal runners draws on Mason and Tatz, ch.3; in particular, the account of Charlie Samuels relies on Mason, p.76 and Tatz, p.19, that of Lynch Cooper on Mason, pp.78–9. The material on Perkins, Moriarty and Williams draws partly on Tatz. The quotation from Roger Cawley is from *Australian Sporting Hall of Fame*. The material on Jerry Jerome and Ron Richards is based on Tatz's account; that on the Sands brothers, and on Mundine and Thompson, is derived from Blanch. The account of Darby McCarthy draws mostly on Owen's article in *Racetrack*. The material on Australian Rules is indebted to Tatz, pp.71–2. Elsewhere the material is from the author's own research.

CHAPTER 7

BEAUTY AND THE BEAST

Jim Webster

Annette Kellerman changed the rules for women's bathing costumes when she wore a 'brief' one-piece swimsuit in Boston in 1907. The Australian endurance swimmer became a star in Hollywood silent films in Neptune's Daughter *(1914) and* A Daughter of the Gods *(1916). From her book* Physical Beauty — How to keep fit
Mitchell Library

She was a child of nature, a daughter of the seas, and in her own inimitable fashion she was one of the first Australian women to cock her nose at convention and assert her independence. Through her spirit and athletic ability, Annette Kellerman (born 1887) was said to have had a liberating influence on millions of women, not only in this country but all over the globe.

Kellerman started swimming as a child, at Robinson's Baths in Sydney's Domain, to rebuild legs which had been crippled by polio. She made such startling progress that she went on to set several distance swimming records. Her first Australian marathon was swimming 6.4 km in the Yarra. She then went overseas where she swam 27.4 km in the Thames in England and 37 km in the Danube in an amazing performance which took her 13 hr. 11 min. Kellerman also made three unsuccessful attempts to cross the British Channel, each time trying the most difficult route from Dover to France. Although she failed, she was the first Australian ever to try a Channel swim.

While the young Sydney woman gained some recognition for these endurance feats, she earned international notoriety and made history when she was arrested on a beach in the American city of Boston in 1907 for wearing a brief one-piece swimsuit in defiance of the current seaside laws, which demanded neck-to-knee shirt and bloomers for ladies. Subsequent publicity which accrued to the case not only started a rush for one-piece bathing suits but was instrumental in the relaxation of laws governing women's swimwear.

Thereafter, Kellerman became a star of Hollywood silent films such as *Neptune's Daughter* (1914) and *A Daughter of the Gods* (1916), initiating a genre which the 'Million Dollar Mermaid' Esther Williams continued into the 1950s. On the vaudeville stage, Kellerman rubbed shoulders with such stars of the footlights as Maurice Chevalier, Jimmy Durante, Sophie Tucker, Al Jolson and scores of others. She played her last show in Germany at the age of 72, returned to the United States to say goodbye and finally came home to Australia, retiring to the Gold Coast where she eventually died in 1975 aged 89 years.

She will always be remembered as the woman who set a new standard; who gave other Australian sportswomen the lead in speaking out, in shaking loose of officialdom, in being liberated. She was a liberating wedge in those early 1900s and others soon followed.

Among them was Sarah 'Fanny' Durack, coincidentally another swimmer and the

Blood, Sweat and Tears

daughter of a Sydney hotel-keeper. She was also a member of the pioneering family celebrated in Mary Durack's *Kings in Grass Castles*, and the hardy and uncompromising nature of her ancestors was to surface in the fights she would face over female acceptance.

Durack had broken several world records before the 1912 Olympic Games in Stockholm and obviously deserved to be included in Australia's team for what was to be the first Olympic swimming event for women, the 100-metres. In a period when male chauvinism was still so dominant, Durack was not included in the five-strong swimming team. Nor was her great rival Wilhelmina ('Mina') Wylie. Australian Olympic officials thought it an absurd waste of time and money to send women to Stockholm. But Durack had attracted public sympathy and her exploits over the previous twelve months had proved she had a chance of winning. Australian women cried out for her inclusion and petitioned so strongly for her that eventually male prejudice was swept aside. Swimming officials relented and Fanny Durack, with her sister Mary as chaperone, sailed with the team. Three weeks later Mina Wylie, then only 15, was also allowed to join the team, escorted by her father who had paid her fare to Stockholm.

In the fourth heat of the second round, Durack swam 1 min. 19.8 sec. to break Englishwoman Daisy Curwen's world record and also beat her comfortably; she beat Curwen in the semi-finals also. Durack led the final from start to finish and won by almost 4 metres in 1 min. 22.6 sec. It was to prove one of the easiest wins in the history of Olympic 100-metre events. Wylie passed several swimmers towards the end to pick up the silver medal, with Englishwoman Jenny Fletcher third.

History was made. Australian women in swimsuits which covered most of their shoulders and reached almost to their knees had been part of the Olympic competition, and an Australian had been the first female winner of a swimming event. Durack went on to break more world records and at one time held every world record from 50 yards to 1 mile.

World War I prevented Durack and Wylie from winning other Olympic medals, as the cancelled 1916 Berlin Games were to have included more swimming events for women. When the war ended, the two Australian women set themselves for the 1920 Antwerp Games and in 1918 they went to America for a series of swim meets.

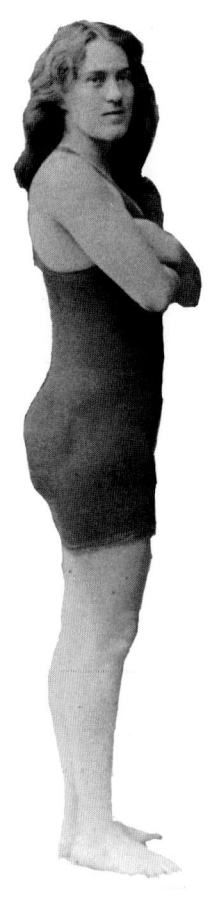

Sarah 'Fanny' Durack, the first Australian to win an Olympic swimming event, at Stockholm in 1912. The daughter of a Sydney hotel keeper, she had broken several world records before 1912, but had to fight officialdom to gain a place in the Games Team
Mitchell Library

Fanny Durack's great Australian rival, Wilhelmina 'Mina' Wylie, seemed slightly embarrassed to be caught by the photographer in her bathing suit. She won the silver medal for the 100 metres at the Stockholm Olympics, and later travelled with Durack for a series of swimming meetings in America
Mitchell Library

Beauty and the Beast

Their trip was sponsored by an unidentified Sydney sports lover and, as such, did not have the sanction of the Australian Swimming Union. When they reached America they were told they were there without permission and would jeopardise their amateur status if they competed. They returned home. The next year, 1919, they set off for America again, this time with official permission, but they encountered trouble at every corner. Initially it was asserted that their coach was a professional and they were told either to get rid of him or to go home. The two Australians reluctantly decided to stay on, irritated that they should be so pressured. The irritations continued. At their third swim-meet in Philadelphia, Durack finally became exasperated with the Americans who she believed were shunting the Australians around without giving them time to recover from their swims. She waited until the day of the swim before a packed house to inform officials that she was not going to swim. The Americans told her she faced disqualification from all future international swimming — including the Olympics — if she did not swim. So Durack took off her swimming robe and, without hesitation, dived in and took off down the pool. Halfway down, she swam to the side, climbed out and defiantly informed swim officials: 'There, I swam, didn't I!' They were too stunned to do anything about it.

The events in America made Durack more determined than ever to show the Americans that she was the best in the world. She returned to Australia to train harder than ever for the Antwerp Games. But two weeks before the boat was to sail for Europe, Durack developed appendicitis and was rushed to hospital. Her Olympic career was over. Durack was 29, and did not feel she could wait four years to make another Olympic challenge. She retired from swimming to run a Sydney hotel.

Fanny Durack steps out proudly among the competitors of the Australasian team at the Olympic Games in Stockholm in 1912
Mitchell Library

Blood, Sweat and Tears

At the same time she continued to teach young children to swim. She died in 1956, aged 64, six months before the start of the Melbourne Olympics when Australian women swimmers won six out of a possible seventeen medals. She would have been immensely gratified by their success.

Back in 1912, Fanny Durack had been a trail blazer for Australian women competing in the Olympic Games and, if nothing else, she prodded women into thinking of a life beyond family and work for those daring enough to venture away from the household.

Breakthroughs like Durack's were uncommon in those days. Women weren't really wanted in sport: that was a man's domain. They were considered eccentric, brash and even a trifle risqué if they showed any desire to become involved in boisterous physical exercise. Sport, for women, was looked on as being a form of light recreation where they had neither to remove much clothing nor exert themselves to the point where they might perspire or — dare one say it — sweat. Heavy female sporting activity ran contrary to all Victorian principles.

Acceptable forms of sport for women were those like croquet, archery or tennis, where the cumbersome skirts did not interfere too much with such pastimes, and perhaps an occasional spot of horse-riding in the park, or some cycling. But nothing much beyond that. Besides, they were supposed to be ladylike and to cultivate their appeal to men. Because of these attitudes — and most women seemed more than happy to abide by them — the inroads women made into the more traditional male sports were very slow in coming.

The first organised athletics event for women, for example, did not take place until 1926 when the New South Wales Amateur Athletic Association organised a meeting for women athletes in Manly. The meeting was staged mainly to determine whether there were any athletes of sufficient standard to be sent to the 1928 Amsterdam Olympics, and standards were disappointing. Only one New South Wales sprinter, Edie Robinson, was selected. She competed in the 100- and 800-metres, finishing third in a semi-final of the 100-metres and fifth in her heat of the 800-metres in the first Olympic track events held for women. A 16-year-old American high school student of the same surname, Elizabeth Robinson, won the Olympic 100-metres gold medal.

The Kooyong Archery Club in Melbourne, Victoria, posed for this handsome photograph in 1908. Archery was among the handful of pastimes considered suitable for ladies
La Trobe Collection, State Library of Victoria

Beauty and the Beast

Right:
A very civilised day's outing! A tennis party takes the mountain air at Tilba Tilba, New South Wales, early this century. From the W. H. Corkhill Collection
National Library of Australia

Below:
The graceful gardens of the Sydney mansion 'Craigend' made a delightful setting for this ladies' game of croquet. The crinolined and bustled ladies in this mid-19th century photograph all seem about to hit the ball simultaneously, a novel twist in this usually tranquil game
Mitchell Library

> **Women Now Star in Many Sports**
>
> **Sensible Attire Has Raised Standard of Play**
>
> *IS ROWING TOO STRENUOUS?*
>
> (By ROSE C. GOODMAN)
>
> *The Referee*, Wednesday, February 18, 1931

A plea for some sense in women's sport, and women's sporting attire, is made in this Referee *article by Rose C. Goodman in 1931. As she says: 'What a contrast our modern hockey girl presents. Her trim tunic, shirt and bloomers leave little to be desired by way of freedom and comfort, while, as a consequence, the standard of play has improved out of sight'*

It was not until 1932 that the Australian Women's Amateur Athletic Union was founded. 'Women's associations in Victoria (1929), Queensland (1931), New South Wales and South Australia (1932)' now had a co-ordinating body.

In the early 1800s cricket was the first organised team sport which women played. Cricket was considered quite acceptable: women weren't required to go around half-naked, as they were in swimming and athletics, and there was a certain dignity and an immense tradition surrounding this fine old game. There was nothing too hectic about it and cups of tea and scones were taken at the lunch and tea breaks, much the same as was done at any afternoon tête-à-tête. The first account of a match involving women appeared in the Melbourne *Argus*, which reported a one-innings match in Bendigo as early as 1874, the players wearing calico dresses and red and blue jackets. The first match of any importance was played on the Sydney Cricket Ground in 1886 between the Fernleas and Siroccos, both considered very strong clubs, and the first interstate match took place in 1890 between New South Wales and Victoria in Sydney. In 1891 Miss Rosalie Dean scored a century in each innings (195 and 104) of a match played at the Sydney Cricket Ground.

Victoria formed a Women's Cricket Association in the 1923–4 season and New South Wales followed in 1927. The Australian Women's Cricket Council was established in 1931, with Queensland joining Victoria and New South Wales.

Long before this, women's cricket had bestowed on the male version of the game

Beauty and the Beast

the art of overarm bowling. An Englishwoman, Christina Wills, found that her wide skirt impeded her when she tried to bowl underarm while giving her brother batting practice. She bowled out her brother with an overarm delivery which so impressed him that he introduced it at Lords in 1822. He was promptly 'no-balled', so he left the field, got on his horse and rode out of first-class cricket for good. But thirteen years later, in 1835, Marylebone Cricket Club officially recognised overarm bowling. So women's almost forgotten contribution to the most popular sport among the Commonwealth countries should be recognised.

However, in the 1930s and 1940s Australia remained a nation in which sport, whether it be participating or watching, was considered largely a male preserve, although women were starting to attend sporting events in growing numbers as spectators.

If women did excel — and there were many noteworthy examples such as golfer Pat Borthwick, swimmer Clare Dennis, sprinter and long-jumper Decima Norman and sprinter-hurdler Shirley Strickland — then it was more through their unrelenting determination and excessive talents than the encouragement and direction given them by the male-oriented sporting system. Men did not want women intruding into their domain. A woman's place was in the kitchen, not ploughing up and down a pool, or jumping and running, or hitting a tennis or golf ball. Besides, it was felt that if women played too much sport they would become muscle-bound and nobody, particularly the women themselves, would want that.

There was no better example of the existing sexual discrimination than in golf clubs, where women could only become associates, not members, and had limited playing times.

The media did its part to nourish the tender female image, embellishing the feats of Australia's male sporting heroes and relegating what women's sporting results they did report to the fine print. This despite women's achievements on the home front during World War II and, in the case of nurses, even in the battle zones.

The 1952 Helsinki Olympic Games first began prising open Australia's closed attitudes. No one did more towards fostering that new thinking in Helsinki than Marjorie Jackson, that shy girl with simple tastes and a wide grin, from the coalmining town of Lithgow, on the other side of the Blue Mountains. She had first gained

New South Wales golfer Pat Borthwick was described by the veteran Burtta Cheney as 'the best woman golfer ever to play in Australia'. She was Australian champion four times and NSW champion six times in the late 1940s and 50s
Herald & Weekly Times

Shirley Strickland was the first Australian woman to win a place in an Olympic athletic event — third in the 1948 London Games 80 metres hurdles. She ran a world record for 100 metres of 11.3 seconds and won the 80 metres at the Helsinki Olympics in 1952 in a world record 10.9 seconds
Herald & Weekly Times

notoriety when in 1949, at the age of 17, she beat the flying Dutchwoman, Fanny Blankers-Koen. She beat Blankers-Koen not once, but twice, on the second occasion with a faster time than Blankers-Koen ran in winning the Olympic 100-metres gold medal the previous year in London. She recalls: 'When I actually beat her it was about a yard faster than the time in which she won the Olympic final. To me that was unreal because I had never run 100 metres before. We only ever used to run 100 yards. To actually beat her over 100 metres and better the time (11.9 seconds) which she did at the Olympics was really great. Goodness, she was so famous and so very much taller than me, and I guess I was a very shy country girl in those days — still am a bit — so it was a great honour and a great thrill.'

Jackson went on from that success to the Auckland Empire Games in 1950 where she contested ten races — heats and finals — in three days and won them all. They included four gold medals, the 100- and 220-yards, the 440-yard and 660-yard relays. She equalled the world record in both the 100- and 220-yards. Subsequently, Jackson lowered the world 100-yards record to 10.4 seconds. When Helsinki came round, the 'Lithgow Flash' was on everyone's lips. In Helsinki, Jackson would again face Blankers-Koen, then 34 and the mother of two children.

In Jackson's 100-metres semi-final, she equalled the world record, running 11.5 seconds. Blankers-Koen had to withdraw from her semi-final because of a carbuncle on her heel and food poisoning. Six runners faced the starter in the final. Jackson gives a vivid description of pre-race butterflies: 'I know that I was very nervous before the start and when I get nervous I tend to want to natter a lot. The finalists were all down in the rooms and we had to wait about two and a half hours before the actual final. Of course, nobody would speak and I wanted to talk so it seemed like about two days that I was down there. I got up and heaved everywhere in the sink, I was so sick with nerves. When I finally came up from underground and into the middle of the arena I knew what it must have been like to be a Christian who was about to be fed to the lions. To see over 100 000 people; it was just so unreal because here in Australia, if you saw 200 at an athletic meeting, that's what they classed as a crowd.'

The finalists were a South African, an American, a German and three Australians, Jackson, Shirley Strickland and Winsome Cripps. Jackson streaked away from the rest, turning a 2-metre lead at the halfway mark into a 3-metre victory. The South African, Daphne Hasenjager, won the silver and Strickland the bronze. Jackson's time, 11.5 seconds into a headwind, equalled the world record again. It was Australia's first gold medal of the Games and the first the nation had won on the running track, male or female, since Edwin Flack's successes in 1896.

Jackson tells of her feelings after the race: 'When I went through that tape my grin just must've swallowed the whole of the world because I was so, so excited. And just excited for everybody, because there was so much sacrifice on a lot of people's parts for me to be there and to my wonderful parents who sacrificed everything and the people of Lithgow who had built me a running track to train on before we went to Finland . . . and Jim Monaghan who had trained me. I really felt that that first gold medal was for all of them. I know Australia went mad. Lithgow had a planned minute of noise at three o'clock in the afternoon when I won and everything that could make a noise made a noise. They had fire engines tearing up and down the street and even the little triangles in the primary school, all the kids went out and donged those. And to know, so many thousands of miles away from home, that they were just so proud of me, it made me proud to be an Australian, and to see our flag go up was a very moving thing for me. It was a moment in time that was mine, that can never be taken away from me. I'll always cherish it and always remember it.'

Strickland, who won the 80-metre hurdles final in a world record of 10.9 seconds, did not run in the 200-metres and, with Blankers-Koen again withdrawing, the event looked a gift for Jackson.

The longest-lasting women's track and field world record was set by Stanislawa

Walasiewicz on 15 August 1935 when she/he (an autopsy performed after she was caught in the middle of a robbery attempt and shot to death showed that she was a man) ran the 200-metres in 23.6 seconds. Almost seventeen years later Marjorie Jackson tied that record in the first round of the 200-metres at Helsinki and in the first semi-final she ran 23.4 seconds to finally break it. In the final she reached the tape 5 metres ahead of her nearest rival. Disappointment was to follow. The Australians, with three sprinters from the 100-metres final, and Verna Johnston, as the fourth runner, were strong favourites to win the 4 × 100-metres final. They looked unstoppable.

But in the final, as Cripps passed to Jackson on the last leg with the gold medal a certainty, the unthinkable happened and, in one anguished moment, the baton was knocked from Jackson's right hand. Jackson explains: 'All the press wrote it up that it was a dropped baton but it wasn't. I had actually run 3 or 4 yards with the baton in my hand ... Unbeknownst to me, Winsome was still running behind me ... This grin came on my face because I knew we were home and hosed and thought this was our gold medal and then suddenly I just didn't have the baton any more and I really didn't know what had happened, but as my arm went back with the baton in my hand, her knee came up and knocked it clean out of my hand. And that's really what happened.'

Amazingly the baton fell on its point and bounced back up as Jackson bent to grab it, but too much time had been lost. She streaked after the field and helped Australia into fifth placing.

The Helsinki Olympics had much meaning for Jackson besides what occurred on the running track. She met Australian cyclist Peter Nelson on the plane to the Games; sixteen months later they married. As Mrs Nelson she went to Vancouver for the 1954 Empire Games, where she added another three gold medals, in the 100- and 220-yards and the 4 × 110-yards relay. Jackson walked off the plane at Sydney Airport to announce her retirement. Her medal count stood at two Olympic gold and seven Empire Games gold medals.

Marjorie Jackson had provided all Australians, men and women, with their greatest post-war champion. Equally important, she further helped break down many of the barriers to women in sport. Everybody was so proud of the 'Lithgow Flash' and what she had achieved; no longer were women quite so alienated from the sporting world.

Four years later a united Australia basked in the reflection of the gold medals from Dawn Fraser and Betty Cuthbert at the Melbourne Olympics. Between them, these two champions have won or shared eight gold medals over three Olympics. Dawn Fraser's life and success touched everyone's hearts. Born in the blue-collar suburb of Balmain, she overcame social bias and financial deprivation to reach the pinnacle of sporting excellence, ruffling more than an occasional official feather on the way. She was a rogue, but a lovable one. And through the waves of disappointment, which included her mother's death in 1964 shortly before the Tokyo Olympics and her banning by the Australian Swimming Union for indiscretions, Fraser continued to plough forward to immortality; her three gold medals for the 100-metres freestyle at three successive Olympics may never be equalled.

After her third gold medal in Tokyo in 1964, Dawn said that just what she had achieved didn't occur to her immediately. 'It was about four days later that I realised that I had created history. I'd won three successive Olympic medals over the 100-metres freestyle and ... I can remember when it finally dawned on me. I was sitting in Tokyo doing a documentary film for Australian television and all of a sudden I looked at my gold medal and I realised that it was mine. It was my third one in succession and I just sat there and cried, which is something that I don't usually do. I was in front of a television crew and all of a sudden I burst into tears. And the crew were, you know, quite concerned that they had said something and I just said "No, I'm really just overjoyed at the fact that this is actually mine" and I showed them my

Dawn Fraser waves to the Melbourne crowd after winning at the 1956 Olympics. Her three wins in the 100 metres freestyle at three successive Olympics — a span of eight years — is a feat unlikely to be equalled
Herald & Weekly Times

gold medal. And it was a wonderful feeling and, you know, all of a sudden I just said "Well mum, this is for you".'

Betty Cuthbert was the quiet type, the demure daughter of a nurseryman from Ermington. She won gold medals in the 100-metres, 200-metres and 4 × 100-metres relay at the 1956 Melbourne Olympics, was injured four years later at Rome and then came back to triumph again over the 400-metres at the 1964 Tokyo Olympics. The two women, whose sporting lives had crossed so much but who were so different in character, were inexorably drawn together. When, in 1978, Cuthbert announced publicly that she had been found to have multiple sclerosis, among the first people on the phone was Dawn Fraser. 'Righto Bet, how can I help? If you want a few dollars you can have whatever I've got. Or if you want me to drive you somewhere just give me a call.'

Cover girls! The front cover of the Australian Women's Weekly *shows Marlene Mathews and Betty Cuthbert displaying their silver and gold medals for the 100 metres at the 1956 Melbourne Olympics. They both took gold in the 4 × 100 metres relay*
Australian Consolidated Press

Below:
The 'golden girl' of Australian athletics Betty Cuthbert heads for the tape to win the 100 metres in the 1956 Olympic Games at Melbourne.
Australian Broadcasting Corporation

Beauty and the Beast

Flanking Dawn Fraser's and Betty Cuthbert's achievements during the 1950s and 1960s was a growing number of female champions in other sports: Margaret Court, Heather McKay, Marlene Mathews, Lorraine Crapp and Ilsa Konrads. On the tennis court, there was none greater than Margaret Court, who won three Wimbledon singles finals — in 1963, 1965 and 1970. She became the first Australian woman to take the coveted Grand Slam, when she won the Wimbledon, US, French and Australian singles titles in the same year, 1970.

Margaret Court was perhaps the first Australian woman consciously to align herself with men in the way she trained. She tried, fairly successfully as it turned out, to emulate their power. She worked enormously hard at increasing her strength and with it the ferocity of her tennis strokes. 'I enjoyed training in tennis. I think in those earlier years I loved it . . . Sometimes I think I enjoyed that side of it more than the actual playing of the game. I loved going to gymnasium. I went to Frank Sedgman's gymnasium five mornings a week and trained with the men, and then when I was on court, Harry Hopman used to let me train with the Davis Cup players. I loved every minute of it. I was really dedicated in that area and I lifted heavy weights. I think probably my training kept me in the game as long as it did, because I was in the game for about twenty years and I hardly ever had an injury, particularly in my first fifteen years . . . I believe a lot of that had to do with my fitness.'

Heather McKay was another to follow this regimen of hard physical work. It worked for her as well, for McKay remains unchallenged as the greatest woman squash player in history. Born the eighth of eleven children at Queanbeyan, outside Canberra, McKay won the British women's open title (considered the world championship) a record sixteen times between 1962 and 1977, the Australian women's amateur title a record fourteen times and, after turning professional, won the inaugural world women's title in 1976. McKay was defeated only twice in her long career. (She lost to Yvonne West in the 1960 New South Wales title and in England to Mrs Fran Marshall in 1962, in five games on both occasions.)

Below left:
Margaret Court, winner of three Wimbledons, the Grand Slam in 1970 and countless other titles, worked hard at increasing her already formidable strength and the ferocity of her strokes. She attributed her ability to stay at the top in tennis for nearly twenty years to her strength and fitness
News Limited

Heather McKay, the greatest woman squash player in history. She won the British Women's open title a record sixteen times between 1962 and 1977, and the Australian women's title fourteen times. She also represented Australia in hockey
Herald & Weekly Times

McKay, who was also an Australian field hockey representative, says it was a combination of hard work and ability which made her so extraordinarily dominant. She subscribes to Margaret Court's philosophy when she explains: 'I'm sure I had a lot of natural sporting ability, coming from a very sporting family. But I would say that, except for maybe one or two other squash players in my time, I would have worked harder to get myself fitter than any other woman. So I think that hard work and ability, the determination and just because I wanted to do it were my reasons for success'.

Heather also used to practise against men, though not against champions like Geoff Hunt. Here, in Margaret Court and Heather McKay, was starting to emerge the model of the physically strong woman. Other sportswomen also began to enjoy the thought of being strong. Perhaps it was partly reaction to repression in the past, but women began taking up body-building and power-lifting.

Others, meantime, continued to prefer the less physical approach. An Aboriginal girl from Barellan, on the banks of the Murrumbidgee River, was one such person. Evonne Goolagong was always as placid as a pond on a still morning. Maybe her Aboriginal nature was somewhat responsible, or the blissful childhood she recalls: 'Growing up in Barellan . . . was probably the happiest years of my life. I remember having lots of fun doing the weirdest things like climbing up wheat silos and trying to catch pigeons and getting into lots of trouble, but mostly playing a lot of tennis. I spent a lot of time hitting a ball against a brick wall and that's how I got started. We lived right next door to a tennis club and I spent a lot of time on the courts there too'.

The Goolagongs didn't have much money, but she says 'I never thought of us as being poor because, if anything, we were probably very rich in being happy'. Goolagong's personality and natural reticence were evident in the way she played tennis. There was minimal, if necessary, aggression; caress and direct was more her approach. She enjoyed what she was doing, rather than seeing it as a way of life. 'I guess I liked to sniff the flowers on the way, so to speak', she says. 'I was the type of person that liked to go practise, go play my matches, do my press conference, leave and go and do something else completely different like shopping or go sightseeing, really see the places that I visited. I didn't like to hang around tennis courts too often.' Goolagong gives a revealing insight into her nature when she says that even when she lost 'I still remembered the points that I thought I played perfectly and I was satisfied. So I think that's why I didn't brood about losing and why I still felt, well, there's always another time'.

It was hardly surprising that Goolagong, who won Wimbledon in 1971 and 1980, became so popular with the crowds, for in her they saw a fresh-faced, uncomplicated youngster, not too affected by sport's pressures or dejected in defeat, but someone who looked so feminine, reacted so naturally to everything and was successful all the same.

Another person of similar nature was Shane Gould: gentle, reserved and one who never enjoyed the limelight which sport thrust upon her. Gould took over Dawn Fraser's mantle as Australia's queen of swimming and wore it very proudly and successfully. In 1972, when only 15, she lowered the world 100-metres freestyle record to 58.5 seconds, won every Australian freestyle championship and during the year set world records for every freestyle distance. She went to the Munich Olympics that year carrying the expectations of all Australia and the attention of the world sporting press focused on her.

On her arrival in Munich, a large group of German media people were at the airport along with the Australian media who had preceded the team's arrival. All wanted to speak with Shane Gould, who had held every world freestyle record until just a short time before. As she emerged into the public area the German and Australian reporters gathered, asking questions. How was she feeling? Was it true she was going to swim in five individual events? Which swimmers might stand in

Beauty and the Beast

A triumphant 15-year-old Shane Gould hugs her kangaroo mascot as she completed her tally of three gold and one silver medals at the 1972 Munich Olympic Games
Photobank/All Sport

her way of winning them all? One of the questions was asked by a heavily accented German and Gould surprised him (and everyone else) by replying in German! She proceeded to conduct the rest of the press conference in two languages, answering questions in German with lengthy, comprehensive replies. She was learning German at school, but at the age of 15 to have the courage to test her knowledge of it in this sort of company was a measure of the girl's character.

If she had inner strength, she needed physical strength too for the enormous programme which she had been set. Many thought it was asking too much of her to swim the heats and finals of five individual events with a few relays thrown in for good measure. But Gould thought she could win them all; the coaches thought she could too; only a bunch of American schoolgirls believed they could stop her.

Gould won three gold medals — the 200-metres medley, 400-metres freestyle and 200-metres freestyle — setting world records in each of them, and won a silver medal in the 800-metres and a bronze in the 100-metres freestyle. By the time the Games finished she had swum twelve races in eight days, logging 4200 metres of competitive swimming. Even though Gould continued swimming — six months after the Games she became the first woman to break 17 minutes for 1500 metres — she was becoming increasingly tired of the relentless training and competition.

Early in 1973 she gave up competitive swimming and fled the pressures of Sydney to continue her education at the New England Girls' School in Armidale. After leaving school she worked for a while with the Adidas sportswear company. That did not provide Shane Gould with the satisfaction in life which she sought. In 1975, she met and married Neil Innes in Sydney. They had met at a Jesus Teach-in the year before, when Shane discovered the joy of being accepted simply as herself and not as a public figure. The couple moved to Perth, working initially as shearers' rouseabouts and farm labourers before buying a 40-hectare farm in the State's south-west. Her wedding and subsequent departure to the west occurred quietly, with Shane doing all she could to ensure there was little publicity. Shane Gould has never questioned the wisdom of this move and, at the time of publication, the couple still lives there, quite self-sufficient and wonderfully happy. Gould says: 'We live below the poverty line, but we're rich in some respects. We eat very well and we own everything we have. Our furniture and most of our clothes are second hand and if we find we're spending too much money, we re-evaluate. We're living for a reason — simply, so others may simply live.'

Swimming has since had two more exceptional female champions in Michelle Ford and Tracey Wickham. That they emerged about the same time was a shame, for at various stages each was forced to share the spotlight with the other when individually they were two superb champions. Wickham was a great swimmer, certainly among the greatest of all time, and her world records of 8 min. 24.6 sec. for 800 metres and 4 min. 6.28 sec. for 400 metres took a power of beating. But she never won the ultimate, an Olympic gold medal, for she withdrew from Australia's team for the 1980 Moscow Olympics after the enormous pressure exerted by Prime Minister Fraser. She maintained that her reasons for withdrawing were not politically motivated. 'I really didn't go because of a lot of personal reasons. My mum and dad had broken up at that stage and, being the eldest daughter, I was more or less the shoulder mum cried on and I had a lot of problems with sickness as well . . . I really decided that it wasn't the best time for me to compete because I wasn't ready and I never swim a race unless I'm a hundred per cent ready.' She used the political situation as her excuse.

At the Moscow Olympics, with Tracey Wickham at home in Australia, a consequence of those boycotted Games, her arch rival Michelle Ford chose three events: the 200-metres butterfly, the 400-metres and 800-metres. Her first event produced a bronze medal in the 200-metres butterfly behind two East Germans. The East Germans again dominated the 400-metres, in which she came fourth. Ford scolded herself for allowing her opponents to dictate the pace in the 400-metres.

Beauty and the Beast

Two fine Australian swimmers, Tracey Wickham and Lisa Forrest, display their medals at the Edinburgh Commonwealth Games. Wickham held world records for both the 800 metres and 400 metres, but she denied herself the chance of an Olympic Gold Medal by withdrawing from the politically entangled Moscow Games
Roger Gould

The 800-metres would be different, she determined, and so it was. Ford took the lead after 250 metres and pulled away to break the East German gold medal monopoly and win by almost 4 seconds in 8 min. 28.90 sec., an Olympic record. Tracey said: 'I always feel that it could have been me that won the gold medal at those Games. I congratulate Michelle; she did a very good job. She swam an excellent race. But I know I had the chance of winning that, but I took the other option. I decided not to go and knew, or was about ninety-nine per cent sure, that she was going to win the gold medal. And she did, which was great. Good on her.'

Another female champion of those times was golfer Jan Stephenson, who fought considerable opposition from amateur female, not male, administrators because of her glamorous ways and outspoken manner before turning professional and heading for the US in 1974. Since then she has accumulated well over $1 million in prize-money and has won just about everything the game has to offer, including the 1983 US Women's Open.

While there have been these female champions in sports with wide acceptance of their sex at the highest competitive levels, the 1970s also began to see women participating in more traditional male sports. If men can do it, why can't we they asked. Scientific tests had shown women as possessing greater powers of endurance and the ability to withstand intense stress for longer periods. And so the pathfinders began to emerge, those determined to question male dominance in one sport after another.

Some women, like Marie Lyndon and Beverley Buckingham, chose horse-racing. Others have followed, until women have become regular riders in this fast, demanding and exceedingly dangerous business. Even Roy Higgins, twice the rider of Melbourne Cup winners, accepts their presence, if with some reservations. He says: 'There is a place somewhere out there in racing for women jockeys. They do worry me a lot. I was a bit fortunate that I was coming towards the end of my career when women started to emerge as female jockeys. The thing that really concerned me, and I got to speak to a lot of doctors and professors in medicine about it, was they were saying the female body is not really structured to develop the strong bone and muscle and the strength of the male. That's a very dangerous profession out there, race riding. You've got to remember that you're talking about probably 100 to

Above left:
The glamour girl of Australian golf, Jan Stephenson, turned professional in 1974 and has since based herself in the US, where she has earned more than $1 million in prize-money. She won the 1983 US Open
Action Graphics

Above right:
Jockey Pam O'Neill, resplendent in her silks before a race. Women have become regular riders in the dangerous and demanding sport of horse racing. Former jockey Roy Higgins says that women jockeys have adjusted their style to compensate for their comparative lack of strength: 'The majority are out leading and they have won a lot of races like that,' he says
Martin King Sportpix

112 pounds of human flesh trying to control a dumb animal and a massive and highly excitable thoroughbred that at times can weigh up to 1300 or 1400 pounds. It only takes one misguided movement during the running of the race, or a horse that is far too powerful for the jockey and it clips another animal's heels and jockeys can be killed out there'.

Higgins says female jockeys have recognised this and have begun making adjustments in the way they ride. 'In every second ride of a female on a thoroughbred — especially distance races — the majority are out leading and they have won a lot of races doing that . . . if they do go on a horse that pulls hard they just can't restrain it. You see them getting a long way out in front and leading by quite a long margin.'

Higgins believes that while there is a place for women on the backs of racing thoroughbreds, there's an even greater role for them in the training and preparation of horses. He sees them as far kinder than men: 'the thoroughbred responds better to the female than they do to the male. The female is not aggressive to the animal, where the male strapper can be'. He says a lot of today's strappers are only in racing to get their wages and then get out, whereas the female strapper does it because of her love of animals. Colin Hayes is a good example of someone who has recognised women's talents. He employs an enormous number of female staff and Higgins maintains that this great trainer has probably some of the best-natured horses in Australia.

Another of the most rigorous sports into which women have followed men is the triathlon, a pastime which originated in Hawaii and consists of a swim, bike-ride and run over enormous distances, each of them an endurance feat in itself. Even the short-distance triathlon, consisting of the 1.5 km swim, the 40 km bike-ride and

10 km run, would take the élite athlete from 1 hr. 50 min. to about 2 hr. 10 min., depending on the terrain and the day's conditions.

Such competition, because of its arduous nature and variety of skills, requires considerable training. Louise MacKinlay is prepared to do all that is required to achieve success. She works as hard as any male triathlete. In fact, she has a training schedule which would make the average Australian male cry for mercy. MacKinlay begins her day at 4.30 a.m. by cycling 60 km from Westmead to Dural and back. In the afternoon after work she has a 15-kilometre run, a workout at the gymnasium and then swim training. If she's lucky, she might be home by 9 p.m. 'A triathlete can get away with as little as ten to twelve hours training a week', she says nonchalantly, adding that the professional triathletes train about 35 hours a week.

Many males might question why a woman would become interested in such an excessively demanding sport, but they are physically capable and the desire for competition is equally strong among the élite athletes of both sexes. MacKinlay says: 'It's a good sport for someone who wants all-round fitness and for someone who doesn't want to just run or cycle or swim. It's a great sport; you've got a lot of variety; it enables you to meet a lot more people and it is a lot of fun. I myself got into triathlons when I was a runner who was looking for something different and had a little bit of extra weight on. So I bought a bicycle and went from there'.

She thinks that in Australia about 30 per cent of the field in triathlons are now women and that there's a tendency for more and more women in the 25-35 age group to become involved in the sport. She, for one, intends competing for some time to come. Her only regret is that in the distribution of prize-money men are paid much more. 'I get angry when I think of the difference, and I know a lot of the other women resent it as well.'

With women of the 1980s possessing the determination, the commitment and the dedication to enter all sports, the time will soon come when they will compete against men in everything. Most books of sporting records include about seventy Australian sports. At the turn of the century, women would have competed in no more than a dozen of them. Now they compete in almost all.

There are notable exceptions. Of the football codes, there seem to be no records of women seriously playing Australian Rules, Rugby League or Rugby Union, except for playing touch football where hard physical contact is disallowed, even though Rugby has a growing number of women's teams in the US.

The objection to women playing football in the unabbreviated form is probably more because of the damage it would do to male machismo than the physical hurt it might inflict on women. It would deprive football, still the pre-eminently Australian male game, of its masculinity. So any suggestions of females playing football (not that there appear to have been many), have not been taken up. Yet, who is to say that in years to come, as male society comes to accept more female involvement in sport, there won't be women's teams in these three codes, joining the large number of women who already play soccer and obviously enjoy it.

Other sports which women have not yet entered in any number are baseball, boxing, ice hockey, modern pentathlon, motor cycling, motor racing, polo, polocrosse, speedway, weightlifting and woodchopping. But times are changing. For the first time, women's cycling was held in the 1984 Los Angeles Olympics and the competition was extended in Seoul. It had remained a male preserve in Olympic competition since the first Games in Athens in 1896.

The surf lifesaving movement is another area where changes have taken place rapidly since women were first allowed to sit in 1980 for the bronze medallion, which allows a person to become a patrolling lifesaver. Four women actually qualified as surf lifesavers in Wollongong in 1914, but the rules were later tightened and the opposition to their joining the movement was based on the flimsy argument that there were no separate facilities in club houses for women. It was a convenient excuse. However, the groundswell of women wanting to become lifesavers finally

Above:
Water polo was once considered to be a 'men only' preserve, but the successful adoption of the sport by Australian women culminated in a World Championship win to the Australian team at Madrid in 1986
Live Action: Acikalin

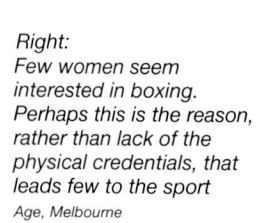

Right:
Few women seem interested in boxing. Perhaps this is the reason, rather than lack of the physical credentials, that leads few to the sport
Age, Melbourne

This women's Australian Rules football team from Western Australia is believed to be the social club of a department store. They are an isolated representation, however, as the game has never escaped from male domination on an organised and continuing basis
Battye Library, Western Australia

caused a breakthrough and a visit these days to any Australian surf beach on a summer afternoon will confirm women's increasing involvement in surf lifesaving. Those standing guard, waiting for a swimmer's distress call, will inevitably include several women or young girls.

Their numbers are constantly increasing. The Surf Life Saving Association of Australia in the late 1980s had nearly 63 000 members of whom 15 000 were females. There were over 16 000 active lifesavers — those who are over 15 years of age and who form the patrols — of whom over 2500 were women. By far the largest concentration of females was among the Nipper movement, where the membership number of just over 18 500 included nearly 7000 girls. At the time of publication, there was only one surf lifesaving club in Australia, Maroubra, which still did not have female members.

Even in the dangerous sport of motor racing, women are becoming known. An intriguing fact is that the first Australian to compete in the world-famous Le Mans 24-hour race was a woman. Joan Richmond of Melbourne drove as a member of Captain George Eyston's team in the 1936 Le Mans. There have been other famous women drivers since: Mary Seed, who had many successes in the 1950s in an AC Bristol sports car; Christine Gibson, who won many races in 3-litre touring cars and in 1978 came close to winning the Rothmans 500 Classic at Oran Park with her husband Fred; Sue Ransom, who successfully mixed circuit racing, rallies and international Go-Kart racing in the 1970s; and Robyn Hamilton, who became a top racing-car driver in the late 1970s and finished fourth in the 1980 TAA Formula Ford championship.

While no woman is currently driving in Formula One Grand Prix events, it is inevitable that we shall eventually see a woman lining up alongside the future Alain Prosts, Nigel Mansells, Nelson Piquets or Gerhard Bergers, buried inside a Ferrari, the engine shrieking, nerves jangling, the crowd hushed, waiting for a Grand Prix start.

In some sports women are already edging very close to men in their standards of performance. For example, the women's rate of improvement in swimming is much more dramatic than that of men, particularly in distance events.

This watercolour by Percy Spence, depicting women lifesavers demonstrating the line and reel method in 1910 at Manly beach, is a little premature. Although four women qualified as surf lifesavers in 1914, the rules were tightened to exclude them. The situation has evolved today into a complete integration of women into the lifesaving movement
Manly Art Gallery and Museum

The differences between some of the world records in track and field are not as great as they used to be. The men's high-jump world record is, at the time of writing, Patrik Sjoberg's 2.42 metres and the women's record is 2.09 metres by Stefka Kostadinova. That's only 33 centimetres' difference. And the fastest of the women marathoners can finish well up these days in any mixed field. Australia's Lisa Martin demonstrated this in January 1988 when she won the Osaka International Women's Marathon in 2 hr. 23 min. 51 sec. It was the seventh fastest time in history by a woman and the best ever run on a point-to-point course. Even by male standards it was a fairly fast time.

There are some sports which women have developed as their own and have increased their expertise in them to a point where they would probably be too efficient even for rival teams of men competitors. Netball is the best example. There are 370 000 registered players with the Australian Netball Association, none of them men. Often described as the women's version of men's basketball, netball is played between seven-a-side teams on a much smaller court, measuring 30.48 long × 14.23 metres wide. It's a sport which lends itself to the Australian way of life and now, with so many women playing it around the nation every Saturday afternoon, they have lifted the standard to where Australia has dominated the world.

Australian captain Anne Sargeant explains: 'Netball has its origins in England and was started as an opposition sport to basketball. It was felt that women needed to have a sport that had a slightly different flavour, that they could compete in and play in for themselves. It's developed from there, and is very much entrenched as a traditional sport in our school system. I guess in terms of international competition it's a modern phenomenon. The international body has been in operation for something like twenty-five to thirty years. The first world tournament was held in 1963 and Australia has been to the forefront of that type of competition. Netball

Above:
A women's surf lifesaving team takes part in a surf carnival march past. Women are very much a part of the lifesaving organisation, in both competition and rescue operations
Roger Gould

Right:
Joan Richmond was the first Australian woman to compete in the famous Le Mans 24-hour race, as a member of Captain George Eyston's team in 1936. She is pictured here crossing the finish line at Calder track in Victoria in the Riley she raced in the 1930s
News Limited

Anne Sargeant, captain of the Australian women's netball team, proudly displays her trophy as New South Wales Sportswoman of the Year. The sport has boomed in Australia, with around 370 000 registered players. The game is played between seven-a-side teams on outdoor courts. It is cheap and accessible, for juniors and seniors alike
News Limited

lends itself to the Australian climate. It's an accessible sport in terms of being played outdoors. It's easy to get a court put down; it's easy to get to a court; it's cheap and it's played through all sorts of weather . . . so it has boomed in Australia from these origins'.

From the beginnings when women fought the dogmatism and ostracism of male society, in this nation they have emerged to produce in Dawn Fraser and Betty Cuthbert two of the greatest sporting champions of all time; Australian women are demonstrating their athletic efficiency in all but a few sports; they have some sports unique to their sex.

There is some way to go before full sporting equality is achieved. Golf remains one of the last sports where women continue to be treated very differently. There is still a significant division between members (who are men) and associates (who are women). There are large differences in fees — the annual subscription for a leading Sydney golf club is $1152 for members and $576 for associates, though the associates are given quite restricted use of the course. However, challenges are now being mounted in various clubs around Australia by women wanting to become members — with the much wider access to their courses which membership confers — and men applying to become associates because of the cheaper fees and being quite happy to play less.

In this case the moves towards equality are coming from different directions, but it would seem that in the not too distant future men and women will compete equally in all Australian sports — a long way from the days of Annette Kellerman and Fanny Durack.

Sources and references

The material for this chapter is derived from the author's own information and research and consultation of the following books:

John Blanch, *The Ampol Australian Sporting Records* (Budget Books, rev. edn 1981); Gary Lester, *Australians at the Olympics: A Definitive History* (Lester-Townsend, 1984); Jim Shepherd, *The Winfield Book of Australian Sporting Records* (Rigby, 1981).

Interview transcripts of the television series 'Blood, Sweat and Tears':

Evonne Cawley, Margaret Court, Dawn Fraser, Roy Higgins, Marjorie Jackson, Louise MacKinlay, Heather McKay, Anne Sargeant, Tracey Wickham.

IMAGE MAKERS

Richard Sleeman

Greg Norman is the face of sport in the modern era. It is a face and a name and a talent, packaged and marketed like one of the Ferraris in the garage of his Florida mansion. Image is everything — the finely chiselled features, the shock of blond hair that gives the impression of a surfboard rider who happened to stumble on a set of golf clubs on his way to the beach, the lifestyle of an internationally famous golfer. Not many television hours go by without the instantly recognisable Norman visage appearing on screen, whether he is wielding his clubs in some faraway tournament, plugging McDonalds and Swan beer, or talking thirteen to the dozen on some chat show.

Stories about Norman, his children, his wife, his golf, his health, abound in the media. What all this adds up to is the fact that Norman is one of the richest people in the history of sport. In 1987 he earned $12 million — more in 1988 — and less than 10 per cent of this comes directly from tournament prize-money. Norman might provide the initial talent, but it takes the professional image maker to turn it into cold, hard cash. Graham Hannan is the Australian and New Zealand vice-president of the International Management Group (IMG) which helps mastermind Norman's profit-making. Hannan said: 'Greg has led a revival of interest in golf in this country. The better he plays the better the publicity. And the more publicity he gets on television in particular and in the media in general, the better the product he is endorsing sells. He is that rare sportsman who has both ability and charisma'.

This is what image-making and a touch of talent did for Norman in 1987. He made more than $5 million to act as Australian spokesman for Qantas and Hertz; another $5.2 million with Daikyo, which runs the Palm Meadows resort in Queensland, for doing not much else than saying nice things about the place and making occasional personal appearances; a further $2 million for a series of television commercials for Alan Bond's Swan brewery; another $3 million from a clothing contract with the fashionable leisure wear outfitters, Reebok; an arrangement with Akubra hats which could be worth $1.5 million if the product sells extensively in the US; a $700 000 contract to endorse Epson computers; and a $650 000 advance for an instructional golf video, as well as a $650 000 advance for a book, *Shark Attack: Greg Norman's Guide to Aggressive Golf* (Macmillan, 1987). Far from being over-exposed, Norman is being fed out and farmed off to others almost by the day — a multi-million dollar contract to act as an international spokesman for McDonalds was signed at the end of 1987, and a host of other deals is being considered.

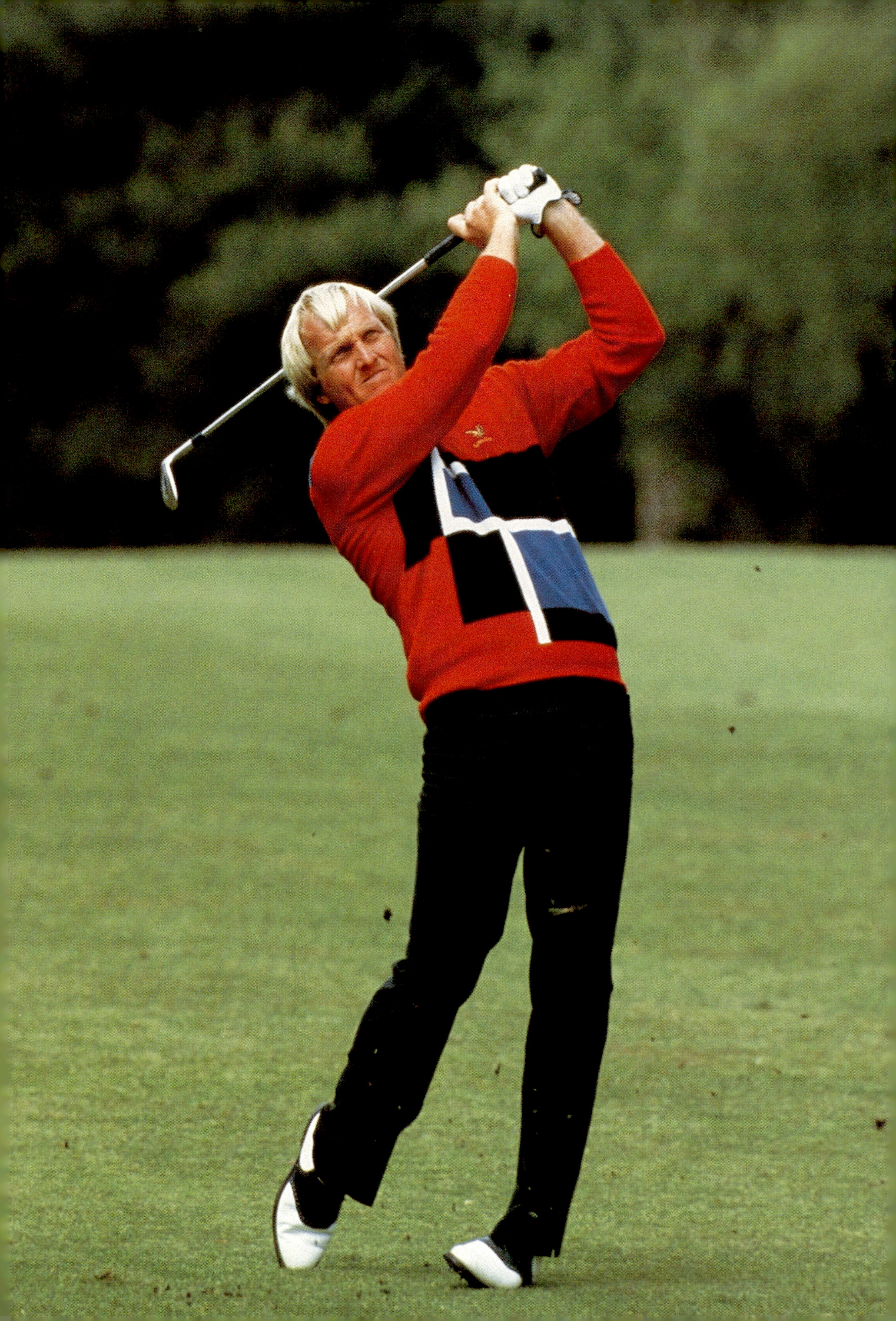

Image Makers

Greg Norman is the ultimate sportsman and a sponsor's dream. His presence in any Australian golf field guarantees big crowds and complete media coverage. His move to the USA has not affected his Australian following
Photobank/All Sport

According to Norman's international marketing agent, Hughes Norton of IMG: 'Greg only wants to be with blue-chip companies. We've turned down a whole lot more offers'. For tax reasons, Norman has to flee to the US to keep house at Lost Tree Village, near Palm Beach, Florida. There are two Ferraris, an Aston Martin and a Rolls Royce in the garage, and from all reports, each is used until there's dust on the duco and then replaced with a new one, even faster and more expensive. Said Norton, 'Greg is a natural. None of it is put on. He exudes all the essential qualities in this new age of sports image-making. He's a winner, for a start, of major tournaments like the British Open and the Australian Masters, and the most gifted player in the world; he's good-looking, attractive to women yet not threatening to men; he smiles most of the time, yet is a man's man who takes no lip from abusive elements in the crowd'.

The 'Great White Shark', as he is known internationally, works hard at this positive image. He has infinite patience with autograph hunters: he lives for his family — children Morgan-Leigh and Gregory, and wife Laura. Rob Grant has covered golf for Australian Associated Press all over the world, and knows why the image of the 'Great White Shark' continues to gleam. 'He is the complete sportsman', Grant said. 'He knows what a sponsor or a member of the media requires and provides it. He is always accessible, always friendly. He's a star who doesn't behave like one. He never objects to tough questions. You can ask him anything and he'll respond'. In fact, it wasn't always that way. At Norman's first appearance in the British Open a decade ago, he played a poor round at the Sandwich course and hurried away from reporters at the end of it. Norman made a couple of reporters chase after him for a quote, placing them in an embarrassing situation and, after one of them objected strongly in print, Norman realised he should pay more attention to his image. Abuse the crowd or the clubs or the caddy, if you like, but not the media. It can be too costly in dollars and cents.

The televised tournament has made it much easier to sell Norman. Modern technology means that Norman's triumphs and tragedies from the British Open and the US Open and the Masters are beamed live into Australian and international lounge rooms. The viewer is either elated or pained right along with him. Instantly. Again, it wasn't always like that. The Honourable Michael Scott, an English amateur living in Victoria, was Australia's first Open golf champion, playing at the Australian Golf Club's Botany links in Sydney on 2 and 3 September 1904. Thousands of fans followed his progress. The *Sydney Mail* did its best to bolster an image of Australia's first golfing hero. It reported: 'The Hon. M. Scott is a pocket-sized Hercules, possessed of remarkable muscular strength . . . He comes from an athletic family. His sister Lady Margaret Scott retired unbeaten after thrice winning the British Ladies Championship, in which she was regarded as invincible. Her portraits, showing a remarkably supple swing, are familiar to all readers of golf literature'.

There was such a thing as the sponsored golfer, then, as well. One such, Scott's arch rival Carnegie Clark, along with 300 other young men, emigrated from the little township of Carnoustie, Scotland, at the turn of the century to teach and play the game of golf all over the world. Clark sailed into Sydney by steamer in 1902 to fulfil a three-year contract with a retail store, and never returned to his country of birth. He gained fame as a player and clubmaker, and remained Australian right down to his Niblicks until his death in 1959 at the age of 78 years. Clark won the Australian Open in 1906, 1910 and 1911, worked as a professional at Royal Sydney Golf Club for twenty-seven years, and is rated in Terry Smith's *Australian Golf* as the 'pioneer of the sport in this country'. Another Scot, Victor East, perfected his golf in Australia, and became our first touring professional, going to America in 1921. He is best remembered for his classic book, *Better Golf in Five Minutes*. The media was already forming images of sports heroes in the minds of its readers, because this helped to sell newspapers. Dr Reg Bettington, a triple Oxford blue and captain of the New South Wales cricket team, won the Australian amateur golf crown in 1932.

Grant Kenny's strength and skill in and on the water, as well as the arduous running on the sand, have amazed and entertained us all. His bronzed good looks and winning smile — seen often in television commercials — have charmed, as has his easy-going and modest manner
Live Action: Acikalin

Smith's Weekly reported: 'He is huge and hairy, and known to caddies at Royal Sydney as Tarzan. Although Dr Bettington swings and slogs like a navvy, he has a delicacy of touch around the greens that would make us unhesitatingly place our life in his hands'. Dr Bettington took the title from the Greg Norman of his day, Harry Williams, a tall, slim youth who won the national title at 16 years of age. Players then didn't have the image makers to turn their talent into cash. Williams committed suicide in 1961. According to *Australian Golf*, the kitchen where he died was gas-filled and the refrigerator empty, except for a single lettuce leaf.

The champions followed in golf, as they did in other sports — men like Norman von Nida, Ossie Pickworth, Kel Nagle, Peter Thomson, Bruce Crampton and David Graham, each earning more out of the game as communications technology widened their impact on Australians and the rest of the world.

Cricket is probably the sport which best demonstrates the effect of the image makers. Kerry Packer in the 1970s gave cricket a whole new image. In the first days of electronic media the old-time cricket images were from radio on so-called 'synthetic' Tests. Alan McGilvray, Australia's fabled cricket commentator, knew nothing of comfortable cricket commentary boxes and instant pictures when he 'called' the Test series between Australia and England in 1934. McGilvray and his team were 13 000 miles away in an ABC studio. McGilvray recalled: 'We had a man sent over there named Eric Scholl, and he'd send the cables every over. Now that came into a deciphering room we had. There were about five or six deciphering; they were all sent in code. Every other station would get the same message, all in code. Now they were deciphered, put on to paper and we'd get a brief comment like "Hammond, Fleetwood Smith, uppish, four, straight". Now we knew that the ball was hit by a full toss from Fleetwood Smith to Hammond, hit uppishly, past the bowler who nearly caught him, then down the ground for four'.

Image Makers

Australian cricket captain Allan Border is subject to the closest scrutiny by cricket followers, as his every on-field action is seen in close-up on television and his words and deeds are reported in the press. His phlegmatic character and his masterful batting have helped him to withstand the pressures. In 1989 Border became the first Australian captain to recapture the Ashes in England since 1934. During his triumphant tour Border scored his 8000th test run. He later surpassed Sir Garfield Sobers' total of test runs to become the third highest scorer ever behind Sunil Gavaskar and Geoff Boycott
The Photo Library

'The next one would say so-and-so caught by Hassett. Now we knew where Hassett was. We knew whether he was at cover or slip. We had the positions of every fielder known to us in the studio at all times. It was on a board in front of us, and old Charles Moses of the ABC insisted on accuracy. If it went to a certain fieldsman, then by golly, it had to go to him, and no other, on the broadcast. And we were never to go in front of the score. On some other stations you'd hear the score from two for 180 to two for 184, only to find out that a third wicket had fallen at 181, and that put them right in the soup. We insisted on not going past the score, because if we did make a mistake, the true score would be reported in the paper. So you see, we had the cables, but had to make our own picture out of it. We had a photo of the ground right in front of us, say Lords or the Oval and we knew the areas like which was the nursery end or the gasometer end or whatever. My fellow commentators, Vic Richardson and M. A. Noble, were lucky in that they had been to these places. Halford Hooker and myself had not. We had to go by the pictures in front of us. I had to get used to tapping the lump of wood that Charles Moses had designed for the sound effects of bat on ball. It was a round piece of wood, and we used to tap it with a pencil. Charles was so meticulous that before each broadcast, we'd practise until the sound was perfect, usually by stifling it with a rubber-band around the pencil or some such . . .

'In fact, by the last Test we were only one minute behind the ball that was bowled in England and as the next ball was coming in, we were talking about the previous ball. Moses wanted us to be even slicker than that. He said we should listen and call at the same time. Moses tried it himself and realised it was absolutely impossible to listen to something coming in and talk about something else at the same time. Then of course, the rain would come and stop play, so we had to talk for hours. Vic was marvellous at that. Halford and I closed out on that because we'd never been away. We left it to the two Australian captains. Not everyone in the audience thought that we were ethically correct in doing what we did. So Moses took the whole studio out to Fox-Movietone in Missenden Road, Camperdown, and assembled it there to show the public how it was done, and that we were not deceiving them. Vic and I would go for a walk from time to time and watch the crowd's reaction as they listened to the commentary coming through on shop radios. Vic would go and say "what a lot of nonsense those people are talking", and one time when he did it, a lady hit him over the head with an umbrella. She was so mad.'

What a far cry from the heady days of World Series Cricket Telecasts! Channel Nine increased the number of television cameras from four to eight. Colin Tatz described the Channel Nine telecasts as 'commercial TV giving the audience what the telecasters thought they wanted — sex, violence, thrills, spills, nationalism, flags, noise, blare, fanfare, booze, colours and lights'. Lynton Taylor of PBL Marketing, which led cricket into this modern era, said: 'We capitalised on what was a vacancy for sports watchers. We identified cricket with the children and wives of the past two generations. We presented the game in an attractive, vital, exciting manner on TV, appealing to the modern mind. Then we made cricket suitable for the housewife to watch'.

Richard Cashman charts some of the changes that World Series Cricket has brought: 'World Series Cricket had a very significant effect on the type of people who came to cricket, but it wasn't just class, it was also gender. A lot of women didn't come to cricket before WSC, but WSC and television explain cricket a lot more to women, unlock a lot of secrets of the game . . . I think the biggest change was slow-motion replay. Cricket is a very secretive game and a lot of people who haven't been brought up with it don't understand it . . . With slow-motion replay they can actually see swing and spin. If they go to the ground they wouldn't understand what was happening. Radio never explained cricket as much as television does'.

Image Makers

Above left:
The doyen of Australian cricket commentators, Alan McGilvray who retired in 1986 after describing cricket all over the world for fifty-two years. McGilvray recalled how in their 'synthetic' Test calls of the 1930s they would tap a piece of wood with a pencil to simulate the sound of bat on ball
News Limited

Above right:
Alan McGilvray knew cricket from inside and out, as he was captain of the New South Wales Sheffield Shield team. He is pictured at the crease in 1936
News Limited

Today it's television that shapes the image of sport: the skills of an army of sporting, marketing and technical men and women is brought to bear on a tradition that has been shaped through hundreds of years. The European ethos of sport and sportsmanship was handed down to Australian colonials by their British forebears; they in turn had inherited it from classical antiquity, where Greek and Roman alike celebrated the warrior's physical prowess and the spirit of competition. In the Middle Ages these ideas mingled with those of chivalry; the tail end of it was to be found on the playing fields of Eton, where prowess, courage, nobility, courtesy were seen to be blended in an ethos of enormous influence. The British upper classes, the inheritors of this long tradition, pursued sports such as cricket and athletics for recreation but also for the building of courage, 'character' — which included the capacity to accept defeat gracefully — and *esprit de corps*.

In New South Wales, among the gambling-mad colonials these sports became less a pursuit of the aristocracy and more an outlet for the ragamuffins. Early reports of cricket matches indicate that the colonials did not mind trying to hoodwink the umpire if they could get away with it. Scarcely a sport was played without the introduction of a side-wager. In these unpromising circumstances many nevertheless carried on the old ideals. It is highly significant that missionaries taught cricket to the Aborigines on their missions as a way of 'civilising' them: sport was seen as an indispensable part of Europeanness. Later on, the ideals of 'muscular Christianity' in which a healthy body and mind were seen as the equally necessary basis for sound religion, were promoted with great vigour. In the early decades of the twentieth century the physical culture movement flourished at all levels of society. Its motto *Mens sana in corpore sano*, a healthy mind in a healthy body, encapsulates the prevailing spirit. Schoolchildren were taught games assiduously as part of their total development.

The newspapers, before radio and television, had sports coverage to themselves. Sport sold newspapers, and newspapers promoted sport, still largely in the serious way demanded by the tradition. Newspapers were influential also in the evolution of games.

The history of the national game, Australian Rules, was shaped in this manner. Printed match reports and agitation for reform in rules and standards of fair play turned the game into the national passion it is today. In 1869, the *Australasian* newspaper suggested that a half-time change of ends would give players a much fairer game. The practice at the time was to change ends after every goal was scored. A year later, the newspaper's suggestion was instituted as a rule, and carried forward to this day. The writer who came up with the suggestion wrote under the nom de plume of 'Fair Play'.

As the nineteenth century came to a close, the Melbourne press agitated against crowd misbehaviour in a manner that would make today's headlines of violence and terror look like a warning of child's play. One paper wrote that 'grounds must be fenced off to keep larrikins off the field'. The sport's officials gladly obliged since it led to their being able to charge admission. Other, more radical organs openly encouraged the louts. The *Bull Ant* magazine featured a character called Ginger Steve who bet on matches, attacked umpires and fought the opposing team's supporters. He reserved his best insults for what he called the 'straw boater teams' like Melbourne and St Kilda.

Each team had an image to be shaped and marketed. It was the same in Rugby League. South Sydney, for instance, was the team of the battlers when it entered the professional rugby code in 1908, and still bears that image to this day. The players began the image by their very professions. Their nickname of the 'Rabbitohs' came about from the old South Sydney Rugby Union days when many players used to sell rabbits during the week, while wearing their football guernseys. Such was the start of the battlers from South Sydney that the first club treasurer, George Ball, handled the princely sum of $178 for the entire 1908 season. Their home ground was known in those days as Nathan's Cow Paddock, later to be called Redfern Oval. It is now surrounded by Housing Department high rise dwellings, and populated with umbrella-wielding, wild-eyed supporters, bedecked in the club's red-and-green colours. Souths produced some great players like Clive Churchill, Harold Horder, Cec Blinkhorn, Ron Coote and John Sattler. But the image, maintained in the League press, never changed. Manly-Warringah, from Sydney's ritzier North Shore, became the 'silver tails', an image given to them by the League coach and commentator Roy Masters. It wouldn't have been appropriate in the early days. Max Whitehead, the second-rower who captained Manly in its first premiership match at Brookvale Oval, on 12 April 1947, was a professional wrestler who moonlighted as a chicken sexer.

Football commentary today is the realm of past players. Rugby League's best known commentator is the king of tautology, Rex Mossop. Mossop once took to heart comments about his slips of the tongue. He used to take it as a personal insult when people would point to comments like 'making forward progress' and 'I wonder if that's a portent of things to come'. On talk-back radio, he was even interviewed by Mike Gibson about his objection to nude bathers at Reef Beach near Mossop's Sydney home. Mossop told Gibson: 'I don't want male genitals shoved down my throat.' Then, in keeping with the new image makers of sport, Mossop found he could trade off these gaffs, and indeed, make a handsome living out of it. He switched from the Channel Seven Network to Ten, lost the Rugby League commentary because of increasing inaccuracies, but retained a lucrative role as the sports news presenter. The Ten executives see Mossop's role as that of an entertainer, rather than an expert able to articulate the skills and pressures of sport. And that is very much in keeping with the new image of sport. Mossop's Melbourne counterpart in Australian Rules is Lou Richards, once described by a *National Times* writer as 'Australia's biggest ocker'. Like Mossop, who was an international in both Rugby Union and Rugby League, Richards had a strong sporting background, having played 250 games for Collingwood between 1941 and 1955. He gained a start as a media sports star on the long-running 'World of Sport' live television show on Sunday mornings in Melbourne. According to Brian Stoddart, in *Saturday Afternoon Fever:*

> Rapid-fire, staccato, unscripted, bumbling, opinionated and infectious, Richards has passed from the pre-commercial to commercial age of football, apparently unconscious of what has happened around him. He now uses statistics (but is uncomfortable with them), and never seems to know what to think about the latest structural changes in the game's organisation and financing.
>
> One key to Richards's survival is his willingness to do anything that will maintain his popularity and notoriety. Elected king of the Moomba Festival, he modestly remarked that he had always expected to become a king one day. To honour wagers contracted in the heat of commentary, he has performed such stunts as sweeping Collins Street with a feather duster, and carrying the VFL's heaviest player the length of a city block. He is an entertainer rather than a simple sports informer. And the result? The boy from working-class Collingwood now lives in fashionable Toorak, inadvertently playing out the myth that sport can open all doors in Australian society. In 1984, for example, his views on the federal budget took up a considerable part of page three in the Melbourne *Sun* the morning after the document had been brought down in Parliament.

Richards sees himself as striking a balance between entertaining and informing. 'I think if you go overboard, then all you worry about is your own personality and you tend to overlook the game. There have been dares that I've done in the course of my commentary.

The irrepressible Lou Richards, who captained Collingwood and played 250 games as a rover between 1941 and 1955. Richard's distinctive commentating style and his 'kiss of death' selections have made him a household name in Melbourne. His crazy vows to back up his selections have put him in hilarious situations, but they always make good pictures and good copy in the Melbourne Sun
News Limited

'I rowed Billy Goggin, the coach of Geelong, across the Barwon River in a bathtub, and we had 7000 people there. I'm quite sure that people still see the funny side of sport. Sport, basically, to my way of thinking, is having fun. I know that the participants and the administrators that run football haven't got much of a sense of humour. In the course of having fun, if money comes along, then that's a bonus. On the eve of the grand final, I said that if Carlton beat Hawthorn, I would juggle three meatballs in one hand and half a plate of ravioli in the other while eating a pizza, but it was nearly impossible to do so. We had 2000, maybe 3000 up there in Lygon Street. That's what makes me happy. Sport is having fun. It's not the third world war, or anything. I think the commentator plays a very big role in making popular whatever game he's associated with.'

Another of the entertainers, known more for controversial statements than outrageous ones, was Sydney's Ron Casey. Even the more cerebral commentators — men like Mike Gibson — know the value of entertaining, rather than informing. In his days as one of the nation's finest sports writers, Gibson would never have let the words 'by gee, by jingo, by crikey' flow from his typewriter, but in television the phrase has become his trademark as parodied by comedians.

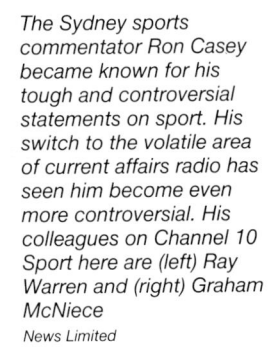

The Sydney sports commentator Ron Casey became known for his tough and controversial statements on sport. His switch to the volatile area of current affairs radio has seen him become even more controversial. His colleagues on Channel 10 Sport here are (left) Ray Warren and (right) Graham McNiece
News Limited

Modern sports writing in Australia is stampeding along the entertainment trail. The *Daily Mirror* in Sydney saw its rival, the *Sun*, go under in 1988. The *Mirror* unashamedly bases its sports writing on attention-grabbing headlines, accompanied by as few words of explanation as possible. There is a real skill in ferreting out those headlines, but this is sports writing as a new art form, completely alien to the aims of Australian sports commentary when it was born in the nineteenth century. Brian Stoddart writes of the conservative nature of commentary:

> R. W. E. Wilmot typified the sports writers employed by the mainstream, socially conservative print organisations of the late nineteenth and early twentieth centuries. One of Australia's earliest prominent sports writers, Wilmot had a most respectable background: Melbourne Grammar, then Trinity College at the

University of Melbourne. At 20, he joined the *Argus* . . . and the *Australian*. He was a university cricket blue in 1891 . . . He was also soon involved in a range of socially important activities: secretary to the Royal Humane Society of Victoria, secretary to the Atheneum Club, work in organisations such as the Hospital Society. Sport was a natural companion to 'good works'. His sports writings reflected the positive values of games in maintaining traditions, conventions and the status quo.

The conservative traditions exemplified by such a background were maintained by a strong sporting press. *Bell's Life* was published in both Sydney and Melbourne; Sydney also had the *Sportsman* and the famous *Referee*, founded in 1886.

Chris Cunneen points out the importance of newspapers like the *Referee*:

The founding of the *Referee* was a significant early sign of the role newspapers, and especially sporting journals, were to play in the burgeoning interest in and devotion to sport which began in the late decades of the nineteenth century. Its stated aims of elevating and recording sporting achievements were basic elements in the role of the press towards sport. The broadcasting of individual and team sporting feats was an essential ingredient in the modern preoccupation with sport. Comparisons, records and all the publicity for sporting organisation were to a large extent dependent upon press publicity.

The *Referee* allowed some well-known novelists and other writers to get a grounding as sports commentators. One of the most notable of these was Nat Gould. Gould's novel *The Double Event* was serialised in the *Referee* before publication, and established his reputation as a sports novelist. Over a hundred popular novels, mainly on sporting subjects, followed. Another famous reporter on the *Referee* was William Corbett who joined the paper in 1895, writing on boxing, bowls and swimming under various pseudonyms. As Stoddart remarks, Corbett was immensely proud of Australian sporting achievements and his columns showed it. 'Corbett had a flair for a story and an angle, but did not sensationalise . . . Although not himself a prominent sports performer, he was knowledgeable in many sports and became widely known to the public as an authoritative sports writer. He realised that sport was of serious public concern, and that good sports writing could sell newspapers.'

R. L. 'Snowy' Baker, on the other hand, was a sports performer, one of the best all-rounders in the country. His sporting prowess, his journalism and a book *General Physical Culture*, published in 1912, marked his beginnings as a commentator.

However, a new brand of sports journalism was developing through a scandal sheet called the *Dead Bird*. This and *Truth* diverged from the strong tradition of positive social values espoused by the *Referee*: they combined sport, gossip and sexual innuendo to entertain the masses. The purchase of the *Referee* by entrepreneur Hugh McIntosh in 1916 helped to establish this new trend of sensationalism-cum-entertainment in sport.

McIntosh was a colourful character whose father had served during the Indian Mutiny of 1857. As a young man his chain of cheap food shops led to richer entrepreneurial pursuits with his staging of the Johnson–Burns world heavyweight fight in Sydney. Indeed, it is in boxing that his name as a promoter leaves an indelible mark on Australian sports history. As well as making massive gate-takings from this famous fight, McIntosh sold the film rights for £80 000, a large amount even by modern reckoning. McIntosh built the ring and surrounds himself, with wood he borrowed on a promise of giving it back at the end of the fight. And to make sure there would be no cries of 'we wuz robbed', McIntosh refereed the bout himself.

Four years later, McIntosh had soured of sports promotion and entered theatrical production, but he was soon lured back to his first love by purchasing the *Referee* and *Sunday Times* in 1916. McIntosh's downmarket leanings reduced the influence and respectability of the *Referee*, partly because of the rise of the *Sun* as a new daily rival. At the same time, the public still had available to them a large range of the more solid sporting publications.

Radio brought in a new era. Introduced in 1923, and with a rapidly growing number of radio sets sold during the 1920s, radio confirmed the trend towards sports as entertainment. In America, sports broadcasting was the new direction of image-making. Marconi himself broadcast the *America*'s Cup races; the writer Damon Runyon delivered his memorable view on the yachting classic over the airwaves. Sent north to Newport when he would much rather have stayed in New York to cover the baseball, Runyon said: 'The only way to make this interesting is to start it just up-river from Niagara Falls'.

In the 1920s there was scarcely an Australian pub on a Saturday afternoon that didn't have a radio blaring the race results and the football. It became an Australian tradition that has persisted to the present day, except that now many pubs have racing by satellite on Skychannel television screens, with live racing from every capital city. By early 1925, 3LO in Melbourne had regular race broadcasts, but as early as 1923 a Melbourne experimental station had broadcast the Grand National Steeplechase. It paved the way for the nasal, excitable and world-famous Australian race callers for, again, it was horse-racing that was in greatest demand from listeners. Racing clubs and governments hated them at first. The clubs thought they kept people away from the track, while governments and wowsers figured that live race calls would increase the rate of illegal off-course betting. Saturday afternoons meant a regular game of cat-and-mouse between callers and clubs, the latter often assisted by police. Until a court case in 1937 established the caller's right of entry to racetracks, men like Cyril Angles, Lachie Melvile and Ken Howard called events from nearby roof-tops, or from scaffolding or trees outside the fence. Outside Pakenham racecourse for his calls, Howard climbed a tree only to find it was being cut down by police as he tried to continue. 'Listeners', he said, 'we're about to get

The Sydney race caller Ken 'Magic Eye' Howard earned his nickname for his ability to call close finishes. Some of his sayings, particularly 'London to a brick on' became part of the language. Howard, who retired in 1973, called thirty-seven Melbourne Cups
Herald & Weekly Times

the chop'. Howard began his sporting career as a race reporter on the *Truth* and *Daily Telegraph*, and became a legend in his own lifetime. He broadcast races for thirty-seven years, equally adept at the horses, greyhounds and the trots. He joined 2SM in 1936, and later worked at 2UE and 2GB. 'Magic eye' Howard earned his name from his ability to pick close finishes, and some of his sayings like 'London to a brick on' became part of the national lexicon. He called thirty-seven consecutive Melbourne Cups until his retirement in 1973. And when Ken Howard called the 1941 Melbourne Cup won by Skipton, a tape of the broadcast was sent to Europe so that it could be played on Italian radio for Australian prisoners of war.

Others followed the lead of the great early callers. Bert Bryant concentrated on colourful calls, with sayings like 'hanging like grandma's teeth', and 'pulling like a Collins Street dentist'. Bryant described horses as 'carrying enough bandage to start their own field hospitals'. He said one tout had 'more tips than a can of asparagus'. Bryant started his career at the age of nine, calling races from a fruit box painted to resemble a radio. At 14, he got a job in radio at Dubbo, in the New South Wales central west, and in 1948, began working for 3UZ in Melbourne.

These were the racing specialists, but there were other notable callers of general sport. Probably the first top personality in sports radio was Norman McCance who called wrestling from 1926 on 3LO in Melbourne. McCance was a refugee from the *Argus*, and started as a broadcaster by calling a wrestling bout between 'Professor' Walter Miller and Al Karasick. McCance, like so many broadcasters since, turned certain phrases into household usage. Stoddart remarks: 'For thousands of people, McCance's "he *can't* get out of it — he *can't* get out of it — he's *out* of it" became a familiar cry.'

Callers like McCance had sports fans drifting away from the established press. By then fans could also see newsreel footage of the action, and didn't need to rely on the press for information. The dozens of sports-oriented papers and magazines of the first quarter of the twentieth century had dwindled to just a few by the onset of World War II. The influence of the press was soon to be depleted even further by the arrival in Australia of television in 1956 — deliberately timed to coincide with the Melbourne Olympics. At first, television's impact was limited by lack of the sorts of technical equipment and expertise available today, but given Australia's many wins, particularly those of 'Golden Girl' sprinter Betty Cuthbert and the great women swimmers, the new medium brought immediacy and involvement that would never be lost. The arrival of colour television and the technological advances that followed ensured television's unbreakable grip on the fortunes of sport, both within Australia and internationally. By 1975, television had a stranglehold on sport. It would bring its influence to bear on the administrators to change rules; it demanded certain venues and starting times; in some cases, its needs even determined the make-up of Australian teams.

World Series Cricket is the obvious example. After failing to gain exclusive rights to cover Australian cricket, and having to share them with the ABC instead, Channel Nine's Kerry Packer provided the patronage and cash for what has come to be known as the Great Cricket Hijack of 1977. The cornerstone of WSC was one-day cricket played at night. It fulfilled Packer's wish to turn the popular view of cricket as 'baseball played under valium' into high drama. Traditionalists slammed Packer's influence as an outrage. Bill O'Reilly said the game had been taken over by a 'band of assassins' and that it amounted to a 'national disgrace'. But so successful was the new, updated marketing of cricket that a 1983 McNair Anderson survey revealed that cricket had replaced football as the nation's most popular sport. There is little doubt that the 'giggle box' of television was totally responsible. Despite moral indignation from the likes of Bill O'Reilly, Packer and WSC had given the people what they wanted.

Administrators, for so long pandered to by the media for fear of upsetting them, were brought into line, starkly, with changed social circumstance and need. They

Blood, Sweat and Tears

Former Australian Test captain Richie Benaud is in the vanguard of the presentation of cricket to the public, heading up Channel 9's commentary team for Test series and one day internationals in Australia
Photobank/All Sport

were also made aware of the vast earning potential of televised sport. If Packer was prepared to sacrifice millions of dollars on WSC then the exclusive rights he so dearly wanted must have been worth a fortune. Indeed, they were. By 1985 advertisers were putting more than a million dollars into Channel Nine's coffers during televised cricket. Two years later the major sponsors were contributing more than twice that amount.

While radio and newspapers never had to pay much for the right to describe and write about sports, suddenly there were whole new financial avenues for sports administrators. Rupert Murdoch's minions were scoffed at for purchasing the rights to the 1984 Olympics in Los Angeles for $10.6 million. The critics weren't laughing quite so loudly when it was revealed that total advertising rates for Channel Ten's Olympic coverage surpassed $30 million. Little wonder then that Ten pitched for, and won, the rights to provide exclusive Australian coverage of the 1988 Olympics from Seoul.

The relationship between sports and the media was suddenly in turmoil. The media had been tolerated in the early years. Now it was clear that television in particular had to be actively cultivated if a sport was to survive and prosper. Stoddart writes:

> Astute sports organisations, or their advisers, slowly became aware of their value to the channels, and negotiated figures for the rights to particular sports rose steadily at first, then dramatically. As the sums climbed, so did the channels' expectations of being given more professional service and consideration. Individual clubs, meanwhile, sought similarly lucrative deals with individual sponsors and also found themselves subject to increasingly stringent demands from those firms putting up the money. The players themselves were almost the only group to lose out on this monetary explosion.

Cricket may have been the most obvious vehicle for change in sport due to the effects of television coverage, but it is by no means the only example. By 1979 the sports getting most cash and coverage were tennis, VFL, Rugby League, golf and motor racing. As the sports grew in popularity, commentators were warning that reliance on television was a double-edged sword. Sydney's Ron Casey said: 'Rugby League, for instance, has suddenly discovered what it is to make huge amounts of money via television commitment, and is heading fast towards being on television four nights per week. We have a 16-team competition and they all want to have television exposure because they all have sponsors to look after. Over-exposure will be a very big problem. What's the incentive for people to go and see a match?

'Okay, so they're winning on television at the moment. But three or four years down the track, and television will control Rugby League, just as it does cricket. Rugby League administrators are making a lot of money, but they don't seem to realise that their game is slowly but surely being sucked into the same situation as cricket. Rugby League is already starting to accommodate television in every way that it can. For example, the mid-week competition is played in four quarters to fit in a certain quota of TV advertising. Television, when it takes over, starts to tell sports how and where to play. Now that in itself is not such a bad thing. As long as sports administrators understand what is happening to their sports.'

So the made-for-TV Rugby League State-of-Origin series is marketed in the same way as the WSC cricket. It is certainly an exhibition of the skills of the game, but it is marketed as sheer bloody war; the players, built up into the same frenzy as the spectators, can accommodate the hype by turning the game into something little better than a pub crawl.

Rugby League's John Quayle maintains that sport hasn't become more violent since the advent of television — it just looks that way. 'Television has brought the game so close to the public over the last few years with instant replays. If we go back a few years, games were covered by one camera. Replays are in slow motion. People forget that on the field of play, that happens in a split second. When they watch it at home in a lounge room, it is replayed in slow motion, which gives it the wrong aspect altogether . . . I believe that the hard physical contact of defence, the skill of an individual player, his kicking skills, his passing skills, by far outweigh the sight of a person coming off the field with blood on his head.'

However, the warnings of a drop in spectator interest at the playing field have not been lost on the administrators of both Rugby League and VFL football. Expansionism is the antidote to the falling attendances which are the result of television overexposure. Rugby League brought teams from Canberra and Illawarra into the competition, then expanded to the Gold Coast, Brisbane and Newcastle. The VFL sent the Swans to Sydney, and took in teams from Brisbane and Perth. The marketing of the sports in new areas has learnt the lessons of television. Far from its roots as the working man's game, Rugby League is sold as a bright, educated, sophisticated corporate vehicle. The Brisbane Broncos are given elocution lessons to smarten up their performances in front of the camera and the microphone. According to marketing manager Richard Winten: 'If a couple of players stuff it up, we are going to lose corporate Queensland'. The players are dressed up like dandies in double-breasted country shirts, casual trousers, suede jackets and Akubra hats, and they are told to hold down a regular job as well as play football.

Live Sunday television in Melbourne of the Swans' games in Sydney was the financial saviour of that team. Marketing whiz Bob Pritchard used the lessons of WSC and sold the games as highbrow entertainment. Half-time entertainment was a full Hollywood production, complete with Swanettes teams of leggy dancing girls. It didn't matter if the team couldn't play; the fans got value for their entrance dollar regardless, and the club got the live television money from Melbourne. To top it off, the Swans even had a high-profile 'owner' in Dr Geoffrey Edelsten. His gaudy lifestyle, which featured surgeries complete with chandeliers and grand pianos, admirably suited the Swans' need for media exposure in a climate of general opposition to all things that emanated from the southern State. Much of the media and public attention focussed on the most visible player, Warwick Capper, complete with flowing blond locks, white boots and shorts so tight he must have found it painful even to cough. Private ownership of the Swans continues.

South Melbourne's Bobby Skilton, now a football commentator, had been on the receiving end of some on-field unpleasantry when he received the news that he had won the Brownlow Medal for 1968. It was his third Brownlow win, a feat equalled by only three other players
Herald & Weekly Times

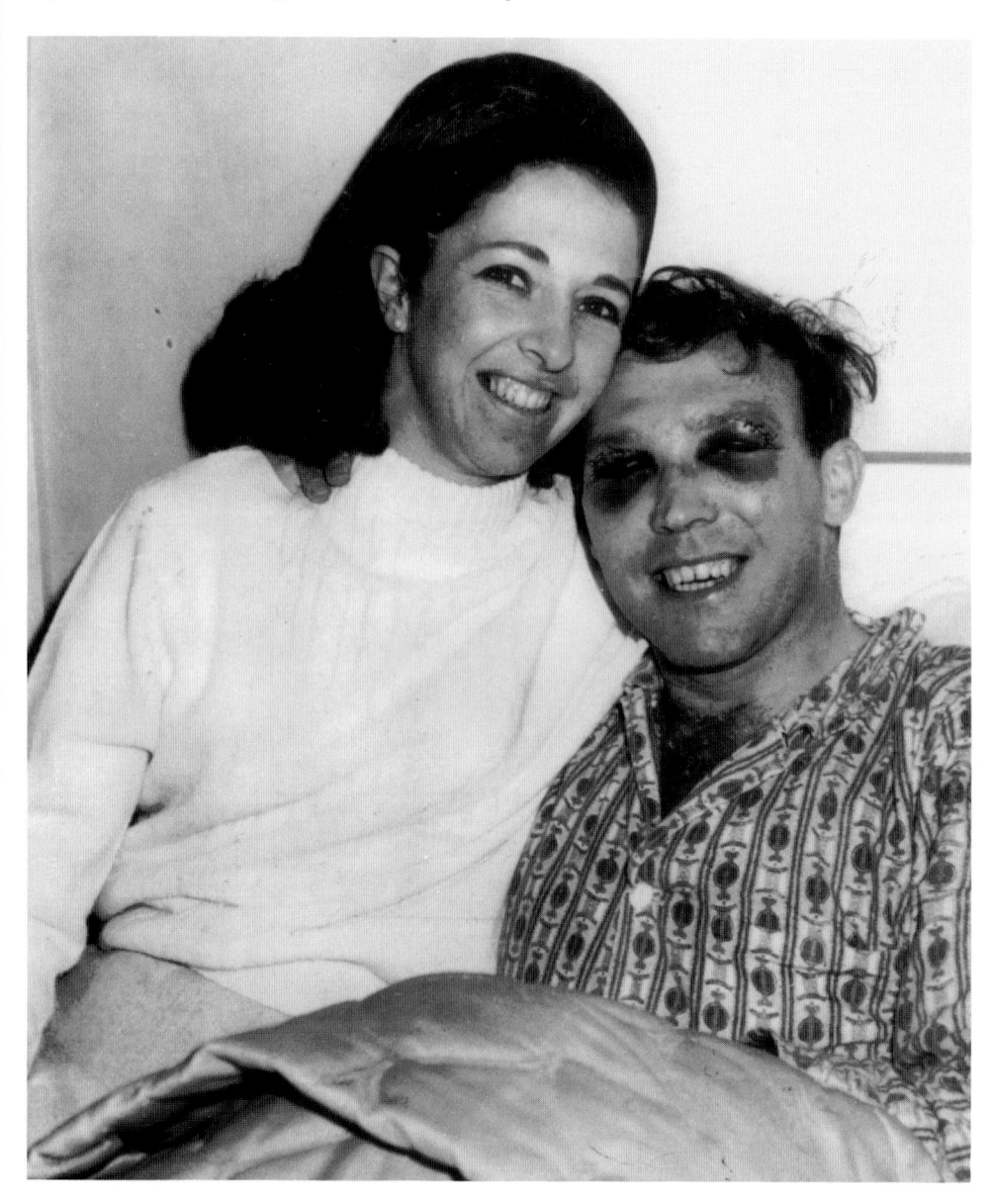

Image Makers

So television has come down to sport with gimmicks. Sometimes the gimmicks are purely technological, like Channel Seven's imaginative Racecam camera mounted for the first time on cars at the 1980 James Hardie 1000. It was pioneering stuff, not accepted internationally until some years later when the American Broadcasting Corporation bought Seven's camera and expertise to highlight their coverage of the Indianapolis 500. The ABC chairman wrote that motor racing without Racecam was like 'Australia without Crocodile Dundee'. The basis of the system was the linking of a video camera, lightweight, aerodynamic and moveable, mounted on a race car, to a helicopter travelling overhead.

Such advances have accelerated the rise of sporting superstars. Who would have thought, for instance, that Australians would have sat glued to television sets at all hours of the morning to watch a yachting race, as they did for the last of the *America*'s Cup events in 1983? Or that millions of viewers would endure the two hours or more of a marathon foot race as they did for Robert de Castella's Brisbane Commonwealth Games win in 1982 and again for his world championship win in Brussels?

We all shared the triumphs and the trials of Robert de Castella. His courageous string of successes in the early 1980s put marathon running on the map and 'Deek' into our hearts
Roger Gould

The inimitable 'Jacko' made the most of his football talents, but his on-field antics didn't necessarily help club solidarity at the four VFL teams he played for. He kept the turnstiles moving with his strong man style and unpredictable behaviour, and made a lot of money with novelty records, advertising contracts and even a TV series in the USA
Herald & Weekly Times

The coverage has also made the sports star the new business king or queen. *America*'s Cup skipper John Bertrand turned his triumph into a personal fortune with books, endorsements and a foot in the door of big international business. De Castella is earning more than a million dollars a year, including a sizeable sum from Adidas, the producers of leisure footwear.

The new wealth of sports stars has given rise to a new figure in sport — the agent. Mark McCormack is the biggest of them all, even controlling Wimbledon as its marketer, negotiator of television rights, and controller of most of the top competitors. In Australia, McCormack's International Management Group has several offices. Their clients include Pat Cash, John Bertrand, John Newcombe, Greg

Image Makers

Norman and Robert de Castella. The modern agent arranges events, negotiates appearance fees, makes travel arrangements, seeks and negotiates endorsements, and tries to control the public image of the client, and in some cases, create one. They are the new image makers. Former VFL player Mark Jackson is a prime example. His image as a loud-mouthed ruffian has helped earn him hundreds of thousands of dollars from such obscure endeavours as an international battery commercial for television, and a US television series. Footballers, once used and abused by club administrators, now mostly have managers to make deals and invest the money properly. Football club secretaries are slow to accept them though, principally because their appearance means the secretaries can no longer pressure naive players into unfavourable contracts. Like television, the influence of agents will only increase as the seasons unfold.

Made-for-television sport produces a new brand of spectator. Not as well informed on accurate analysis as his early twentieth century predecessor, the new spectator is often as violent and mindless as the way in which his game is marketed. The Rugby League State-of-Origin matches, particularly at Brisbane's Lang Park, are invariably marred by violent displays among the crowd. Lang Park is said to be the only sports ground in the world where fans line up for half an hour to buy cans of beer to throw at each other. In the second match of the 1988 series, full cans were used as missiles to hurl at the referee and at New South Wales players after Queensland's hero, Wally Lewis, was sent from the field. Lewis was accused of inciting the crowd to riot by arguing with the Sydney referee over many penalty decisions, and then racing 20 metres to enter a one-on-one scrap, thus converting it into a ten-man mêlée. 'Southerners are all alike', he said. 'They're always whingeing.' Such is the confused relationship between sport, television and the behaviour of crowds and players that no one is quite able to determine which is the cause and which the effect. There was violence in New South Wales–Queensland clashes before television marketed the match as war, but was it more or less than now?

The not-so-pleasant face of sports promotion at Brisbane's Lang Park stadium gave new meaning to the phrase, 'I can feel a Fourex coming on'. In the second round of the 1988 Rugby League State-of-Origin matches, full cans were used as missiles after Queensland hero Wally Lewis was sent off
Action Graphics

Blood, Sweat and Tears

Opposite:
The legendary barracker from the Sydney hill 'Yabba' has his voice stilled for once as he enjoys his lunch during a Test match in 1936. Yabba coined some famous barracking phrases, such as 'git a bag' and 'your length's lousy but you bowl a good width'
News Limited

Perhaps the difference is that brawls, crowd punch-ups, arguments with referees and so on become taken for granted because, like violent scenes on the news, they are colourfully presented in everyone's lounge room.

The commentators, aware that this sort of television pays their million-dollar contracts, lap it up. 'Biffo', Rex Mossop calls it. 'A good punch in the mouth never hurt anyone' is one of his favourite sayings.

There used to be interaction between players and spectators. With the new form of marketing violence in sport, players can sometimes get carried away. Greg Chappell almost single-handedly won a match for Australia against England, and left the field swinging his bat close to the heads of adoring fans. It was lucky no one received a fractured skull. In the 1920s and 1930s spectators seemed to have their love of sports stars returned to them. The most famous barracker of them all was nicknamed Yabba. He was a Balmain rabbit hawker whose real name was Stephen Harold Gascoine, and he entertained crowds and players alike for thirty years from his base camp on the Sydney Cricket Ground Hill. He appeared at every SCG cricket match, head covered in cloth cap and with a sweat rag tied around his neck. There was no swinging a bat to keep Yabba at bay. The English immortal Jack Hobbs, in his last Test in Sydney, was presented with a souvenir boomerang by the crowd on the Hill. At the tea interval, Hobbs walked around the ground, paused at the Hill, and called Yabba out for a chat as the crowd cheered their appreciation. Hobbs told reporters: 'He is a lot of fun. It's a pity there aren't a few like him at Lords. We might not take ourselves so seriously if there were'. Yabba put some of his barracking calls into the language of the nation. 'Git a bag' was Yabba's rebuke for some hapless fielder who missed a catch. There were others. 'You'll have to get the fire brigade to get him out' and 'Your length's lousy but you bowl a good width'. Modern cricket has replaced the likes of Yabba with flag-wavers and those who drape message-bearing banners over grandstands, or wave them enthusiastically — all, of course, for the sake of the television cameras.

Sources and references
Publications consulted for this chapter are:
   Chris Cunneen, 'Elevating and Recording the People's Pastime: Sydney Sporting Journalism 1856–1939' in Richard Cashman and Michael McKernan (eds), *Sport: Money, Morality and the Media* (NSW University Press, 1981); Gary Lester, *The Sun Book of Rugby League* (John Fairfax & Sons, 1983); Terry Smith, *Australian Golf: The First 100 Years* (Lester-Townsend, 1982); Brian Stoddart, *Saturday Afternoon Fever* (Angus & Robertson, 1986).
Interview transcript of the television series 'Blood, Sweat and Tears':
   Ron Casey, Alan McGilvray, John Quayle, Lou Richards, Colin Tatz.
The quotations from Graham Hannan and Richard Winten are from interviews conducted by the author. The quotations from the *Sydney Mail* and *Smith's Weekly* are from Smith, pp.19 and 27 respectively. The quotations from Stoddart are at pp.109, 88, 89, 93 and 102; that from Cunneen is at p.164. The author is indebted for the material on the early sporting press to Stoddart. Material otherwise is derived from the author's own research.

CHAPTER 9

BOUGHT SPORT

Richard Sleeman

In the continuing commercialism of sport in Australia, World Series Cricket (WSC) stands out as the event that led the way. It earned the name of the Great Cricket Hijack when news broke that television proprietor Kerry Packer had bought his own troupe of sixty-six top players. Cricket — indeed, sport — would never be the same again. WSC did more than just introduce the white ball, coloured clothing and night cricket. It blasted sport out of the hands of amateurs and placed it firmly in the care of entrepreneurs and private enterprise. Television and the sponsorship dollar would become gods.

In his book *The Great Cricket Hijack* Christopher Forsyth examined the remarkable origins of WSC. It began as a germ of an idea in the mind of Paul Hogan's manager and comedy straight-man, John Cornell. Cornell and his former colleague on the *Perth Daily News*, Austin Robertson, kicked off a thirteen week World Masters Snooker tournament which was launched on Packer's National Nine network. The series pioneered sports sponsorship to some extent in that Berger Paints was the chief backer. It was an important first step, since Packer would eventually commandeer WSC and Berger would become a major sponsor. Cornell recalls in *The Great Cricket Hijack*:

> 'The cricket side [of our discussions] just wouldn't go away . . . One night we got talking about it again. We were really probing how far we could go with cricketers. I knew we wouldn't be loved by the cricket authorities if we signed up a whole team of cricketers. But suddenly I got to thinking, Why not? What was the Australian Cricket Board anyway? We could do our own thing. It wasn't God or a judge or a policeman — nothing like that. From that point I realised the ACB couldn't stop us.'

At the time, Cornell and Robertson were managing the interests of cricketers Dennis Lillee, Rod Marsh, David Hookes and Tony Greig. Having established the strength of the players' feelings who considered they were being underpaid by the ACB, Cornell and Robertson set about finding a way to get their plans off the drawing board.

> 'By November 1976 I was really caught up in it', said Cornell. 'We knew a lot of players were disaffected with the current pay system. I felt that we had something going for us — with the right idea and, of course, a lot of money for

John Cornell, the journalist turned entrepreneur who conceived World Series Cricket and signed up many of the players. He has also been Paul Hogan's manager, his television straight man as 'Strop' on the Paul Hogan Show, and co-writer and producer of the Crocodile Dundee films
John Fairfax & Sons Ltd

Bought Sport

Kerry Packer, the man who changed the face of cricket, settles down to enjoy the game on the opening of the first World Series Cricket match between Australia and the Rest of the World on 27 November 1977. WSC ultimately brought cricket television rights to the Nine Network and provided the base for the huge popularity of international one-day cricket
News Limited

backing. So, as we stayed up all night discussing ways of getting a better deal for cricketers, I gradually came to the conclusion that the future lay in television. From that point on everything led to Packer. First, I knew him, second, he was in television, third, he had the money — and what's more he had a demonstrated interest in television sport with his million-dollar outlay on the Australian Open Golf Championship. So I went to Kerry.'

As much by chance as anything else, Cornell could not have picked a better time, or a better person to approach. Packer was angered by the ACB's decision to award Test cricket television rights to the Australian Broadcasting Commission for $207 000 over three years. Packer wanted the rights exclusively, not shared; he had been down that road, and failed. The public associated cricket telecasts with the ABC, and once before when the coverage was shared Packer's Nine Network had been trounced in the ratings. Packer had to have cricket to himself. Into this atmosphere walked John Cornell. Packer was immediately taken with the idea. Cornell recalls that he said: 'Why not do the thing properly? Let's get the world's best cricketers to play the best Australians'.

Kerry Packer had a fine teacher in the use of television to promote sports events. His father, Sir Frank Packer, used to order incessant replays of horse-races in which his own gallopers were victorious, and, when his yacht *Gretel* surfed down an Atlantic swell to win an America's Cup race off Newport, he ordered his station to air early in the morning so viewers could see the triumph.

Blood, Sweat and Tears

Between mid-January and April 1977, Robertson signed up thirty-five of the world's best players — a cricket head-hunter in a Sackville suit, as Christopher Forsyth described him. In the division of WSC's $1 shares, Robertson had 15 and a directorship; Cornell was a director with 16 shares; Paul Hogan had 16 and Packer had two. Forty-eight shares were held by a Packer subsidiary, Publishing and Broadcasting Limited, so Packer would always maintain the controlling interest. Robertson worked in secrecy, helped by former player Bob Cowper and the man they had earmarked as their captain, Ian Chappell. It fell to Chappell to choose the players he wanted, and Robertson to do the leg-work in getting them. On 10 January, Lillee signed the eight-page WSC contract guaranteeing him $35 000 a year for three years. Cornell joined Robertson on a trip to New Zealand to sign Greg Chappell and the crowd-pleasing Doug Walters. With a signing-on fee of $11 666, Chappell was to get $35 000 a year for five years plus a $5000 consultant and commentator's fee and, as well, WSC would purchase Chappell's Brisbane home from him for $65 000.

Doug Walters recalled the methods of the WSC head-hunters in his autobiography:

> I first heard of World Series Cricket in Auckland during the Second Test on the 1977 tour of New Zealand . . . I remember Dennis Lillee telling me John Cornell wanted to see me in one of the bottom dressing rooms during the lunch break. When I walked into the room I didn't know what he wanted to see me about. Austin Robertson was with him . . .
> John and Austin . . . told me about the concept they had for playing international cricket in Australia. They didn't have to talk long. I told them to count me in. Sure the $75 000 I was guaranteed for three seasons had plenty to do with that decision but, let's face it, cricket had become a professional game in everything but the players' payments. Players had become the poor relations . . . When they spoke to me, no other players' names were mentioned and I was told the matter had to proceed with the utmost secrecy.

Walters signed his contract in the dressing room during the Melbourne Test in the same year. He and the other players who had committed themselves to WSC saw themselves half-seriously as 'renegades' to Test cricket. Players from the English team also signed up. The captain, Tony Greig, lost his captaincy as a result.

To the cricket establishment WSC was no joke. There were bitter reprisals. Jack Pollard recounted some of them in *Australian Cricket*:

> In Melbourne Ray Bright was barred from grade cricket in 1977–78 and had to play for Footscray Technical College to get practice . . . In England Tony Greig found his daughter in tears when he went to pick her up at school. She had been excluded from a children's party because of what her father had done. Another of the rebels, Derek Underwood, said: 'It was a terrible time for me and my family . . . I sensed that people considered me disloyal, a traitor, a money-grabber and worse, when the truth is, all I was trying to get was a degree of security for my wife and two daughters.'

On a larger scale, as Pollard relates, WSC was not allowed on most of Australia's cricket grounds, and some players were banned from district cricket or from practising with the State squads. But established cricket also learnt a lesson about paying players decently: the Australian Cricket Board enlisted sponsors to reward the cricketers who had remained loyal to it. WSC had forced a nexus between big cricket and money. A major sport was now well and truly bought.

When Packer's lights, erected at the Sydney Cricket Ground at a cost of $1.3 million, were turned on for the first time on 28 November 1978, Ian Chappell led an Australian WSC team on to the field in front of 58 000 spectators. Bought sport had found a new audience. They brought big banners, cheered loudly and abused or

Opposite:
The Sydney Cricket Ground (top) entered a new era with the installation of lights in 1978. Here a vast crowd fills the stadium for a day-night match between Australia and England. The MCG's lights were to come later, in 1985 (bottom). One-day cricket, while decried by the purists, has boosted crowds and brought a flood of money into cricket
Live Action/Roger Gould

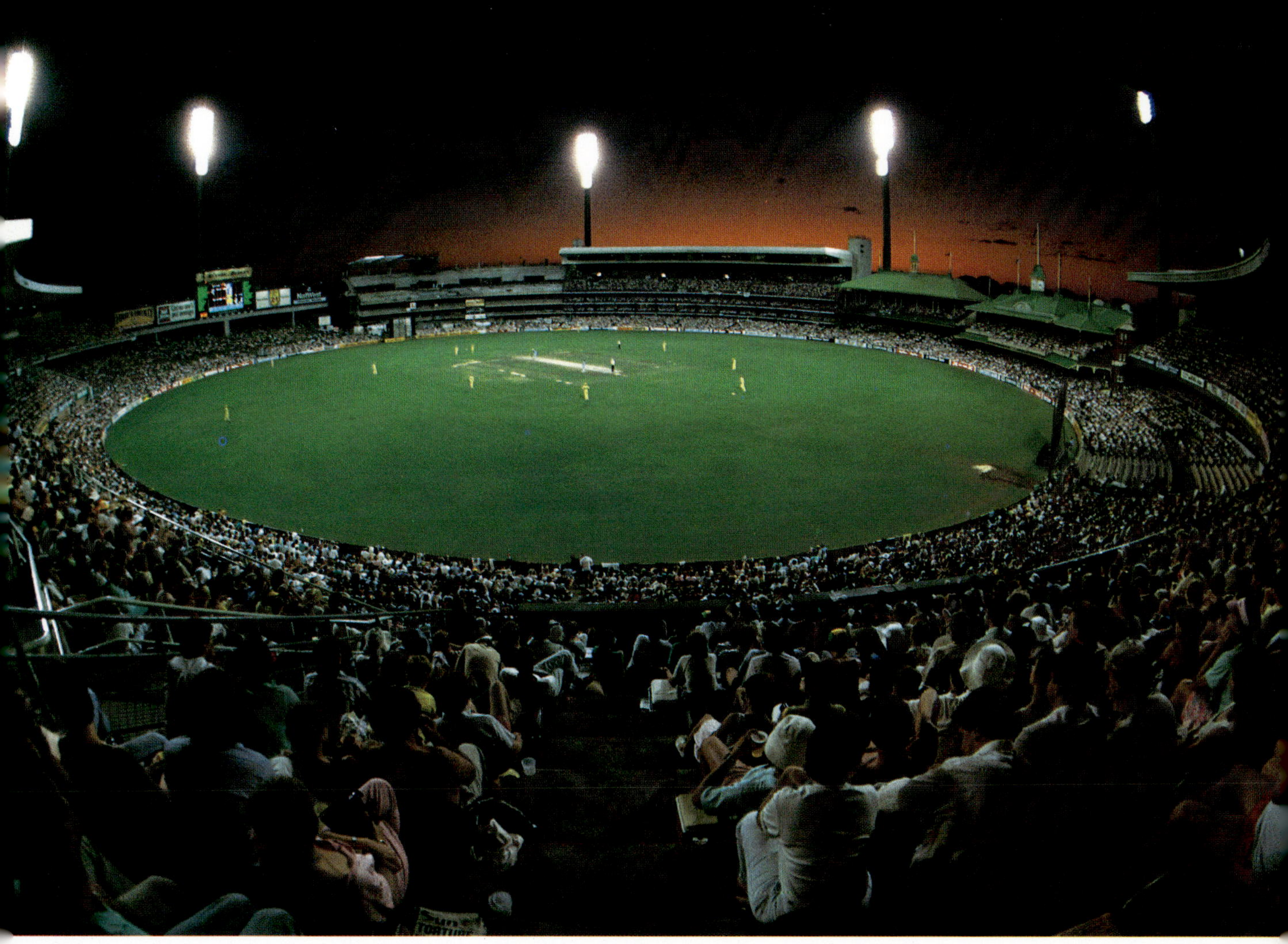

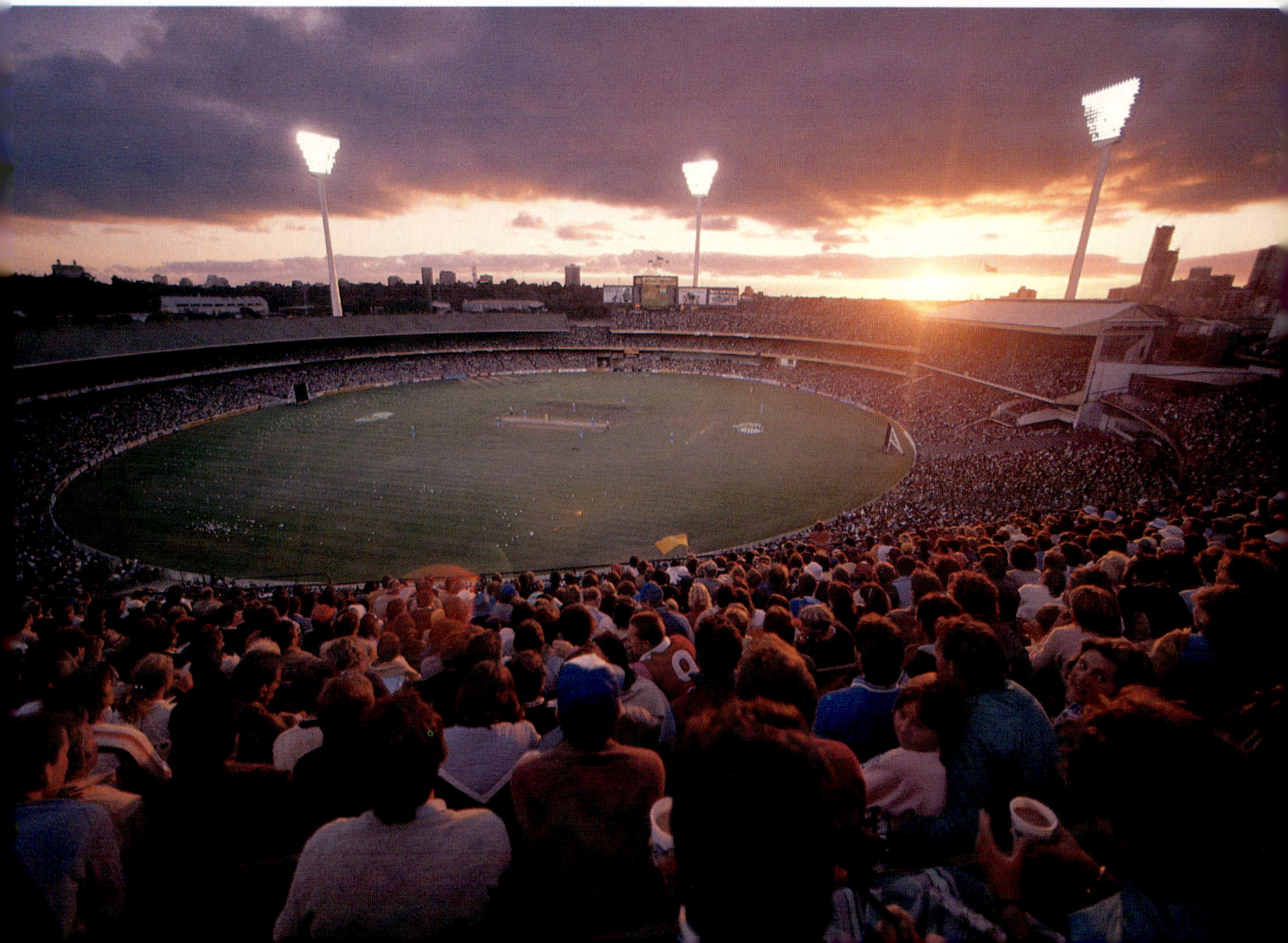

praised the players vehemently. The atmosphere bore little resemblance to established ideas of cricket. Gone was the purity of the white clothing, the leisured stateliness and its connotations of upper-class Englishness. Restraint had given way to hype. There was a white ball; players wore brightly coloured clothing, coloured pads, coloured helmets. The audience was younger and rowdier, and came expecting entertainment.

It wasn't all beer and skittles for Packer. He lost an estimated $4 million on the first year of WSC, and sought to rescue the finances by bringing in more corporate sponsors. He lost far less the second year. During that time he had an enormous personal win. Jack Pollard tells the story:

> When the International Cricket Conference announced that they intended to ban all WSC players from official Tests for two years after their last appearance for WSC, Packer took them to court. The High Court hearing in London lasted thirty-one days and judgment took 5 hours 30 minutes to deliver. The court ruled in Packer's favour, basically on the ground that banning his players was an unreasonable restraint of trade.

The ICC and England's Test and County Cricket Board had to pay costs of more than $A300 000. By implication the victory was also against the Australian Cricket Board, which regarded WSC as an intrusion on to its legitimate territory. The ACB opposed Packer and WSC in every way it could, but after three years of negotiations Packer got what he wanted: exclusive rights to televise big cricket in Australia. The ACB, having suffered crippling financial losses during this time, conceded that it needed WSC's promotional expertise. It was a case of the wheel having turned full circle, and the end forever of an amateurism which cared for officials before players, sponsors and the public.

Other players had been bought and sold well before Kerry Packer's time. The partners in a Melbourne catering firm, Spiers and Pond, were English migrants who understood cricket, and understood how to make a pound out of the game as well. When they failed to entice the novelist Charles Dickens to Australia, they hired a cricket team instead. They brought out the first English touring team, which arrived just before Christmas 1861, after sixty days at sea. Often they played against as many as twenty-two locals, at such obscure venues as Castlemaine in Victoria. It was reported that the tourists drank a little too much of the sponsors' fine wines, and lurched to losses against Castlemaine, among others. But Spiers and Pond didn't lose. The tour made £11 000.

The Aboriginal cricket team, which toured in Australia and then in England, is similarly an early example of sponsorship. Pollard has noted that 'the Melbourne match was conceived more as a contribution to Aboriginal welfare than as a financial venture', but the story, which is told in the chapter 'Black Diamonds', records their exploitation as much as their athletic feats. Interestingly enough, there were some gimmicks on the side in the English tour that might be seen as paralleling Packer's colourful razzmatazz today.

It was a decade before the first white Australian team arrived in Britain, and they too displayed a form of professionalism. Forced to play every day to alleviate the costs of the tour, they refused to play before noon or after 6 p.m. In a newspaper of the day, the *Lillywhite's Companion*, a writer said the Australians 'seriously and perceptibly aggravated the symptoms of a commercial spirit in cricket'. They took half the gate-money and often made sure that a game entered a third day so they could collect another day's money. Even then, top players were attuned to earning a quid from the game, though they were strictly amateurs. The feeling that the colonials wanted to break out of the British harness of strict amateurism boiled over again in the side to tour England in 1911 when six players refused to go because of the terms offered.

An early form of sponsorship pays off as the 1862 All England Eleven is greeted with rapture by the Melbourne crowd outside the elegant Café de Paris. The tourists were sponsored by caterers Spiers and Pond and drew big crowds wherever they went

National Library of Australia

So the roots of rebellion were planted very early. It was television, though, that brought cricket, and sport generally, into the modern era. Television provided potential sponsors with valued exposure. There was no need to beg for money for players or promotions with the introduction of televised sport. The Benson & Hedges tobacco company was among the first to realise the potential of having the company's name plastered all over a televised sports event like cricket that held a captive audience for five days. In 1984, Benson & Hedges pledged $15 million for the next five years for televised sports coverage. Annual prize-money and promotion is set at $2 million.

Just why did television hail a new era in bought sport? Glennys Bell wrote in the *Bulletin*:

> Sport, the way it is played and the conditions under which it is conducted, have been revolutionised by television. A force that has schedules to keep, commercial breaks to observe and ratings to maintain has seen to this.
>
> In tennis, it favors the indoor tournament where weather never upsets play. The synthetic surfaces, which play more slowly than grass, have changed the pace of the game and create problems for players who have to adjust back to grass or clay. In the US Tennis Open, the 90-second change-over period has often been extended to more than two minutes to allow the television networks to play its commercials.

Television likes action. So in Rugby League, rules about scrums and tackles have been changed to quicken the pace of the game. The unlimited tackle rule became the eight-tackle rule, then the six-tackle rule. The same happened in the Victorian Football League where not only the pace of the game but the colour co-ordination of uniforms, even those short shorts, were designed with both colour television and female television audiences in mind.

Television likes prime-time viewing where it can charge bigger advertising rates. Hence the popularity of night games. The men's singles at the Australian Open tennis go well into the night, from daylight to artificial light, bad for players but great for the Seven network that pays $1 million annually for the rights. Sunday used always to be a rest day at Wimbledon. But even that holy ground of tennis now plays its men's singles final on a Sunday as a concession to television audiences worldwide. In cricket, television loves the one-day game — the audience gets a result before it goes to bed.

The need for television to provide advertisers with large audiences has been one of the most powerful forces for change in the nature of televised sports. While aficionados brave every kind of weather and discomfort, television viewers simply push a button. It is this large and ignorant audience which, Bell says, led Christopher Lasch, in *The Culture of Narcissism*, to maintain that sport degenerates as spectators become less knowledgeable. 'They become sensation-minded and bloodthirsty', he wrote. On the other hand television has the power to capture and hold an audience. Television treats sport like any other form of entertainment and promotes it like any other programme against which it may have to compete for viewers, ratings and advertising dollars.

Just who was giving the orders in cricket was evident after the West Indies and Australia played out a tie in front of 98 000 spectators in a one-day final at the Melbourne Cricket Ground. The fact that officials then made a highly suspect attempt to force the West Indies to play a third and technically unnecessary final may only show that commercial pressures were dominant. The public, though, wasn't as gullible as officials hoped. Only 16 000 turned up to watch the game.

Just about every major Australian sporting event has its sponsor. The Australian institution known as the Melbourne Cup has been Fosterised — sponsored by the beer brand of Foster's — to the tune of $10 million over five years, starting with the 1985 event. Carlton and United Brewers struck the deal with the Victorian Racing Club, which led the way for a break in the VRC's traditional attitude to sponsors. The time-honoured Hotham Handicap became, simply, the Dalgety. In 1987 there were four horse-races worth a million dollars each. None would have been so without corporate backing. Apart from the Foster's Melbourne Cup, the others were the Foster's Magic Million at Southport, the Toohey's Golden Slipper in Sydney and the Swan Premium Australian Derby in Perth. Once one institution was sold off, others followed lamely.

The brewers are far and away the biggest buyers of big-time sport. Foster's won the Adelaide Grand Prix in a $6 million deal over three years. The Foster's name was plastered all over the racetrack, as a capacity crowd of 107 000 and viewers in thirty-five countries watched live on television. As a marketing tool on the road to Foster's chairman John Elliott's pledge to 'Fosterise the world', the buying of this event was a masterstroke, if a costly one. Hundreds of millions of potential Foster's drinkers around the world were glued to the event on television.

In amateur sport — which, of course, is amateur in name alone — Adidas is the sugar-daddy. Athletes such as Carl Lewis command as much television time as an Ivan Lendl, and earn almost as much money. Some of the methods of tying up these top-level competitors are straight out of a spy book. It is known that at the world championships in Brussels, a prominent athlete was met by a representative of a shoe manufacturer as the athlete made his way from the dressing room, along the tunnel, to the track. After an exchange of words and a bag containing a pair of shoes and a huge sum of money, the athlete returned to the dressing room, changed his footwear, and went back out into the tunnel.

In 1985 only three international athletes made more than US$5 million. They were boxers Larry Holmes, Marvellous Marvin Hagler and Thomas Hearns. By 1988 there

A triumphant Wayne Gardner raises his trophy in the winner's stand after winning the Swan Premium 500cc Motorcycle Grand Prix at Phillip Island in 1989.
Live Action

Bike fans from all over Australia gathered at the highly successful inaugural motorcycle racing Grand Prix at Phillip Island, Victoria, in 1989.
Live Action

were at least ten times as many, with technological advancements in television coverage bringing wider exposure internationally for tennis players like Ivan Lendl ($9 million) and Boris Becker ($6 million), and golfers like Greg Norman and Sevvy Ballesteros ($7 million). Australians were swept up in the money spiral. In 1987 Norman was the highest earning sportsman in history, but there were other Australians closing quickly. When he won the world 500cc motor cycling championship in 1987, Wayne Gardner freewheeled his way to a $4 million fortune. The *Bulletin* reported:

> It may be apocryphal, but the story of Gardner's rise from unemployed fitter-and-turner to world fame is said to have started when he walked into the office of former International Management Group consultant Harris Barnett in London. Gardner is supposed to have dumped his only money in the world on Barnett's desk, divided it equally into two piles — one for his fare home, and the other for Barnett to represent him. The agent gambled on the brash young Aussie who now leaves a $165 000 Porsche garaged in Australia, some Hondas in England, and a $250 000 Ferrari Testarossa for use in Monte Carlo, which he now calls home.

Japanese, French and Australian companies are all doing business with Gardner these days. Endorsements and licensing contracts are held with the chic Kusihtani Leather boutiques in Japan, Rothmans, Honda, Gaerne Boots, Shoei, Michelin tyres and Swan Lager. Over three years Swan will pay Gardner some $4 million for his endorsement. In the heart of television and technology in electronics, Gardner is movie-star material in Japan. His life-story, in Japanese, is a runaway bestseller. There is a W. Gardner's signature range of RayBan sunglasses and even Wayne Gardner jigsaw puzzles. Other Australians earning more than $1 million annually are Wimbledon champion Pat Cash ($2 million) and veteran golfer Bruce Crampton ($1.2 million). Television has prompted a rash of nostalgia events, and Crampton is earning many times more now on the televised veterans circuit than he ever made in his youth.

On Boxing Day 1986 the VFL announced that the Sydney-based production company controlled by Basil Sellers' Linter Group, Broadcom Australia Ltd, would have exclusive rights to 'wholesale' domestic and international TV and video rights to Australian football for six years. The figure was $24.55 million. In order to whet the appetite of international viewers, the VFL went overseas with its product. It played an international football challenge in Ireland, the Courage Cup between Carlton and North Melbourne at The Oval in London, and Aussie Bowl '86, a Grand Final replay at the Yokohama Stadium near Tokyo. The game was on sale and display internationally.

There is always an inherent danger for the sponsor. Terry Maher, writing in the *Financial Review*, summed up the dilemma:

> Unlike death and taxes, the only thing predictable about sport is that its elemental and human characteristics make it unpredictable. Like any other business, you can hedge your exposure by investing in an outfit run by professional management with the organisational ability and resources to hit a mass market. But even skills and money don't necessarily buy success on a competitive field of play. The first rule in placing a bet on a sports sponsorship is to be prepared to lose your dough as well as face. Sports investments are definitely for life's risk-takers.

Almost every major sport is moving toward television and international exposure for its future. The tobacco industry, with no avenue for direct television advertising, now sponsors about twenty-three different sports at an annual cost of around $15 million. Other smaller companies have joined the headlong rush.

Even the minor sports like 18-foot skiff sailing are finding sponsors. Grand Prix sailing, as it is known, is presented by Michael Edgley International at a cost of $8 million. Basil Sellers, a multimillionaire businessman, has an interest. Foster's has a skiff. Alan Bond's Swan Premium kicked off the first leg of Grand Prix sailing in Fremantle during the America's Cup campaign. The event then moved on to New Zealand, America, Yugoslavia and finally Sydney. Everywhere, sponsors are clamouring for sports packages to buy — but only televised ones with a wide exposure. Foster's chief executive Peter Bartels explained why: 'We are looking only at major ticket items like the Australian Grand Prix and the Melbourne Cup. There is not a lot of sport left to buy in Australia. We'll be looking more towards overseas events with an international flavour that we can bounce back to Australia. We may have plateaued Foster's as a brand in Australia but our growth is coming from the south of England and the west coast of the US. I rank that Foster's Adelaide Formula One Grand Prix our single most successful sponsorship in 1986. It got us to an international audience of 500 million beer drinkers.'

Suddenly, a year later, the brewers were scaling down their involvement. Bill Widerberg, chief executive of Bond Brewing, said the company had jumped in to support everything from lawn bowls to hang-gliding and marbles. 'When you get the amount of criticism alcohol markets get from sections of the community for involvement in sports, plus astronomical price rises in sports sponsorship, then cap it off with a research report that questions its worth, you have to look at the dollar value you are getting.' The report he referred to was commissioned by Bond Brewing, Carlton and United Breweries, Ford Australia and Philip Morris, and advised that 'the value in terms of company profile in supporting anything but major televised events is questionable'. It also said that there was a substantial fall in the proportion of people who claimed that sponsorship would increase the interest in a sponsor's product — from 22 per cent in 1983 when sponsorship was still reasonably novel, to 13 per cent in 1986. It concluded that the impact of sports sponsorship had clearly lessened.

Anyone who went to the biggest sports event in Australia's history — the 1986–7 *America*'s Cup in Fremantle — would not have known that sports sponsorship might be under question. The Cup was the corporate Olympics, no doubt about it. And somewhat ironically, too, since yachting has long been the last bastion of good, old-fashioned amateurism. Sir Frank Packer, the first Australian challenger with *Gretel* in 1962, was a blunt, stubborn, high-powered media magnate. He was born rich, and could afford to back the challenge without outside sponsors, and since television in Australia was barely six years old, there wasn't the exposure to interest a sponsor. Yachtsmen, skipper and staff were all enthusiastic amateurs. Sir Frank's next challenger *Dame Pattie* probably pioneered *America*'s Cup sponsorship when Bradford Cotton Mills Ltd unveiled a new cloth, Kadron, and announced it would weave sails for *Dame Pattie* out of the new material.

It was the first little step into a sports marketing event that would be unrivalled in Australian history. Seventeen yachts took part at Fremantle. Sponsorship of the six Australian contenders totalled $51 million. The American footwear company Nike, for example, was a sponsor of the *Kookaburra* syndicate. It used the Cup as a chance to market an entire new line of sailing gear, including deck shoes, shirts and pants.

Despite advertising restrictions, the *America*'s Cup still offered corporations the opportunity for unparalleled international exposure. Additionally, sponsors could, as analyst Peter Ruehl suggested, 'simultaneously appear magnanimous about it'. Construction costs to yachts and accommodation for additional tourists cost around $100 million. Money spent on operations and other equipment such as public transport and facilities cost another $120 million. The *America*'s Cup becomes sport no longer. In terms of working hours, the nautical madness in Fremantle generated the equivalent of 14 400 jobs with a total income of about $244 million.

Alan Bond's business empire enabled him to pour millions into the successful bid for the America's Cup in 1983, and his unsuccessful defence of it in Perth in 1987. Even in yachting adversity the mass exposure of the Bond breweries' Swan Lager boosted recognition and sales
Photobank/All Sport

Australia's contenders were sponsored to the yard-arm. *Australia III* and *IV*, carrying Alan Bond's hopes for a successful defence, sailed into battle on a sea of Bond Brewing dollars — some $18 million. The Bank of Hong Kong and Amway weighed in with an additional couple of million, while the Nine Network paid for rights to film exclusively from the deck of the boats and for access to racing headquarters. *Kookaburra II* and *III* had $15 million from Parry Corporation, the Seven Network and Digital Computers. *South Australia* had $8 million from Woolworths, Ampol and Australian National Railways, while *Steak 'n' Kidney* had $10 million from Powerplay and the owner and property developer, Sidney Fischer.

The battle on water paled into insignificance beside the battle in the sponsors' boardrooms. Carlton and United Breweries had to have an answer to Bond Brewing's saturation exposure in the *America*'s Cup. So CUB tipped in $4 million to the *Kookaburra* challenge. It was money exceptionally well spent, since *Kookaburra* eventually became the defender. Throughout the world during the final series, it was the Foster's name that 250 million viewers saw internationally, not the Black Swan symbol of Bond Brewing. Even the losers were happy with their portion of 'bought sport'. Ian Chrichton, national marketing manager for Bond Brewing, said he was 'particularly happy' with the results. Referring to a survey by the Roy Morgan Research Centre into Cup-associated brand awareness among twelve major sponsors, he said there had been '48 per cent unprompted brand awareness'. Chrichton said: 'You can't beat that. For a big event such as the *America*'s Cup, there is only room for one association, and we came across head and shoulders above every other sponsor. It was instrumental in establishing a new, full-strength beer into the Australian market. It gave us a credible vehicle to promote Swan Premium as a national brand.'

As in all 'bought sport', there comes a time to pay the piper. The *Australia* defence was often inconvenienced by having to give time, yachtsmen and facilities over for the sponsor's use. It wasn't just because of a slower boat that the *Australia* defence effort was sunk by the *Kookaburra*. Commitments to Bond Brewing of the kind mentioned took no small effort. Also, the majesty of *America*'s Cup racing — for so long the domain of the rich and powerful — lost a considerable amount of its highbrow status by selling off to brewers. Harold Vanderbilt or Sir Thomas Octave Murdoch Sopwith must have been rolling in their graves as *Stars and Stripes* sailed back to a tumultuous victory welcome in Fremantle flying a Budweiser beer spinnaker.

In the lesser sports, sponsors aren't quite so demanding, simply because the sums involved are nothing like those of the *America*'s Cup or Grand Prix racing. But the sports body sells its soul, nonetheless. The Australian Athletic Union was supported by a $1.7 million deal over three years between 1984 and 1987. The Australian junior team, sponsored by the sugar industry, finished fifth at the world championships in Athens, behind the traditional athletics nations, the USA, the USSR, East Germany and West Germany. It represented a highly credible result, one which would not have been possible without corporate financial backing of the trip. As the time drew near for renegotiation, the sugar industry's deal began to taste not so sweet. Marketing manager John Payne said: 'In terms of pure public relations we have struggled with this sponsorship. Athletics is not exactly what you would call a high profile event. People were generally disappointed with the numbers which turned up to events. At the Nationals, which is the biggest athletics event in Australia, you might get 2000. And they are friends and relatives of the competitors. Australian athletics doesn't have any personalities. If I asked you now to name the top athletics personalities, you'd say Darren Clark, Robert de Castella and Clayton Kearney, and be pretty much stuck after that. It would be nice to be involved with a sport which has a higher profile. But most of the major sports have been taken and the money is out of our league anyway.'

Events don't come much larger than the Olympics, and it isn't just the events which have been bought. Most of the players and competitors — the most prominent ones at least — were bought well before they reached Seoul for the 1988 Olympic Games. Australia chose several highly paid competitors in its Seoul team. Marathoner Robert de Castella had contracts with a number of sponsors including Adidas; Grant Kenny was part of a widely circulated Kelloggs NutriGrain campaign, swimmer Jon Sieben was contracted to Fury Ford car sales, cycling world champion Martin Vinnicombe to Les Edwards Transport, and swimmer Janelle Elford sported the colours of Club Méditerranée. The old stickler for amateurism, Avery Brundage, would have done cartwheels about this situation in his days as International Olympic Federation chairman.

Perhaps there had been a precedent in the gifts and riches showered on Spyros Louis, the small-framed Greek post office messenger, who beat Edwin Flack at the first modern Games in 1896. Women took off their jewellery and hurled it at Louis's feet, doves with small Greek flags attached were let loose, and Princes George and Nicholas ran to greet the winner, accompanying him up the straight to the finish. One man offered the hand of his daughter and a dowry of a million drachmas; another a barrel of sweet wine; a tailor offered to clothe the winner for life. A barber offered a lifetime of free shaves and the owner of a chocolate factory offered 2000 pounds of chocolate. Even the peasants arrived with sheep and cattle as gifts. Spyros Louis never raced again. He was forever tainted as a professional.

Australia's first brush with professionally 'tainted' Olympians was in Paris in 1900. Donald Mackintosh of Melbourne, 'the best shot in the world at the present time' according to the *Grand World of Sport*, is not officially listed. It was alleged that Mackintosh received stake money. He competed for a stake of up to £200, as well as a trophy, and that is the only apparent reason for his non-inclusion on the

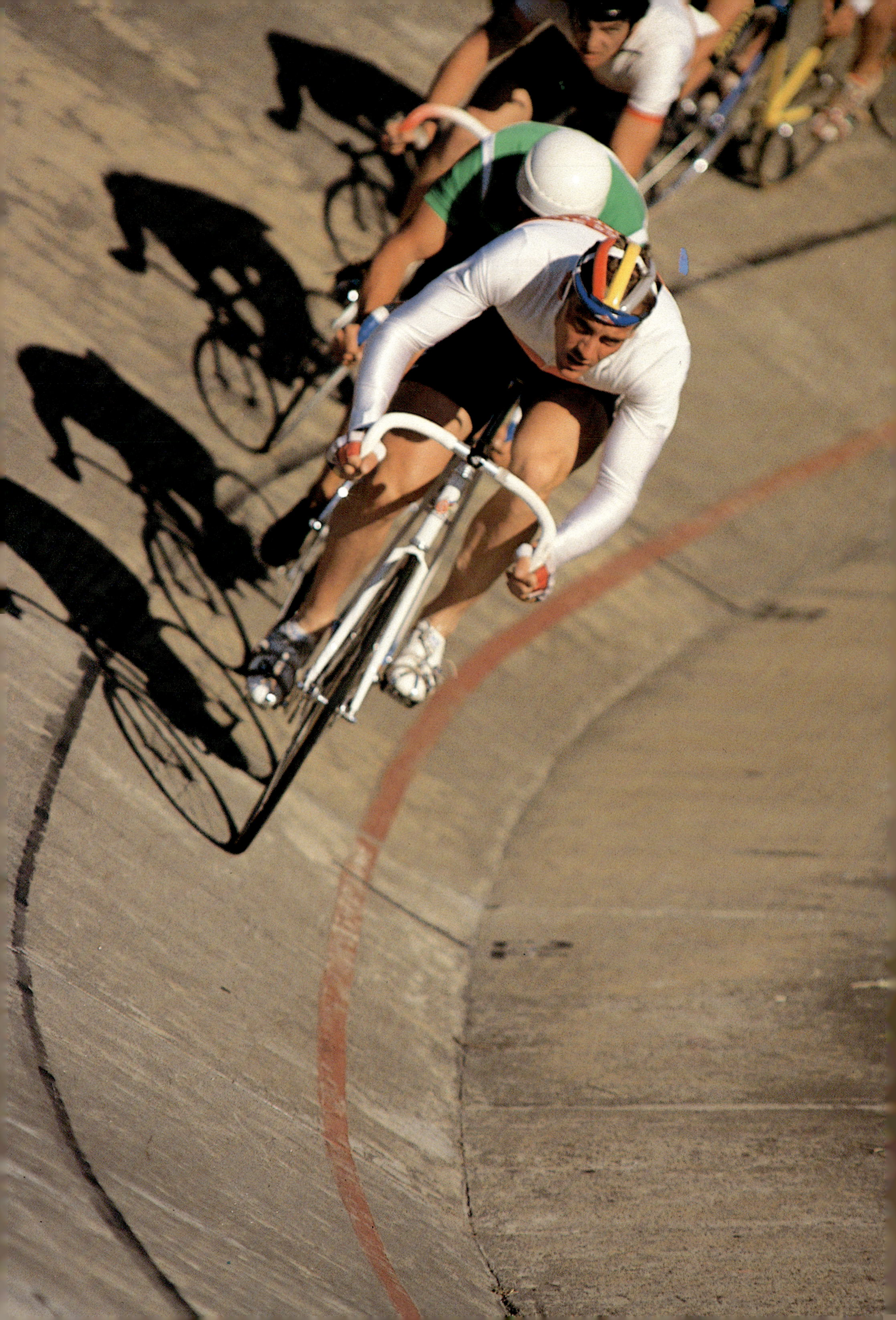

World champion individual time trial cyclist Martin Vinnicombe is among a number of Australians with lucrative contract arrangements which are structured so that they are able to stay within the newly defined boundaries that enabled them to compete for their country in the 1988 Olympic Games at Seoul, South Korea. Vinnicombe was a silver medallist in his event at the 1988 Games.

Live Action: Acikalin

official register of Olympic champions. By the London Olympics in 1908, any idea that Australians may have been 'bought' was well and truly quashed. The London team, comprising fourteen athletes and the 1908 Wallaby Rugby Union team, survived on £200, and had to pay its own fares. The 1912 Olympics in Stockholm became one of the most notorious for professionalism — or, at least, for over-reaction to it from officials. The American Indian, Jim Thorpe, became a legend, winning the decathlon and pentathlon gold medals, but in January the following year they were withdrawn when officials discovered he had been paid $60 a month to play basketball. Forty-one years later, on his deathbed, Thorpe had his amateur status returned, his name re-enlisted in the record books, and the two gold medals given to his family.

Many times throughout Australian sports history individual sportsmen have fallen foul of officials for allegedly being bought by sponsors. Not the least of them is the greatest sporting name of all, Sir Donald Bradman. Back in 1930, the song 'Our Don Bradman' was composed during the Don's innings of 309 in a day at Leeds. It was written by Jack O'Hagan (who also left us the classic 'Road to Gundagai'), and the sheet music sold 40 000 copies within its first week. Bradman was sent £1000 by a businessman. General Motors gave him a Chevrolet. Predictably, the Australian Cricket Board hauled him over the coals. Bradman also had a commercial contract with a sports store and provided newspaper and radio commentary. Sports historian Brian Stoddart: 'The Australian Cricket Board tried to ban that kind of income being derived from sporting success. Bradman toughed it out and said that if the Cricket Board was going to adopt that attitude, then he wouldn't be able to play in the Test Series in 1932–3. The Cricket Board backed down because they knew very well that Bradman was the one person who made the difference to the Gates, and the Gates were then what determined the Cricket Board's financial success. So Bradman was a very early example of the sorts of commercial pressure that could be mounted upon sports associations that were trying to maximise their income.'

In the early days, competitors tried to maximise their incomes, too, but more often than not by deception or trickery. Turn-of-the-century sport was accompanied by a great deal of gambling. And competitors would do almost anything to ensure they finished with some of the funds. It was as much a case of bought sport as any of Kerry Packer's pyjama cricket matches. Take the day at the Melbourne Cricket Ground, for instance, when 30 000 people turned up in 1901 for the final day of the Austral Wheel Race. No single sporting event had attracted more spectators in Australia's history. The big drawcard was a colourful Irish-American named 'Plugger' Bill Martin. Martin first appeared in local competition in 1895, and was said to have spent thirteen days in Adelaide Gaol for thumping an official. Although a veteran at 42, Martin won the race, and the bookmakers paid out huge sums. Everyone suspected that Martin had bribed most of his opponents. The sporting purists danced on the grave of professional cycling, and some other big-betting sports like foot-running. They claimed that as soon as money entered into sport, that would be the end of it.

Some sports survived the domination of money. Rugby Union — its players known as 'Lilywhites' because of their enduring amateurism — still claims to be unaffected by money. It's nonsense really. Even the Australian team was sponsored in 1988 by Ricoh cameras to the tune of $400 000. Any player wanting to go to South Africa can earn a giant pay cheque. South Africa has bought entire cricket teams and is planning the same for Rugby Union.

Sometimes athletes can be paid not to do things. Rugby Union's most capped player Simon Poidevin was set to earn $30 000 from Carlton and United Breweries for a television commercial, endorsing a socially responsible product, namely low alcohol beer. CUB's bitter rival, Toohey's, was a major sponsor of Rugby Union, and secret talks were held to prevent Poidevin from doing the commercial. It is understood he knocked back the commercial in favour of a promise from the Australian

Rugby Union that he would have the national team captaincy. In fact the Wallaby Grand Slam-winning captain, Andrew Slack, made an unexpected comeback, and was awarded the captaincy in preference to Poidevin. Later, under bitter and controversial circumstances, Poidevin retired from international rugby.

During the height of the drama surrounding Australia's participation in the boycott ridden Moscow Olympics, it was again money that stopped certain competitors from going. Former Federal Sports Minister John Brown said: 'The fact that some Australian athletes were paid not to go was an obscenity. Now I'm not in any way detracting from the record of those great Australian athletes like Tracey Wickham and Raylene Boyle who succumbed to that temptation. But it was an under-the-lap payment by the Government which to me was bordering on the obscene and it should never have happened.'

Brown is also outspoken on the role of sponsorship in sport: 'I'm pleased to see the tobacco companies' influence in Australian sport is waning. When I became the Minister back in 1983, the national budget for sport was about $6 million, the contribution then by the tobacco companies to sport throughout Australia was $13 million and it was quite ludicrous for the then Government to be criticising tobacco companies.

'There is not the same urgency now to have tobacco sponsorship in sport. And the more it retreats, the better — the happier I am. But tobacco companies and breweries apart, there are a lot of other corporate identities in Australia that have now seen the value in having their name associated with sport. And I think that's a very healthy move. I like to see our élite athletes and even our battling athletes, the kids in the juniors, having an opportunity to play sport with funding, not only from Governments and public bodies but also from private institutions, companies and private individuals. It's a healthy move.'

Mr Brown's views have found a few critics, especially traditionalists like the world's oldest living Test cricketer, Australia's Hunter 'Stork' Hendry. On the occasion of his 93rd birthday, Hendry said, ' big money has ruined sport . . . We have moved away from the origins of sport in general and cricket in particular. It's a completely different game today to what it was when I was playing. And the intrusion of money is to blame'. John Brown countered: 'There are people who think that the private dollar can corrupt sport. I don't think that is necessarily true. For instance, there has been a continuing argument surrounding Rugby League, the fact that it is called the Winfield Cup. I don't think that anyone is going to go out and buy their first packet of cigarettes because they see the Winfield Cup or Winfield sign on a fence. I've objected to good-looking girls handing out cigarettes at the gates to the football, and the tobacco companies have now withdrawn that practice, which is good. But I've never believed that the name Rothmans or Philip Morris or Peter Jackson or something is going to start people smoking . . . The concept of pure amateurism was obviously something that most sports lovers cherish. But amateurism had to go because it's very difficult for someone who is not extraordinarily wealthy to maintain the rigour of training excellence to compete on the international level unless they have been heavily sponsored. It's not a matter of amateurs competing for money. It's a matter of needing that professional financial back-up if they're going to achieve excellence on the world stage.'

There could be no pastime more typically Australian, nor more fundamentally amateur than surf lifesaving. In the early days people had to bathe secretly out of the back of English-style bathing boxes on wheels, and only before 6 a.m. or after sunset, and never on Sundays. Then in 1902 William H. Gocher advertised on three successive weeks that he would defy the law and surf at noon on a Sunday. On the third Sunday, a police sergeant waded in to arrest him. The Police Commissioner listened to Gocher's pleas for individual freedom to surf without restriction, and decided that police should not interfere provided bathers were discreetly dressed. There was an outcry from pious coastal dwellers who preferred the 'rapture of the lonely shore' to watching bathers. Probably the last of the arrests was that of the Rector of St Mary's, Waverley, at Bondi beach and, when he was prosecuted, a group of would-be bathers rallied to his cause, forming the Bondi Surf Bathers' Lifesaving Club on 6 February 1906 — the first surf club in the nation. The stillwater lifesaving methods of Dr Hall were recommended for surf lifesaving. These included advice to 'promote breathing by exciting the nostrils with snuff, hartshorn or volatile salts, or by tickling the throat with a feather'.

The first surf carnival — starting an Australian tradition recognised the world over — was at Manly in 1908 when spectators were reported to 'howl with laughter' at the march-past of men clad in flannel underwear. Now there are 2000 clubs and half a million lifesavers. And how times have changed. The iron man event is the focal point of competition. When Hayden Kenny of Alexandra Headland won the the first national iron man title in 1966, he was showered with praise and sand, but precious little else. His son, Grant, started a successful iron man reign by winning first in 1980 and, with the onset of sponsorship and television coverage, the victory turned Grant Kenny into a wildly wealthy, instantly recognisable, national celebrity. His contract to endorse NutriGrain breakfast cereal was reported to be worth $130 000 annually. He set the scene for others to follow. Coalminer's son Darren Mercer won the first iron man Grand Prix series and $80 000 in prize-money. Guy Leech earns well in excess of $150 000 annually from prize-money and endorsements.

As in every sport where money has taken hold, it has brought huge controversy with it. Most clubs are administered by well-meaning but amateur officials. They want to keep their sport that way, while the national and State bodies know they can only prosper with television and sponsorship. Leech and a number of iron men quit the famous Manly club in search of a better deal in Queensland. Australia's fastest man on sand, Clayton Kearney, quit another traditional club, Coogee, because he wasn't paid the percentage of prize-money which the National Council recommended. National Council spokesman Ian McLeod said: 'We are trying to educate the clubs about sport in the modern era. But tradition dies hard'.

Surfboard riding has undergone just as drastic an overhaul, due solely to sponsorship and television coverage. When Bernard 'Midget' Farrelly won the world's prestige event, the Makaha International in 1963, he returned proud and penniless from Hawaii. By 1986, with Australia having produced world champions like Mark Richards and Tom Carroll, the 24-event world circuit was worth $735 000 in prize-money. Australia staged eight of these events, worth $235 000. The 'Big Australian', Broken Hill Proprietary Company, pumped up its sagging image in the industrial city of Newcastle by staging the richest event in the history of surfing, and chalked up another first by having it covered live by NBN 3 television. Beaurepaire successfully introduced night surfing and attracted 50 000 spectators to Cronulla beach for an event marred only by the untimely arrival of a southerly buster. Former world champion Richards flogged beer. The current champion, Carroll, sold yoghurt and Alfa Romeo motor cars. Later he was to sign a package for sponsorship for allegedly more than a million dollars.

Surf Association spokesman, Graham Cassidy, has seen the sport grow and prosper with the introduction of cash. He said: 'Surfers used to live by the seat of their boardshorts. They only survived by camaraderie, billeting each other and sharing transport. Their schedules were more hectic than tennis or golf and they were busting a gut to make a buck. For the top sixteen, at least, times have changed. When I look at Mark Richards's four consecutive world titles under those early conditions, I see a far greater feat than Bjorn Borg's five Wimbledons'.

Surfing has spawned an enormous industry. When the 1912 Olympic 100-metre freestyle gold medallist, Duke Kahanamakou, rode the waves at Freshwater in Sydney in 1915, he used a board designed by him and built by Hudson's timberyard in Sydney. He finished it off himself, sanding it to the required shape. Now the surfboard industry is worth hundreds of millions of dollars annually. The surf

Blood, Sweat and Tears

Guy Leech, winner of the Coolangatta Gold iron man event in 1984 and 1985. Leech earns well in excess of $150 000 annually from prize-money and endorsements, and the exploits of the iron man have done no harm to tourism of Australia's Gold Coast
Live Action: Acikalin

clothing industry is worth hundreds of millions more. Cassidy said: 'We can offer a pretty attractive package these days to the potential sponsor. In the past, we used to talk about lifestyle and the youth market, but we've become more pragmatic. Now we talk about surf contests as sales vehicles. We have the ability to stage a major event on a beach in the heart of a major population centre for six or seven days and promote the heck out of it. We can get council approval to seal off the area and blanket it with promotional material. What we're really selling is on-site exposure plus a vehicle to string a sales promotion around. Sponsors can use that to launch a new product or to reinforce product image. The fact of the matter is that the novelty value of surfing has gone. Now we're talking dollars and cents'. Such is the effect of this cash infusion that the 1960s image of a surfer as a drop-out and layabout has changed to the stage where they are high-level executives.

Whether in man or machine, the mighty dollar has blanketed sports arenas and

The spectacular start of the Coolangatta Gold: a perfect Gold Coast setting
Live Action: Acikalin

television sets. If the Australian motor racing Grand Prix is the biggest single sponsored event in the nation, it is interesting to see how the sport survived in the year that television came to Australia, 1956. It was the year of Australia's then-largest motor racing crowd, estimated at 125 000, for that year's Grand Prix, won by Stirling Moss at Albert Park, Melbourne. There was no such thing as a sponsor like Foster's. The promoter was the Light Car Club of Victoria and its efforts sold more than 75 000 tickets. But swindlers and counterfeiters sold and printed tens of thousands more, while others entered through makeshift hessian fencing around the track. The Light Car Club of New South Wales, formed in 1931, persuaded the Bathurst City Council to develop a scenic strip of road on Mount Panorama into a motor racing circuit. Farmers considered the noise of motor cars would prevent their cows from producing sufficient milk and formed a committee of protest. Construction went ahead though, and was completed in 1938 at a cost of $55 000.

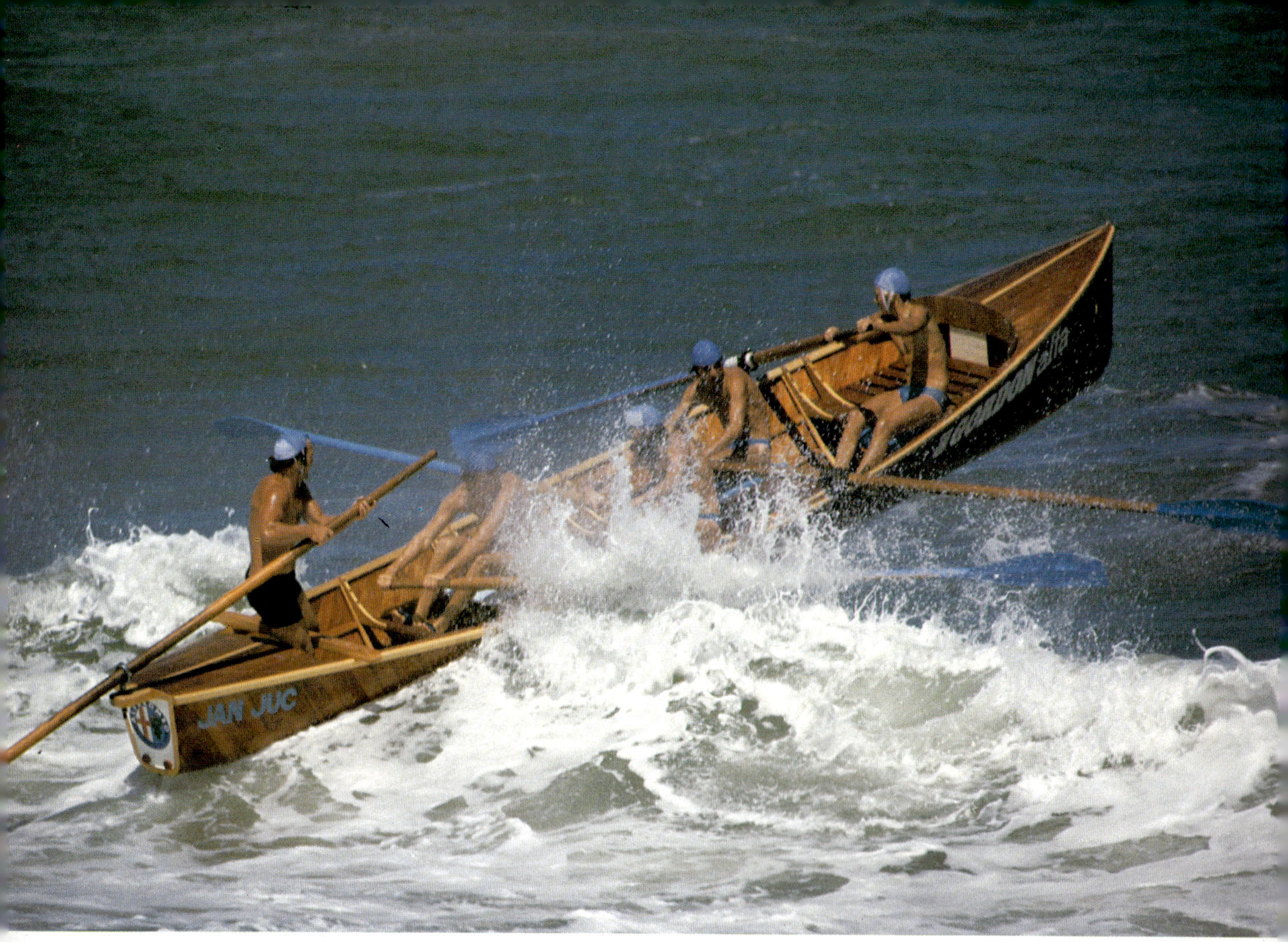
JAN JUC

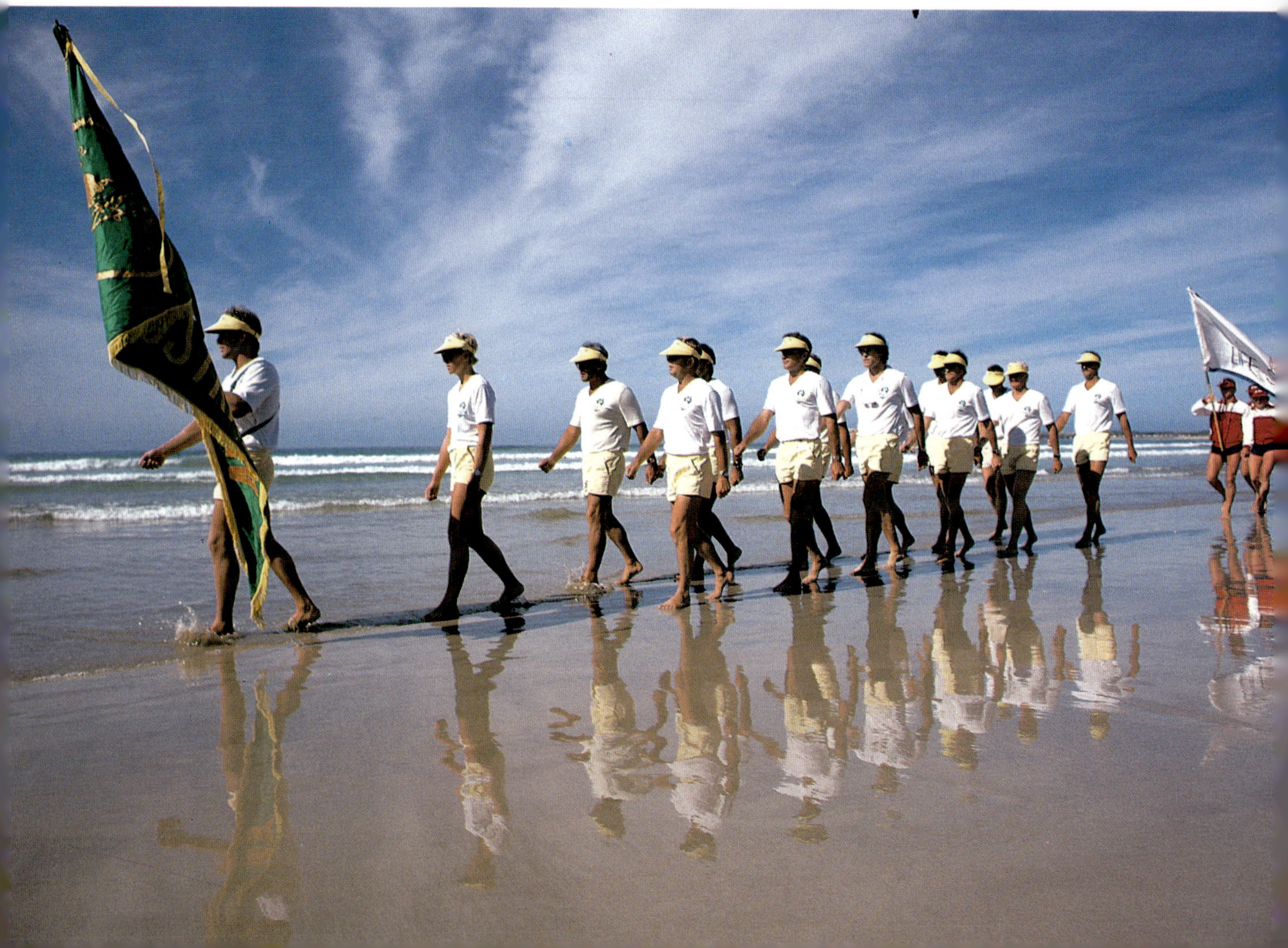

Bought Sport

Opposite, top:
Spectacular action in a surf boat race at an Australian Carnival, a part of the Australian summer tradition. The volunteer surf lifesaving clubs have to battle for funds, but the 'iron man' competition, which was once just part of the fun, now carries a fortune in prize-money and endorsements
Roger Gould

Opposite, bottom:
The teams stride out in a march past, a part of every Australian surf carnival. The Australian Surf Lifesaving team competing against the Rest of the World in the 1985 Australian Games at Ocean Grove, Victoria. The first march past in 1908 brought 'howls of laughter' at the men in their baggy flannels. Aside from their carnival competitions, the lifesavers make many rescues each year in dangerous conditions
Live Action: Acikalin

Right, top:
Champion Australian surfer Tom Carroll is a picture of strength and poise as he competes in a competition on the Australian 'circuit', now the most lucrative in the world. Commercial sponsorship of surf riding is plainly evident. Carroll won world titles in 1983–4 and 1984–5, but his refusal to go to South Africa cost him a chance at the third title
Live Action: Acikalin

The first Australian to make the 'big time' in world surfing was Bernard 'Midget' Farrelly, who in 1963 won the Mahaka International at Hawaii, the biggest international contest of the time. The first properly organised world championships took place at Manly, New South Wales, in 1964, and again Farrelly won. He took the title brilliantly, riding the last possible wave before his time expired
News Limited

Adelaide turned it on with their first Formula One Grand Prix in 1985: Australian and former world champion Alan Jones hurtles around a corner
Live Action: Acikalin

Englishman Peter Whitehead won the first race on the circuit, without a helmet so he could hear his motor revving, and in front of a crowd of 30 000, at an average speed for 40 laps of 70 miles per hour. When Australian Alan Jones won the world championship for Grand Prix drivers in 1980 he estimated it was worth $2 million to him. At the height of his career, Peter Brock's eight-time Bathurst-winning career sparked a $35-million-per-year operation backed by Holden. In motor cycling, Australia's first world champion, Keith Campbell, rode a 350cc bike to the top in 1957, made practically nothing from his efforts and was later killed in a high-speed crash at Cadours, France, in 1958. When Wayne Gardner won the world championship in 1987, it was worth an estimated $8 million to him in prize-money, sponsorship, and endorsements, and when SBS television showed his races live in Australia, it was the network's highest-rating show.

Tennis was a big money-spinner well before the professionals took over. But the money, and the rules, were made by the officials not the players. When tennis arrived in Australia in the 1870s, women were advised to have 'the cleanest and prettiest of white underskirts, as these show when running for a stroke far more than one would imagine'; financial interests, rather than the players, were firmly in control. The first Davis Cup challenge round staged in Australia was in 1908 when Australasia beat the United States at the Albert Ground, St Kilda, Melbourne. Total gate receipts were $2440, and each team's share of the spoils a princely $566. By 1954 tennis was ripe for the financial revolution that came with the onset of professionalism. In that year, a world record 25 578 spectators turned up to watch the Davis Cup challenge round at Sydney's White City courts where the United States beat Australia. Some 10 000 spectators were turned away at the gates. Over three days, gate takings were $340 000, with each team's administration receiving $65 000.

It was time the players got more of the money. One of Australia's tennis champions, Ken Rosewall, took up the story. Rosewall said: 'I moved into the professional ranks six months before Lew Hoad did. We played our last Davis Cup match together in Adelaide in December 1956 and at that time, American Jack Kramer, who was controlling professional tennis, felt that both Lew and I would be good for his game. I decided to make the move and I think the opinion around Australian tennis was pretty much supportive. I challenged a player called Pancho Gonzales, who was an awfully tough character. I didn't have much of a choice really about turning professional. I was 21, had just been married, and didn't have much financial backing. On top of that, I'd given up a few years of education to concentrate on playing tennis. I felt it was in my best interests to go into the professional ranks to try to substantiate my financial future. It was the right decision. The administrators were very down on professional tennis, but then I was able to make a comeback to the international game at a later age, so it wasn't too bad'.

Rosewall never won Wimbledon, but his professional partner, Lew Hoad, won it twice in succession in 1956 and 1957. Hoad recalls: 'I was given the offer by Jack Kramer to turn professional and at that particular time I wasn't too secure in my family life and as to what I was going to do in the future. Kramer made me a pretty substantial offer. I can remember that when I turned pro I had nothing. I didn't have a house, I didn't have a flat, I didn't have a car, but I had about £300 in the bank which I thought was pretty good.'

Open tournaments did not begin until 1968, so the early professionals were denied a crack at the world's major tournaments for a long time. But they blazed the trail for today's tennis players, who are among the highest earners in any business pursuit on earth. In a best-of-three challenge series at the Hordern Pavilion in Sydney and Kooyong in Melbourne, Bjorn Borg and John McEnroe shared more than $1 million. When Lew Hoad won Wimbledon twice, he had, by his own admission, just £300 in the bank. When Pat Cash achieved the same feat thirty years later, he was worth $10 million.

While officials once condemned the dual devils of cash and television, they now welcome them with open arms, aware that it is the only open-ended road for sport. The Australian Olympic team for Seoul numbered a record 270, and with government assistance alone it is doubtful whether the Australian Olympic Federation (AOF) would have ratified a squad of such magnitude. Much of the cash came from the old enemy, television. A telethon in May 1988 raised almost $10 million. The Olympic Games are perhaps the last remaining bastions of the old times where the competitors see very little of the huge amounts their performances generate. The AOF's marketing arm has raised some $10 million from the private sector. Much more will be raised through public donation. The AOF charges a big licensing fee for use of the Olympic rings logo. Not even gold medallists are allowed to display the Olympic rings for financial gain unless they are licensed to do so. The way is open for the Games to be hijacked, just as tennis and cricket and a host of other sports have been. It must only be a matter of time before the Games go open and fully professional.

AOF boss Phil Coles is a strict believer in the Olympic movement. Coles said: 'We removed the word 'amateur' from our charter a few years ago because things have changed. Things change dramatically over the years as to what constitutes an amateur. There is no reflection in the modern society as to what an amateur is. I mean if someone said you did an amateurish job, it would be regarded as an insult. So we had to relax the conditions which apply to Olympic entry quite dramatically. Athletes receive financial rewards now under certain conditions under Rule 26 of the Olympic charter. Athletes are now eligible to be compensated for loss of salary and they can be compensated for air travel, accommodation, meals, training expenses and coaching fees while they are preparing for the Olympic Games. Some athletes are as hungry today as they were thirty years ago. But I've seen a deterioration in desire and commitment in Australia. Unfortunately the infusion of money in the form of financial reward is a double-edged sword. It can be good. But it has its

Blood, Sweat and Tears

Pat Cash's supreme moment, as he holds the 1987 Wimbledon trophy aloft. Apart from increasing Cash's riches with prize-money and endorsements, the win continued to attract big money and support for tennis in Australia
Photobank/All Sport

*Below:
Paul McNamee and Peter McNamara hold their matching Wimbledon Men's Doubles trophies. They were twice Wimbledon Doubles winners in 1980 and 1984, and Paul McNamee and Pat Cash were Wimbledon Men's Doubles runners-up in 1988*
Roger Gould

Bought Sport

Cricket is everywhere in an Australian summer — and this Yellow Cab keeps up the momentum with its advertisement of the one-day international cricket finals
Photobank/All Sport

bad moments. But the Olympic movement is looking good. We'll be around for a long time to come.'

So there remains one last target to be bought. Money and television have changed the face of sport over the past thirty years to such an extent that some sports are almost unrecognisable. Cricket — especially the one-day game, made for television — is the prime example. Television has even created sports for the masses, such as indoor cricket and soccer. It has turned television into the main object of interest for sports viewers, and made many competitors household names and multi-millionaires.

Lew Hoad, comfortable in his Spanish villa, deserves the last word, typical of the sentiments of world-class sporting stars from his era. 'I wish I'd been born thirty years later.'

Sources and references

The following books were consulted:
  Christopher Forsyth, *The Great Cricket Hijack* (Widescope, 1978); Jack Pollard, *Australian Cricket; the Game and the Players* (Hodder & Stoughton/ABC, 1982); Doug Walters, *The Doug Walters Story* (Rigby 1981).
Interview transcripts from the television series, 'Blood, Sweat and Tears':
  John Brown, Graham Cassidy, Phil Coles, Lew Hoad, Ken Rosewall, Brian Stoddart.
The material on the origin of WSC is derived from Forsyth, chs 2 and 3; the quotation from Walters is from pp.140–1; the quotations from Pollard are at pp.1138–9, 1139–40, and 21; the Glennys Bell article is in the *Bulletin*, 13 January 1987. The material otherwise is derived from newspaper files and the author's own research.

CHAPTER 10

WINNERS AND LOSERS

Brian Mossop

For all our armchair Norms, Australians and sport are synonymous. Losing at sport is not something we accept with good grace. Unlike our British forebears, it is not enough to have played the game. When we do play we want to win, a desire which places a great deal of undue pressure on our athletes, pressure which can often be inhibiting.

We are adept at idolising, at putting sporting heroes on pedestals, at glorifying. It is part of our national psyche that we gain as a nation from the successes of our athletes. This is not in itself a trait peculiar to Australians. What is perhaps peculiar is our readiness to turn our backs on those same sporting heroes the moment they falter, our readiness to cut them off at the legs.

This peculiarity, an aspect of the 'tall poppy' syndrome, is not confined to sporting personalities. There is a perversity about us which takes some sort of solace from the fact that even an apparently successful businessman can have his faults. It is the same sort of perversity that would make an ordinary club golfer, while thrilling at the shot execution of a Greg Norman, delighted to see him take three strokes to extract himself from a bunker. It brings the Normans of the world back to the pack; makes them human.

Our contradictory nature is such that while we can secretly hope for a mistake, we make little or no allowance for the fact that mistakes can occur, or even for the fact that an opponent might just happen to be better than our particular fancy. Robert de Castella won a string of marathon races in the early 1980s, filling us all with pride when he took the world championship in Holland and the Commonwealth Games gold medal in Brisbane with a stirring finishing burst. The moment he failed to finish first — not once, but in a number of subsequent races — he was written off as a has-been. He deserves, surely, to be remembered as a great athlete.

We revelled in Greg Norman's victories, in Pat Cash's Wimbledon success, in our mid-1970s dominance of world cricket, in our Rugby League superiority, in our soccer team's win over world champions Argentina in the Bicentennial Gold Cup in 1988. We also adopted a 'told you so' attitude to the failures of Norman and Cash, to our tumble from cricket's pedestal, to a Rugby League Test loss to Great Britain in 1988. And in spite of our pride, we did not really expect to beat Brazil, nor did we, in the Gold Cup final. Somehow we treat the troughs in our sporting roller-coaster of fortune with something akin to disgust. We do not take kindly to defeat. Nor need we. We could, however, adopt a less critical attitude, be more supportive of those

Dean Lukin lifting successfully for gold at the 1984 Los Angeles Olympics also 'lifted' the profile of the sport of weightlifting in this country
Live Action: Acikalin

who try so hard to bring us the pride which goes with success. Australian emotion, which hit an all-time high when businessman Alan Bond brought yachting's *America*'s Cup back from the United States in 1983, was hardly visible when we lost the Cup to the Americans in 1987. Once again, we placed a team of sportsmen under a great deal of pressure, expecting the world from them and shrugging with an 'I knew they couldn't do it' attitude when they lost.

The long leap of Debbie Flintoff took her to her total of three gold medals at the 1986 Commonwealth Games in Edinburgh
Live Action: Acikalin

Australians are not easy to please when it comes to sporting performances of their teams, be they club, State or national. The State-of-Origin Rugby League clashes between New South Wales and Queensland usually bring a keen following in Sydney, while in Brisbane Lang Park is always filled with a crowd which borders on frenzy. Queenslanders are so emotional about their sport that it is generally considered that if they ever win cricket's Sheffield Shield the premier will declare a State-wide holiday.

Even if Australians are quick to dismiss their champions when they falter, the role of sport in the nation's development has always been significant. Australia's fighting men — at the Boer War, during the world wars — won for Australians a reputation for gallantry and for being tough and fair. But so have its sporting men and women.

This reputation has been enhanced by Australia's cricketers, of whom Donald Bradman was an outstanding example; by its tennis players who, along with the

Winners and Losers

Americans, turned the Davis Cup into something of a two-nation duel; by squash champion Heather McKay; by swimmers, athletes, boxers and hockey teams. It was a reputation which even in defeat was never sullied. And while it is the winners of whom we generally boast, Australia has had its share of champion losers — perhaps not losers so much as champions who, for one reason or another, never quite achieved what the public perceived as their potential. In most such cases, the perception was that the hero had only to turn up and go through the motions to set the record, to take the gold. It is one of the major drawcards of sport that nothing, absolutely nothing, can be taken for granted.

Neville Penton, author of *A Racing Heart*, recounts one such occasion: the defeat of the mighty racehorse Ajax which won eighteen races in a row but is remembered mainly as the greatest loser of all time. All because he was beaten, at 40–1 on, in a three-horse race at Rosehill, the Rawson Stakes, in 1939. Ajax was the shortest-priced favourite ever to start, and the race is talked about still.

Ajax was such a certainty to equal the record of nineteen consecutive wins held jointly by Desert Gold and Gloaming that the bookmakers made him a totally unattractive punting proposition. Even for a certainty it is a bit much to ask for a massive outlay in order to pick up a winning crumb. The punters went up in the stands and sat down, says Penton:

> So away they went. Ajax and one of the other runners named Allunga. They were at each other early on, and for most of the race they raced neck and neck while Spear Chief, the other runner, sat behind and waited. What everyone expected was that at any point Ajax's rider, Harold Badger, wanted, he would just pull out and stroll away from the field ... But when they got into the straight Allunga had had enough, and Ajax had had enough too. Spear Chief just drew up alongside Ajax and went away from him, as easy as that.

The huge crowd at Rosehill races is dumbfounded after the great racehorse Ajax, a 40–1 on favourite, is beaten in the Rawson Stakes in 1938. In the foreground of this picture from the Referee are part-owner E. L. Baillieu, trainer Frank Musgrave and part-owner A. W. Thomson. The loss is considered the greatest 'boilover' in Australian racing history

---

THURSDAY, THE REFEREE MARCH 30, 1939

"Warrawee" Says Ajax Did Not Look Himself

Has Had Enough Racing For Present

I SEE it suggested that "the only explanation of the defeat of Ajax was that he was having his first race the right-handed way."

Ajax won his first race right-handed (the Sires' Produce Stakes at Randwick) at two years.

At three years he won the Rosehill Guineas, having his first right-handed race that season.

BEFORE the Rawson Stakes on Saturday Ajax appeared to me to have lightened off considerably since last season. This was noticeable behind the saddle. His coat lacked something of its usual lustre, looked rather dry, in fact. Here, I think, is the explanation of Ajax's indifferent display. He has had enough racing for the present.

It should not be overlooked that it took Ajax nearly a mile to shake off Allunga. The Ajax that made Royal Chief look second-rate in the spring would have had no difficulty in getting a break of ten lengths on a slow beginner like Allunga

"AND STILL THEY GAZED AND STILL THEIR WONDER GREW!" Rosehill racegoers on the rails after Ajax had been beaten in the Rawson Stakes, at 40 to 1 on. In foreground, Mr. E. L. Baillieu is seen "laughing it off," but veteran trainer, Frank Musgrave (centre) fails to see the joke. Mr. A. W. Thompson is dumbfounded.

HAROLD PARK TROTS

Fields For Monday

(The following are the final acceptors for the New South Wales Trotting Club's meeting to be held on April 3, 1939).
Trial Handicap, 1¼m: Invitation, Tom's Image, Machine Boy, Marmalyn, Barter, Some Swank, Pergola, Billy Blano, Clareton Lad, Dadnuman, Black Nut, Pete's Machine, Realistic, Forest Dixie, Don Again, scr.
Glebe Unhoppled Trotters' Handicap, 1¼m: Flying Peter, Bullawalla, Talking Peterwah Direct, Altimeter, Sterling Alto, Buckwood, scr; Drifting Home, Davy's Ribbon, Satin Don, 24yds bhd; Heroic Voyage, 36yds bhd; Rock's Image, 60yds bhd; Great Cross, 84yds bhd.
Approved Handicap, 1¼m (1st Div.): Derby Adonis, Rock Beauty, Fourex, Louis Desire, Glenlivet, Young Wilver, Marble View, Golden Grove, Flying Johnnie, Lord Marvin, scr.
Second Division: Gay Polly, Van Wilver, Delavan Boy, Wildgee Bells, War Chief, Albena Derby, Arisus, Gleam of Silver, Callaghan, Ribbon Mac, scr.
Flying Handicap, 1m: Jim's Boy, Harabond, Royal's Best, Lonely Mint, Kernel Lu, scr., Joe Delavan, Remember Me, Childwood Direct, Royal Linda, Lucy Again, Machine King, Don Fan, 12yds bhd; Marble Ridge, Bobbie Ribbons, 24 yds bhd.

Selections For Monday
(By "TIERCEL")
TRIAL HANDICAP: Marmalyn 1, Tom's Image 2, Don Again 3.
GLEBE TROTTERS' HANDICAP: Heroic Voyage 1, Flying Peter 2, Satin Don 3.
APPROVED HANDICAP.—First Division: Flying Johnnie 1, Marble View 2, Louis Desire 3.
APPROVED HANDICAP.—Second Division: Gleam of Silver 1, War Chief 2, Van Wilver 3.
FLYING HANDICAP: Kernel Lu 1, Royal Linda 2, Remember Me 3.
TRAMWAY HANDICAP.—First Division: Mollison 1, Rock Globe

Blood, Sweat and Tears

Ajax subsequently ran and won twice at Randwick, and was shaded in the W. S. Cox Plate at Moonee Valley on 26 October 1940, his farewell race. Ajax had raced forty-six times for thirty-six wins, seven seconds and two thirds, and while he is remembered as a great champion, he is remembered most of all for the day he lost the Rawson Stakes at Rosehill.

By the 1960s Australia had a sensational runner in Ron Clarke who at one stage held every world record from two miles to 10 000 metres, but in two Olympic Games and a Commonwealth Games he was unable to win a gold medal. Short on international experience when he went to the Tokyo Olympics in 1964, he was relegated to third place in the 10 000 metres won by American Billy Mills with Tunisia's Mohammed Gammoudi second. After making the pace in the 5000 metres Clarke had nothing left for the last lap and finished ninth, as he did in the marathon. In the Commonwealth Games at Kingston, Jamaica, in 1966, gold was again elusive, Naftali Temu beating Clarke home over six miles, and Kip Keino finishing too strongly for him at the end of three miles.

While he never won a gold medal, Clarke was held in high regard by those who knew what went into his many achievements. The great Czech runner Emil Zatopek, farewelling Clarke at Prague Airport in 1966, slipped a small package into his pocket, whispering, 'Not out of friendship — you deserve it'. When Clarke boarded the plane and opened the package he found Zatopek's treasured 10 000 metres gold medal from the Helsinki Olympics of 1952.

The loss for which Clarke became best remembered happened in the agonising altitude of Mexico City two years later, when he collapsed after finishing sixth in the 10 000 metres.

A young Ron Clarke has the world at his feet as he lights the Olympic flame at the Melbourne Olympics in 1956. Clarke broke seventeen world distance records in a four-year span but failed to win either a Commonwealth or Olympic Games gold medal. His collapse after finishing sixth in the 10 000 metres at Mexico City in 1968 marked the end of a gallant competitive career
Photobank: All Sport

If any Australian wants any more inspiration than that provided by Edwin Flack, Don Bradman, Dawn Fraser, Betty Cuthbert, Herb Elliott or the *America*'s Cup win then they should give some thought to Ron Clarke's performance at the 1968 Olympic Games in Mexico City. Because Mexico City sits 2239 metres above sea level, those Games added a dimension never before seen in the quality of some of the performances. Bob Beamon's 8.90 metres for the long jump, Tommie Smith's 19.83 seconds for the 200-metres, in which his average speed was 10.101 metres per second, and Lee Evans's 43.86 seconds for the 400-metres remain among the greatest performances in track and field history. Indeed at the time of writing the feats of Beamon and Evans were still world records, while Smith's time was still third on the world's all-time list. Twenty years later!

But while the gasping altitude was of such assistance to those in explosive events, it was the reverse in the endurance events for those not born at such altitudes. Never was this more clearly demonstrated than in the 10 000-metres final, the first track and field event to be decided. Ron Clarke was running in this for Australia — a man everyone had come to admire greatly for the succession of world distance records he had created. At the same time it seemed he couldn't win a gold medal at the Olympic or Commonwealth Games. He was known quite simply as the runner who could thrash the clock, but not human beings. And in what he said would be his last Olympics, he found himself unfairly penalised by the altitude. He knew from medical evidence that those in the race from 'altitude' countries had a decided advantage over him.

With six laps of the final to go, two runners had already been carried away on stretchers. With 800 metres remaining, the only runners still in contention were Mamo Wolde of Ethiopia, Clarke, Naftali Temu of Kenya, and Mohammed Gamoudi of Tunisia. Then Clarke began fading fast. He was fighting his own private battle to stay alive. The race was won by Temu, the long-legged Kisii tribesman from the high country of Kenya. He beat Wolde after the two of them staged the most unbelievable fight over the last lap, sprinting as if doing a solitary lap instead of coming to the end of twenty-five laps of torture. Temu, after chasing a stride or two behind Wolde, caught and slithered past him just 60 metres from the tape. Third was Gamoudi, a silver medallist in the same event at the previous Olympics, followed by Juan Martinez, of Mexico, and Nikolay Sviridov, of the Soviet Union, and then Clarke. Just as predicted, the men from the mountains had triumphed.

Clarke was distressed, ashen-faced and tottering. He fell flat on his stomach on the grassed centre area a moment after dragging himself over the line. A blanket was thrown over him by a first-aid attendant. Australian team medical officer Dr Brian Corrigan hurdled the stadium fence and raced to Clarke's aid, helping the attendant administer oxygen to him. Clarke whiffed 60 litres of oxygen in ten minutes before coming to. Corrigan explained later to the media:

> He just ran beyond his capabilities. The idea was for him to run at a steady rate early and then to cover the last four laps much quicker. But in the last two laps he was in trouble. He got a sense of tiredness and weakness. In the last lap he found severe difficulties. His vision was affected and his concentration wandered. Anybody else would have given up, but he kept going. And because he kept going he had a circulatory collapse. When I reached him he was ashen-faced and completely unconscious. His heart was beating irregularly. There was just not enough oxygen for him at this level. He ran past the limits of endurance.

So Clarke had missed out on the medal he wanted so dearly. He wasn't defeated by other mortals this time but by the accident of his birthplace. The crowd felt for him, so much so that people cried unashamedly when he fell. Years later, Clarke was forced to undergo open heart surgery and there was firm medical opinion that the need for it could be traced back to that race in Mexico City. That he ended his career without a gold medal was grossly unfortunate, because his great front-running had helped set new long-distance running standards. And what he did that day in Mexico City should be more than enough inspiration for any Australian.

For the boyish Kim Hughes, captaining the Australian cricket team had been a long-nurtured dream which, after a stop-start beginning, took on permanency when Greg Chappell stood down after the Test series of the 1983–4 season. In attaining the position many an Australian sees as the ultimate sporting honour, Hughes achieved the heights. But what started out as the fulfilment of a dream turned into a nightmare which ended in a tearful resignation on 26 November 1984, following the loss of the second Test — the second loss of the series — against the West Indies.

Greg Chappell, Rod Marsh and Dennis Lillee had retired at the end of the 1983–4 season to leave Australia without its most seasoned players; there was constant criticism of Hughes, and the Western Australian batsman had been struggling for some time to get among the runs. The pressure, not helped one iota by the fury of the West Indies, built up daily. Something had to give. Not even at the post-match press conference in the players' lunch-room at Brisbane's Woolloongabba was there any indication of the bombshell to come.

There was some banter aimed at easing the tension of another loss. When a television journalist asked Hughes if he intended announcing his resignation, there was indignation all round. The conference proceeded as usual with questions and answers about where it had all gone wrong, what Australia had to do to become competitive again, what pluses, if any, could be found in the performances. Hughes rose to leave the room — and then startled everyone when he said, 'Gentlemen, before you go I have got something to read'. Reaching into a back pocket he withdrew a piece of paper, unfolded it, and began reading his resignation to a hushed and disbelieving group of reporters.

He made it only halfway through the text before his voice broke. Tears welling in his eyes, Hughes handed the sheet of paper to team manager Bob Merriman and hurried from the room. Merriman finished reading the text, and an era in Australian cricket captaincy had ended. Hughes may never have ranked as one of the great leaders, but he was a victim of his time — a time of turmoil and rehabilitation as cricket attempted to put behind it the turbulent years of World Series Cricket, the Kerry Packer-backed breakaway which took most of the leading players out of the 'traditional' game for two years.

The text of Hughes's letter of resignation was as follows:

> The Australian cricket captaincy is something that I've held very dear to me. However, playing the game with total enjoyment has always been of greatest importance. The constant speculation, criticism and innuendo by former players and sections of the media over the past 4–5 years have finally taken their toll. It is in the interest of the team, Australian cricket and myself that I have informed the ACB of my decision to stand down as Australian captain. I look forward to continuing my career in whatever capacity the selectors and the Board see fit with the same integrity and credibility I have displayed as Australian captain. Gentlemen, I wish not to discuss this matter any further, and I will not be available to answer any further questions. KIM HUGHES.

It was a disappointing exit for Hughes who genuinely loved captaining his country, and a step along the road which would eventually lead him to South Africa and leadership of the team of Australians who chose to play there in the 1985–6 and 1986–7 seasons. It is testimony to the strain champions suffered once they were in the spotlight.

There was disappointment too for Australian Rugby Union, or at least for its followers. Having won the Grand Slam by beating England, Ireland, Wales and Scotland in 1984 under the guidance of coach Alan Jones, the expectation was high every time the Australians took the field. As seems to be the nature of the Australian

Kim Hughes, one of Australia's most gifted batsmen, nurtured an ambition to captain Australia. The dream turned sour when, dogged by a series of poor performances and the repeated failures of his team, he resigned in 1984 in the middle of a West Indies tour. He later turned his back on official Australian cricket to lead two rebel tours to South Africa
Martin King Sportpix

sports follower, success is everything. There is no room at all for defeat. For a while, all was well. Australia strode world rugby like a colossus, even bringing home the coveted Bledisloe Cup, symbol of supremacy in competition between Australia and New Zealand and a kind of Holy Grail.

Nineteen eighty-seven brought a fall. Success eluded Australia at the Hong Kong Sevens tournament and at the inaugural World Cup; the Bledisloe Cup returned to its usual resting place across the Tasman; and even the anticipated destruction of Argentina on the South American tour did not eventuate. In the first Test, Australia escaped with a draw when Hugo Porta failed with a conversion attempt in injury time. In the second Test, it was all Porta as the veteran five-eighth chalked up 23 points from five penalties, two field goals and a conversion. Although the Australians scored two tries to one after making five changes to the team, Argentina won the match and the series. As far as most Australian rugby followers were concerned — and it is a puzzling attitude — the year had been a disaster. The triumphs of a recent past counted for nothing, or so it seemed.

In her farewell appearance in 1982, Raelene Boyle at the Commonwealth Games brought the crowd at Brisbane's QEII stadium on their feet as she stormed to a magnificent win in the 400 metres. The win helped to make up for her failure in Edinburgh when she broke twice to be disqualified from the 200 metres.
Roger Gould

Adair Ferguson's early sports hopes lay in the field of athletics, but it was single skulls that led her to a world championship and to gold in the Edinburgh Commonwealth Games
Live Action: Acikalin

When it comes to certainties beaten, Australia's 4 × 100 metres women's relay sprint team at the Helsinki Olympic Games in 1952 ranks among the most memorable. Marjorie Jackson, already the 100 and 200 metres gold medallist, headed the four runners, Jackson, Shirley Strickland, Winsome Cripps and Verna Johnston, but the one fear of relay runners, a dropped baton, came to pass, and the Australians lost. The disappointment of the relay team was only one of many in the long history of Olympic competition. Few were accompanied by such controversy as the disqualification of sprinter Raelene Boyle from a semi-final of the 200 metres in Montreal in 1976. A medal prospect and a triple silver medallist, Boyle was the victim of a rule rarely invoked in Olympic competition — the first step on the way to her disqualification.

Crouching on the blocks awaiting the starter's gun in her semi-final, Boyle rolled her shoulders. The starter, Englishman Jack Fisher, noted the movement, pulled the runners back from the blocks, and informed Boyle that her unsteadiness constituted a false start. Back on the blocks for the second time, Boyle broke, the false start invoking a mandatory disqualification. Her quest for gold was over.

Fellow athletes were shocked by the decision to penalise Boyle for the shoulder roll, pointing out that it was usual at international meetings for the transgressing athlete to be given a warning. Even Boyle was unable to explain why she broke the second time when all she needed to qualify for the final was to finish in the first four. In fact her brush with officials was not confined to the 200 metres. She was a member of the Australian 4 × 100 metres relay team disqualified for allegedly causing interference to a runner from another team during the first semi-final. Replays showed it was not an Australian who was guilty, but a member of the French relay team. The Australian team of Barbara Wilson, Debbie Wells, Denise Robertson and Boyle contested the final in which they finished fifth behind the gold medallists, East Germany.

Cricket has produced more than its share of disappointments, for players and spectators alike. While it was merely one moment in a career filled with many highlights, it was utter shock which accompanied the last innings dismissal of the great Donald Bradman for a duck. Given a standing ovation and three rousing cheers by the English crowd as he walked to the wicket to take strike for the last time at the Oval in 1948, the Don must have been cognisant of the occasion. Perhaps he was a little blinded by it. He needed just four runs to walk away from a magnificent Test career with the astonishing average of 100 runs per innings. It was not to be. Eric Hollies, a brisk and accurate purveyor of leg breaks, was the bowler as Bradman strode to the crease. The crowd was ready to sit back and enjoy another great offering from the blade of the master batsman, and the rustle of anticipation was evident as Bradman offered a dead bat to the first ball, a leg break. The second ball, a googly of perfect length, bowled the great man. A stunned hush settled on the ground. Bradman had been denied a century Test average, and would have to settle for 99.94.

At least he wasn't alone in making a duck, even if for him it was a rather rare occurrence. Keith Stackpole recorded a 'pair' in his last Test against New Zealand in 1974; so did Richie Benaud at Leeds thirteen years earlier; and a string of seven ducks in Tests and one-day matches during the 1981–2 season befell even the great Greg Chappell. The list is endless: a badge of perhaps dubious distinction, but a badge which at times brings even the best players back to the ranks of mere mortals.

One of the greatest controversies in cricket surrounded the Victorian left-arm pace bowler Ian Meckiff, no-balled out of the game in the Brisbane Test against South Africa in 1963–4 after enduring for much of his career the jibe 'chucker'.

It was a label attached to Meckiff by English pressmen searching for a scapegoat after the Australians had shattered England in the Melbourne Test of the 1958–9 Ashes series. Following the Imperial Cricket Conference in London in 1960,

The crowd of 30 000 at the Sydney Cricket Ground cheered with abandon when, on 16 November 1947, Don Bradman scored his hundredth century in first-class cricket. Bradman's first three innings for South Australia at the start of his career were 117, 233 and 357. The ninety-nine against his name was a prophetic figure, as he finished his Test career with an average of 99.94 runs. In one sequence of 48 innings in 1938–9, Bradman hit 27 centuries and 10 fifties
News Limited

The action of Ian Meckiff, the Victorian and Australian fast bowler who was barred from first class cricket in 1963 because of his alleged throwing action. Controversy about the umpire's calls raged for years, as many believed Meckiff had merely a loose bowling arm and a bent elbow at delivery
News Limited

the Australian Cricket Board chairman, Bill Dowling, a man known for his fair-mindedness, commented: 'The attacks being made in England on the Australian fast bowlers Ian Meckiff and Gordon Rorke amounted to intimidation of umpires. They have been prejudged and condemned as throwers without ever having been seen in England. It is contrary to every principle of fair play that feeling should be whipped up and that sportsmen should be condemned out of hand before ever appearing in a country'. Dowling noted he and Bradman had been shocked at the way public opinion, particularly where Meckiff was concerned, had been aroused by the press.

Meckiff bowled with a left arm that could not be fully straightened, and consequently had a bent elbow at the point of delivery. It did not stop him from generating considerable pace. Melbourne Cricket Club secretary Ian Johnson, in an article in the Melbourne *Herald*, suggested that if Rorke and Meckiff were called under Law 26 relating to throwing, then so too should Statham, Loader, Lock, Trueman and many others have been. Johnson said both Rorke and Meckiff had whippy actions that jerked and had relaxed elbows at the moment of delivery because both were loose-limbed, but emphasised that these things were not apparent to umpires, and only showed on slow-motion films. Meckiff had been called twice in Sheffield Shield matches, but never in seventeen Tests, so it came as a surprise to everyone when he was called by umpire Col Egar during the Brisbane Test against South Africa in 1963–4 and not bowled again in the match by his captain, Richie Benaud. It seemed that Meckiff had been sacrificed in order to appease the furore created by the publicity.

Golfer Kel Nagle did not have his career sacrificed, but he did throw away what chance he may have had of winning a tournament in Ireland in 1969 when he

Golfer Kel Nagle lost his winning chance in a tournament in Ireland in 1969 when he signed an incorrectly marked card and added 31 strokes to his score. Nagle had many golfing successes including victory in the British Open in 1960
Herald & Weekly Times

signed an incorrect card. Playing at Portmarnock he shot a four on the 9th hole. But his playing partner, Irishman Christy O'Connor, accidentally marked his outward total of 35 in the space for the 9th hole score. Nagle signed the card without checking, and so added a massive 31 strokes to his score. Being Nagle, the error was shrugged off and chalked up to experience.

The Australian cricketers also had to chalk up to experience the disaster of the Old Trafford Test in 1956 in which the England off-spinner Jim Laker claimed an amazing 19 wickets at a cost of 90 runs on a pitch variously described as 'disgraceful' and 'horrendous'. In *The Game is Not the Same* former ABC commentator Alan McGilvray offers a colourful description of events in that fateful match, noting that Laker's capacity for wreaking havoc amongst the Australians had been revealed in the third Test at Leeds when he took advantage of a difficult pitch to claim eleven wickets and wrap up the match by an innings. 'Perhaps', said McGilvray, 'that performance affected the judgement of the groundsman at Old Trafford, for when the Australians arrived there for the decisive fourth Test, the pitch was an abomination. Clouds of dust swirled about it from the first day, and the ball did such weird and unpredictable things the Australians could hardly lay a bat on it'.

England won the toss and batted first to score 459. By the time the Australians went in all the unhappy portents for a horror pitch had proved spot on; the ball was doing amazing things as Laker bowled to the conditions. It was without question, according to McGilvray, the worst Test wicket he had ever seen. Not surprisingly, the Australians were bundled out for 84 in the first innings, and for 205 in the second to lose by an innings and 170 runs. Even the English, it is said, were embarrassed by the state of the wicket and its consequences. It remains one of the mysteries of Anglo–Australian cricket. It assured Jim Laker of a place forever in the history of cricket, and left the Australian Ashes quest in tatters.

Difficult as it may be at the time, dignity in defeat can sometimes turn a loss into something of a victory. So it was with John Landy at the Empire Games in Vancouver in 1954. Landy had run 4 min. 2.1 sec. in late December of 1952 to be one of a number of athletes knocking at the door of the first sub-4-minute mile. The knocking got louder in 1953 with Landy and several other runners pressing consistently at around 4 min. 2 sec. But it was Englishman Roger Bannister who secured a place in history when he burst through the barrier at Oxford on 6 May 1954. It came as a surprise even to Landy, but served to pave the way for a turn of events which would help the Australian.

The effect of Bannister's run, said Landy, was to remove a barrier. It was possible to run a mile in under four minutes. As Landy recalled, 'I think people thought "Well, that's as fast as it's likely to go for a while"'. Chris Chataway, a fine three-miler, and Chris Brasher, later to win a gold medal for the 3000 metres steeplechase at the Melbourne Olympics, had acted as pacemakers for Bannister's record and barrier shattering run at Oxford. Landy was training in Finland at the time, and the Finns, aware that they could make some mileage out of a well promoted mile event, invited Chataway to run. 'Chataway came over and people said he was going to pace me. Of course he came over to try to beat me — which is what he should have been trying to do. I had been running in Australia essentially on my own. I had not had a competitive situation nor had I run with a pacemaker, and the race against Chataway was the first in which I was confronted with a real competitive environment. I didn't see Chataway in the race at all. But he clung very close to me and, particularly when we began the last lap, I was aware he was there and all I was trying to do was beat him. I had no concept of what time I was running, not the faintest, although I knew it was going to be a fast time. As it turned out, it was well inside Bannister's record. It was 3 min. 57.9 sec., and in addition I ran the world record time for 1500 metres. That, of course, created the ideal circumstances for a clash because Bannister and I were due to meet in Vancouver in August of that year. But this happening, the fact that he had broken the four-minute mile and established the record, and then I had done it within forty days and reduced his record, created an ideal circumstance. Who was going to win this match race of two people who had run inside the four minutes for the mile?'

With that as the background, the stage was set for fireworks in Vancouver. The pressure on the athletes was tremendous. Landy said: 'It was like a world title fight. It went on for weeks: how would I run the race, how would Roger Bannister run the race, who would win it, what the time would be, was the track going to be good in Vancouver? It was a very big occasion for those days in track and field. You could say it was unique. It was interesting too because it was the first time any sporting event had been televised right across the United States. It was the first sort of national or continental hook-up. They hooked up from Vancouver to Seattle and beamed across to New York and, although it sounds very small these days, there was a 70 million TV viewing audience — and that's back well over thirty years ago.

'As a pawn in that game, if you like, as one of the people who had to put on the performance, it was pretty stressful. We took a good-humoured attitude to it, but people never left you alone.

'I guess the race itself went fairly predictably. Although I wasn't going to say what I was going to do, it was pretty inevitable that I would have to lead and Bannister follow. My aim in the race was pure and simple. I was going to try to run Roger Bannister off his feet. Bannister had a great finishing sprint. He was a very long-striding runner, slightly taller than I was. Essentially he ran a waiting race and usually made a long sprint with about 300 metres to go. I, on the other hand, had won my races by running fairly evenly, but nearly always taking the lead. And that's what happened.

'As I said, my aim was to run Roger Bannister off his feet, and to do this I felt, since he was going to be much more formidable than Chris Chataway, I would have to set a faster pace than I had in Finland. Moreover, I would have to continue to apply pressure, particularly in the last lap, beyond what I normally would have felt to be a sensible thing to do. In other words, my aim would be to convince him that I was not going to slow down.

'That, in fact, is what happened, except that initially I gained a big advantage over Bannister — something of the order of 15 yards which I held right up to the half mile when Bannister began to inch back. So I was aware that I had a diminishing lead. When they rang the bell for the last lap, I could suddenly see him on my shoulder. I knew the worst had happened in the sense that I hadn't really got right away from him and that I then had to apply another tactic. I thought he would go with 300, so even though I was running out of strength, I made an effort at 300 and began to move away. I think a lot of people thought I was going to win it. Frankly, I was dubious because I was extremely tired.

'Coming down the back straight I was aware where Bannister was because the sun was in the right position to show our two shadows, and I could see myself moving away from him a little. I guess I wasn't thinking clearly at that stage about the position of the sun and the fact that you wouldn't always see the shadows. When I came around the corner approaching the 1500 metre point, say with 120 yards to go, I was aware that Bannister's shadow had disappeared. My first reaction was one of hope, that I had got away from him — and that's when I couldn't resist looking back. I looked to the left because that was the position I would be able to see where he was if he was (as I thought he might have been) about 15 yards behind me. I looked, and he wasn't there. I looked a bit further — all in a split second of course. When I looked up the other way he was going past my right-hand side and of course the race was all over.

'A lot of people have said if I hadn't looked around maybe I would have won the race. Well, of course that's nonsense. It would perhaps have made some difference, but the surprise element set me back a bit. When I tried to get back into gear, there was no gear to get into. He was off and away. If you look at the times for the sections of the race you will find it was a matter of who slowed down first — and it was me rather than Bannister who did that.'

Although Landy had run with a deep gash in his foot held together by four stitches, he refused to use the injury as an excuse for his loss. 'It's the sort of thing people look for in a situation like that where so much depends on it. They're looking for explanations. Now the explanation of the result of that race was that Bannister, in the way the race was run and in the circumstances, was the better runner. There's no doubt that at the time I was disappointed that I didn't win, but the truth of the matter is if you're not good enough, you don't win, and that's precisely what happened.'

World mile record holder and one of the favourites for the 1500 metres at the Melbourne Olympics in 1956, Landy did not have a good preparation for the Games. He had been beaten over two miles, and had grave doubts about his ability to win the 1500. He was in fact the slowest qualifier for the final. As it happened, the final was a cluttered race with little more than 10 metres separating the field at the bell. Irishman Ron Delany made his move with about 300 metres to go and Landy, wondering just where he could finish in the field, came round the final bend and looked up to see the tape. Realising he had a lot left, he began a sprint. It was too late. The gold medal went to Delany, and while he almost caught the German runner, Richtzenhain, Landy had to settle for bronze. Sportsman that he was, Landy had nothing but praise for Delany. 'It was a wonderful race of Delany's. He was a super individual, a lovely guy, and he was also a wonderful tactical runner. But that

John Landy came close to re-writing the record books in the 1950s. He missed becoming the first to break the four minutes for a mile by 46 days. England's Roger Bannister got there first, and then beat him in an epic encounter in the 1954 Commonwealth Games at Vancouver
Ern McQuillan

Blood, Sweat and Tears

was easily the best performance he had put up, and it was the time to do it. You get one chance to win an Olympic Games, usually. I competed in two (the first as a raw youngster in Helsinki in 1952) and had no chance in the first one. But you get this chance and you've got to be able to deliver the goods on the day, and that's exactly what Delany did.

'As a competitive athlete I was disappointed at not having won a gold medal, but there was no excuse. I don't believe I was at my best in that race although I would not say that about any other race. I wasn't at my best for faults of my own. I trained wrongly and did not run a very good race. But I believe that on the day, no matter how I had run, Delany would have won. I would not have beaten Delany. I come back to the point I have always made. Winning Olympics is not about having run the fastest time in the world; it is not about being rated as the best runner in the world for that distance. It's about delivering your best performance in a particular instance of the utmost importance. I was not able to do that and the fault, or the inadequacy, lies with me and nobody else. Yes, I was disappointed not to win a gold medal — but I accept that Delany was the better runner on the day.'

Landy at least got the chance to go for gold. It was more than the Australian water polo team got in the 1968 Olympics. Even before the Games began in Mexico City the Australians were the centre of controversy over the refusal of the Australian Olympic Council to endorse their entry. The team went anyway, members paying their own way via Europe where they performed with a good deal of credit. When they arrived in Mexico they were housed privately and were extended facilities for training while the International Olympic Committee decided their status. The IOC ruled against the inclusion of the Australians in the competition.

For swimmer Georgina Parkes there was the frustration of swimming in the shadow of Lisa Forrest to whom she finished second in the Commonwealth Games in Brisbane in 1982 in both the 100 and 200 metres backstroke. But the determined Parkes stood on the winner's dais at Edinburgh four years later clutching a gold medal and shedding tears of pure joy. She, at least, had the satisfaction of overcoming bitter disappointment to make her mark.

If swimming hard-luck stories could fill a book of their own, so too could those surrounding boxing — amateur as well as professional. One such tale concerned Tony Madigan who fought in three Olympics — Helsinki, Melbourne and Rome — and emerged with one bronze medal from Rome. A middleweight, Madigan was the only boxer of five in the Australian team to win a fight at Helsinki. Forced to stop sparring for several weeks before the Games because of a sprained knuckle in his left hand, Madigan had a first round bye and easily beat the Russian, Silchev, on points in the second round. He could not find his touch in the quarter-finals, and was outpointed by the Swede, Sjolin. He again came unstuck in the quarter-finals at Melbourne, going down to the Russian light–heavyweight, Mouraouskas. It was a heart-breaking loss for Madigan who had lost only four of sixty-eight contests in eight years. Feeling he had let down his countrymen, the dejected boxer announced after the fight, 'This is it, I'm through'. Four years later, at Rome, he was to give a young American light–heavyweight by the name of Cassius Clay his toughest fight. It was in a semi-final and, while Clay took the bout on points, the judgement in favour of the eventual gold medallist was an extremely narrow one.

Also beaten in Rome, in the second round of the flyweight division, was a youngster named Rocky Gattelari who would turn professional and become a controversial figure in Australian boxing without ever managing to take a world title. Twenty-four years later another young fighter, Jeff Fenech, would falter in the Olympic ring at Los Angeles and go on to amass three world titles in the professional ranks, so fulfilling the promise he always felt should have been recognised at his only Olympic appearance.

One Olympic gold medal most Australians counted on was that in hockey at Montreal in 1976. It was taken as a foregone conclusion once the team had beaten

Australian boxer Tony Madigan had come closer than he thought to greatness when he won the silver medal at the Rome Olympics in 1960. His opponent was Cassius Clay!
Photobank: All Sport

Pakistan to reach the final. New Zealand had other ideas. The Australians had overcome forty years of Olympic history in beating India in extra time in Mexico eight years earlier to reach the final — only to lose to Pakistan and have to content themselves with silver. When they beat Pakistan in the semi-finals in Montreal, they faced a New Zealand side which had never been in an Olympic final and which had not beaten Australia in seven years. But in a match which left no room for the faint-hearted, the New Zealand defence held firm. The Kiwis won 1–0. An equaliser by Australian Terry Walsh with three minutes to go was disallowed by the German referee as the ball had been struck on a rising trajectory. The decision was hotly disputed, but it stood.

There was both triumph and tragedy for cyclist Russell Mockridge, a participant at the London and Helsinki Olympics. Mockridge, an introspective athlete, had poor eyesight and risked danger whenever he rode at high speed on steeply banked tracks. The Victorian, regarded as the finest cyclist in the world — amateur or professional — when he won two gold medals at Helsinki, almost didn't make it to Finland. He refused to sign a £750 Olympic bond required by the Australian Olympic Federation guaranteeing he would remain an amateur for two years after the Games. Although a gold medal prospect, he was dropped from the team when he went to compete in Europe several months before the Games — and was only restored to the side when the Mayor of Geelong guaranteed the bond money and the AOF reduced the post-Games amateur term from two years to twelve months. Mockridge won gold in the 1000 metres time trial and the 1000 metres tandem — and a year and two days later turned professional. Tragedy struck in 1958. Mockridge was competing in the 224-kilometre cycling Tour of Gippsland when he approached an intersection, skidded under a bus, and was killed. He was just 30 years old.

When it comes to tennis, Ken Rosewall, a champion in every respect, is widely regarded as perhaps the greatest player never to have won the coveted All England

Cyclist Russell Mockridge, a dual gold medalist at the Helsinki Olympics, had poor eyesight and risked injury whenever he rode at high speed on steeply banked tracks. He was killed in an accident while taking part in a road race in Victoria in 1958
Herald & Weekly Times

Championship at Wimbledon, in spite of the fact that he appeared in four finals on the hallowed centre court over a period of twenty years. He won the French title in 1954 and 1968, the Australian in 1955, 1971 and 1972, and the US in 1956 and 1970. But in Wimbledon finals he lost to Jaroslav Drobny in 1954, to his tennis 'twin' Lew Hoad in 1956, to John Newcombe in 1970 and to Jimmy Connors in 1974. Tony Roche, winner of the French crown in 1966, played in losing Wimbledon and US finals without ever making a final of the Australian championships. But he did go close in Brisbane in 1969. In what those who witnessed it describe as an epic match, the left-handed Roche went down to his left-handed countryman, Rod Laver, the eventual title-winner.

Journalist and author Bruce Matthews, in *Game, Set and Glory*, describes the match thus:

> For nearly five hours the left-handed pair shrugged off Brisbane's murderous humidity and searing heat before Laver eventually claimed the 90-game struggle 7–5, 22–20, 9–11, 1–6, 6–3. In a match where one set lasted 87 minutes, the result would be decided on who got the breaks. The dubious call came in the 88th game as Laver's cross-court backhand return was thought to be wide. No call came and Roche lost concentration and the match.

Johnny Raper, the great St George and Australian Rugby League lock, knew only success throughout his playing career. A member of the St George team during its golden era when it won eleven straight Sydney premierships between 1956 and 1966, losses were few and then not when it really mattered. It was a different matter when Raper began coaching at Cronulla. And losing was not something which Raper suffered well. As he puts it: 'Losing is the lowest thing in the world. It's something that gets you down — especially when, like me, you have had greatness all around you. I had never played in anything bar winning sides, I had never played under a losing coach'. On reflection, Raper feels that, having been part of such a great side as St George, he expected too much from his players at Cronulla. While he might approach the job differently in the light of subsequent experience, being on a losing team was harrowing.

There are far more losers in sport than winners. St Paul's axiom is always true: many run for the prize, but only one wins the race. For every champion there are dozens more who never expect to achieve greatness, who never expect to stand on a dais and accept a gold medal, who never expect to make the first team never mind represent their State or their country. There is, however, a contribution made by every competitor at every level to his or her sport. Participation encourages growth, and the growth — and achievements — of sport in Australia have been little short of phenomenal.

Sources and references

The following books have been consulted:

Neville Penton, *A Racing Heart: The Story of the Australian Turf* (Collins, 1987); Gary Lester, *Australian at the Olympics: A Definitive History* (Lester-Townsend, 1984); Alan McGilvray, *The Game is not the Same* (ABC, 1986); Bruce Matthews, *Game, Set and Glory: A history of the Australian tennis championships* (Five Mile Press, 1985).

The quotation from Penton is at p.116; Hughes's letter of resignation is reproduced in Chris Harte and Warwick Hadfield, *Cricket Rebels* (QB Books, 1985) facing p.81. The quotation from McGilvray is at p.105. The Matthews quotation is at p.79.

The quotations from John Landy and Johnny Raper are from interview transcripts for the television series 'Blood, Sweat and Tears'. The chapter draws also on the author's own research.

CHAPTER 11

YOU'VE GOT TO HAVE HEART

Don Hogg

Opposite:
An early morning swim in all weathers by the 'Bondi Icebergs' is based on the 'mind-over-matter' principle. A still from the television series, 'Blood, Sweat and Tears'
Paul Tatz

It cannot have been easy for a Collingwood football supporter since 1958 when the team won its last VFL Grand Final, probably Australia's highest-profile, and certainly its consistently best-attended sporting event. In the intervening thirty years to 1988, Collingwood played in seven Grand Finals, losing three of them by less than a single goal and tieing one, only to be beaten in the replay.

Last time the team made the Grand Final, in 1981, against Carlton, its arch enemy, it lost by twenty points. Many Collingwood supporters left the Melbourne Cricket Ground in tears. Along the street a small boy dressed in Collingwood livery was leaning against a shop wall sobbing. An elderly woman dressed in the same colours, also crying, approached him and gently put her arms around him. 'C'mon son, I know how hard it is, but you've got to have heart — there's always next year. You've got to have heart.'

Every champion, all those whose names loom large in Australia's sporting history, know that. And the administrators, the also-rans, the spectators — everyone who ever pulled on a football guernsey or held a squash racquet or oars or the reins of a racehorse knows that to participate in sport at a competitive level, let alone become an elite achiever in it, you need to have heart. It's the strength of will that matters quite as much as the strength of body.

For every one of those sportspeople who take their activity seriously enough to aspire to reach the top of the heap there are literally thousands more who simply play for the sake of it; for the benefit the activity brings to mind or body, or perhaps for no other reason than that in the pursuit of their chosen sport they may broaden their social opportunities, enhance the quality of their lives.

For there to be champions there has to be, of course, a base from which they may spring, a common denominator from which measurement of achievement may properly be made. It has been estimated that as many as six million Australians engage in one sport or another each weekend the whole year round. That means nearly 40 people out of every hundred is at play for those two precious days of competition, leisure and recreation each week.

Some of the statistics surrounding sport in Australia are astounding. In 1988 there were 750 000 men and women, boys and girls playing netball. Basketball boasted 200 000 registered players with a further 100 000 unregistered participants. Lawn

You've Got to Have Heart

bowling authorities claimed that on every day of the year there were 550 000 bowlers using the tens of thousands of greens around the nation. An interesting statistic also provided by the lawn bowling administrators was that in 1988 the average age of lawn bowlers was 42 years. Fifteen years earlier, in 1973, the average had been 48 years.

The establishment of bowls clubs and regular competition went on apace through the late 19th century. These Hobart bowlers of the 1890s are smartly attired in club jackets and hats
Archives Office of Tasmania

You've Got to Have Heart

Bowls was taken up early in Australia's life after settlement, as a recreational sport for gentlemen. This diverse group of citizens in seen playing at the Melbourne Bowling Green, Chapel Street, Prahran in 1865. The artist is S. T. Gill
Mitchell Library

Below:
These participants in the Amputee Games in Sydney are a dedicated band among the legion of lawn bowlers who take to their beautifully manicured greens every day in the summer in the southern States and throughout the year in the north
Live Action: Acikalin

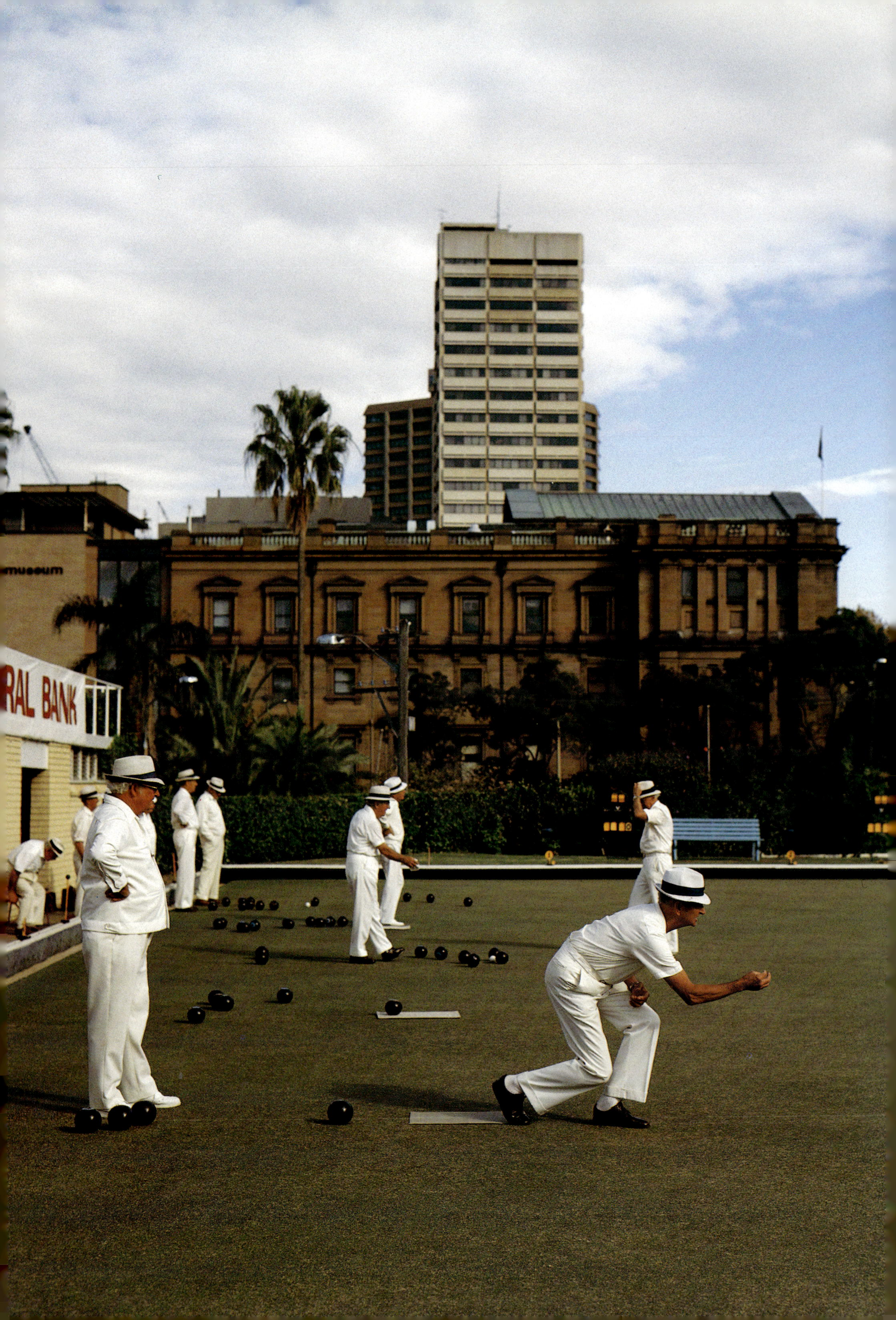
museum
RAL BANK

Opposite:
As Australia's population ages and leisure time increases, the already popular sport of lawn bowls is booming, but conversely the average age of bowlers has dropped by six years (to 42) since 1973
Photographic Library of Australia

Below:
A twin-hulled power boat surges through Port Phillip Bay off Brighton. Ocean racing in high-powered speedboats is hard on the body as well as the bank balance. The high spot of the year is the Sydney to Newcastle race
Roger Gould

The 1960s, 1970s and 1980s had seen an explosion in the number of sports and leisure activities. Orienteering captured the imagination of thousands of Australians from the middle 1960s. Water skiing and grass skiing arrived and immediately attracted hordes of adherents. Children took to BMX cycling and skateboarding with enthusiasm and the colourful, triangular sails of sailboards in their thousands gave a new excitement to the lakes, harbours and even the dams of the Commonwealth. Each weekend the owners of four-wheel-drive vehicles headed bush to tackle the creek crossings, the deserts and mountains, and the buzz and sputter of trail bikes ripped at the former quiet of the green belts surrounding the cities. Offshore motor-boat racing appeared for the first time on television screens. Hot air ballooning, sky diving and parachuting offered new experiences to Australians seeking both the satisfaction of participation and the thrills of competition. Glider pilots were happy to travel hundreds of kilometres in a weekend in search of thermals to send their machines soaring, and rock-climbers challenged the silent dangers of the earth's very shape. The traditional, long-established, high-profile sports such as cricket, athletics, swimming, football in its various codes, golf and tennis have had to compete with a host of sports made possible by the affluence of the Australian

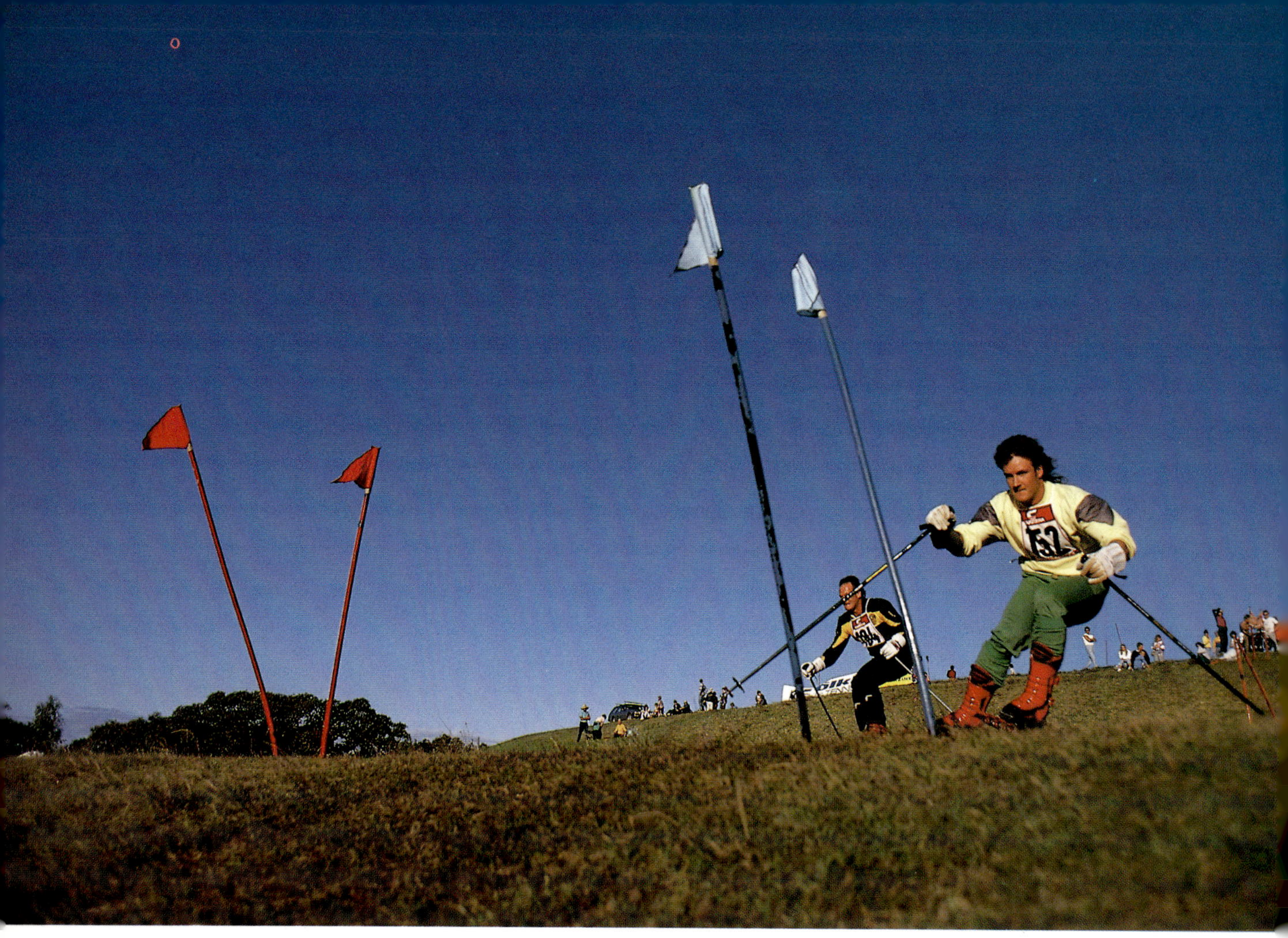

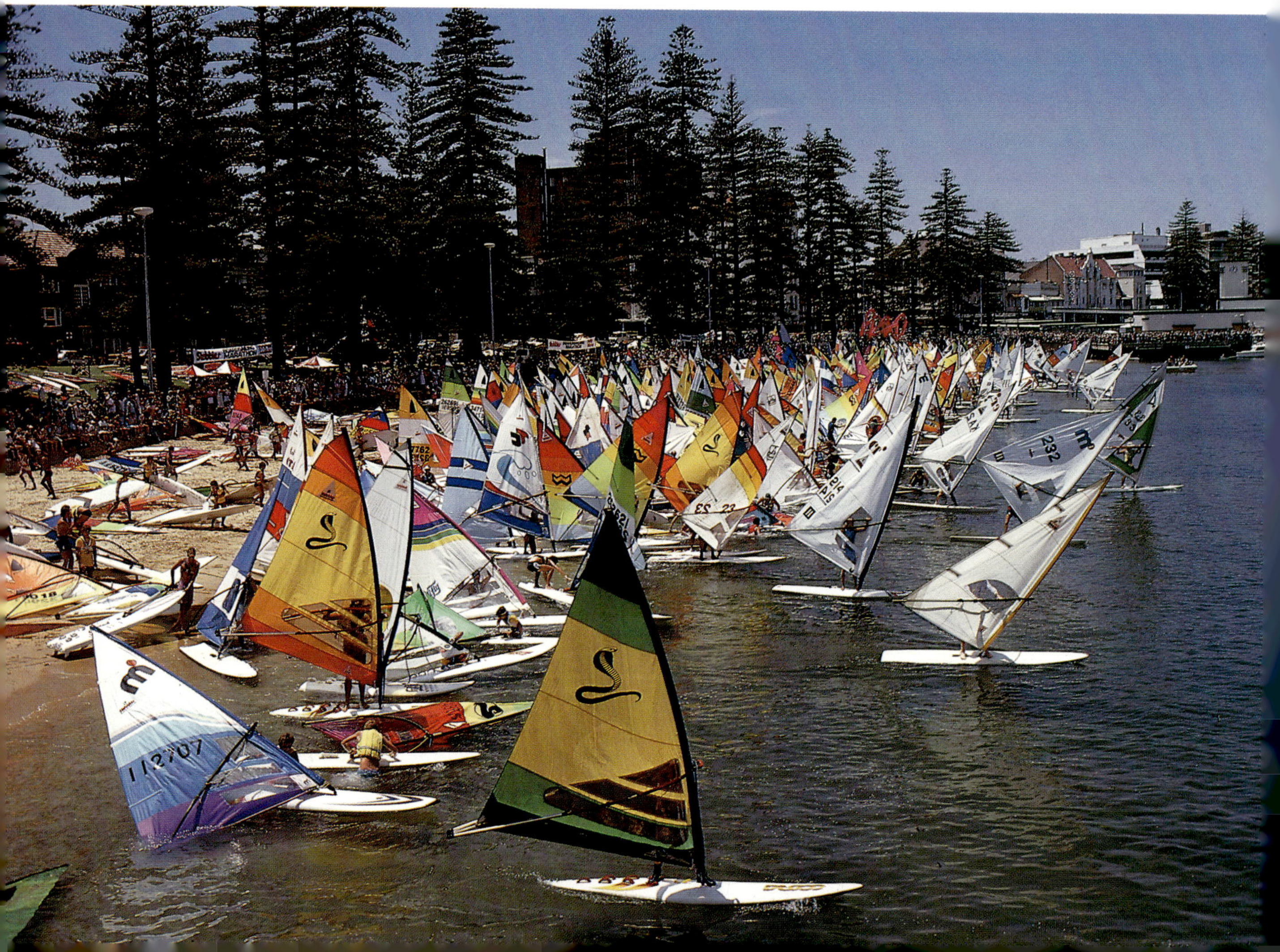

Opposite, top:
The range of ways to seek out danger is ever increasing in Australian sport. Australian champion Craig White takes off on a downhill run at Moore Park in Sydney
Martin King Sportpix

Opposite, bottom:
Windsurfing has brought cheap thrills for sailors young and old alike. A mass start to a race at Manly beach, Sydney, provides a rich spectacle
Live Action: Acikalin

community, the ease and speed of travel and the staggering advances in technology. You couldn't have been an off-road four-wheel-driver thirty years ago because there were only a handful of four-wheel-drive vehicles. And you couldn't have been a grass skier because grass skis hadn't been invented. Advances in modern plastics and lightweight fabrics made the sailboard a reality, and lightweight, relatively cheap and reliable motorcycles meant trail-bike riding was possible.

Of that great body of Australians who engage in sporting activity in all its forms, the majority are at play simply for the fun of it.

Bill Moyes, one of the world's hang-gliding pioneers and one of the sport's champions, says that as a five-year-old he dreamed of running and jumping from a rock ledge with a set of wings. 'When I first got hold of a hang glider it just fulfilled that dream.' Moyes made his first flight with a hang-glider, or kite as he calls it, in 1966 and within six weeks he had set a new world altitude record.

Moyes has flown over the Grand Canyon, set endurance and new altitude records since his early days with the sport. He talked of another dream. 'At my age I don't think it's possible to climb Mount Everest with a hang glider. But I could fly up there with a disposable balloon and release the balloon when we were in a suitable position. You'd have to launch the balloon and glider upwind and fly over the top of the mountain and release the balloon and then fly to the summit, land on it and then take off again before you were short of oxygen and equipment . . . it's only possible to take a certain amount of gear on a flight like that. My ultimate dream is the big one, and that's Mount Everest.'

The term 'social player' was not uncommon in golf, tennis, squash and many other sports; indeed tens of thousands of Australians belonged to sporting clubs for social reasons — the opportunities to meet people and develop relationships. For the great majority of sporting Australians the game was the thing; they were not looking for reward by way of riches or recognition but for self-satisfaction.

From the early days of the nation there had been professionals, particularly in cycling, boxing, foot racing, Rugby League and horse-racing, but their numbers were few. Amateurism had been the thing for most Australians, and until fairly recent times there had been the almost universally held view that there was something wrong with professionalism in sport, that the real sportsmen and women were amateurs. For the greater part of Australia's sporting history a stigma marked professionalism.

Television, perhaps more than anything else, has changed this view; at the same time the medium has caused a rush to professional status. With the big money that television brought, a career in professional sport began to look a more and more realistic option. Slowly, ever slowly, professional sports people grew respectable in the eyes of the country's sports fans.

In the 1950s, before the advent of television, American tennis stars, once amateur, recently turned professional, and led by the former Wimbledon champion Jack Kramer, toured Australia annually and played to big houses. Australians, among them the legendary John Bromwich and Dinny Pails, joined the troupe and the Australian tennis fans tut-tutted. It seemed it just wasn't on for Australian sporting heroes to make money from the game that had made them famous.

Less than twenty years on, the great tennis tournaments of the world, traditionally events restricted to amateurs only, opened their entries to professionals and the great Australian players of the time one by one turned professional. There was to be an even greater shock. The Davis Cup competition, one of the last bastions of international amateur competition, the world's greatest tennis trophy, admitted professionals. Tennis purists were appalled. What they failed to see, it seems, is that tennis was much more than just a game for its leading proponents: it was a living. The participants at the very top had ceased being simply players; they were entertainers as well, via the medium of television, and were demanding appropriate payment for that role.

While the men took up bowls in times past, the ladies turned to croquet. This charming scene is at a croquet club in Perth, Western Australia. The sport of croquet has declined in modern times, while the number of lady bowlers has increased markedly
Battye Library

Of the youngsters who start out to become professionals in the whole range of sport, lured by the dream of fame and wealth, how many make it? There is no real way of knowing. The only certainty is that only one in thousands of aspirants in cricket, tennis, motor racing, lawn bowls, soccer, Australian Rules or any other pursuit will ever make a living from it.

Walter Lindrum, the humble Melbourne man who became the greatest billiards player the world has known, was forced by his father Fred to practise for as many as fourteen hours a day when he was little more than a child. The young Lindrum, his back aching from six or seven hours practice, would plead with his father to be allowed to leave the billiard table. His father, convinced that perfection may only be achieved through the subconscious mind, would send the boy back to work.

Fred Lindrum believed both the mind and the body had to be punished to arrive at a condition where both would react automatically. Walter Lindrum became a professional billiards player at the age of 14. Throughout his career he continued to subject himself to long, daily practice sessions despite the fact that his mastery over the game so far removed him from the abilities of his rivals that the games' administrators were compelled to change the rules to bring him back to the field.

Jim Collins, a contemporary of Lindrum, and a close personal friend says: 'There were many facets to Walter's success. He had sheer determination to succeed which became an obsession with him. At no time did he ever seek to reduce his

You've Got to Have Heart

Above:
Walter Lindrum, second from left, looks an unlikely hero as he poses with his family in 1925. Mr Lindrum's family was infatuated with billiards and Walter became the world's greatest player, achieving more than thirty breaks of 2000, two of 3000 and one, in 1932, of 4137
Herald & Weekly Times

Walter Lindrum at the height of his power. His mastery of the nursery cannon forced the English administrators of the game to alter the rules in an attempt to curb him. It made little difference to his supremacy. When he died in 1960 he still held 57 world records
Herald & Weekly Times

Opposite:
Boiling out of the city streets of Sydney thousands of athletes compete in the annual City-to-Surf fun run. Fun runs in Australia have become a highlight of the joggers' lives, and have the advantage that they usually raise money for a deserving cause
Photographic Library of Australia

hours of practice; he thrived on it. The game itself imposes an awful strain on your back, but he had very strong back muscles and he withstood the arduous routine of hour after hour of practice without any difficulty. But perhaps the biggest material factor was his determination to succeed and keep on that dull, monotonous routine that would take him to success.' Lindrum had the motivation to take the arduous training into himself and become a champion.

Sir Jack Brabham, three times Formula One motor racing champion of the world and the first Australian to win the title, lived with his wife in a shabby, one-room London flat and earned a few pounds by selling racing car parts to friends back in Australia while he embarked on the long, slow road to recognition. He understands the sacrifices needed to achieve success. He retired from his sport with impaired hearing and in poor health.

Perhaps more than most professional sportsmen, jockeys understand what hard work and sacrifice is. To succeed they must carefully control their weight, which for many means daily visits to the sauna — the sweat box as they call it — and they must be at the racetracks at dawn most days to put the horses through their training programs. And on racedays they risk their lives.

Certainly the financial rewards of success in some professional sports in recent years have been huge. Wendy Turnbull, the evergreen tennis player, boasted career earnings of more than $1 million, and top players in the Victorian Football League were being paid between $100 000 and $150 000 a season, with players of lesser ability getting over $30 000. There was money to be earned from stardom in virtually all sports, especially those with big television followings, and more and more Australians were becoming cognisant of the fact.

With little thought of glory or reward, Carole Grahame took up body building 'because I was very skinny and shapeless and I wanted something that would help me improve my looks. I knew that there was a choice between being fat and skinny, but I wasn't happy with either, I wanted something in between. Then I discovered body building could shape you in all the right places — you could still have a small waist and good curves, so I decided I'd get involved in it.

'I decided to be more feminine and body building has given me that. Body building has been wonderful to me. I've travelled the world several times, I've met lots of people and I've been able to pass on to other women what body building can do for you, and that's been a great thing for me. Women's body building is a lifestyle, it's something you can do forever . . . It's the most feminine thing you can do for your body, it shapes you, it works your whole body and you can have exactly what you want out of the sport.'

Explaining why he began his career in marathon swimming, Des Renford says, 'At the ripe old age of 39 I felt that I was getting into middle age and life was passing me by. A Melbourne newspaper was running a 25-mile race across Port Phillip Bay and I entered. I led for 17 miles and then I became exhausted and I finished up coming in third. I was mentally, physically and emotionally distraught and I spent two days in Frankston Base Hospital. I knew right from that very moment that if I gave myself the right sort of training I'd be a pretty good marathon swimmer, and that's how it all developed.

'The most satisfying swim of my life was the first time I swam the English Channel. It was the culmination of three and a half years' work from January 1967 to August 1970, thousands and thousands of swimming hours behind me, thousands and thousands of hours pounding the pavements punishing your body, and all of a sudden in twelve and a half hours you've achieved that goal you've set yourself. I don't think I could explain the sense of euphoria and personal achievement that I got out of it.

'In the early days when I was starting out I used to run raffles down at the Maroubra Bay pub to try and get some money to finance my swimming. We used to run bodgie raffles — we used to get a bloke, one of our own, and give him the

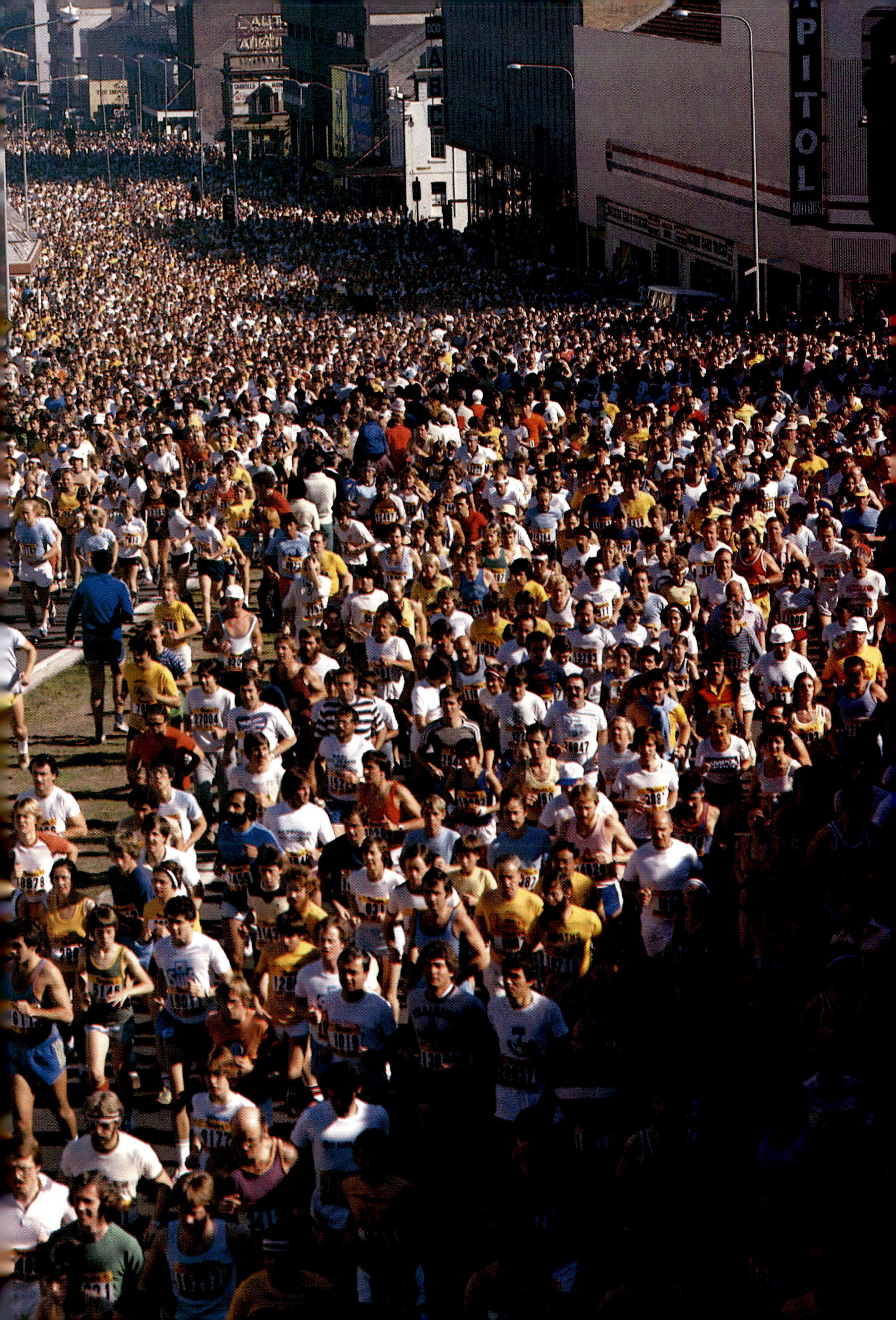
APITOL
ABC

winning ticket and he put it into his ring finger and he'd pull out the prize so we wouldn't have to give the prize out and we'd carve the meat up among ourselves and still get the money. I ran gambling nights and I'd do all sorts of things, and my friends also gave a lot of help to get me there. And the Maroubra Seals Club and the Coogee RSL Club helped me.

'It was just a damned hard battle, but that made it all worthwhile. I had to do three jobs on the side and I had to raise a family, so I was a salesman during the week and on Fridays and Saturday mornings I'd work in a butcher's shop. On Saturday afternoons I used to pencil for an SP bookmaker to get a few extra bucks, and that's how I got over to Europe for my channel swims, and I think the only way an Australian can do it is by bloody hard work.'

In 1988 Des Renford was 61 years of age and in his long career he had held most of the world's recognised titles in long-distance swimming. Why had he set out to, among other things, swim the English Channel? 'There's only one Stawell Gift, there's only one British Open in golf, there's only one Wimbledon, there's only one Melbourne Cup and there's only one English Channel. Of all the swims I've done around the world there's nothing that can emulate a swim across the Channel. It has a tradition dating back to 1875 when Captain Matthew Webb first conquered the Dover Straits and nothing can capture that.'

Renford believes man can achieve any goal 'as long as it's an achievable goal'. Discipline, dedication and devotion are totally necessary in any area of life, not only sport, he says. 'I've often thought there's not much difference between a sportsman and a businessman. A banker or a businessman has money as his working capital, and a sportsman's got time for his working capital. The sportsman has to budget his time like the businessman budgets his money otherwise he'll wonder where it's all gone.

'Man's got to keep striving, he's got to have a goal to strive for and to drive for. If you haven't got a goal you run round in circles. If you've got a goal you make things happen instead of letting things happen to you. And each and every one of us has to test ourselves to the limit.' So that, it seems, is what made Des Renford swim.

Richard Sibthorpe was another Australian who set out to do something that had not been achieved before. His goal was to run a marathon in the Antarctic. A keen jogger in Canberra, his work took him to the Antarctic in 1983 and he continued his running, but this time on the sea ice. 'I was running out there on the sea ice one day, in the vicinity of the camp and on this particular day I sort of lost myself and I'd run around in circles. I was calculating how far I'd run and I worked out that it was about ten miles which was about the furthest I'd ever run at that stage and I thought "what an odd place to do that". The next thought that came to me was the marathon in Antarctica. The guys I used to run with said, "that's stupid, that's impossible", but therein the seed was sown and I thought about it and I said "why not?"'

With one of his colleagues, the camp diesel mechanic Ian McDonald, Sibthorpe trained for the next ten weeks with a view to them both running a marathon at the end of the Arctic winter. Sibthorpe says: 'On the day of the race it was a really heavy track. We had an unfortunate heavy snowfall and no strong winds to blow it away so it was a really tough track and I was gone after 18 miles — it was just too tough for me. But Ian, being the tough bird that he is, plugged on and got the distance and in the history of mankind he's the first person to get the 26 miles in Antarctica, a wonderful effort. I guess I was a bit disappointed although perhaps I didn't show it. When I decided to go back to Antarctica, the moment I was given the green light to go there, the marathon was in the back of my mind and I started training again. I knew there were to be no Nellie Melbas this time, it had to be all or nothing. So it was a very serious business for me.'

Sibthorpe returned to Antarctica in 1986 and resumed training. 'You have to put the miles in irrespective of where you are. That's as true down there as anywhere

You've Got to Have Heart

Body-building has traditionally been a male preserve but the last few years have seen an increasing number of girls and women redefining their bodies. Carole Grahame is one of the leading exponents of the beautiful body brigade. A still from the television series 'Blood, Sweat and Tears'
Paul Tatz

Life begins at 39! Des Renford has compiled an amazing career record since he first began marathon swimming in 1967 at the age of 39. He has swum the English Channel a record fourteen times (both ways). His advice? 'Man's got to keep striving!' A still from the television series 'Blood, Sweat and Tears'
Paul Tatz

else. I had to run when the weather permitted and run consistently. It might have been after a heavy snowfall or when it was extremely cold, I had to go out there and do it. That's part of the deal if you're serious about it.'

Sibthorpe says he was very nervous leading up to his second attempt. 'On race day I knew I was right, I knew I was fit, I'd had a good preparation and the weather was good. The track itself was pretty fast out over the sea ice and I was pretty confident I was going to get there, nevertheless it had to be done. On the day everything went beautifully. I really had the support of the chaps on the station there. Like all marathoners, having the crowd on the side of the road makes a big difference. I perhaps may not have been so successful without them.'

To prevent dehydration during the run Sibthorpe needed to drink large amounts of water. At each of his regular drink stops he drank three cups. Because of the heavy clothing he was wearing against the cold the sweat could not escape easily, but the moisture worked its way to the outside of his clothing and turned to ice. At the end of the successful attempt on the marathon distance Sibthorpe weighed 2.5 kilograms more than when he had set out.

Asked whether he would do it again he said, 'I wouldn't have the urge to do it again. I have overcome having to do it again. I've achieved it. I'm really very proud that I have'. For the run this remarkable young man wore thick-soled joggers, two pairs of thick woollen socks, two sets of long woollen underwear, football shorts under woollen pants, a woollen shirt and jumper, mitts and scarf. That was Richard Sibthorpe's idea of fun. At the same time it was his contribution to Australia's sporting history.

Not everyone, of course, tackles their sporting activity with the same single-minded will to succeed. In the pubs and clubs of the nation nightly great numbers of Australians, young and not so young, play competitive darts or pool. Some take their places in their pub or club sides seriously and practise assiduously; others approach the activities in a much more casual way, seeing their participation as an opportunity to do little more than enjoy a good night's outing in an environment of good companionship to which the thrill of competition has been added.

The Bald Rock Hotel in the inner western Sydney suburb of Rozelle, like literally hundreds of other hotels around Australia in 1988, fielded darts teams. Each of the Bald Rock's two teams was made up of six players with two reserves. Each Tuesday night the hotel hosted a side from another hotel while the other team played its 'away' match. Sixteen hotels were represented in this particular competition which was divided into summer and winter tournaments and into two groups according to player skills.

The drinkers gather round each Tuesday night to watch their heroes play. The pub's reputation is seen as being on the line. Such a simple thing as a game of pub darts is treated as a matter of great moment. Two hours or so later when the final dart has been thrown, the result of the contest known and accepted, the players mingle over a convivial beer or two. Which is not to say a beer or two hasn't been consumed during the course of the competition, but the beers following the match are the ones the players have really come for. They are the ones over which there's the opportunity to discuss every dart in the match, to analyse the finest little detail, and to make new friends. While winning to these folk is a sweet and pleasurable thing, losing isn't a bitter experience. It's the playing that has mattered, not to mention the outing itself.

At the village of McLaren Vale on the Fleurieu Peninsula south of Adelaide the Aussie Rules team meets at the hotel after training twice a week and the talk is exclusively of how they're going to go about beating whichever surrounding village they meet next Saturday or Sunday. And on the day of the match more people than you would think live in the district turn out to cheer their boys on. The scene is repeated, whatever the sport, across the country each weekend.

Richard Sibthorpe on a training run for his most difficult and dangerous challenge, a marathon in the Antarctic. His training diary from May to September 1986 records temperatures from −6°C to −30°C. He writes 'the weather was the boss here'
Matthew Gould

Is there anything different about jogging in the Antarctic? Richard Sibthorpe says you can never relax: 'You are always concentrating on where your next footstep will land: the ground may look good but can have a few inches of give in it with each footfall. One eye is forever searching for better ground, while the other is monitoring the plateau horizon for any fuzziness indicating drift or weather'
Grahame Canterbury

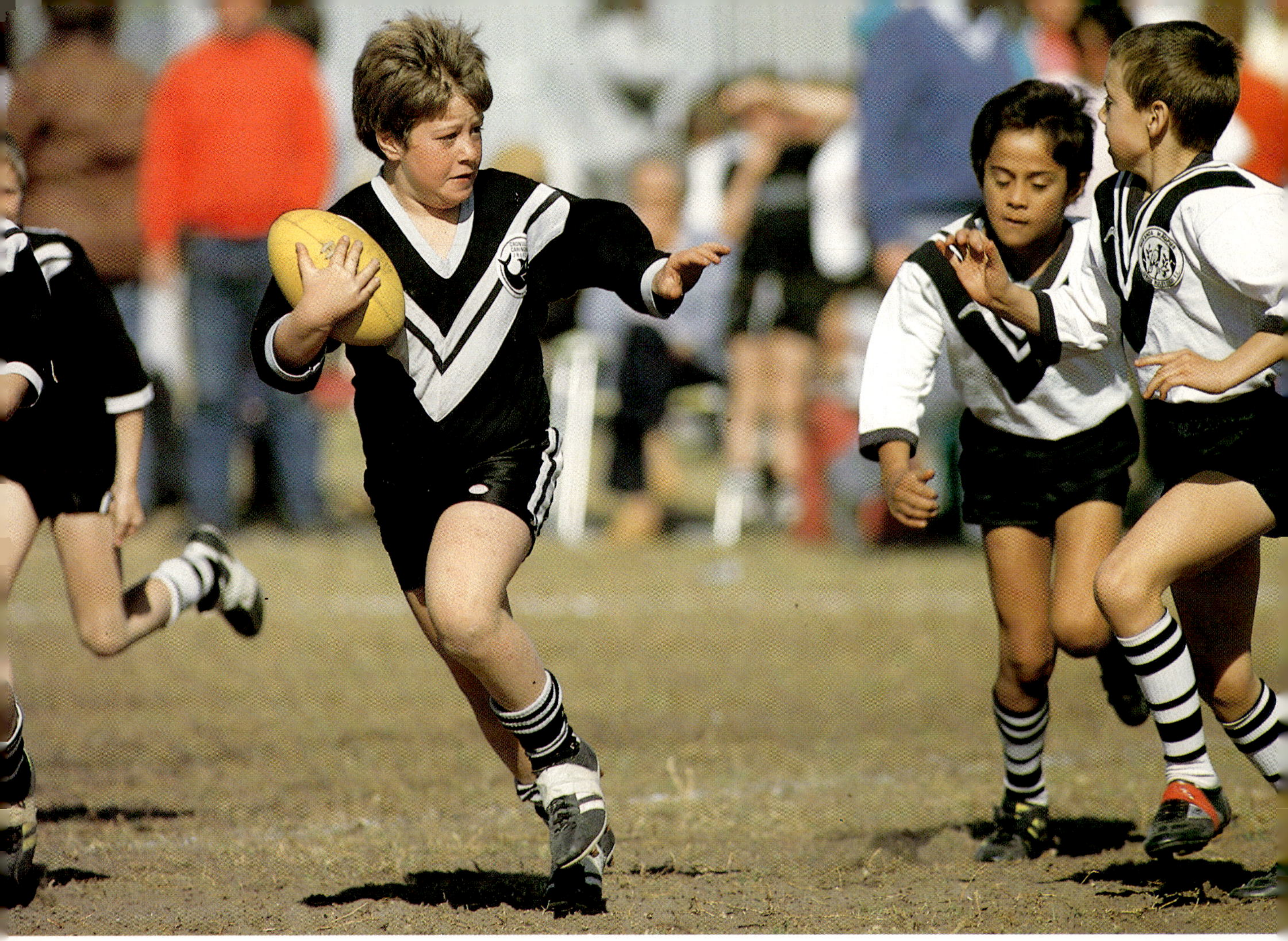

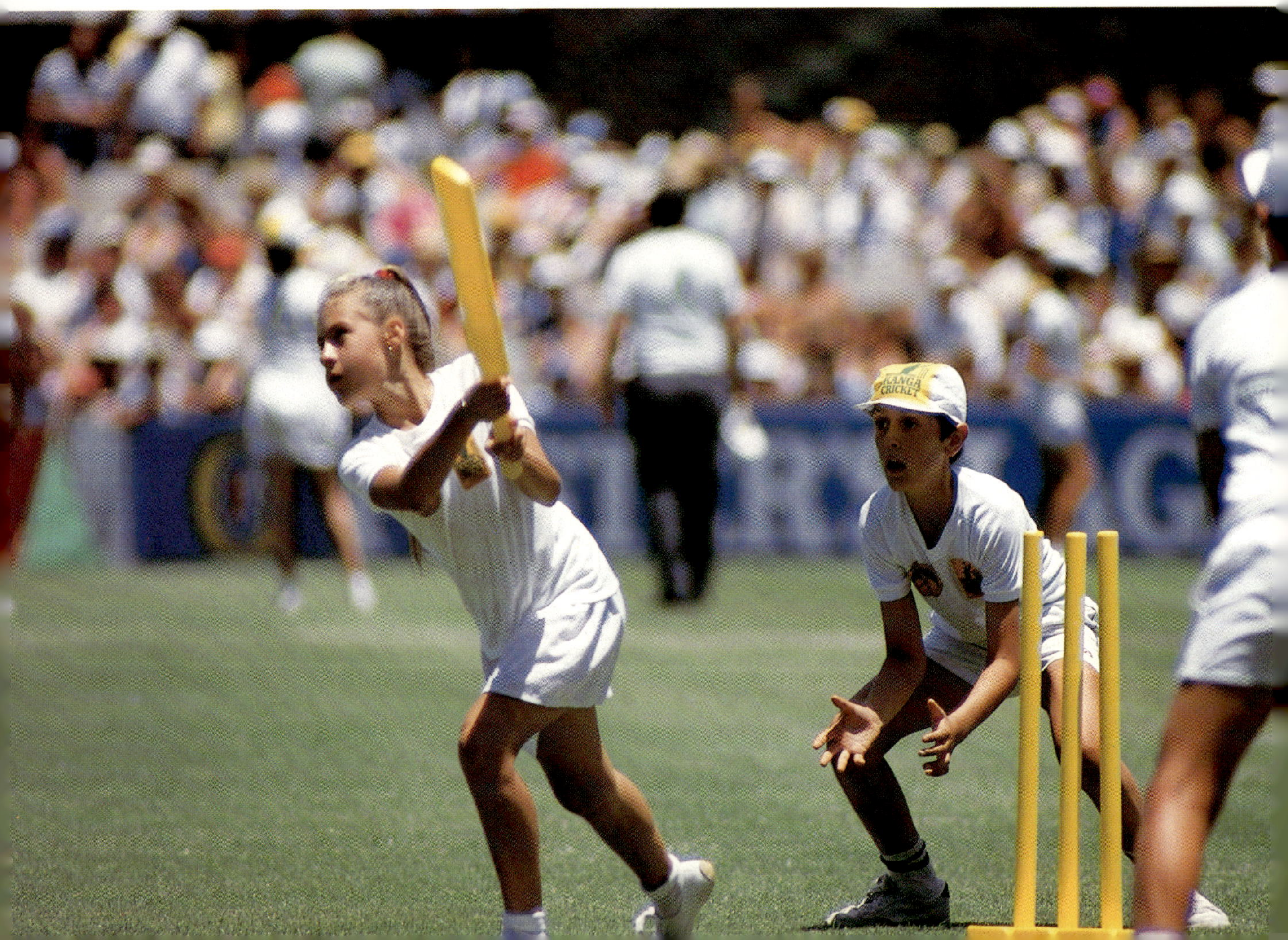
KANGA CRICKET

Saturday morning excitement as these Sydney juniors give their best in a Rugby Union game. Saturday morning club sport brings many Australian families out as their girls and boys take part in swimming, netball, football, hockey and a host of other sports. In schools at least one morning or afternoon a week is set aside for sport
Action Graphics

While all the evidence seems to suggest that Australians take sport seriously, Martin Weeks, a management consultant and former director of the Australian Sports Commission, writing in the *Sydney Morning Herald* in June 1988, suggested quite the opposite. Weeks argued that sport is, as a total enterprise, largely unco-ordinated. He pointed to the fact that government agencies concerned with sport are largely not coordinated and in some cases overlap. Nobody in Australia, he said, can tell you how many people play sport, how many sporting facilities there are, how many people are employed in sporting enterprise or how much is spent by people playing or watching sport. If you were foolish enough to ask, he said, you would have surprising difficulty discovering how much each State government spends on sport. 'And all of this of an activity which at a best guess contributes about one per cent of Gross Domestic Product to the nation's wealth, employs up to 150 000 people and involves about six million Australians as active participants.'

For as long as anyone can remember, most of Australia's sporting administration has fallen to those who give freely of their time and experience to help run the local club. Often these folk have retired from their chosen sport as active participants, and now seek to give something back to the sport and to use their involvement in administration to enhance the quality of their lives. To them falls the responsibility of discipline, recruitment, management and, by no means the easiest of their tasks, fundraising. The sporting club raffle and bazaar, the weekend dance and the fund-raising nights have become institutions in the Australian way of life.

Mums and dads, big brothers and sisters, uncles and aunts can be seen on any Saturday morning taking the little Australians to sport. Four- and 5-year-olds going to swimming, 7- and 8-year-olds in their smart, new uniforms off to the local oval for footy or cricket; little girls going to gym-basketball, their bigger brothers and sisters crowding the buses and trains heading for their chosen pursuit.

In the schools at least one morning or afternoon a week is put aside for sports and all the mainstream (and some not so mainstream) activities are actively encouraged and nurtured. Inter-school and intra-school competition is something most young Australians see as an important and desirable part of the school curriculum. It's possible to be a local hero, an envied member of junior society at eight or nine years of age. Certainly among most young Australians proficiency at sport is seen as a desirable social asset.

In many schools there has been a dramatic change of attitude to sport in the 1980s. Writing in the *Bulletin* of 19 April 1988, Tony Abbott said:

> School sport in Australia was once straightforward: jocks in one corner, swots in the other — and cultural activities bundled unceremoniously out the back door. It was all firmly rooted in the British Rugby School tradition, a private school ethos in which sport predominated and exam marks could go to hell. In state schools it was much the same — only the sporting codes were different. And the girls cheered from the sidelines.
>
> All that has changed, but in unexpected ways. Sport is still up there, but sharing the arena. If no-one quite accepts these days that sport is the making of the man, fewer still insist that it breeds barbarians.
>
> State schools crave the prestige and high morale that sporting success brings. Private schools — which once bred 'rugger buggers' — now hold that cultural pursuits must complement bat, ball and book.

Young cricketers swing into action during the lunch time break in an international one-day match. Despite the proliferation of other sports opportunities, cricket remains the most popular summer sport in Australia
Live Action: Acikalin

In 1987 a survey conducted by the Australian Council of Health and Physical Education found that 90 per cent of all boys aged 15 and 87 per cent of all girls of the same age played sport. It was Abbott's view that 'in the fight for attention between study, culture and the various fads, educational or otherwise, which seem to find their ways into schools, sport is winning'.

Not everyone shares this view. It is comic to observe that the behaviour of parents at fixtures was causing some education department officials concern. Indeed in

Blood, Sweat and Tears

May 1987, the New South Wales Minister for Education, Mr Rodney Cavalier, was moved to suggest that badly behaved parents should be asked to leave sports fields.

Announcing a code of behaviour covering players, teacher–coaches, parents, spectators, the media, officials and administrators, Mr Cavalier said the code was aimed at ensuring participants in all games played within the rules with a sense of responsibility for the safety of all. He singled out parents who criticised rival teams. 'The moronic behaviour of some parents urging their children on in weekend games will be unacceptable in school sports', he said. 'I expect our teachers to give our parents prompt marching orders if they step over the mark in barracking.' Such parents should be told politely they were unwelcome and asked to leave. 'Everyone involved in the good of the sport will make it clear that barracking that is unfair, fails to recognise the merits of the other team or places unfair pressure upon the team they are supporting, is simply not acceptable.'

A rosy future for Australian athletics seems assured when we look at these fit and enthusiastic young people at the opening ceremony of the World Cup Athletics in Canberra in 1985
Photo Library

Explaining why he thought a code of behaviour was necessary the minister said: 'A number of Greater Public Schools have been particularly concerned about the way in which their Rugby Union matches became approximations of the Battle of Gettysburg'.

The most noticeable development in school sports in recent years has been the shift away from the traditional sports — football, cricket and athletics for boys, netball, hockey, athletics and swimming for girls — to a range of sports catering for all interests. To the traditional sports had been added sailing, gymnastics, canoeing, trampolining and lawn bowls. An Australia-wide programme called 'Aussie Sports' involved 500 000 primary school children. Its purpose was to develop skills rather than introduce children to a particular sport. Under this programme the notion of winning is played down; instead the emphasis is on teaching children to catch, run, pass and kick well.

Competitive games for both girls and boys have been introduced, among them football without tackles and cricket played with a soft ball. The New South Wales Department of Education reported that in 1987, the year of its introduction, mixed-touch football, a game in which boys and girls compete on the same basis, became the third biggest State school competition behind Rugby League and soccer.

There has also been the emergence of national school competitions and a much greater emphasis on women's or girls' sporting activity. According to Abbott there were, in 1988, 'commendably fewer sex and class distinctions'. Developing that theme, Abbott reported:

> The general rule promulgated by education departments is that boys and girls must be treated equally. In primary schools where boys and girls are treated as physically equal, no sex based discrimination is allowed unless clearly necessary to avoid disadvantaging girls.
>
> Boys' sport too has changed. Geoff Hornibrook, a sports officer with the Queensland Education Department, says that mothers make more decisions about their sons' activities. This has meant a wider range, with less stress on rugby and Aussie football. Another factor in the diversification has been the increasing number of women teachers in boys' schools.

By 1988 corporate sponsorship was playing an important role in school sports. In New South Wales and Queensland the Commonwealth Bank sponsored Rugby League competitions; in South Australia Australian football sides competed for the Pizza Hut Cup. Coca-Cola supports cricket in Western Australia and South Australia; and Gillette entered the field in 1988 with a promise to provide $250 000 for a national schools cricket competition for the next five years. Colgate-Palmolive joined the corporate sponsors in 1988 with a commitment to donate $1 million over the next five years. Their interest is in promoting and assisting sports played by both boys and girls.

In the *Sun Herald* of 14 April 1986 Melbourne journalist and writer Keith Dunstan wrote:

> I went to a school deeply steeped in the traditions of Dr Arnold. If one was to acquire a pretty badge on one's pocket or rise to the extraordinary heights of prefect or house captain, it was essential to be able to kick a football with great skill or run with the utmost speed.
>
> You might be able to get away without ever learning the names of the Australian Prime Ministers, but football, cricket and cross country running was compulsory. There were two spectator activities which were also compulsory, chapel six days a week, and taking part in the ritual of observing the school play against other schools.

The one time he refused to watch the school team in a football match against Melbourne Grammar, he was publicly castigated.

Deahhne McIntyre, Young Australian of the Year in 1988, Australian Junior Track Wheelchair Champion
Live Action/Acikalin

It is worth noting that Mr Dunstan grew up to found, in Melbourne, the Anti-Football League, a group actively devoted to the diminution of football as a topic of conversation and to a lessening of the time and space devoted to it by the media. The league seems to have failed in its efforts.

Times have changed since Keith Dunstan's unhappy experiences with school sport. Many of the attitudes surrounding children's sport and recreation appear to have changed. Noting the change, the wit and raconteur Mungo MacCallum observed, in 1986,

> There have been times in recent Australian history when the term 'children's sport' has come perilously close to being a contradiction in terms.
>
> From being a healthy outdoor activity designed to make children physically confident and fit, games have been played with a frighteningly competitive intensity, and have led to so many injuries that a number of families have withdrawn their children altogether. But the good news is that in the last couple of years there has been a quiet revolution in the area.
>
> Probably few people not directly involved have noticed it, but the whole pattern of community children's sport has undergone a radical change. New sports, devised specifically for children, have been invented, largely by modifying the rules for the old ones. Kanga cricket, played with modified equipment, in which everyone is guaranteed a decent bat and bowl, is an example.

> There is still competition, but it is far less ferocious than it was, and children who would normally not have been considered talented enough to make the teams are flocking back to the playing fields in droves. Other non-contact sports, like netball and softball, have virtually trebled their participation in the last year. So far this has been achieved almost entirely by the local sporting associations. The government has provided nothing but moral persuasion and support.

MacCallum then reported how the Federal government would, in the 1986 budget, allocate $400 000 to help promote sport in primary schools, the emphasis being on the new children's sports. 'For the non-athletic children for whom sports days used to be a source of fear and embarrassment, this is good news indeed', he opined. Children's sport may soon be again what it always should have been — fun!

Sources and references
The material in this chapter is derived from the author's own research and observation, with the use of interviews and newspaper articles.
Interview transcripts of the television series 'Blood, Sweat and Tears':
   Jim Collins, Carole Grahame, Bill Moyes, Des Renford, Richard Sibthorpe.
Newspaper quotations:
   Martin Weeks, *SMH*, 9 May 1988; Mungo MacCallum, *Sun-Herald*, 13 April 1986; Keith Dunstan, *Sun-Herald*, 14 April 1986; Tony Abbott, *Bulletin*, 19 April 1988; Rodney Cavalier, *SMH*, 1 May 1987.

POLITICAL FOOTBALL

Brian Mossop

It is worth noting at the outset that two western politicians who advocated boycotts of the Moscow Olympic Games in 1980 — Malcolm Fraser of Australia, unsuccessfully, and Jimmy Carter of the United States, successfully — lost subsequent elections. They may well have lost them anyway, but their respective stands on the Olympics did them far more electoral damage than even they might care to admit.

Both cases served to illustrate the point that, unlike oil and water, sport and politics do mix. However much we may like to think of the two as separate philosophies to be dealt with separately, they are inextricably bound. They always have been, long before Moscow deemed it prudent to march into Afghanistan. Because of the widespread interest in sport — particularly so where Australians are concerned — it follows that sport is more readily subject to manipulation for political ends; that it is more likely to become involved in politics.

As Brian Stoddart argues in his book on sport in the Australian culture, *Saturday Afternoon Fever*:

> To believe in, let alone argue for the separation of sport from politics in modern Australia is, at the very least, to be overoptimistic. At every level of Australian society there is a political dimension to sports activity. And as local, state and federal funds become increasingly significant for the development of Australian sport, those dimensions are widening and deepening. Internationally, it is futile to argue that sport and politics should be separated — many would wish it *were* so, few can argue strongly that it *is* so.

Emerging African nations have discovered what far older nations have long known: that sport can be a most effective weapon when it comes to making a point. Even the superpowers use sport for political point-scoring. The Olympics may still cling to an ideal which most appreciate but there is no denying that, while it is better to confront each other in a sporting amphitheatre than in a theatre of war, when East meets West in international sports events such as the Olympic Games, the medal count means far more than having merely played the game.

Australia is no different from the rest of the world when it comes to how sport is viewed within the community. Financial assistance from government for national teams to compete in events such as the Olympics may be relatively new — there was little of any significance until the 1950s — but the nation has long taken pride

Political Football

Two New South Wales governors had a hand in the shape of racing in Australia. Sir Thomas Brisbane (below left) was the patron of the Sydney Turf Club when it was established in 1825. However, a later Governor Sir Ralph Darling (below right) claimed he was insulted at a Sydney Turf Club dinner in 1927. He withdrew as the club's patron and public servants in the club resigned to form a new club, The Australian Racing and Jockey Club
Mitchell Library

in, and benefited from, the achievements of its athletes. From club to State to nation, sporting bodies are often political in nature because of the kudos which can flow from being associated with a team. Such is the case with many of the leading businessmen in the community — and certainly so with Australian prime ministers who, while they usually have an affection for sport, see in it too the thread which can bind them to the electorate.

While we may regard such pursuits as horse-racing and rifle shooting as the sporting endeavours they are, the two had far broader meaning among colonial governments of the nineteenth century. To be able to shoot straight meant a preparedness in case one should have to confront the enemy; and to have thoroughbred horses at one's disposal meant a potential for mobility. In essence shooting — hunting may be included — and the breeding and racing of thoroughbreds were matters pertaining to national defence and, as such, were fondly encouraged.

The Sydney Turf Club, established in 1825 under the patronage of the governor, Sir Thomas Brisbane, ran into trouble when the far less popular governor, Sir Ralph Darling, took over patronage — which he withdrew in 1827. As the privately run STC folded, so the Australian Jockey Club was born, the 'gentleman's club'. Racing clubs sprang up with the development of the other States, but as a rule they were private clubs which only came under colonial control much later. The STC itself had bloomed again between 1880 and 1905, and was resurrected once more, in 1943, through the insistence of the Labor Premier, William McKell.

McKell wanted to close down proprietary racing clubs and do away with privately owned courses, earmarking Kensington for what today is the University of New South Wales. The premier faced strong opposition, from within and from without the Parliament, but felt he could put the privately owned land to better use. He was not happy with the fact that, in spite of the war, the Associated Racing Clubs, comprising Ascot, Roseberry, Moorfield, Rosehill and Victoria Park, maintained their policy of obtaining whatever profits they could for the benefit of their shareholders. The Australian Jockey Club, on the other hand, had made valuable contributions to charity and patriotic funds. The STC, like the AJC, would be non-proprietary. By abolishing the Associated Racing Clubs there would be added fixtures for the AJC. In spite of the opposition of the Upper House, McKell got his bill through, albeit in a watered-down form, and established the STC. Financial support for the new club came from a compensation fund which extracted 5 per cent from racing revenue, and which helped compensate employees of proprietary racing clubs who lost their jobs. McKell appointed William Hill, a prominent businessman and an outstanding amateur footballer and athlete, as chairman. Extremely capable, as well as popular, Hill and his committee began from scratch and quickly turned the club into a successful venture. Today the STC and the AJC coexist peacefully enough, but both under the watchful eye of the State government.

Sport is political, and no amount of wishing will make it otherwise. It is through sport, as well as the presence of Australians in wars ranging from the Crimean and Boer to Vietnam, that Australia has won an image as a physical, outdoors nation. It is a reputation we sometimes find difficult to live up to, but one we enjoy none the less.

It was war, World War I, which, far from bolstering the reputation of one of the true giants of Australian sport, left it somewhat impaired — until his death in 1917. Boxer Les Darcy, established as the finest middleweight in the country, found himself a helpless target in an amazing conscription campaign. He wanted to enlist, but had been rejected once on health grounds. He was also concerned about sick parents and his nine brothers and sisters — and his mother was against him enlisting until he was 21. Offered a large sum of money to fight in the United States, Darcy approached the Army with a proposal that he be allowed to post a bond, visit the US, and enlist on his return six months later. When the authorities refused, Darcy secreted himself on a steamer and made his way to New York.

The discovery that he had left in 1916 brought an amazing amount of invective as the press turned on him. He was stripped of his titles and, with reports reaching New York branding him as a 'shirker' and a 'deserter', he was unable to secure fights. Darcy was more readily accepted in Memphis, Tennessee, and joined the Flying Corps in April 1917. A month later the persecuted boxer died in a Memphis hospital of septicaemia, the result of a broken tooth sustained in an earlier Australian heavyweight title fight.

The public was divided in its opinion of Darcy in the period up to his death. While he was vilified by the middle-class opinion-makers, he was a hero of the Irish-Catholic anti-conscription forces, rivalling Archbishop Mannix as an important symbol for many working-class Australians. The same public which had been unsure of Darcy in Australia made him a national hero when his body was returned home. Tens of thousands filed past his body as it lay in state in Sydney before a huge funeral in Maitland where he is buried.

Darcy was a victim of public pressure and the inflexibility of the authorities. It was not an episode of which Australians can be proud.

When teams marched in an opening ceremony at the Olympic Games for the first time in London in 1908, Australians represented Australasia. Although Australia had competed as such at Athens (1896), Paris (1900), St Louis (1904) and at the Interim Games in Athens in 1906, it contested both London (1908) and Stockholm

Political Football

The tragic hero of Australian boxing, welterweight Les Darcy. Born of a poor family at Maitland, NSW, Darcy had a stream of stunning main bout victories before the age of 18. He was, however, branded as a draft dodger from World War I recruitment and died at the age of 21 in America before he had a chance to redeem his reputation
Mitchell Library

After his death in America in 1917 Les Darcy, vilified in life, became a national hero. His body lay in state in Sydney before a huge funeral in Maitland, New South Wales, where he is buried. A crowd is gathered here for a memorial service in 1967
John Fairfax & Sons Ltd

(1912) under an Australasian banner. Not until the Games resumed after World War I, at Antwerp in 1920, was the Australian flag in evidence, although team members were still paying their way, either from resources of their own, or from contributions made by members of the public. Government, although making vast contributions to the development of sport at a local level, remained reluctant to commit State and Federal funds.

An illustration of the way government viewed sport came during the Paris Olympics of 1924. Andrew 'Boy' Charlton was one of three Australian gold medallists, causing a sensation in a record-breaking win over the great Swedish swimmer Arne Borg in the 1500 metres. A New South Wales Member of the House of Representatives in Canberra, F. A. McDonald, noting the importance of swimming as a national pastime, suggested a message of congratulations should be sent to Charlton. The reply from Prime Minister Bruce was that there had been so many achievements of note in sport by Australians that to send such a message would be to set a dangerous precedent. So, while Australians were long accustomed to success at cricket as well as many other sporting pursuits, government tended to remain aloof.

Sport had, nevertheless, established its ties with politics, at home and abroad, long before this. 'International relations' meant ties with England. In cricket it was a Melbourne catering firm, Messrs Spiers and Pond, owners of the Café de Paris in Bourke Street, who were responsible for opening relations between Australia and England. Thwarted in their attempts to bring Charles Dickens to Australia in 1861, they settled on an English Eleven, led by H. H. Stephenson. Seven years later, the first Aboriginal cricket team toured England. Although it may not have been viewed as such, it was in fact a cultural exchange and therefore political in nature.

Cricket had begun in Sydney at the Domain, then a part of Hyde Park, and was also played at the Albert Ground in Redfern. That it would eventually settle at the

Sydney Cricket Ground was due in part to local government initiatives. The colonial secretary approached the assistant military secretary in 1851 seeking a grant of land near the Victoria Barracks. When an intercolonial match was played there in 1878 between New South Wales and Victoria, the ground was established as the home of big cricket. The Melbourne Cricket Club meanwhile had run into a problem with its ground bisected in 1854 by a train line running from the city to what is now Port Melbourne. Governor La Trobe appreciated the club's problem, and granted it an adjacent enclosure of approximately ten acres — the site of the present Melbourne Cricket Ground.

While cricket seemed to be well catered for, rugby and soccer were having to do the best they could. The grounds they played on were mere paddocks, and it was all the players could do to keep from stepping into holes or cowpats. Even in their earliest days the various football codes were fighting for the best facilities. Local councils and State and Federal governments have come to appreciate the need to provide recreational facilities, whether for the public generally or for the serious athlete specifically.

Sir Robert Menzies was a politician who made his presence felt in the sporting sphere, both by his love of cricket and by his preparedness to intervene in cricketing matters which in his view might have broader implications. As Brian Stoddart tells us, some of Menzies's correspondence now reposing in the National Library, Canberra, reveals the former prime minister's previously unknown role in a number of matters related to cricket and the West Indies.

He is believed to have played a part in seeing that an Australian team toured the West Indies in 1955 following the suggestion of a British governor that such a tour might have diplomatic value. Nine years later Menzies helped secure a release for Gary Sobers from a contract with South Australia following a request from an influential West Indian politician.

While Menzies was able to bring political pressure to bear, particularly in the field of cricket for which he had an abiding passion — perhaps for its link with the English for whom he had such a soft spot — he did it not only directly, but also more subtly by his evident personal enthusiasm for the game. Most Australians shared his feelings. The successes and failings of the Australian cricket team were felt equally by the prime minister and the man in the street. The effect of this common bond played not a small part in Menzies's long and popular political career.

Municipal councils have long been the major source of sports facilities, taking it on themselves to provide playing fields, pavilions, stadiums, tennis and netball courts and swimming pools. As late as the 1950s and 1960s State government assistance was at best meagre, sport being viewed in the main as a private pursuit best left to the local community for funding. It took until the 1970s for sport to achieve large-scale funding by the States. The Federal government funded the National Fitness Council in 1941, assisted financially the Royal Life Saving Society and the Surf Life Saving Association from 1951, and provided grants to assist in the organisation of the Melbourne Olympic Games in 1956 and the Commonwealth Games in Perth in 1962.

Australia's failure to win a gold medal at the Montreal Olympics in 1976 — for only the fourth time — prompted Canberra to look more seriously at allocating a bigger slice of the budget to sport. The tally was one silver medal and four bronze. Sporting standards were declining, the Confederation of Australian Sport was an effective lobby group, and there was a need to ensure that the Commonwealth Games in Brisbane in 1982 would be a resounding success. In 1981 the Liberal government of Malcolm Fraser established the foundations of the Australian Institute of Sport — an institution for the development of elite athletes which was backed to the hilt by Bob Hawke's Labor government when it came to power in 1983.

Carlton captain and coach Ron Barassi presents a long-time supporter, former Australian Prime Minister Sir Robert Menzies, with his jumper as the No. 1 ticket holder of the club. Sir Robert's love of football, and the Carlton Club, was only surpassed by his devotion to cricket
Herald & Weekly Times

Australia's Institute of Sport was soon regarded by many countries as a facility *par excellence* for the development of the elite athlete. But it was the Hawke government, under Brown's administration of the sport portfolio, which broadened the concept of the AIS to include high-level coaching, sports medicine support including psychologists, improved training and live-in facilities, and the time to develop skills. As Brown points out, 'The irony of sport in Australia is that, despite the extraordinary level of success we have had at international events, most of our sportsmen and women, particularly Olympians, until 1984, competed almost with an arm behind their back'.

The $100 million spent in establishing and maintaining the AIS, the $2 million-plus the 1988 Olympic team received from the Federal government compared with $1.4 million in 1984 and $200 000 for the besieged Moscow Olympics in 1980 are just part of an improving pattern of Federal involvement in sport. Brown maintained that when he took over as minister in 1983, Federal funding amounted to about $6 million. He boasted that in the first budget of the Hawke government he was able to increase the amount for sport to almost $40 million.

The Australian Sports Commission was set up with a twenty-two member board of leading business and sporting figures to administer the new injection of funds. It is now a smaller body incorporated in the board of the Institute of Sport, but still with a watchdog role on how the public money is spent by sporting administrators. Importantly, however, sport was at last being recognised for the role it played, and continues to play, in our society.

Government is quick to make capital out of its willingness to spend money on facilities for sport. The establishment of the Australian Institute of Sport in Canberra is one example among many. The New South Wales government upgraded the Sydney Cricket Ground and developed the Sydney Football Stadium, Parramatta Stadium and the sports complex at Homebush. The South Australian government saw their way to promote a leg of the Formula One motor racing circuit. All these

Political Football

Successive Australian governments have been ambivalent in their approach to sport — unwilling to spend too much but aware of the electoral benefits of sporting success. The establishment of the Australian Institute of Sport in 1981 in Canberra has created a continuing involvement in the training of elite athletes
Roger Gould

were developments worthy of praise in a nation keen on promoting its sporting flair but not as obsessed with it as some of the countries of the Eastern bloc. It intervened to break a deadlock and make possible the construction of lights at the Sydney Cricket Ground by the start of the 1978–9 World Series Cricket season; the Victorian government entered a dispute about whether VFL Grand Finals should be played at VFL Park or the Melbourne Cricket Ground, ruling in favour of the MCG; and deemed it prudent to help the Lawn Tennis Association of Australia to finance a magnificent new National Tennis Centre in Flinders Park — a move it could justify by the fact that the centre is available for a host of events other than tennis throughout the year.

In getting behind a bid to stage a motor racing Grand Prix in 1986, and in making Adelaide a model for Formula One racing, the South Australian government saw value to the State and a means of attracting vast revenue. But there was another motive behind Premier John Bannon's push for the Grand Prix. Success in staging it was to lead to the more important success at the ballot box.

The Queensland government turned the Gabba into a smart greyhound racing venue as well as a fine cricket ground. The Western Australian government has assisted the Western Australian Cricket Association in redeveloping the WACA Ground. The Tasmanian government has done the same with the TCA Ground in Hobart and with developing major cycling facilities.

FOSTER'S
FOSTER'S
5
1:24
157
1
1:25
973
25
Marlboro
Marlboro
Reporter
SIMOD

Political Football

Above:
The new football stadium, developed with the support of the New South Wales government, is the main stadium of Rugby Union in New South Wales. Support of Federal and State governments has helped in the upgrading of facilities and the creation of new centres, such as the National Tennis Centre in Melbourne
Live Action: Acikalin

Opposite:
The McLarens of Prost and Johannsen fly around the street circuit in the Adelaide Grand Prix of 1987. In its first year as host city Adelaide was voted 'Best Grand Prix of 1985' by those connected with the Formula One sport — a marvellous accolade and one that ensured subsequent Grand Prix would be huge successes.
Roger Gould

Commercial recognition had been evident for well over a century. But while State governments made small contributions to early Olympic teams, it has only been in relatively recent years that the Federal treasury deemed it prudent to add a contribution. If that is because politicians see the value of association, or sport as a diversion to be encouraged, it does not matter — as long as the funds continue to be forthcoming.

John Brown is the first to admit that politicians, as well as others, have used sports personalities 'either consciously or otherwise because of the great public appeal that sportsmen have'. As he puts it: 'It has been a criticism of the present government . . . that Bob Hawke and myself were often seen with sportsmen. It's a criticism people can make. I guess the point worth making is that whether we were politicians or not, we have always sought the company of sportsmen and women because we are sporting nuts. And I think the public have accepted it that way'.

As a world stage, the Olympic Games — conceived, ironically, as a means of better understanding between nations — has been continually manipulated for political purposes. Berlin, 1936, was a showpiece for Hitler; when London staged the 1948 Olympics, both Germany and Japan were absent; some fifty nations threatened to withdraw from Mexico City in 1968 if South Africa was reinstated following the ban imposed four years earlier; Mexico was also the venue at which America's 200 metres gold and bronze track medallists, Tommie Smith and John Carlos, gave their Black Power salute, each with a clenched black-gloved hand raised high; 1972 saw the massacre of Israeli athletes at Munich by Palestinian guerillas; Montreal in 1976 was boycotted by African nations angered by the presence of New Zealand whose rugby team was touring South Africa; the Games went ahead in Moscow in 1980 without the Americans who were protesting the Russian invasion of Afghanistan, and with Australia marching in the opening ceremony behind the Olympic rather than the national flag.

The politics of race have been well to the fore in sport in recent decades. The defiant black power salute given by black American athletes, in this case the victorious USA 4 × 100 metres relay team at Mexico City in 1968, was a symptom of the racial struggles back home.
Photobank: All Sport

In 1980 the Fraser government had taken what was to be a controversial initiative. In protest against the Russian invasion of Afghanistan, Malcolm Fraser urged the Australian Olympic Federation to withdraw its team from the Olympic Games in Moscow. Public opinion was split. Fraser stopped short of ordering Australians not to participate — unlike President Carter of the United States. But his pleas instilled doubts in the minds of many athletes, most of whom only get one chance in their lives to compete in an event such as the Games. It was psychological warfare, and the casualties were Australia's sporting men and women. Although the AOF refused to withdraw from the Moscow Olympics, some sporting bodies voted not to send teams, and some individuals chose to stay at home. Some also had their decision rewarded with special payments by the Fraser government.

John Brown, sports minister in the Bob Hawke Labor government from 1983 until 1987, saw the Fraser government's pressure on the AOF as heavy-handed. It was, said Brown, 'the grossest example of the intrusion of politics into sport. It offended me and it offended most Australians who loved their sporting stars'.

Baron Pierre de Courbertin, the founding father of the modern Olympics, never envisaged such turmoil. It was nothing new. Even the Melbourne Olympics of 1956, the first staged in the southern hemisphere, did not escape the overtones of politics. Apart from the fact that the Federal government quite naturally saw the conduct of the Games as helpful in the promotion of the nation both overseas and at home,

Political Football

it was difficult to ignore the feeling among Victorians that they had managed to go one better than the other States, which indeed they had. The result was sports facilities which would do Melbourne proud for many more years.

Several nations absented themselves from Melbourne. But the most blatant display of politics at work came in the pool when Russia and Hungary met in a semi-final of the water polo. The Russians had used tanks to quell the Hungarian uprising, and the feeling among Hungarian athletes was such that emotions boiled over in one bloody moment. Gary Lester quotes the *Sydney Morning Herald*:

> A fierce water polo match between Hungary and Russia today ended in the ugliest scene of the Olympic Games after a Russian player punched a Hungarian player in the eye.
>
> Only the sudden appearance of police, who had been obviously waiting out of sight, prevented a riot. The incident occurred late in the second half, and above the noise, the announcer's voice could be heard declaring the match finished, with Hungary winning by four goals to nil. Throughout the match players of both sides exchanged kicks and punches. The referee ordered five players out of the water — three Russians and two Hungarians. There were several incidents early in the second half when a Russian player was punched or kicked. But the final demonstration began when Valentine Prokopov, of Russia, swam up to Ervin Zador, of Hungary, and punched him in the eye while the ball was at the other end of the pool. Zador climbed out of the water with blood streaming from two deep cuts. Several spectators and Hungarian officials jumped the barrier on to the concourse yelling and shaking their fists at the Russians.

There was bloodshed too in the lead-up to the Mexico City Olympics in 1968 as protesters, mainly students, wandered the streets demonstrating against the Mexican regime and its decision to spend vast sums of money on the Games while the country wallowed in poverty. Just ten days before the Games began, a military display of force resulted in the deaths of some 300 in a city square and injury to another 1000. There were those who felt the Games should be cancelled, but they went ahead anyway and there was no further trouble — other than the Black Power salute given to the crowd, and the watching world, by Smith and Carlos.

In Australia, cricket has provided many instances of an uneasy relationship between sport and politics — in interstate as well as international terms. The tour by the Fifth English team captained by Lord Harris in 1878–9 resulted in an invasion of the pitch by the crowd, the first such major disturbance, when Billy Murdoch was given run out by a Victorian umpire, George Coulthard, in a match at the Association Ground, now the Sydney Cricket Ground. Murdoch, the crowd favourite, had batted through the first innings to score an unbeaten 82 in the New South Wales first innings. When he went cheaply in the second innings, it was too much for many in the crowd who, according to the *Sydney Morning Herald*, caused a 'most disgraceful scene'. The English team was quickly surrounded by an ugly mob, and both Lord Harris and Coulthard were struck. When a second attempt was made to resume play, the crowd again surged onto the field, and play was eventually abandoned for the day. A combination of intercolonial and anti-English feeling was already simmering, and the signal by a Victorian that Murdoch was out was all the spark needed to bring it to the boil. The incident served to make life difficult for the next Australian team in England.

The friction between players and administrators flared into violence as preparations for the 1912 Australian tour of England got under way. In fact what happened was a battle to establish responsibility for the control of cricket in Australia — a rivalry as much concerned with interstate politics as with the differences between players and administration.

In 1905 a meeting of delegates from New South Wales, Victoria and South Australia in Melbourne had resulted in a constitution for a cricketing Board of Control. One of the clauses allowed that: 'The appointment of Manager of any Australian team visiting England or elsewhere shall be made by the players interested and submitted to the Board for confirmation'. It was no more than a cunningly worded bit of frippery — window dressing to keep the players on-side. It would take until 1912 for them to discover that.

East Melbourne bowler Frank Laver had been asked to manage the 1905 tour of England in which he also played in all five Tests. He managed the team with skill, and was a member of a delegation of Australian players who met with the Marylebone Cricket Club committee at Lord's to discuss the future of tour exchanges. The MCC was not prepared to recognise the Australian Board of Control which it felt did not represent the interests of all parties. It would, however, continue to welcome to England teams representative of Australian cricket.

The players, concerned that there might be no tour by the MCC to Australia in 1907, signed a letter asking the Melbourne Cricket Club to bring out a team from England. Ray Robinson noted, 'Piqued, NSW officials disqualified all the senior State's players who signed the letter. With this bludgeon of authority officials inflicted a slow-to-fade bruise on relationships in the game. [Joe] Darling and [Clem] Hill, saying they would not play in Sydney until their victimized Test mates were reinstated, caused a hurried backdown by officials, gulping hard'.

South Australia, the home State of Darling and Hill, rejoined the Board of Control in 1907 with Darling, a former Australian captain, as its delegate. Darling was unimpressed with the way the board conducted itself. Laver again managed the 1909 Australian team in England. But instead of the players choosing the touring party, the board appointed two lesser lights — Frank Iredale and Peter McAlister. McAlister, who felt he should have been chosen for an earlier tour, selected himself and made himself vice-captain. The board's hand was clear, but it was only a portent of things to come.

Matters came to a head with preparations for the 1912 tour. Double-cross, double talk and half-truth paved the way for the eventual departure of a makeshift team minus six of its star players: captain Clem Hill, batting idol Victor Trumper, all-rounder Warwick Armstrong, left-hand batsman Vernon Ransford, fast bowler Albert Cotter and wicketkeeper Hanson Carter. The Board of Control was doing what its name implied.

The dispute, which was to cause bitterness for many years, began with a resolution aimed at getting rid of Frank Laver, the team manager to England in 1905 and 1909, and a man held in high regard by the players. The board was still smarting from Laver's part in discussions with the Marylebone Cricket Club seven years earlier in which the MCC declined to recognise the authority of the board. While the players thought they still retained the right to appoint the manager, the words 'subject to confirmation by the Board' had been added to the original clause.

The wresting of all control of the game from the players had been going on for some time. All hell broke loose at a meeting of the selectors in Sydney to choose a team for the fourth Test against England in Melbourne during the 1911–12 season and the team to go to England in March, 1912. The selectors were Clem Hill, the Australian captain, Peter McAlister, who leaned towards the board, and Frank Iredale. Also present was the board secretary, Sydney Smith. Before they met, Hill sent a telegram to McAlister which read: 'Macartney all right. Think must have left-arm bowler. Suggest Macartney and Matthews in place of Whitty and Minnett. Minnett twelfth'. McAlister's reply was cutting: 'My team as forwarded yesterday. Still opposed Macartney's inclusion. If Iredale agrees with you, favour yourself standing down and not Minnett'.

Tension filled the air when the selectors got together. Hill threw in Laver's name for the fourth Test, much to the annoyance of McAlister who suggested Kelleway and Minnett, neither of whom appealed to Hill who found his leadership of the Australian team under fire from McAlister. The argument developed into the most bitter, most violent and most controversial selectors' meeting ever held. What happened was to have remained a secret for the good of the game, but it was impossible to keep the events of that night from becoming public.

As Robinson records it, the meeting degenerated into a physical altercation. Hill struck McAlister after one taunt too many, and McAlister, invited by Hill to retaliate, made his move. 'Rushing around the table, McAlister grappled with Hill. Locked together, they swayed around the room, crashing against the table and the walls.' The pair fought for the next ten minutes, blood staining their clothes as they traded punches. When it was over, an unmarked Hill was standing over McAlister, lying flat on his back on the floor. As Hill left the room, McAlister called him a coward. Hill informed Smith he could not continue to act as a selector alongside McAlister, and was asked to put his resignation in writing. It was accepted the same evening, and the remaining two selectors chose the team for the fourth Test — still omitting Macartney — and named a preliminary ten players for the England tour. Hill was given a rousing cheer when he walked to the wicket in Melbourne six days later, as he was in Sydney in what was to be his last Test. Deprived of the chance to lead Australia in a triangular Test tournament in England, he called it a day.

Hill was one of six players who insisted on Laver going to England as manager — one of six who were replaced in the team when, despite intervention by the governor of New South Wales, Lord Chelmsford, and the premier, J. S. T. McGowan, they rejected a compromise proposal. There were faults on both sides. The board was heavy-handed and the players pig-headed. Johnnie Moyes, a prominent cricketer, writer and broadcaster, commented in his *Australian Cricket*:

> Back in the days of the big fight my sympathies were with the players, for Clem Hill was our hero in Adelaide. I believed they had justice on their side and were not well treated, but at the same time I could see that some Australia-wide control of cricket was essential. The Board at that time knew it must win or die and it fought bitterly . . . The Board would have become defunct or merely a museum piece if it had not won at once. It needed a knockout blow, not a points decision.

There would be other differences over the years, but none so acrimonious. And no one will ever convince those who choose to think otherwise that there are not times when trade-offs are done between national selectors representing different States.

It was the tour of Australia by England in 1932–3, etched in history as the Bodyline tour, which really set the cat among the pigeons. At the heart of it all was an apparent desire to curb the prolific run-scoring feats of Donald Bradman. The upshot was an exchange of strongly worded messages between the Australian Board of Control and England's Marylebone Cricket Club, organisers of the tour. There were even rumblings of a possible break in diplomatic relations between the two countries, but it is doubtful this was ever seriously canvassed — in spite of the fact that there were discussions between the British representative in Canberra and Australian Prime Minister Joe Lyons.

Bodyline produced extraordinary reaction among players, administrators and the general public. And when the Australian board's initial complaint about unsportsmanlike bowling angered Jardine and his men to the point where they refused to play the fourth Test in Brisbane unless the cable was withdrawn, the board did so in the last of a series of cables to the MCC. The problem was that the board was making a fortune from the series — far too much money to consider abandoning it as the first cable had suggested. But it did sour relations for a while, and has certainly been an oft-recounted episode in the history of Anglo–Australian relations.

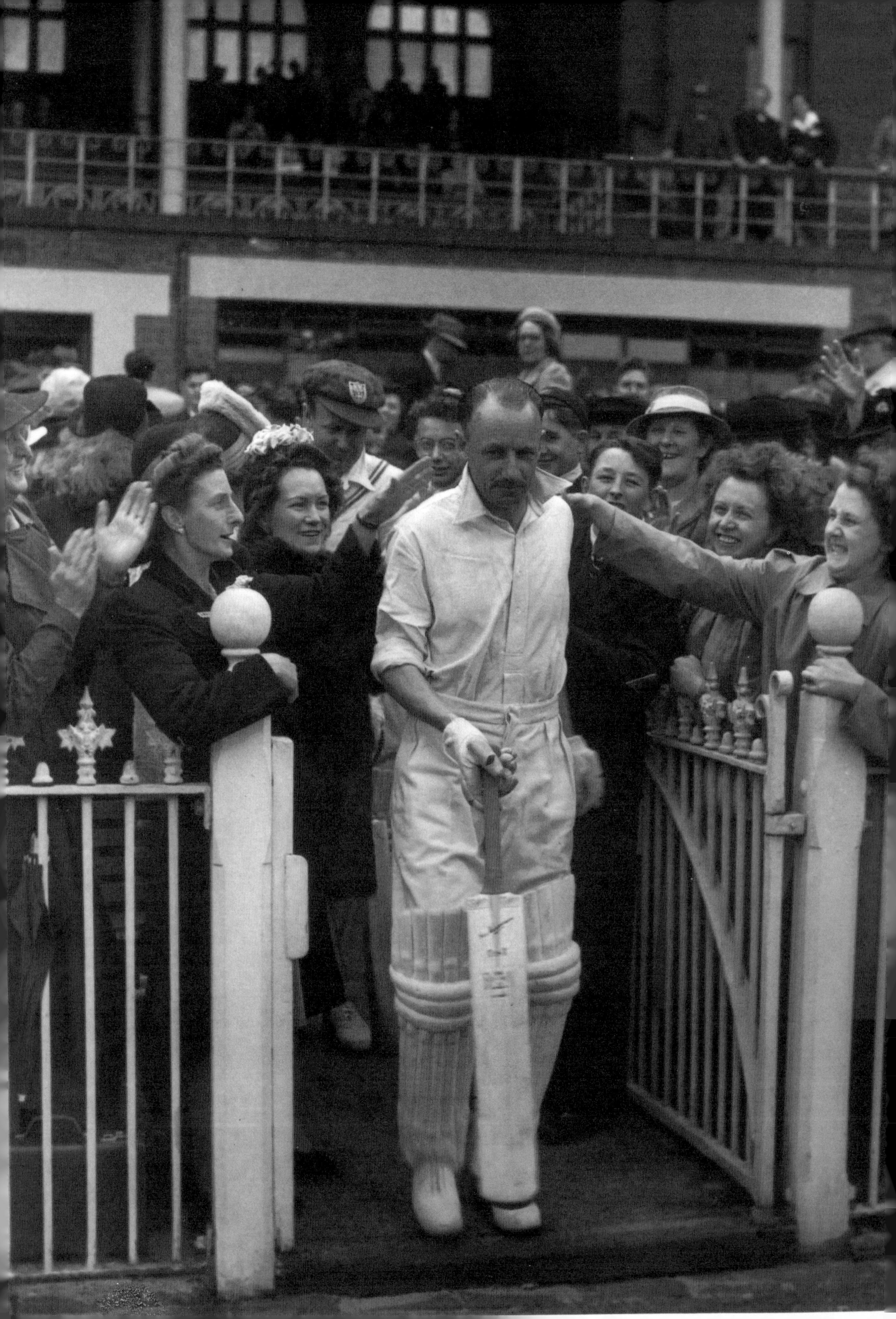

Political Football

Our Don
Courtesy *Herald and Weekly Times*

It happens not only in cricket. There is perhaps not a sport which is not affected by interstate jealousy — a battle of the administration boardrooms which sometimes manifests itself in a surprise selection. There were accusations that the reason for the lack of success of the 1981–2 Wallabies in Britain was differences between New South Wales and Queensland factions within the team which led to disharmony and therefore an inability to perform to maximum potential. Whether there was any serious basis in those accusations is not important. What is important is that the climate still exists for such claims to be made — and always will.

It was the questionable decree of the swimming authorities which kept Murray Rose, a gold medallist at Melbourne and Rome, from competing in the Tokyo Olympics in 1964. Although not in itself a political decision, the contention of those in power that Rose had to return to Australia for trials was conveniently never conveyed to him. It was an oversight which smacked either of incompetence or of intent — intent to produce the result it did. Even though he was swimming world record times for the 400 metres, and may arguably have won yet another gold medal for Australia, he was not added to the squad. Those same authorities also took it on themselves to mete out a ten-year ban on the remarkable swimmer Dawn Fraser for her part in a flag-stealing incident in Japan. Twenty years later another questionable decision prevented Moscow gold medallist Michelle Ford from swimming in Los Angeles. And athletics officials showed an equally peculiar outlook on selections when they failed to include Marlene Mathews in the Australian relay team at the Melbourne Olympics in spite of the fact that she had taken the bronze medal in both the 100 and 200 metres to stamp herself as the third fastest woman in the world. These actions by officials may not have been political in the true sense of the word, but they were actions which portrayed, at best, a stubborn outlook almost designed to show who held the whip hand.

While the Olympics have been used by many nations as the focus for expression of a national viewpoint through non-attendance, South Africa is more often than not at the root of protests involving sport.

There are few more emotive issues than South Africa. The weapon which is used throughout the world to try to fight the racial inequality which prevails within that country is sporting isolation. As in Australia, sport is important to South Africans. Inability to flex their sporting muscle against international competition leaves them frustrated, and their retaliation, at least where cricket is concerned, has been to arrange unofficial 'rebel' tours. There remain some areas of contact — surfing, squash, boxing, snooker and minimally, rugby. South Africa has felt the international sporting pinch most intensely since being barred from the Olympic Games in 1964 and from international cricket since the refusal of Prime Minister John Vorster in 1968 to accept a Cape coloured, Basil d'Oliveira, as a member of the MCC team.

Sport is open to attack as a 'soft' option for countries keen to see liberalisation of attitudes by South Africa's ruling white government to its black and coloured citizens. In making sport a focal point, economies are not affected; trade may continue while the world has visible evidence that someone is making a stand against what are undoubted injustices. The upshot has been the gradual exclusion of South Africa as a nation from almost every form of sports competition, although there is still tolerance in many parts of the world to South Africans competing as individuals.

Australia and South Africa have had ties stretching back to the Boer War and, in the case of plants and animals which were brought from the Cape to the fledgling colony of New South Wales, since even before that. The two countries were in at the start of the Empire (later Commonwealth) Games in 1930 which, at that stage, could hardly have been seen as anything other than a 'Whites Only' club. Australia lent what support it could, through Prime Minister Sir Robert Menzies, when that country sought a return to the Olympic fold in the 1960s.

International opposition to South Africa's apartheid policies was growing. England refused to send a cricket team to South Africa in 1970 following that country's objection to d'Oliveira, and Australia withdrew its invitation to the South African cricketers the following year. No one, certainly not the Federal government, foresaw the bitterness which the 1971 Springbok Rugby Union tour of Australia would engender. It not only split the Australian public, it also saw protests more savage than any during opposition to the Vietnam war. It led to an offer from then Prime Minister William McMahon to use RAAF personnel to fly the Springboks around the country, and a state of emergency being declared in Queensland. There were baton charges by mounted police, protesters tossed marbles and tacks under the hooves of horses, barbed wire fences were erected to keep the crowds off grounds. It was a case of sport gone mad.

It was also a public issue, the like of which had not been seen before in Australia. Australians found themselves pitted against one another as the bitterness, and at times even hatred, spilled over into violent confrontation. It was not the fault of the Springboks themselves; they were merely a team of sportsmen bent on doing their best, as is the endeavour of all teams everywhere. But they were a catalyst. Many Australians were alerted to the fact that it was better to take a stand than to sit idly by and wish that South Africans would liberalise their views on treatment of some of their own people.

Neither the Australian politicians nor the rugby officials realised the degree of hostility the tour would evoke. Smoke bombs, fire crackers, flares and whistles were common. Sharpeville, where sixty-nine black Africans had died at the hands of the South African police, was a name intoned wherever the Springboks played or stayed — and which prompted the National Socialist (Nazi) Party of Australia, which was pro-white South African, to lend what they saw as their support to the visitors. Rugby Union officials, players and supporters sided with the police in ugly conflicts involving students, intellectuals, church groups and trade unionists. Barbed wire appeared around playing areas in an attempt to prevent invasion by demonstrators. Football seemed to be not a game, but a focus for opposing forces to present conflicting attitudes and beliefs.

The 1971 Springbok Rugby Union team's tour of Australia brought politics and sport to Australia's own front door. It split the Australian public and caused demonstrations more savage than any during opposition to the Vietnam War. Here demonstrators and police clash at the Sydney Cricket Ground, amid the fumes of smoke bombs
News Limited

Political Football

The hostile crowds gather outside the Sydney Town Hall as South African rugby players attend a civic reception during their 1971 tour. The vehemence of the protests against the South African presence virtually put paid to any further thought of official tours by South African teams to Australia, or vice versa
News Limited

The disturbances underlined the fact that sport and politics, particularly political beliefs, could mix with volatile results, touching almost everybody in the Australian community. It was not to everyone's liking, this blending of two seemingly diverse philosophies, but there was no escaping its impact on the community in general, and on individuals who for perhaps the first time took a public stand on a particular issue.

Political scientist Professor Colin Tatz feels that post-war changes in attitudes towards South Africa, at least where sport was concerned, came from the sports people themselves who said, 'This [apartheid] is intolerable. What we need in sport is brotherhood, equity, equality of opportunity, equality of access . . . We are going to ban South Africa, or embargo South Africa, until they come good with some notion of equality on the sports field'. As far as Tatz is concerned, the Springbok tour, 'one of the most calamitous sporting tours in world history', was only permitted to go ahead because of the intransigence of the Rugby Union bosses. As for the three-week state of emergency in Queensland, Tatz sees it as 'unheard of in world democratic history that a society or a State government or a national government should declare a state of emergency — not in wartime, not during insurrection, not during civil war, but during a three-week rugby visit to a particular set of venues. So all normal law was suspended. All normal writs that are protective devices in our legal system were suspended. Why? Because the Springboks are going to play three matches in the enlightened State of Queensland'.

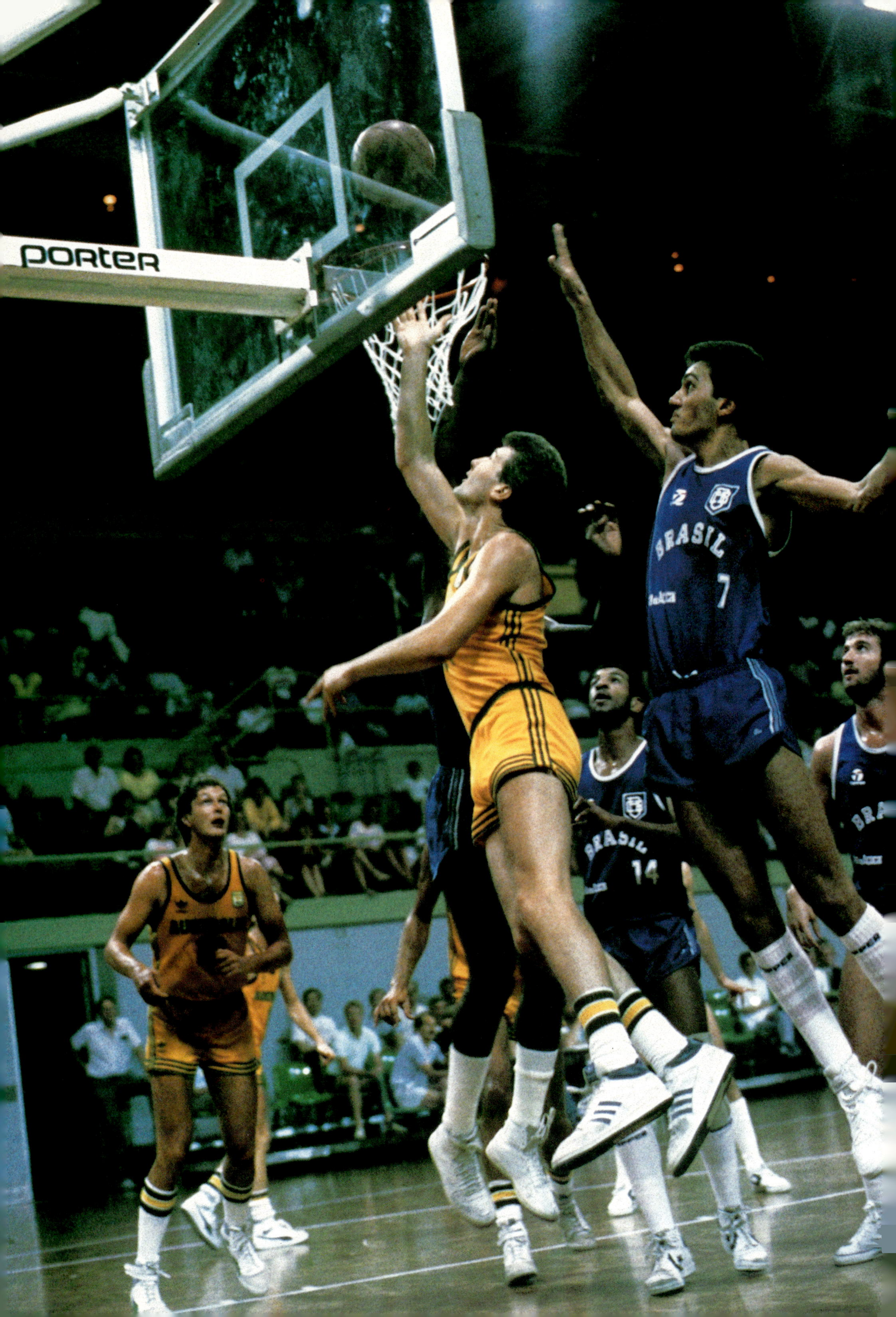

porter
BRASIL
7
BRASIL
14

Political Football

Former Sports Minister John Brown would have preferred that the 1971 tour had never taken place. As he put it: 'It evoked violent feelings in the Australian community, and that brawl we had in Brisbane ... was very undignified. That, of course, was the last South African tour we've seen here, and I'm pleased about that'. If there was a lesson to be learned from that tour, it went over the heads of New Zealanders. And when the Springboks toured New Zealand in 1981, the result was the same as it had been in Australia ten years earlier: New Zealander set against New Zealander.

In 1977, with Australian Prime Minister Malcolm Fraser in the vanguard, all Commonwealth governments put their signatures to the Gleneagles Agreement which, in essence, was an undertaking to put an end to all sporting contact with South Africa. That it wasn't taken as seriously as it might have been was reflected in the visit of the South African rugby team to New Zealand four years later, with the result that there was considerable feeling within the African countries of the Commonwealth that there should be a boycott of the Commonwealth Games in Brisbane in 1982 if New Zealand took part. That there was no boycott was due to moves by the politicians in sport to strengthen the terms of the Gleneagles Agreement by spelling out clearly, for both sportspeople and administrators within the Commonwealth, the steps required to be taken by each country's Commonwealth Games Association in the event of a breach of Gleneagles. Until then, there had been far too many grey areas in the Agreement, allowing room for argument as to whether a particular breach actually did contravene Gleneagles.

At the time, former Australian Test batsman Bruce Francis said the Commonwealth Games Federation's new and stricter code of conduct would not deter him from organising an Australian cricket tour to South Africa 'when the money is available'. Francis was quoted in the *Sydney Morning Herald* of 30 September 1982 as saying, 'The Australian Games Association knows that it can not control me or anyone else on this issue. If they bind themselves to the code, I'll still take a cricket team to South Africa and it will be the association's fault if the federation comes down hard on it'. Francis resented the association's attempt to commit individual Australian sportsmen and women to a code of conduct aimed at tightening the Gleneagles Agreement. Tommy Campbell, executive member of Freedom in Sport, an international body dedicated to separating politics and sport, saw the code as a code of misconduct.

The money Francis was waiting for became available in 1985. A team of West Indian cricketers had already toured South Africa, and in 1985–6 and again in 1986–7, Kim Hughes, disenchanted with the establishment in Australia and seizing the opportunity to earn a substantial amount of money, took a team of Australian players to the Republic. The gathering of the team became a drama almost the equal of the 1977 coup which gave birth to World Series Cricket and changed the face of the game forever. The 'rebel' tour was not quite in the same mould, but it did provoke reaction from the Australian Cricket Board, the Federal government and the public — most of the last wishing the tourists well. Sports Minister John Brown called on the ACB to punish players who accepted contracts to go to South Africa, and drew from Bruce Francis, an unashamed proponent of sporting contact as a means of improving the lot of sportsmen and women of all races in South Africa, the reaction: 'This call for punitive action must be the most obnoxious request ever put by an Australian Government to a sports association. Mr Brown has loaded the gun for someone else to fire, but he would appear to be extremely hasty in his desire to have someone pull the trigger. Bluntly put, it would seem that Mr Brown is asking the cricket board to be his hit man'. There was rhetoric, there were withdrawals by several players, there were writs. In the end the Australian 'rebels' went to South Africa. Strangely, however, the public appeared to take no more than a passing interest in how Hughes and his players fared.

Persistent questions in 1982 about his attitude to playing in South Africa drew from then Australian cricket captain Greg Chappell a statement that, as long as the

Opposite:
Professional basketball is a huge growth sport in Australia, but it has grown out of the national coaching support, and funding, of successive Olympic and World Championship teams. In this action Australia is playing Brazil in the Australia games
Live Action: Acikalin

Blood, Sweat and Tears

Australian Wallabies Gary Pearse and Dick Cocks playing Rugby Union in Umlazi, near Durban, in South Africa. Invited to play before a major scheduled soccer match, the game caused much hilarity to the crowd of 30,000 who had never seen rugby before. These Australian players see playing in South Africa as a way of keeping the communication channels open, and sport as one of the best ways to relate to people, no matter their political beliefs. Durban Daily Mail

Above:
Dick Thornett, pictured above right playing Rugby League for New South Wales against New Zealand in 1967, played with a brilliance equal to that of his better known brother, John Thornett (above), and was a triple international, representing Australia in Rugby Union, League and water polo. John Thornett was captain of Australia in a record sixteen Rugby Union Tests. His 1975 team was the first Australian team to win a series against South Africa since 1934. He was among those players who built up a healthy sporting rivalry with South Africa which was destroyed by apartheid and South Africa's banishment from the world's sporting arena
News Limited

Right:
Anti-apartheid demonstrators gathered Australia wide in violent protest of the Springbok rugby tour of Australia in 1971

WILD START TO SPRINGBOK TOUR

Incorporating "The Sunday Sun and Guardian" (No. 3550) and "The Sunday Herald" (No. 1163)
Telephone: 2 0944   SYDNEY, SUNDAY, JUNE 27, 1971.   144 Pages   TEN CENTS

Demonstrators clash with pro-tour supporters at Perth airport yesterday morning before the arrival of the Springbok side.

Water polo is very much a minority sport in Australia, but our world competitiveness is a tribute both to the dedication of the players, and the government sponsorship of Australian Olympic sport. Australia wins playing Brazil in the Australia games
Live Action: Acikalin

policy of the Australian Cricket Board was to refrain from visiting the country for the wellbeing of world cricket, he would not play there. As he commented at the time, 'It is an unfortunate reality that today sport cannot be isolated from the political environment'. Leading sporting figures such as surfer Tom Carroll, who drew a pat on the back from Prime Minister Bob Hawke, and golfer Greg Norman refused to play in events in South Africa. Tennis player Pat Cash, in a quest for points to enable him to make the Masters, went in 1987. A number of leading Rugby Union players visited the Republic in 1987 to discuss the possibility of a tour by an Australian team, but the howls of protest in Australia resulted in the prospect being shelved, at least for a time.

There is a growing belief by a number of scholars that athletes are beginning to wonder whether playing and competing in South Africa is worth the effort, considering the attendant stigma. Professor Colin Tatz believes governments have the right to stop sportsmen and women from going to countries like South Africa — even private tours if there is a possibility of those being exploited. No matter the guise under which teams do play in South Africa, it is difficult to prevent the promotion of and belief that the visitors represent their particular country. At the very least the South Africans are enjoying international competition, and that is precisely what those opposed to the ideologies of the Nationalist Party are keen to prevent. Tatz argues that if the foreign policy of the state is to boycott, then the state has the right to expect its sporting subsidiaries to go along with the policy.

South Africa has discovered, through a number of cricket tours, that it is possible to obtain a response to cheque-book sport, and is seriously considering turning to professional Rugby Union as a means of attracting the visiting teams of which it has been so starved in that area of its national sport. There is perhaps some irony in that sporting tours in the late nineteenth century were privately sponsored affairs, administrative bodies either not yet having been formed or at least not yet in total control of the sports they administered. But, in the case of cricket at least, the teams even then were considered representative of the country — which leads to the conclusion that sport, in all but a very few exceptions, is a highly public property leaving little or no room for private whim.

Strangely, there is not always consistency in dealing with sportsmen and women who come from South Africa; yet another indication of the fact that sport is an easy way for governments and individuals openly to show their opposition to South Africa's policies. South African tennis players and golfers, although not welcome everywhere, are generally accepted as representing themselves as individuals and not as being representatives of the state. They are not permitted to contest team events such as the Davis Cup or the Eisenhower Cup, but are generally able to ply their trade as professionals. So too are a number of South African cricketers who play in the English county competition. Swimmers and athletes are less acceptable; runner Zola Budd is an example of a young sportswoman who became a target for opponents of the South African regime in spite of the fact that she competed internationally for Britain.

Events such as Commonwealth and Olympic Games, on which many nations of the world focus their attention, are a natural target for civil liberties groups and others.

The Brisbane Commonwealth Games in 1982 gave Aborigines a platform from which to advertise to a wide audience their grievances concerning conditions and land rights. With all eyes on Brisbane, they were able to make their presence and their cause felt without in any way disrupting the Games. It is futile for sport to feel it can stand apart from issues. Sport can draw people together, or force them apart. An extreme example of sport's ability to draw people together is available in the Caribbean: the various islands of the West Indies are governed independently, but virtually the only thing for which they come together under a collective banner is cricket.

There are still clubs which do not allow certain races to become members; clubs for which the fee structure makes them available only to the wealthy. Yachting's *America*'s Cup, for example, can be contested only by millionaires or by syndicates able to attract vast sums of money.

Ironically, it was Australia's success in wresting the *America*'s Cup from the United States in 1983 that brought Australians closer together than anything in a long time. It also provided the sight of Prime Minister Hawke leaping, yelling and being showered with champagne as the wing-keeled wonder *Australia II* crossed the line ahead of *Liberty* to snatch victory. Although Australians became accustomed to the sight, it was strange at the time — a Labor Prime Minister cavorting with the wealthy in the Royal Perth Yacht Club. By the time Fremantle came to host the 1987 challenge for the Cup, many millions of dollars had been allocated by the Federal government to upgrade Perth's international airport, the city of Fremantle, roads, marinas and anything else connected with the challenge. And when the Cup was lost to the Americans, the same Australians who had rejoiced at having won it four years earlier felt that this time the expense was an extravagance the nation could ill afford.

Like it or not, sport is political at all levels of its being, not just nationally. It has been used in the past as an international weapon, and no doubt will be again. It is not possible to keep politics and sport from mixing. National pride will always manifest itself in competition. Sport is a weapon. At the lowest end of the scale it is full of good intentions — intentions which all too often make way for the aspirations of officials rather than the athletes involved — and which at the highest level can be used to make statements and to fashion demands. In the case of Australians, however, it makes striving for the green and gold a no less worthwhile goal.

You can't win them all! Australia's Prime Minister Hawke congratulates American skipper Dennis Connor after America's win in the America's Cup series off the coast of Perth in 1987. The Akubra hat is a present for President Reagan
Photobank/All Sport

Sources and references
Books consulted for this chapter are:
   Keith Dunstan, *The Paddock that Grew: The Story of the Melbourne Cricket Club* (Cassell 1962, rev. edn 1974); Chris Harte and Warwick Hadfield, *Cricket Rebels* (QB Books, 1985); Gary Lester, *Australians at the Olympics: A Definitive History* (Lester-Townsend, 1984); Ray Robinson, *On Top Down Under* (Cassell Australia, rev. edn, 1976); Brian Stoddart, *Saturday Afternoon Fever* (Angus & Robertson, 1986).
Quotations from these books are, in order: Stoddart, p.57; Lester, p.134; Robinson, pp.100–1, 115; Dunstan, p.103.
Interview transcripts for the television series, 'Blood, Sweat and Tears':
   Colin Tatz   John Brown.
The quotation from Bruce Francis is from Harte and Hadfield, p.63. The quotation from Greg Chappell is from a media release.

CHAPTER 13

WEARING THE GREEN AND GOLD

Jim Webster

Surveys show that the three most identifiable Australians abroad in the late 1980s are Prime Minister Bob Hawke, Paul Hogan and Greg Norman — a charismatic, sports-loving politician, an ocker who is seen on the world's television screens advertising beer and prawns and who gave crocs a fresh celluloid image, and one of the world's premier golfers.

This probably tells us much about ourselves: presumably they're also the best-known trio within Australia. Recognition is a natural consequence of the office of prime minister, but what about the other two? We love the image of the Sunburnt Country, even if many of us prefer not to be too active outdoors; we enjoy the roughly-hewn, folksy humour of Hoges, respect the immense sporting talent of Norman and are envious of the collective drive and ambitions of all three.

Our sporting successes have, regularly in the past and occasionally in the present, enabled us to hold our heads up proudly in the competitive and often distressed world in which we live. We are a relatively small nation but known for our sporting achievers. Sportsmen and women the world over know that if they're pitted against an Australian they'll have a tough, uncompromising fight on their hands. Australians won't back off easily: they may not back off at all.

When did all this begin? Have we always had a steady stream of people with sporting talent, sometimes quite exceptional? Have we always wanted to demonstrate it to the rest of the world?

In the early years after colonisation, Australia's international lifeline was tied solidly to the Empire framework. There were natural bonds between Australia and England, or 'Home' as it was referred to, and no firmer were they than in sport.

Rowing was among the first of those sports. Captain John Piper is acknowledged as the founder of Australian rowing. He arrived in the colony aged 19 with the New South Wales Corps in 1792, four years after Captain Phillip's first settlement. Piper had a chequered career in the colony, as he became chairman of the Bank of New South Wales only to be forced into resigning after an investigation of certain of its loans. Piper, for whom Point Piper was named, was for all his faults a great lover of water sports and was instrumental in staging Australia's first rowing events.

Starting in 1818, numbers of young Australians, including Piper, matched themselves in four-oared and six-oared match races against crews from visiting English and American ships on Sydney Harbour.

Edward Trickett from New South Wales became world sculling champion when he defeated Englishman John Henry Sadler on the Thames in 1878. The race was extensively reported in the English press
Illustrated Sydney News

From that beginning, the first international sculling contest took place in 1856 when 20-year-old Dick Green of the Green boat-building business raced the Englishman Jack Dewardt on Sydney Harbour. Green won with ridiculous ease. Then the English sent out another sculler to take him on. His name was Tom Cavendish and Green trounced him too on the Parramatta River in 1857.

It was to be the start of a continuing parade of Australian world sculling champions: oarsmen like Edward Trickett, who became our first world champion when he defeated England's Joseph H. Sadler on the Thames in 1876, English-born

Wearing the Green and Gold

*Opposite, top:
The first eight-oared race in Australian waters was held at the Melbourne Regatta in 1875. In inter-State racing Victoria won twenty-five of the first thirty-one races held between 1878 and 1907*
State Library of New South Wales

English-born William Beach also received the acclaim on both sides of the world when he won the world sculling championship in England in 1886. He received a hero's welcome when he returned to Sydney
Mitchell Library

William Beach and Henry Searle. The British rejoiced in the Australian triumphs just as we did, for the young colony was still seen as an extension of British influence in the southern hemisphere. In Australia, they were sporting heroes, among the first we ever had. The adulation for them was never more evident than when Searle died from typhoid fever on 10 December 1889 in a Melbourne sanatorium after returning from successfully defending his world professional title in London. Searle was accorded the largest funeral at the time in Australia's history, with 175 000 people packing the shores of Sydney Harbour when his coffin went aboard the steamer *Thetis* to sail to his home town of Grafton.

In those days of the Empire, when the British influence spread to the far corners of the globe, there was another sport which dominated all others, which Australians learned from their forebears and which was to bind the parent country and the fledgling colony nothing more tightly than anything else: the game of cricket. In summer, nothing stirs the soul of a Yorkshire coalminer or a North Queensland truckdriver, of a London merchant banker or a grape producer from the Barossa Valley, of the whole of England and Australia, more than cricket.

Cricket is a game bent by the weight of centuries. Its dim origins are obscured by the shadows of the Middle Ages and the Sussex Weald, where shepherds first played the sport with their 'cricc' or staves as the bat. In comparison with that ancient game, international or Test cricket is but a recent arrival.

James Lillywhite's team representing England arrived in Melbourne in 1877 for the first Test between the two countries. The preceding tour of New Zealand had been rocked by scandal; the English regular wicketkeeper Pooley was arrested for assault and remanded on bail on a charge of 'injuring property above the value of five pounds'. So Lillywhite's team had to undertake the tour of Australia without a wicketkeeper — an enormous blow. Undeterred, the tour proceeded and on Thursday, 15 March 1877 about a thousand people gathered at the Melbourne Cricket Ground to watch the match between the All England Eleven captained by Lillywhite and a combined team selected from the colonies of Victoria and New South Wales.

It was the first of the Test matches which have continued to bind and mesmerise the two nations for more than a century. As it turned out, the combined team won outright by 45 runs. There was enormous rejoicing in the colonies at having done so wonderfully well against the might of English cricket, and Australians as a whole became tremendously enthusiastic about continuing with Test matches between the two countries. The formalising of cricket relations between the two bound them more tightly together, as well as ensuring Australia brief opportunities, as in rowing, to express its national identity. Then in 1882 cricketing bonds became stronger still with the Ashes. The third Australian team toured England that year and won at the Oval by 7 runs. At one stage England had wanted only 34 runs with 7 wickets left, and still lost. Next day the *Sporting Times* published the famous obituary notice in which it said the ashes of English cricket would be sent to Australia. Nobody thought much of the notion at the time but it caught the imagination of Ivo Bligh who took a team to Australia immediately afterwards. In a speech in Adelaide he mentioned the ashes. After Bligh's team won the third Test of that series a group of women presented him with an urn reputedly containing the ashes of a burnt cricket stump, the symbolic trophy for which the nations still play.

Rifle-shooting was another sport to encourage this interchange of sporting competition, for most men in the new colony possessed a rifle and organised shooting began with the formation of the Sydney Rifle Club in 1842. The earliest desire of competitive shooters was to compete at the headquarters of rifle-shooting at Bisley in England. Australians first did so in 1902 and our first winner there was Lieutenant Walter C. Addison, who won the coveted King's Prize in 1907.

Australia's sporting interest was so heavily related to England at the time that there was not much attention given to events which occurred outside that realm. There is no better example of this than the Olympic Games. While Australia readily

Wearing the Green and Gold

A modern rifle-shooting success: Elizabeth Felton of Subiaco, Western Australia, took the winner's chair after becoming the first woman in Australia to take the Queen's Prize in rifle-shooting in 1974. She scored a record 348 points out of 355
West Australian Newspapers

accepted Baron Pierre de Coubertin's ideals behind the revival of the Olympic movement Australians were represented at the first modern Olympic Games in Athens in 1896 only by Edwin H. Flack.

It is not easy to determine the exact number of countries and athletes attending those Games, but the most accurate estimates suggest that 311 athletes from thirteen nations competed. Admittedly, many of the athletes had to come to Athens at their own expense. Some of America's best athletes stayed home and not all of Britain's best athletes attended. In some cases athletes competed simply because they happened to be in Athens at the time. Flack, who had been studying accountancy in England, went to the Games as a member of the London Athletic Club. In those times, national teams were not sent as they are today and it was quite acceptable to go as an individual, or as a member of a club. It is almost certain that Flack would not have gone to Athens had his father not sent him to London to further his accountancy, in which case Australia would not have had a representative at all. But there seemed little concern at all for these first Games, for they were in a foreign land and far removed from the Australia–England relationship.

At the Games, Flack first won the 1500-metres, clocking 4 min. 33.2 sec. and winning by 5 metres. He was therefore Australia's first Olympic champion, but nobody at the time seemed to care very much. Flack also won the 800-metres with ease. Also, as often happened in those days, he entered another sport as well: tennis, in which he was unsuccessful. And to round off his Olympic competition, Flack also ran in his first marathon, courageously leading the field for 37 kilometres until retiring. It was a memorable performance and a remarkable ending to his pioneering efforts. Not only did he win two Olympic gold medals, but he forged the first link in Australia's proud record of being one of only three nations to have competed at every modern Olympic Games. Yet the significance of Flack's efforts went largely unnoticed.

Our second gold medal winner was Frederick C. V. Lane, who won two swimming gold medals at the 1900 Paris Olympics. Although he stood a mere 167 centimetres, 22-year-old Lane was nevertheless a fierce competitor and outclassed Hungary's great Zoltan Von Halmay in the 200-metres freestyle, the shortest event on the programme, and later won the 200-metres obstacle race, in which competitors had to alternatively climb over and swim under row boats and punts in the River Seine.

After Lane's victories, the Union Jack was hoisted to the masthead in the medal ceremonies. There was no Australian flag. Australia was still twelve months away from Federation. The fact that the Union Jack was hoisted again didn't seem to worry anybody. Indeed, in a radio broadcast some years later Lane referred to it as the Australian flag. It was consistent with the feeling of the time that Australian sporting success was merely an example of what those under the comforting arm of Britain could do. Whatever we did outside England–Australia contests was merely an extension of British achievements. We were still thought of as being British and had done little to try to alter that notion.

One of the great ironies of our sporting heritage can be found in the colours our sportsmen and women wear so proudly — the green and gold, although until 1984 our official colours were blue and white. The exact date of the adoption of green and gold is hazy, it appears to have been considered to coincide with Federation in 1901 — although it turned up earlier than that. Dr Leslie Poidevin, New South Wales cricketer and Australasian Davis Cup team representative in 1906, suggested to Australian tennis officials the use of green and gold in 1900, a year before Federation. The colours had been used in pennants flown at hotels at which the Australian cricketers stayed during their 1899 tour of England. The acceptance of green and gold as Australia's colours was gradual. Rugby League adopted the colours in 1928; cricket's baggy green cap is generally accepted as having been introduced in about 1926; Rugby Union went green and gold in the 1920s.

Even later on at the 1908 Olympics we weren't overly concerned with having our own identity. Nations marched in their team dress for the first time in an opening parade. Australia had not bothered to equip the team with national outfits. Embarrassed when it was learned that all other nations were properly outfitted for the march, the Australians hastily decided to march in dark singlets and white shorts. Those not owning shorts wore swimming trunks.

We won only one gold medal there, for Rugby Union, beating Britain 32–3 in the final. At the next Olympics in Stockholm in 1912, we won two gold medals — one for the men's 4 × 200-metres freestyle relay and another by Sarah 'Fanny' Durack in the 100-metres freestyle. It should be pointed out that one of the male relay swimmers was a New Zealander, Malcolm Champion, for the two nations competed together at this and the previous Games.

The move away from being an apprentice of Britain to a self-asserting nation eventually began with the cricket tour of England led by Warwick Armstrong in 1920–1. The massively built Armstrong (he weighed 139 kg) had a natural disdain for his English opponents. Beat them at all costs, he maintained. The first signs of a love-hate relationship between the two nations began to show, fuelled by the fact that it had started in cricket, the sport dearest of all to the heart of both nations. It continued in the Don Bradman era, through the 1930s and 1940s, in the cold, methodical and ruthless manner in which he devastated the best of English bowlers. He was apparently unstoppable; people thought of him as a run-scoring machine. At least, that is, until the notorious Bodyline series. On 14 January 1933, the second day of the third Test against England at Adelaide Oval, Australia's captain Bill Woodfull lay on a massage table, badly bruised and in pain. Out for 22, he had been repeatedly struck by short, rising balls from express bowlers Harold Larwood and Bill Voce. When the English team manager came to offer sympathy, Woodfull made his famous reply: 'There are two teams out there on the Oval', he said. 'One is playing cricket, the other is not. This game is too good to be spoilt. It's time some people got out of it.'

The English tactic had not only ruined the series but almost severed Australian relations with England. Australia had suddenly had national identity and independence fully thrust upon it by its oldest and most cherished ally. The Bodyline campaign made Australians more aware than ever before that they were a sporting nation in their own right, with a pride and heritage to be fought for and defended.

While Bradman's presence was turning the cricket world upside down, another Australian of similarly small stature had the English scratching their heads and rewriting the rule book. His name was Walter Lindrum. He was simply the greatest billiards player who has ever lived. Lindrum came from a family infatuated by billiards and was, like Bradman, far ahead of anyone else of his day. During his career, he made about thirty breaks of 2000, two of 3000 and one, in 1932, of 4137. The best his great rival, Joe Davis, achieved in his lifetime was two 2000 breaks. Lindrum's uncanny mastery of the difficult nursery cannon shot forced the English administrators of the game to alter the rules in an attempt to curb him. It made little difference: he was too good. When Lindrum died in 1960, he still held fifty-seven world records, many of which still stand. He was the unbeatable Australian, someone in whom Australians took immense pride, especially because of his mastery — at a time of national stirrings and anti-British feeling — of English players and of the rules devised by English officials. As with cricket, Lindrum's feats in billiards through the 1930s and early 1940s helped enormously to fuel Australia's pride and foster her independence from Britain.

At the time Bradman and Lindrum were ruffling English feathers, another group of Australians was making a name for themselves. This time, they were riding motor bikes. The world's first motor cycle was produced by Gottlieb Daimler in Germany in 1886 and, while some kind of racing must have begun shortly after his invention, documentation of it is almost nonexistent. Motor-cycle speedway racing as we

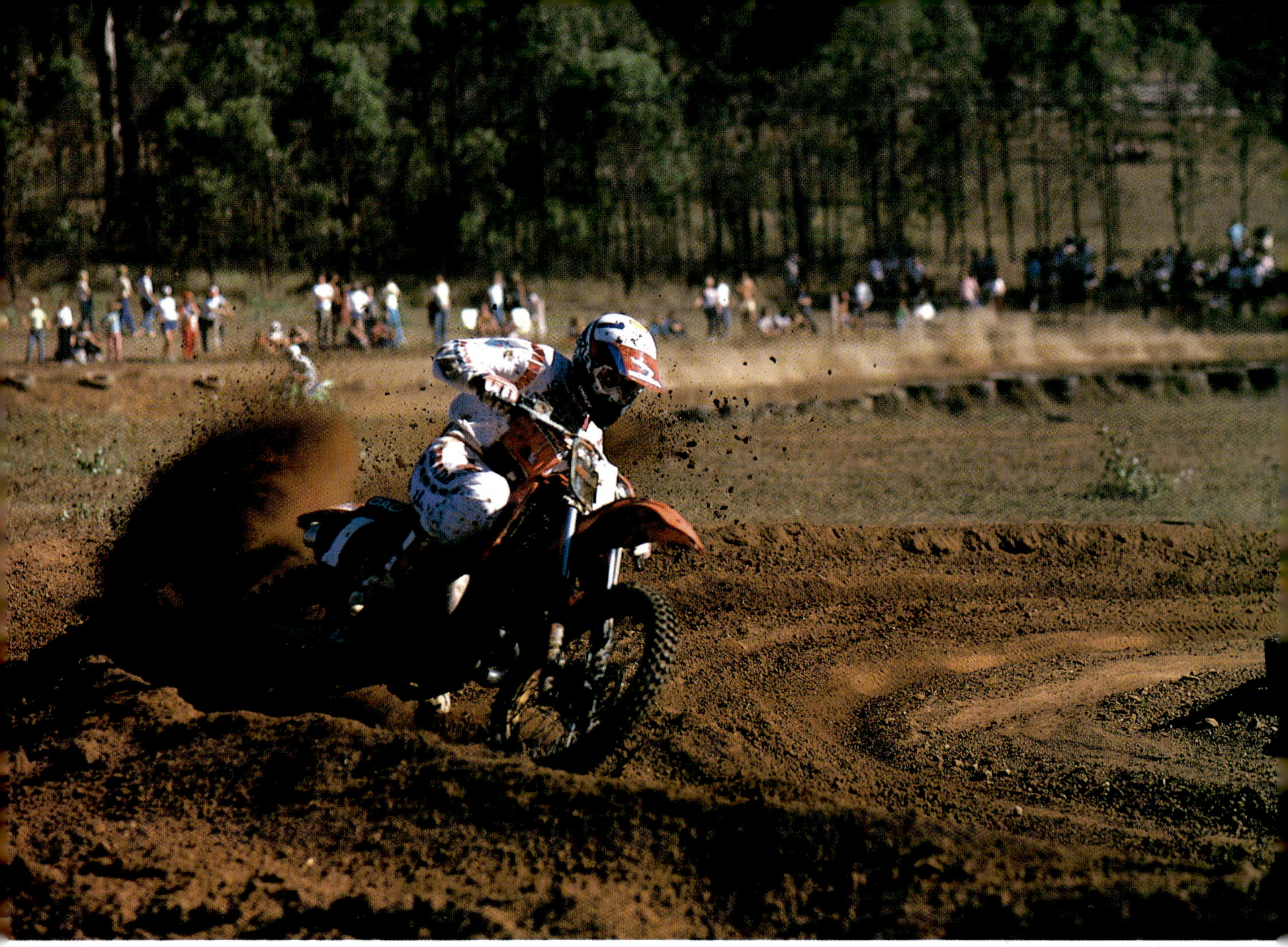

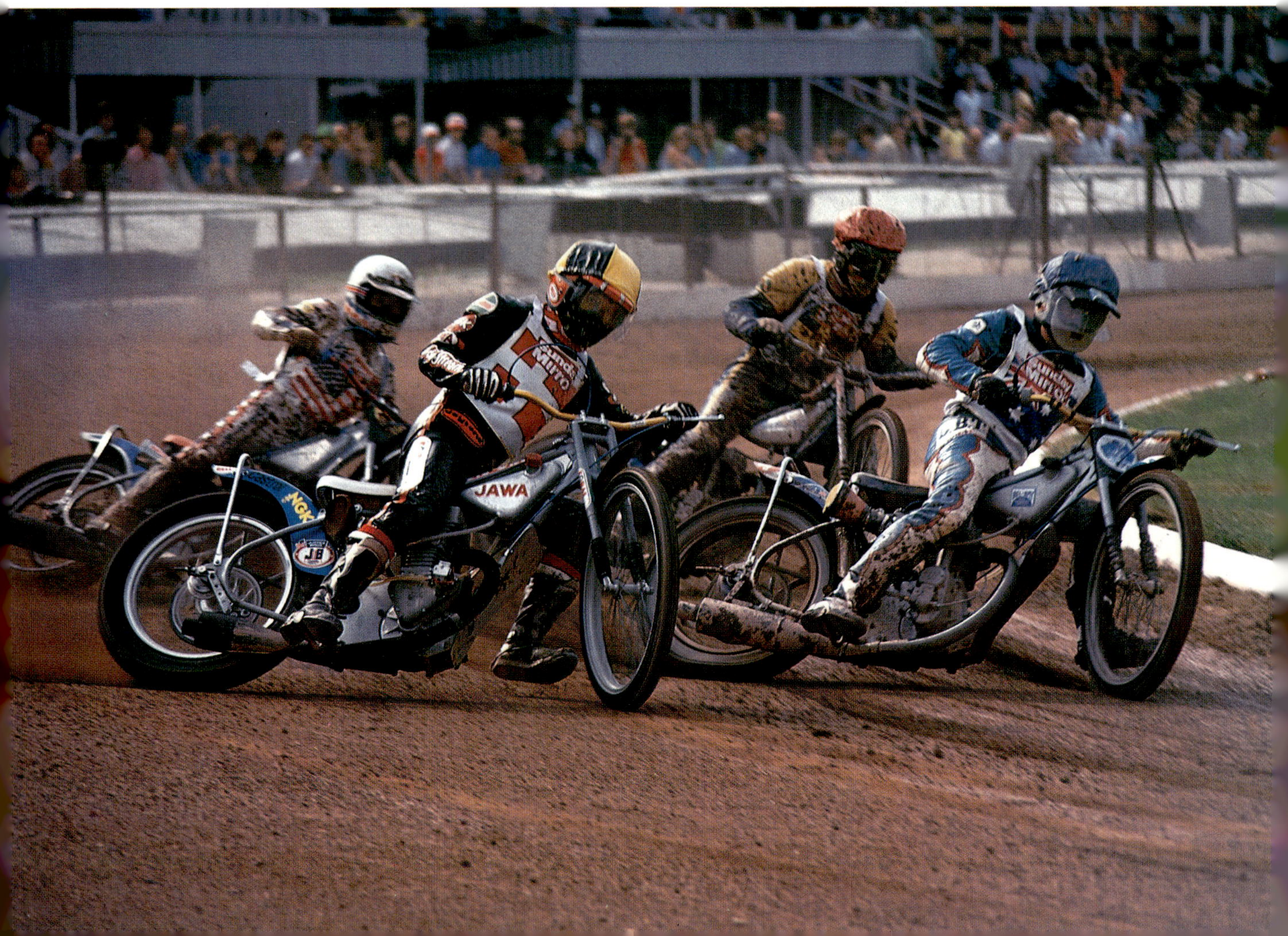
NGK
JAWA

There seems widespread acceptance that racing motor bikes on a quarter-mile dirt track in a speedway originated in Australia: one of our few contributions of a genuinely new sport in the world (top). A natural progression has been to motor-crosse (bottom) — a rough and tumble obstacle race on motor bikes
Live Action/Martin King Sportpix

know it began in the United States and South Africa, but there seems widespread acceptance that racing motor bikes on a quarter-mile dirt track in a speedway, as distinct from outdoors, originated in Australia: one of our few contributions of a genuinely new sport to the world.

It began in Maitland through the efforts of Johnny Hopkins, who came across from New Zealand, set up a dirt track for motor bikes, then took it to England and turned it into a professional sport. It was an instant success. People turned out in thousands, both in England and Australia, to see daredevils screech around the small circular tracks in a curtain of red dust, with death or serious injury only a wheel-touch away. Australians dominated this new sport: prominent riders like Sig Schlam, Ron Johnson, Vic Huxley, Charlie Spinks and finally Lionel van Praag, who became the first official world champion.

Until then most of Australian sport had been related to England, the Mother Country. But Australians slowly began moving into the non-Empire world, thus projecting important views about us in other parts of the world and also helping us form impressions about others. We began showing ourselves to other nations as possessing national pride, as well as being innovative and extremely skilled. Our sporting horizon was broadening and our reputation increasing.

The Davis Cup carried our sporting emergence to other parts of the world, notably America. Our first victory came in 1907 when British supremacy had waned and Norman Brookes and New Zealand's Anthony Wilding (we still often competed together as Australasia in those early days) scored a 3–2 victory over Britain at Wimbledon. The following year, the same players defeated the US by the same score in Melbourne and thus began what was to become an Australian dominance (we eventually parted from New Zealand in 1923) of the Davis Cup through players like Gerald Patterson, John Bromwich, Adrian Quist, Frank Sedgman, Ken McGregor, Lew Hoad, Ken Rosewall, Mal Anderson, Ashley Cooper, Neale Fraser, Rod Laver, Roy Emerson and John Newcombe.

Another individual who began to make a name for himself in different parts of the world in the 1920s and 1930s, thus further developing the international image of Australians as talented sportsmen and women, was Joe Kirkwood, probably Australia's first famous golfer.

Born in 1897, Kirkwood was a boy of eight when he fashioned a golf club out of a gum sapling and hit balls about the Manly course while minding the sheep and goats which were used to keep the fairways trim. He became an assistant professional there when only 13 years of age. Kirkwood had seven clubs in his bag when he won the 1920 Australian Open with a score of 290, carving a dozen strokes off the course record, and he completed a wonderful double by capturing the New Zealand Open that same year. Kirkwood was lured overseas the next year and was thus to become one of the pioneers of golfing global travel. He claimed to have played 6740 courses in his travels and made friends everywhere. The Soviet Union was about the only country he missed. There are many photographs of Kirkwood and his travelling companion Walter Hagen riding camels past the pyramids, playing around kangaroos and cobras, being admired by kings and native girls.

During all this, he did manage to play some very fine golf, for he added the 1933 Canadian Open to his two other national golf titles. But he came to realise that the skimpy golf purses of the day weren't enough to fashion a healthy lifestyle and so he joined up with Hagen as a trick-shot pioneer. Peter Thomson describes Kirkwood as having been the 'great entertainer of golf'. He could do some truly amazing things. Kirkwood could tee up two balls and, with a seven-iron, hit them simultaneously and cause them to cross in mid-flight, one hooking and one slicing. He could play left-handed with right-handed clubs. Another of his stunts was to ask somebody from the audience to lend him his waistcoat watch; he would balance a ball on it and hit it off. Very amusing — if it wasn't your watch. He also claimed to have hit 29 holes-in-one. Another innovation of his was being the first professional to use a wooden tee peg, just as we know it today.

Harry Hopman's name is synonymous with Australian tennis due to his magnificent record as both player and coach. From 1950, when he became Australian Davis Cup captain, he led the team to fifteen wins before retiring from the position in 1969
News Limited

Norman Brookes, who always wore a grey tweed cap while playing and often fortified himself with a tot of brandy between sets, looks on as his doubles partner A. W. Dunlop returns the ball during the 1912 Davis Cup final against Britain in Melbourne. Sir Norman Brookes won Wimbledon twice, and played Davis Cup for Australia in eight challenge rounds
Mitchell Library

The 'Tennis Twins' Ken Rosewall and Lew Hoad carried Australia's tennis hopes in the 1950s and had many thrilling Davis Cup victories. Rosewall, at left, could not emulate Hoad's success in the Wimbledon singles. He was runner-up three times — to Lew Hoad, John Newcombe and Jimmy Connors — over a span of eighteen years
Ern McQuillan

The triumphant 1960 Davis Cup team. From left to right, Roy Emerson, Fred Stolle, Harry Hopman coach, John Newcombe, Tony Roche
News Limited

Australian athletes at the Olympic Games were continuing to show their skills. In 1932, with the world in the grip of the Great Depression, some little joy came our way with three gold medals at the Los Angeles Games — Edgar 'Dunc' Gray in the 1000-metres cycling time trial, Claire Dennis in the 200-metres breaststroke and Henry 'Bobby' Pearce, who won his second successive gold medal in the single sculls.

Our sporting successes became infrequent as World War II approached; we had to wait until the late 1940s and the 1950s before Australian sportsmen and women began creating international headlines once more. But more and more we were projecting — and believing in — the image of Australia as a sporting nation.

Australia's sporting expansion after the war was helped in no small way by the extensive influx of migrants which was starting to take place. While many of them continued to follow sports traditional to their homelands, particularly soccer, some of them did emerge in sports more associated with Australia.

Among those that the stream of evacuees from war-torn Europe gave to Australia were two young Latvian children named Ilsa and John Konrads. Their family was housed in a migrant hostel near Wagga and next door, in an RAAF camp, was a swimming pool. It was there that the two of them learned to swim and developed their passion for the sport. And it was there, incidentally, where young John contracted a mild dose of poliomyelitis. It was fortunately diagnosed early and he spent a month in Wagga hospital. Part of the rehabilitation programme was swimming

Wearing the Green and Gold

The opening ceremony of the Empire Games, held in Sydney in 1938. The first Empire Games (now Commonwealth Games) were held in 1930 in Canada
John Fairfax & Sons Ltd

Ilsa Konrads, one half of the greatest swimming family in history. Her brother John set twenty-six individual world freestyle records and won the 1500 metres at Rome. Ilsa set twelve individual freestyle records. As migrants from Latvia, the Konrads began swimming at an RAAF pool near their migrant settlement camp at Wagga, New South Wales
Herald & Weekly Times

and so his time in, and love for, the water increased even more. The Konrads kids were to become the greatest swimming family in history: John set twenty-six individual world freestyle records and won the 1500-metres gold medal at the Rome Olympics; while Ilsa, though failing to win an Olympic gold medal, set twelve individual world freestyle records.

The creation and development of Australia's identity as a sporting nation and the physical skills which naturally flow from a predominantly outdoor people were all bound to have a cumulative effect. And they did — in the 1950s, the glorious 'sporting' 1950s. Science had also not begun intruding into sport and nations had not yet seen sporting successes as a means of expressing themselves internationally in the same manner as technological achievements. Politics and sport were yet to combine in the way they were later to do. It was one person against another, without any scientific aid or political prompting. Athletes had only God's resources in their pursuit of excellence — and we showed ourselves to be as good as any other nation.

Australia seemed to be able to do no wrong in international sport in the 1950s. At tennis, we reigned supreme. During the 1950s Australia produced several Wimbledon singles champions, and our Davis Cup performances will perhaps never be equalled. From 1950 Australia won the Cup in fifteen of the next eighteen years, overcoming challenges from the US (nine times), Italy (twice), Spain (twice), India (once) and Mexico (once). In this period, Australian tennis players set new standards in physical fitness and tennis excellence.

In boxing, Jimmy Carruthers knocked out South African Vic Toweel in a flurry of staccato punches in the opening round of their fight in Johannesburg on 15 November 1952 to win the bantamweight championship of the world. He went on to make three successful defences of his title against Toweel, Henry 'Pappy' Gault and Chamrern Songkitrat in the next eighteen months.

Cricket began to move into a new era under the guidance of Richie Benaud, and golf provided us with our greatest moments in both amateur and professional ranks. Australia won the World Cup, with Peter Thomson and Kel Nagle, in 1954 and again in 1959, and Thomson emerged as the foremost golfer of the day, winning the British Open in 1954, 1955, 1956, 1958 and 1965. The year of Thomson's first Open triumph also saw Doug Bachli win the British amateur championship and bring unique recognition to the Victoria Golf Club, which had produced them both. Australia also won the first Eisenhower Trophy for men's amateur golf in 1958, when the team of Bachli, Bruce Devlin, Bob Stevens and Peter Toogood tied with the US and then defeated them in a play-off.

The magnificent St George Rugby League team won eleven successive premierships in the Sydney competition from 1956 to 1966, a world record for senior club premierships for any code of football in the world. The late 1950s saw Jack Brabham begin his rise to prominence in the world of motor racing, winning the first of his three world championships in 1959 in his Cooper-Climax. And the sport of rowing was mesmerised by the remarkable feats of that great scallywag Stuart Mackenzie.

Mackenzie was easily the most colourful and controversial sculler that Australia has ever produced. He just missed a gold medal at the 1956 Melbourne Olympics in a tremendous final and even more remarkable post-race incident. The powerfully built Aussie seemed to have the race well in hand, but the Soviet sculler Vyacheslav Ivanov made a sensational spurt with 200 metres to go and won. Eighteen-year-old Ivanov was so thrilled when he was presented his gold medal that he jumped up and down with joy — and dropped the medal into Lake Wendouree. He immediately dived to the bottom of the lake, but came back up empty-handed. After the Games were over, he was given a replacement medal by the International Olympic Committee.

Wearing the Green and Gold

Although Mackenzie missed out on this greatest prize of all, he did win a record six successive Diamond Sculls at Henley from 1957 to 1962. His talent was unique; his showmanship first-class. Mackenzie would often toy with his opponents, slowing down his rating until they caught up and then suddenly clapping on the pace, leaving them stranded. In one race he went out on the water in a top hat and still won convincingly. In another race he was heading for a record but sacrificed it when he stopped to talk to friends. The English found his antics amusing and perhaps a little abrasive. While English sports lovers will never forget him for his six consecutive victories on the Thames, neither will they forgive him for the way he performed. He was something of a brash Australian to them, another example of this independent spirit and exceptional sporting talent which seemed to be exploding in every direction.

Nowhere was this burst of Australian excellence seen more clearly than at the 1956 Olympic Games in Melbourne. When a young Victorian runner named Ron Clarke lit the Olympic flame at the top of the Melbourne Cricket Ground that sunny November morning it was to signal the commencement of our greatest occasion in sport, when Australians were to win our largest-ever collection of Olympic medals. Thirteen gold, eight silver and fourteen bronze. It was a time of enormous pride for everybody, for all Australians and particularly for those fortunate enough to be chosen to compete in those Games. Dawn Fraser recounts her thoughts at marching in the opening ceremony: 'Having that Australian blazer on for the first time and then being part of a team, it just capped off all those months of hard training, three times a day, getting up at 4.30 in the morning and training seven days a week. To actually put on an Australian blazer and march into that Melbourne Cricket Ground was just something. In fact I start getting goose bumps every time I think about it.'

The Melbourne Cricket Ground was revamped as the main stadium for the Olympic Games at Melbourne in 1956. A capacity crowd watches Hungary march past at the opening ceremony
All Sport: Ken Shepherd

Not surprisingly, Australia fielded its largest Olympic team ever of 243 men and 44 women; only America with 298 competitors had a larger team. And with the shift to the southern hemisphere for the first time, the timing of the Games was also moved from July–August — a more suitable time for athletes from the northern hemisphere — to late November–early December, which favoured Australians so much more. The swimming pool was where the Australians had their finest moments. They ousted the US as the dominant swimming nation, winning eight gold medals to America's five.

Never before, or since, have we so ruled an Olympic sport. Australia finished first, second and third in both the men's and women's 100-metres freestyle finals — only the third time in Olympic history that all six placings had been filled by one country, the US having done so in 1920 and 1924. Jon Henricks won the gold medal in the men's 100-metres final, John Devitt the silver and Gary Chapman the bronze. Dawn Fraser captured the first of her three gold medals in the women's 100-metres final, beating Lorraine Crapp and Faith Leech. Fraser still maintains that winning her first gold medal in Melbourne was her most wonderful moment in sport.

Murray Rose, the 17-year-old vegetarian who became known as 'the Seaweed Streak' and made a lot of Australians think about their diets, won the 400-metres and 1500-metres freestyle finals and was the most successful male swimmer at the Games. He won the shorter event fairly easily from the Japanese Tsuyoshi Yamanaka and America's George Breen, but there was concern before the 1500-metres race whether he had the stamina to beat both Yamanaka and Breen again, for he had swum in few 1500-metres events before Melbourne. Breen was an outstanding opponent and set a world record of 17 min. 52.9 sec. in the third heat of the qualifying round. After 800 metres in the final, he, Rose and Yamanaka were neck and neck. Then Rose began to surge. With 100 metres to go, Breen was well back, but it was Yamanaka who posed some danger. He was just 6 metres back and swimming strongly. Down the last lap and Yamanaka was gaining with every stroke. The packed stands were going wild, screaming at their young hero to find something extra. And thankfully Rose held his lead to win by just 2 metres in 17 min. 58.9 sec., 6 seconds outside Breen's world record. The American came third. There was no more disconsolate figure after the event than Breen, who had felt certain of the gold medal after his record-breaking heat swim. 'I'd rather have one Olympic gold medal than all the world records', he lamented. He never did get his wish, for he finished third again in the same event four years later in Rome.

Another gold came in the men's 100-metres backstroke where David Theile became the first and only Australian to become an Olympic champion in this discipline. Yet he would have missed the Melbourne Olympics had the Senate of the University of Queensland not agreed to post-date his scholarship to study medicine. The final was an exciting battle between the two Australians, Theile and John Monckton, with Theile gaining a winning edge through his controversial method of turning, and then drawing further away to win.

The women's 400-metres freestyle continued the Australian dominance. Beaten in the 100-metres final by Dawn Fraser, Crapp had her revenge in the later race. Fraser took her on early; the two Australians swam stroke for stroke over the first 100 metres. Crapp, however, moved ahead by a metre at the halfway mark and from then on was never headed. The talents were obvious then: Fraser was superior over the sprint distances; Crapp was better the longer the race went. To even further emphasise Australia's pre-eminent standing, we also won both relays, the men's 4 × 200-metres with Rose, Devitt, Henricks and Kevin O'Halloran and the women's 4 × 100-metres with Fraser, Leech, Sandra Morgan and Crapp, both in world record times. Crapp always contends that winning the relay meant more to her than her individual gold medals. 'The individual events were a sort of toss-up between Dawn and myself. Whoever got there first on the day was the better swimmer. But the relay; you're working as a team and everyone's working together. That's what was

The 'Seaweed Streak' Murray Rose in the 1962 Perth Commonwealth Games. Rose won gold medals for 400 metres and 1500 metres at the 1956 Olympics and won four medals at the Perth Games. His vegetarian diet was considered strange in the meat-eating 1950s
Sydney Morning Herald

Lorraine Crapp, sprinter and middle distance swimmer, who had many stirring tussles with her Australian team mate Dawn Fraser. She won the 400 metres gold medal at the 1956 Olympics in Melbourne and was part of the winning sprint relay team. At the end of 1956 she held world records at seven distances, up to 880 yards.
Australian Broadcasting Corporation

so good about it'. No Australian woman won a medal outside the freestyle events and yet Australia missed only one final over the entire swimming competition: the women's 200-metres breaststroke.

Track and field provided Australia with many other moments of glory. Betty Cuthbert was the heroine, emulating Marjorie Jackson's sprint double in Helsinki and then going one better by anchoring the Australian team to the relay gold medal. Cuthbert was worried by team-mate Marlene Mathews and Christa Stubnick, an East German police typist, in the 100-metres, but found for most of the race that she was threatened by the black American, Isabell Daniels. With mouth characteristically wide open, Cuthbert kept driving as hard as she could for the line and won in 11.5 seconds. She says the win meant little to her at the time. 'However, Mum must have realised what I had done because I looked up in the crowd just after the race was over and saw her crying her eyes out', she says. Daniels had faded slightly towards the finish, as Stubnick finished second and Mathews third. In the 200-metres final, Cuthbert got a terrific start and went after Stubnick, in the lane outside her, for all she was worth. She caught and passed her after about 80 metres and, for the only time in Olympic history, the medallists in the two sprints finished in exactly the same order. It was during the 200-metres that Cuthbert picked up the name — compliments of the *Argus* newspaper (now defunct) — of 'Golden Girl', the nickname which she has proudly carried with her throughout her life.

Australia also won the relay gold medal with Shirley Strickland, Norma Croker, Fleur Mellor and Cuthbert, following an enormous outcry when Mathews was omitted from the team. The selectors felt that Mellor was a better relay runner, particularly round a curve, and was obviously fresher. At the last change, the British team and Australia were level, but Cuthbert pulled away just before the tape to win the gold medal and the third for herself. The time of 44.5 seconds knocked seven-tenths of a second off the world record. Cuthbert was to go on and win a fourth Olympic gold medal over 400 metres in Tokyo eight years later and so establish herself as one of the greatest competitors in the history of Olympic competition.

Shirley Strickland wound up her illustrious career in Melbourne, winning this relay gold medal and successfully defending her 80-metres hurdles title. In three successive Olympic hurdles finals, she had come third, first and first again. Her complete total of Olympic medals was seven: three gold, one silver and three bronze, providing her with the most medals won by an Australian in track and field.

The only gold medal which Australia won at Melbourne outside swimming and track and field was in cycling, where Ian Browne and Tony Marchant won the 2000-metres tandem, despite having to face a repêchage after finishing third in their first round heat. The Australians then beat South Africa in the quarter-finals, Italy in the semi-finals and cycled brilliantly to beat Czechoslovakia in the final.

Australia's gold medal total of thirteen was more than double our previous best of six from the previous Olympics in Helsinki. It was a time of immense national celebration. Australia was, right there and then, at the forefront of the sporting world. We were known in the far reaches of the globe: this small, island nation with an excess of sporting champions. And what's more, all Australians were very proud of what they had done for us. Every man, woman and child bathed in the reflected glory of the Melbourne triumphs. The momentum created by those Games carried through into the 1960s and 1970s for Australia. Many of those champions stayed around and went on to greater heights: Fraser, Theile, Rose, Devitt and Cuthbert.

The 1956 Games proved the inspiration for a skinny young West Australian boy to want to become a great runner. With his parents, he watched in awe from the stands as the great Soviet runner Vladimir Kuts won the 10 000-metres and then, five days later, the 5000-metres. His name was Herb Elliott, and he was later to wear the green and gold with perhaps more distinction that any other Australian athlete.

Also in Melbourne at the Games was the silver-haired old eccentric Percy Cerutty, who had seen Elliott run in a college mile event at Aquinas College in Perth in 1955.

He had been impressed by Elliott's running and also with his time, 4 min. 22 sec. Cerutty influenced Elliott to remain in Melbourne after the Games. They trained during the week in the city and at weekends he went to Cerutty's seaside training camp at Portsea, where the old man pushed him relentlessly up and down the sandhills and then at night over dinner would instil in him dreams of success and his own philosophies on running. The body was not enough; Cerutty was all the time working on his mind as well.

In his first race under his old mentor, the boy ran 4 min. 6 sec. for the mile — 14 seconds less than his previous best. At the age of 19, and after a year under Cerutty's training methods, Elliott, on 28 January 1958 in Melbourne, ran his first sub-4 minute mile. From then on, he rarely ran a mile over 4 minutes. Late in 1958, Elliott broke the 1500-metres world record, running 3 min. 36 sec.

At the Rome Olympics two years later, Elliott was the undisputed favourite, but knew it was still going to be one of his toughest races with the Swede Dan Waern and the American Dyrol Burleson up against him. After 950 metres, Elliott took off out in front like a hare. His opponents and the 90 000 people in the stadium immediately conceded that he wasn't going to be beaten. But the lanky Aussie refused to look behind. Unaware that he had opened up an insurmountable lead, he was sure that someone was close on his heels.

When he reached the back straight he saw Cerutty standing by the side of the track waving a towel. The prearranged signal meant that a world record was achievable and that Elliott should give it all he had. Cerutty had actually raced out of the stands and dashed across the protective moat that surrounded the track in order to signal his pupil. He was quickly grabbed by police and hauled away. But his effort had been worth it. Elliott, still refusing to turn around and still thinking that he might lose the gold medal, strained all the way to the finishing line and won by 20 metres in one of the greatest performances in Olympic history. His time was 3 min. 35.6 sec., breaking his own world record. And it took the rest of the world seven years to catch up with him. France's Michel Jazy was second in 3 min. 38.4 sec. with Hungary's Istvan Rozsavolgyi third. Waern came fourth and Burleson sixth.

Elliott remembers that incredible performance: 'I remember before the final Percy Cerutty saying "now I will be sitting up here in this particular spot in the crowd and when you get to the last lap, if you see me waving a towel, it means that you've got a chance of breaking the world record or else there's someone on your hammer, so watch out!" and I must admit that I was so distracted by the event coming up that I didn't take a great deal of notice about what he said . . . Anyway, the race started and it's always an enormous relief for an athlete when the gun goes. The nervous tension and the anxiety and the worry that has built up inside you for weeks . . . starts to flow into your event and you start to use it positively . . . My pre-race plan was to sit around for a lap and a bit and just see what the hell was happening and then, with two laps to go, to make a go for it and rely on the reputation that I had established to frighten the other guys off. So the race started and this guy in a blue singlet got out in front. I had no idea who he was, and I settled into maybe fourth or fifth place. And we got to where there was two laps to go, which was my break point, and I remember thinking to myself "God, I'm buggered" and there was a slight moment of panic. The officials were yelling out the lap times in Italian. I had no idea, therefore, what times we'd run the first couple of laps in. In fact, it was ridiculously fast and I would've understood why I was buggered if I'd understood Italian.

'Anyway, that was really a very important decision point, because I either stuck to my original plan of going for it or, because I wasn't feeling quite so good, there was the attraction of sitting back in the field and waiting for a while to see what was going to happen. You really don't think these things through in a logical sense. I guess instinctively I decided to stick to my original plan and off I went. And as it happened, it worked. I sort of got in front and opened up a bit of a gap and the bell

The fanatical athletics coach Perry Cerutty had many of Australia's best athletes at his training camp at Portsea, Victoria. Cerutty worked on his charges both mentally and physically and led them on gruelling runs around the steep sand dunes of the Portsea back beach. He 'discovered' Herb Elliott as a schoolboy miler and coached him to gold medal success.
Herald & Weekly Times

Herb Elliott, Australia's great mile runner. In 1958, at the age of 19, he ran his first sub-4-minute mile and in the same year he broke the 1500 metres world record — running 3 min. 35 seconds. He broke his own record in taking the 1500 metre gold medal in Rome.
Ern McQuillan

went for the final lap and I was pretty well away from the field at that stage of the game. I went around the turn, into the back straight and I remember the wind whistling past my ears, because I was running against the wind. I couldn't hear what was going on behind me because of the wind, so I wasn't quite sure where the other competitors were and I was a bit uncertain about whether I should look around, because that can throw you off balance. At that point I saw Percy waving this towel and I thought "what does that mean?" and I remember thinking "it doesn't matter about the detail, it means you've got to run faster" and indeed I tried to run faster. I'm not sure that I did, but all I remember is coming around into the finishing straight and having a strange mixture of fear and elation. Elation because I knew I had a pretty good chance of winning; fear because there was always that concern that somebody would come up and pip you on the post. I guess the feeling I

Blood, Sweat and Tears

remember most when I did hit the finishing line was sheer and utter relief, because the pressure was finally off. Just relief.'

Between 1954 and 1960, Herb Elliott won forty-four consecutive races at 1500 metres and one mile before retiring from competition. He's still widely regarded as being the greatest miler of all time.

After the 1960s and the early 1970s, our sporting triumphs began trailing off. Australia won eight gold medals, including Elliott's, at the 1960 Rome Olympics, six in Tokyo in 1964, five in Mexico City in 1968, eight in Munich in 1972, including three by Shane Gould, and nil in Montreal in 1976. Australians dominated Wimbledon through much of the 1950s, 1960s and 1970s. Our honour roll of men's singles champions in that period is daunting: Lew Hoad (1956, 1957), Ashley Cooper (1958), Neale Fraser (1960), Rod Laver (1961, 1962, 1968, 1969), Roy Emerson (1964, 1965), John Newcombe (1967, 1970, 1971). Since then, there has been only Pat Cash in 1987. Margaret Court also won the women's singles in 1963, 1965 and 1970. Evonne Cawley took the title in 1971 and then waited till 1980 before doing so again. Since then, nothing.

Similarly, our golfing triumphs declined after Peter Thomson's five British Open wins, four of them in the 1950s. Kel Nagle won the Centenary British Open in 1960 and David Graham the 1979 US PGA and 1981 US Open titles. Then a long quiet. Our cricketers continued to have their ups and downs, although the West Indies tour of Australia in 1960–1 was one of our greatest cricketing summers and produced the first tied Test in the history of Test cricket.

In yachting, we won the second Admiral's Cup we competed in, in 1967, with *Balandra*, *Mercedes III* and *Caprice of Huon*, but then failed in the next five challenges before winning again in the tragic 1979 event (in which the Fastnet race cost

Australia's 'Mean Machine', the 4 × 100 metres relay team, salutes the crowd after taking the gold medal at the Edinburg Commonwealth Games. The team is Greg Fasala, Mark Stockwell, Matthew Renshaw and Neil Brookes
Live Action: Acikalin

Queensland's Duncan Armstrong blitzed the opposition to take gold in the Men's 100m Butterfly at the Seoul Olympics.
Live Action

Australia's golden girls put hockey on the map when they took out gold at the Seoul Olympics.
Time Space/Live Action

Blood, Sweat and Tears

the lives of fifteen yachtsmen), with *Police Car*, *Ragamuffin* and *Impetuous*. In boxing, Lionel Rose and Johnny Famechon brought Australia international recognition between 1968 and 1970 with their numerous title fights. Heather McKay also ruled the world of women's squash for an incredible period, winning the British Open championship a record sixteen times between 1962 and 1977, and Geoff Hunt won the men's equivalent seven times in much the same era.

But the overall frequency and extent of the heady, exhilarating performances was lessening. Rather disturbingly so.

There had been such a glut of them, through the 1950s in particular, that Australians tended to take sporting success for granted. They incorrectly assumed that with the same amount of work and the same amount of money, the upward spiral would simply continue. There was a disturbing lack of foresight.

For world sporting interest had begun stirring through the 1970s and 1980s. Other nations began seeing sport as a powerful instrument by which they could either express their political feelings, as first shown by African nations boycotting the Montreal Olympics because of a New Zealand rugby tour of South Africa, or unify their nation and at the same time project themselves much more forcibly than they otherwise might, particularly among the Soviet bloc countries.

In those nations wanting to expand internationally, governments were prepared to spend vast amounts of money and to turn their scientific and medical resources towards producing better performances. Athletes were fully supported financially by governments: space age equipment was introduced and existing facilities widely expanded and improved; and even some highly elaborate forms of doping were introduced.

Australia, meanwhile, was content to rest on past glories. The attitude was that if we were good once, then there was no reason why that should not continue. Belatedly an Institute of Sport was established after the 1980 Moscow Olympics.

Below:
Geoff Hunt was regarded as the fittest man in Australia as he dominated world squash for more than a decade.
Live Action: Simmonds

Above:
Preparing for the Seoul Olympic Games in 1988. On a misty morning on Lake Burley Griffin, Canberra, the Australian eight set out on a training row. The crew was in Canberra for the opening of the new Parliament House. They are James Galloway (bow), Mike McKay, Sam Patten, Hamish MacLashan, Richard Finlayson, James Thomkins, Jon Popa, Steve Evans (stroke), Dale Caterson (cox).
Live Action: Acikalin

The natural ability of our athletes was the same, the performance levels were the same, but we were being gradually overwhelmed by the massive government-backed scientific and medical growth which sport underwent in other countries.

This change, when it eventually hit home, was hard to accept. Remembering just how prominent sport had made Australia internationally, it meant that when isolated sporting achievements did occur they were grasped and eulogised with far more vigour and enthusiasm than ever before.

Nothing exemplifies this more than our success in the *America*'s Cup when John Bertrand guided the wing-keeled *Australia II* to its emotion-charged victory over Dennis Conner's US 12-metre *Liberty* on 26 September 1983 at Newport, Rhode Island, thus wresting the *America*'s Cup from the New York Yacht Club after an unbeaten 132-year grip on the Cup by the Americans.

Many Australians had two television sets and several radios going to catch all the commentaries towards the end of that final race and a whole nation's early morning peak-hour traffic clogged up as people slowed to hear, and then celebrate, the phenomenal conclusion.

The excesses which went with this victory were very much the result of a nation having been denied the multitude of sporting successes it had once known. Here was the past revisited. Even Bertrand couldn't get over the emotional outpourings. He says: 'If I was dreaming in my wildest imagination, I would've figured that maybe half the response of what we saw was happening in this country. But obviously it was an incredible melodrama and the timing was out of sight in terms of us going down to 3–1 and then the almost impossible dream of coming back to win. Australians love that . . . The concept of Australia taking on the world, particularly the United States, technologically the most powerful nation in the world, all added to the drama of the event. But it still amazes me and bowls me over just how important it was to this country. It's part of our culture now.'

Australia's victorious 1983 America's Cup team look proudly on as syndicate head Alan Bond and Skipper John Bertrand display the 'Auld Mug' won against America in match races off Newport, Rhode Island. America had held the Cup for 132 years and survived a number of challenges from Australia in recent decades.
Photobank/All Sport

Can that *America*'s Cup triumph do anything for us as a sporting nation, to help us retrieve some of those past glories? It was enormously uplifting and inspirational, but is it the prop we need? Bertrand said perhaps not, but at least it gives us hope. 'It's not a change in direction for a country like Australia but it's a glimmer of hope that we can do things far in excess of what we normally set our horizons at. I think Australians tend, on the average, to undersell themselves. You know, this self-effacing type of thing; the attitude that "well, you know, we won, but it was just a fluke" or whatever . . . It's a lovely environment to live in . . . but in places like the United States people are much more up-front and they're much more positive and a part of their culture is that if they win they say "well, thank you" . . . Our *America*'s Cup success . . . showed that we can do something. And it wasn't a fluke . . . I know a lot of companies which started off in new directions as a result of it, saying "well, if those buggers can do it, then we can too" and a lot of people have come to me since the *America*'s Cup and said "look, for the first time we felt part of this country and as a result we became naturalised Australians". That's a fantastic situation to be in.'

Australians have had their isolated successes since then, hopefully some inspiration having been derived from our *America*'s Cup win. Greg Norman finally fulfilled the weighty expectations held for him by carrying off the 1986 British Open golf championship at Turnberry. From that day, Norman has played a dominant role in world golf. (He would also have won a second major had not local boy Larry Mize holed his freakish chip shot at the 1987 US Masters.) And Pat Cash won Wimbledon in 1987. The wins by Norman and Cash were greeted with excessive jubilation, because such triumphs by Australians are now so uncommon. We also became preoccupied with winners such as the Marrickville puncher Jeff Fenech, who was rescued from what looked an inevitable life of crime by kindly policemen and directed towards a boxing ring to vent his high spirits and rebelliousness. And also

Wearing the Green and Gold

Wayne Gardner, who took on the world and beat them in the death-defying sport of motor-cycle racing. Neither sport held a high profile in the public's eye until they came along, but so anxious were Australians for sporting success that they swooped on their world title victories and took them overwhelmingly to their hearts.

Perhaps this excessive desire for champions has, in its own way, been counter-productive. The pressures to produce have been enormous. Australians have wanted their champions to prove that the 1950s were not just a flash in the pan, that we still have acclaimed sporting ability. We have looked longingly to our national champions to become world champions, to lead us back to those halcyon days, and if they have not done so then we have roundly criticised them. For example, the greatest critics of Greg Norman before he eventually won one of the world's major golf championships were Australians. He was seen by many as having the obvious playing skills, but not the inner strength. He was not achieving what we wanted and so he was constantly deemed a failure. Only when he won the British Open did he finally become a national hero.

This pressure is felt by our best competitors. Many talk of it. Many must have felt the risk of failing too great and not been willing to take the chance. Others have been hounded into going overseas, seeking success and the recognition which did not come their way at home.

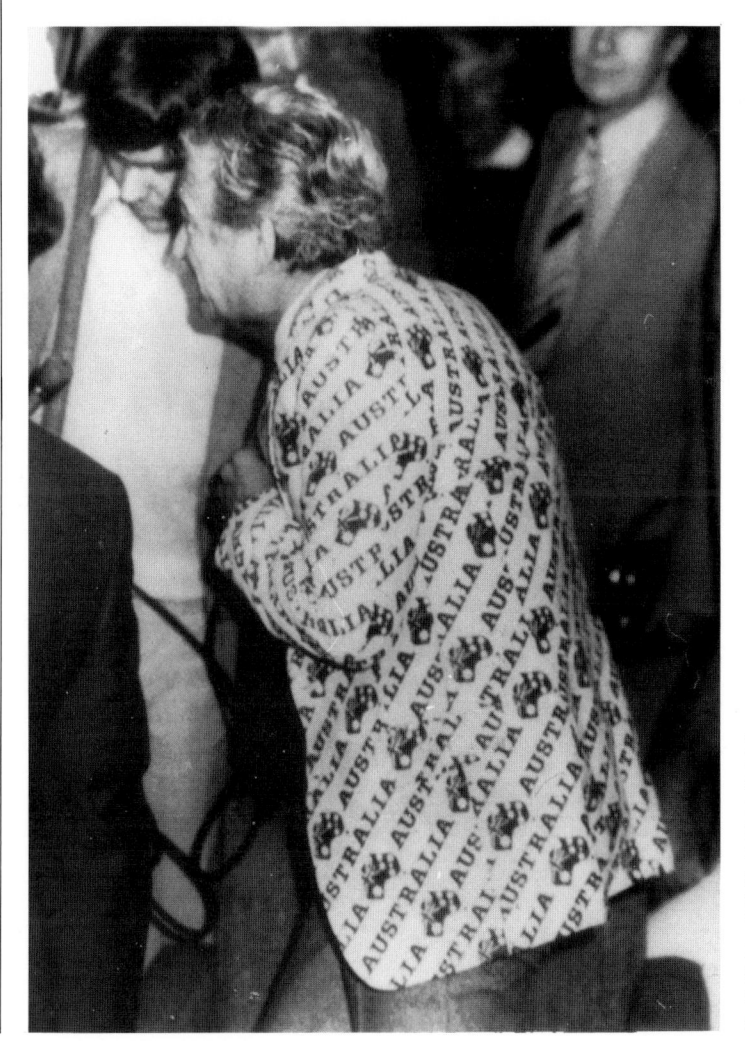

Australia's Prime Minister Bob Hawke is a genuine sports devotee, and he has the habit of being in the right place at the right time when there is a sports triumph to celebrate. He was at the Royal Perth Yacht Club, wearing a monumentally jingoistic blazer, when Australia II *won the* America's Cup.
News Limited

All Australia held its breath in the final minutes of the last heat of the America's Cup in 1983. As Australia II hit the line to win after an intense tacking duel with Liberty, *city traffic in Australia began to clog up as people listened to the race, and then erupted with cheers and a multitude of car horns. The celebrations went on for weeks, and Matilda, the boxing kangaroo, was part of a street parade in Perth to celebrate the event.*
News Limited

Australians need their champions to win at the highest levels because we have been so great in the past. So we will always love, almost idolise, our world champions, even if they are few and far between. The reason 'Matilda' wears boxing gloves on the boxing kangaroo flag (which emanated from our *America*'s Cup triumph) may well be to show the world that while Australian sport might be down, it's still fighting — even against its own unfortunate 'knocking' syndrome.

Or are we kidding ourselves about all this? Have we simply lost the drive and tenacity to be great once more? Have we become indolent; a nation so blessed with wealth, sunshine and a high standard of living that it doesn't really matter any more? History will reveal that.

Sources and references

Books used for this chapter were:

John Blanch, *The Ampol Australian Sporting Records* (Budget Books, rev. edn, 1981); Gary Lester, *Australians at the Olympics: A Definitive History* (Lester-Townsend, 1984); Jim Shepherd, *The Winfield Book of Australian Sporting Records* (Rigby, 1981); Terry Smith, *Australian Gold — the first 100 years* (Lester-Townsend, 1982); Jim Webster, *It's a Sporting Life* (Macmillan, 1986).

Interviews from transcripts of the television series, 'Blood, Sweat and Tears':

John Bertrand, Jim Collins, Lorraine Crapp, Herb Elliott, Dawn Fraser.

Otherwise the material is derived from the author's own information and research.

Index

ABC, 182–4, 191, 201
ABC 'Four Corners' programme, 81
Aboriginal boxers, 102, 145–9
Aboriginal cricket, 204
Aboriginal jockeys, 99–102, 103
Aboriginal sports competitors, **131–56**, 99–103
Aborigines,
  destruction by Caucasians, 132
  discrimination against, 132
  monetary abuse by whites, 137–8
Aborigines in Sport, 132
abseiling, 47
Adams, George, 66–7, 74, 75
Addison, Walter C., 294
Adelaide Grand Prix, 206
Adidas, sports sponsorship, 206, 211
Admiral's Cup, 312
advertising,
  and sportspeople, 143, 179, 196, 206–8
  on television, 193, 206
Age tapes, 80–1
aggression in sport, 47, 49–50
Agua Caliente Handicap, 13
Ajax, 227
AJC, *see* Australian Jockey Club
Albert, Prince, 26
alcohol, effect on sport careers, 102, 103
Alderman, Terry, 109, 110
Allen, 'Gubby', 44
Allunga, 227
amateur sports, 244–51
amateur status, Olympians, 213
Ambrum, George, 154
American Broadcasting Corporation, 195
America's Cup, 1, **111**, 195, 201, 209–10, 225, 315–16
  Australians' attitude to winning, 1, 315–16
Ampol, 210
Amway, 210
Anderson, Mal, 299
Angles, Cyril, 190
animals, imported for sport, 16
Ansett, Bob, 116
Antarctic marathon, 256–8
Anti-Football League, 10, **116**, 264
Anti-Gambling Association, 72
apartheid, effect on sport, 281–9
Arab Hector, 59
archery, 160
Armstrong, Duncan, *313*
Armstrong, Warwick, 278, 297
ashes, cricket, 5, 294
Ashton family, 89
Ashton, Geoff, 88–9
Askin, Robert, 79
Associated Racing Clubs, 268
athletics, 14–15, 62, 63, 127, **176**, **229**, 249, 289, 296, 308–12
  history, 22
  school, 263
  sponsorship, 206, 211
  sprinting techniques, 137
  women's participation, 160, **163–5**
'Aussie Rules', *see* Australian

Rules Football; Victorian Football League
'Aussie Sports', 263
Austral Wheel Race, 213
Australasian, 186
Australia,
  as sporting nation, 55
  early settlers, 25
  rivalry with England, 105–6, 108–9
  sporting colours, 275, 296–7
Australia II, 1, 2, 111, 315
Australia III and *IV*, 210, 211
Australian Athletic Union, 211
Australian Board of Control, 276–7, 279
Australian Broadcasting Commission, *see* ABC
Australian Council of Health and Physical Education, 261
Australian Cricket Board, 109, 200, 201, 202, 204, 213, 285
Australian Cup, 93
Australian Derby, 206
Australian Grand Prix, 209
Australian Hang-gliding Association, 47
Australian Institute of Sport, 3, 13, 271–2, 314
Australian Jockey Club, 94, **267–8**
Australian National Railways, 210
Australian Netball Association, 176
Australian Olympic Council, 240
Australian Olympic Federation, 221, 241, 276
Australian Open, 3, 206
Australian Protestant Defence Association, 75
Australian Rules football, 2, 6, 8–11, 103, 106, 116–21, 133, 140
  Aboriginal participants, 154–5
  amateur, 258
  attendance figures, 114
  clubs, 111–12, 116–21
    rivalry between, 114
  effect of media, 186
  history, 17–18, 111–19
  interstate rivalry, 123
  violence, 51
  see also Victorian Football League
Australian Soccer Federation, 141
Australian Sports Commission, 261, 272
Australian Swimming Union, 14, 159, 165, 281
Australian Women's Amateur Athletic Association, 162
Australian Women's Cricket Council, 162
Australians,
  attitude to sport, **1–22**, 104–12, 224–6
  sporting prowess, 291–319
  tribalism in sport, 104–12
Aylett, Allen, 116

Baby Ortiz, 33
Bachli, Doug, 304
Backhouse, James, 57
Backo, Sam, 153, 154

Badger, Harold, 227
Bailey, Ken, 34
Baker, R. L. 'Snowy', 189
Balandra, 312
Ball, George, 186
Ballesteros, Sevvy, 208
ballooning, *see* hot air ballooning
Bamblett, Les, 155
Bank of Hong Kong, 210
Banner, R. G. 'Dick', 28
Bannerman, Charles, 44
Bannister, Roger, 237–8
Bannon, John, 273
Barassi, Ronald Dale, **10**, **114**, 116, 121, 272
bare-knuckle fights, 15, 25, 30–1
Barlow, Andrew, 136
Barnett, Harris, 208
Bartels, Peter, 209
baseball, 16, 103
basketball, 16, 103, **125**
  clubs, **125**
  numbers participating, 244
Bathurst City Council, 217
'Battle of Brisbane', 43
Bay, John, 53, 54, 55
Beach, William, *293*, 294
Beamon, Bob, 229
Beau Zam, 13, 93, 96
Beaumont, Bill, 52
Beaurepaire, 216
Becker, Boris, 208
Beetson, Arthur, 153–4
Bellinger, John, 62
Bell's Life, 189
Benaud, Richie, *192*, 233, 235, 304
Benson & Hedges tobacco company, 205
Berger Paints, 200
Bertrand, John, 111, 196, 315–16
Betros, Peter, 51
Better Golf in Five Minutes, 181
betting, 15, **56–84**
  legislation, 75–6
  off-course, **72–7**, 96
  SP, 78–9
  type of sports, 62
Bettington, Reg, 181–2
Bicentennial Gold Cup, 224
'Big Artie', *see* Beetson, Arthur
Bigge, Commissioner, 57
billiards, 16, 252–4, 297
bingo (housie-housie) 78
'Black Colossus', *see* Johnson, Jack
Blacklock, Ray, 154
Blankers-Koen, Fanny, 90, **164**
Bledisloe Cup, 231
Bligh, Ivo, 294
Blinkhorn, Cec, 186
'Blood Bath', 43
bloodsports, 15, 16, 25
'Blues', *see* Carlton Football Club
BMX cycling, 249
bocce, 22
body building, women's, 254
Bodyline cricket series, 5, **44**, 105, 107, 108–9, 297
Bold Personality, 56
Bond, Alan, 55, 111, 209, *210*, 225
Bond Brewing, 209, 210
Bondi Surf Bathers' Lifesaving Club, 215

Bonecrusher, 13, 93, *95*
bookmakers, 13, 74–5, 82, 91, **94–5**
boomerang throwing, 15
Border, Allan, *183*
Borg, Arne, 270
Borg, Bjorn, 217, 221
Borthwick, Pat, 163
Botany Handicap, 137
Bottom, Bob, **80–2**
Bowlers, Bill, 44
boxers, 102, **268**
  Aboriginal, 131, 140, 145–9, 147, 148
boxing, 24, 25, **30–6**, 103, 131, *174*, 304, 314, 316–17
  deaths, 35, 36
  injuries, 35
  losses, 240
  Olympic Games, 240
  promoters, 189
boxing kangaroo flag, 319
boycotts,
  of international sport with South Africa, 281–9
  Olympic Games, 170, 276–7, 281, 314
Boyd, Les, 53, 122
Boyle, Raelene, 214, 232, 233
Brabham, Sir Jack, 254, 304
Bracken, George, 145
Bradford Cotton Mills Ltd, 209
Bradley, Rocky, 117, 118
Bradman, Sir Donald, 6, 7, 44–5, 108, 136, 213, 226, 233, 235, 279, *280*, 297
Brady, Mike, 112
Brasher, Chris, 237
Breen, George, 306
brewers, sponsorship of sport, 206, 209, 213
Bridge, Les, 13
Briggs, Eddie, 138
Briggs, Selwyn, 138
Bright, Ray, 202
Brisbane Cup, 93
Brisbane, Sir Thomas, 267
British Open (golf), 312, 316
British Open (squash), 314
broadcasting rights, 192, 200–2, 204, 206
Broadcom Australia Ltd, 208
Brock, Peter, 219
Brockhoff, David, 52
Brohman, Darryl, 53
Broken Hill Proprietary Company, 216
Bromwich, John, 251, 299
Brookes, Sir Norman, 22, 299, *300*
Brother Peter, 44
Brousse, Elie, 37
Brown, Joe, 34
Brown, John, **214**, 272, 285
Brown, Ray, 122
Browne, Ian, 308
Brundage, Avery, 211
Bruns, Neville, 51
Bryant, Bert, 191
Buckingham, Beverley, 171
Buckley, Vincent, 83
Budd, Zola, 289
Budweiser beer, 211
Bull Ant, 186
'Bulldogs', *see* Canterbury Rugby League Club

Index

'Bullocky', 133, 135
'Bumper', see Farrell, Frank
Bunton, Haydn, 140
Burdon, Alec, 18
Burke and Wills, 3
Burleson, Dyrol, 309
Burnell, Alf, 52
Burns, Frank, 147
Burns, Tommy, 32–3
Burton, Mike, 52

Caledonian Games, 16
Callum, Steve, 52
Campaign King, 93
Campbell, Keith, 219
Campbell, Tommy, 285
canoeing,
    dangers, 48
    school, 263
Canterbury Rugby League Club, 122
Capper, Warwick, *8*, 194
Caprice of Huon, 312
'Captain Blood', see Dyer, Jack
Carbine, 13, 60, 72
Carlos, John, 275
Carlton and United Breweries, 210, 213
Carlton Football Club, 116, 117
Carroll, Tom, 127, 215, *219*, 288
Carruthers, Jimmy, 304
Carruthers Liberal and Reform Association, 75
Carter, Hanson, 278
Carter, Jimmy, 266
Casey, Ron, 188
Cash, Pat, 4, 196, 208, 221, 224, 288, 312, 316
Cashman, Richard, 184
casinos, **79**, 80, 83
Cassidy, Graham, 215–16
Catchpole, Ken, 52
Catholics, 69, 70, 75
Cavalier, Rodney, 262
Cavendish, Tom, 292
Cawley, Evonne, see Goolagong, Evonne, 312
Cawley, Kelly, 143
Cawley, Morgan, 143
Cawley, Roger, 142
Cazaly, Roy, 112
Central Board of Protection for Aborigines, 132, 133
Cerutty, Percy, 308–9
Cervantes, Antonio, 34, 148
Chalker, 'Big' Dan, 62
Challenge Cup, 111
Champion Cup, 89
Champion, Malcolm, 297
champions, sports, **224–43**
Chance, 60
Channel Nine, see television, Channel Nine
Channel Seven, see television, Channel Seven
Chapman, Gary, 306
Chapman, Glen, *22*
Chappell, Greg, 5, 7, *46*, 199, 202, 230, 233, 285
Chappell, Ian, 45, **202**
Chappell, Trevor, 5
Charles, Billy, 138
Charles, Jim, 138
Charlesworth, Ric, 7
Charlton, Andrew 'Boy', 270
Chataway, Chris, 237, 238
Chelmsford, Lord, 279
children's sport, 261–4
Chinese, discrimination against, 67–8
Chinese gambling games, 67, 75

Chisholm, Caroline, 69–71
Crichton, Ian, 210
chuck-farthing, 65
Churchill, Clive 'Little Master', 36–8, *37*, 186
Clark, Carnegie, 181
Clark, Darren, 211
Clark, Mavis Thorpe, 138
Clark, Sam, 62
Clarke, Ron, **228–30**, 305
Clay, Cassius, 240
clay pigeon shooting, 103
Cleary, Michael, 7
Clover, Harry, 112
Club Mediterranée, 211
clubs, licensed, 78
Cochrane, Mal, 153, 154
cock-fighting, 15, 26, 60–1
Coles, Phil, 49, 221
Collingwood Football Club, 112, 114, 244
Collingwood supporters, 244
Collingwood Tote, 72, 74, 75
Collins, Jim, 252
colours, Australian sporting, 275, 296–7
commentary,
    cricket, 182–4
    football, 186–8
    horse racing, 190–1
commentators, sports, 182–91
Commonwealth Games,
    Brisbane, 271, 285, 289
    effect of politics, 289
    Perth, 271
    see also Empire Games
Confederation of Australian Sport, 271
Conner, Dennis, *290*, 315
Connors, Jimmy, 242
contact sports, 49–53
Coogee RSL Club, 256
Cook, George, 147
Coolangatta Gold, *217*
Cooper, Ashley, 299, 312
Cooper, Bill, 138
Cooper, Bob, 53
Cooper, Lynch, 138
Coote, Ron, 186
Corbett, James J., 32
Corbett, William, 189
Cornell, John, 200–2
Corowa, Larry, 154
Corrigan, Dr Brian, 229
Corris, Peter, 62
corruption, 78–81
Costigan Royal Commission, 78, 81
Cotter, Albert, 278
Coulthard, George, 277
coursing, see greyhound racing
Court, Margaret, 4, 131, 142, *144*, **167**, 312
Cowie, Chick, 37
Cowper, Bob, 7, 202
Crafter, Tony, 47
Crampton, Bruce, 182, 208
Crapp, Lorraine, 167, 306, *307*
Crawley, Helen, 145
cricket, 4–5, 16, 25, **44–7**, 62–3, 103, 104, **108–11**, 127, 133, 200–5, 249, 294, 304
    Aboriginal participation, 133–6
    Bodyline series, 5, 44, 105, 107, 108–9, 279
    captaincy, 230
    clothing, 162, 204
    colours, 296
    commentary, 182–4
    effect of politics, 277–9
    grounds, 270–1, 273

    history, 17
    international incidents, 108–9
    interstate, 226
    losses, 230, 236–7
    media promotion, 182–5
    national team game, 105, 106–7
    night, 202, 203
    one day, 200–4
    overarm bowling, 162–3
    player aggression, 44–7
    promotion of, 109
    school, 263
    selectors, 278–9, 281
    spectator behaviour, 105–6, 108–11, 199
    sponsorship, 202–4, 213
    'synthetic' Tests, 182–4
    television broadcasts, **191–3**, 201
    'throwing in', 235
    tours, 5, 17, 105, 133, 204
        South Africa, 285–9
    venues, 270–1, 272, 273
    wicket condition, 236–7
    women's participation, 162–3
    World Series, see World Series Cricket
cricketers, 226
    injuries, 44
    payment, 200, 202, 204
    South African, 289
crime, organised, 78–81
Cripps, Winsome, 164, 165, 233
Croker, Norma, 308
croquet, 16, 160, *161*
crowd misbehaviour, 45, 49–50, 105, 106, 112, 125–7, 186, 197–8
Cumes, J. W. C., 71
Cunningham, 'Joffa', *10*
Currie, Tony, 154
Curwen, Daisy, 158
Cuthbert, Betty, 165, **166**, 191, 229, 308
Cuzens, 133, 135
cycling, 103, 160, **241**, 302, 308
    dangers, 48
    women's, 173

Daily Mirror (Sydney), 188
Dalgety, 206
Dame Pattie, 209
Dancey, J., 137
danger in sport, 47–9
Daniels, Isabell, 308
Darcy, Les, 12, **268**, 269
D'Arcy, Tony, 150
Darling, Joe, 278
Darling, Sir Ralph, 267
darts, 258
Davidson, Alan, 127
Davis, 136
Davis Cup, 3, 220, 227, 289, 299, **304**, **312**
    professionals in, 251
Davis, Joe, 297
Dawson, Freddie, 34
Dawson, John, 52
De Castella, Robert, *195*, 197, 211, 224
De Courbertin, Pierre, 276, 296
Dead Bird, 189
Dean, Rosalie, 162
deaths, from sport, 35, 36, **48–9**
Delany, Ron, 238, 240
Delta, 49
'Demons', see Melbourne Football Club
Dempsey, Dan, 43
Dench, David, *130*
Dennis, Claire, 163, 302

Desert Gold, 227
Devitt, John, 306, 308
Devlin, Bruce, 304
Dewardt, Jack, 292
Dewart, Peter, 39
Dick-a-Dick, 134
Dimond, Peter, 39
dinghy-racing, 103
Dipierdomenico, Robert, *10*
dirt track, speedway, 297–9
diving, dangers, 48–9
Dixon, George, 32
dog fights, 26, 60
D'Oliveira, 281–2
Dorahy, John, 122
Dowling, Bill, 235
Dowling, Greg, 52
Drobny, Jaroslav, 242
Duckmanton, Alby, 110
Duelling, 15
Dumas, Charlie, 135
Dunn, Lionel, 64
Dunolly, Peter, 138
Dunstan, Don, 138
Dunstan, Keith, 10, 114, **116–17**, 263–4
Durack, Mary, 158
Durack, Sarah 'Fanny', **157–60**, 297
Duran, Roberto, 34, 148
Dyer, Jack 'Captain Blood', **43–4**, 114

earnings, racehorses, 92–3, 96
East, Victor, 181
economic class, effect on sport, **85–6**, 103
Edelsten, Geoffrey, 194
Edenhope Aborigines, 133
Edwards, Vic, 132, 142, 144
'Eels', see Parramatta Rugby League Club
Egan, Phil, 155
Egar, Col, 235
Eisenhower Cup, 289
Elders IXL, 116
Elford, Janelle, 211
Ella brothers, 132
Ella, Gary, 150–1
Ella, Glen, 150–1
Ella, Gordon, 150, 151
Ella, Marcia, 150
Ella, Mark, 150–3, 156
Ella, May, 150
Ella, Steve, 150, *152*, 154
Elliott, Herb, 229, 308–12, *311*
Elliott, John, 116, 117, 206
Emerson, Roy, 299, 312
Emmett, 106
Empire Games,
    Vancouver, 237
    see also Commonwealth Games
emus, hunting, 26, 27
English Channel, swims, 254, 256
English, Des, 117
equality in sport, 178
Eureka Stockade, 3
Evans, Lee, 229
Evert-Lloyd, Chris, 145, 156
Eyston, George, 175

Fairfax, Russel, 150
Falconer, Peter, 125
Famechon, André, 33
Famechon, Johnny, 314
fan-tan, 16, 75
Farmer, Graham 'Polly', 154–5
Farrell, Frank 'Bumper', 36
Farrelly, Bernard 'Midget', 215, *219*

321

Farrington, Frank, 42
Federal government, 271–2
Felton, Elizabeth, 295
Fenech, Jeff 'Marrickville Mauler', 34–6, 54, 55, 240, 316
Fenech, Mario, 54
Ferguson, Adair, 232
Ferguson, John, 154
Fernleas, 162
fighting, 15
  bare-knuckle, 25, 30–1, 60, 62
  see also boxing; wrestling
film, newsreels, 191
Fine Cotton, 56
Finnane, Steve, 52
Fisher, Jack, 232
Fitzgerald Inquiry, 78, 80, 81
Fitzgibbon, Freddie, 10
Fitzroy Football Club, 140
Flack, Edwin H., 23, 164, 211, 229, **296**
Flannery, Frank, 34
Flegg, Harry 'Jersey', 38
Fletcher, Bruce, 92
Fletcher, Jenny, 158
Flintoff, Debbie, *226*
'Flying Pieman', *see* King, William Francis
football, 25, **36–44**, 48, 103, **106**, **111–24**, 125–7, 249, 304
  Aboriginal participation, 140, 150–5
  Australians' attitude to, 2, 6
  changes in attitude to, 263
  cheer squads, 117–18
  commentary, 186–8
  dangers, 48
  effect of success, 230
  grounds, 271, 272–3
  history, 17–20
  interstate rivalry, 123–4
  losses, 243
  male dominance, 173
  marketing practices, 104, 114
  mixed touch, 263
  school, 263
  spectator,
    behaviour, 11, 105, 106, 122
    rivalry, 49, 112–14
  teams,
    image, **186–8**
    purchase, 193
    rivalry, 114, 122
  television broadcasts, 116, 193–4, 205–6
  touch, 263
  tours, 11, 19, 282–5, 288
  venues, 272
  violence, 49–51
  women's participation, 173, *175*
  see also Australian Rules; Rugby League; Rugby Union; Soccer
footballers,
  Aboriginal, 140, 150–5
  image, 193–4
  injuries, 36–9, 41, 42, *43*, 44, 48, 51
  managers for, 197
  violence, 51, 197–8
Ford, Michelle, 170, **170–1**, 281
Forrest, Lisa, *171*, 240
Foster's, sports sponsorship, 206, 209
four-wheel-drive vehicles, 249
fox hunting, 25
Francis, Bruce, 285
Fraser, Dawn, 7, **14**, **85**, **165–6**, 229, 281, 303, 306, 308

Fraser, Malcolm, 116, 170, 266, 271, 285
Fraser, Neale, 299, 312
Freedom in Sport, 285
Freedom Rides, 141
Freshwater (Harbord) club, 128
Frith, David, 136
Fuller, Les, 33
Furnell, Freddie, 137
Fury Ford car sales, 211
'Fuchsias', *see* Melbourne Football Club

Gale, Scott, 154
Gallipoli, 3
gambling, 15, **56–84**
  attitude of religious orders, **69**, 74
  banned, 75–6
  games, 16, 63, 67
  income for governments, 74, 84
  legislation, 75–6
  money lost, 83
  reformers, **74–5**
  turnover, 83
Gammoudi, Mohammed, 228, 229
Gardner, Wayne, *207*, **208**, 220, 319
Garrison, Zina, 145
Gascoine, Stephen Harold 'Yabba', **198**, 199
Gasnier, Reg, 40
Gattelari, Rocky, 240
Gault, Henry 'Pappy', 304
Gaze, Andrew, *124*
General Motors Holden, 213, 219
Gibbs, Ron, 153, 154
Gibson, Christine, 175
Gibson, Fred, 175
Gibson, Mike, 186, 188
gig racing, 15
Gilbert, Eddie, 135, 136
Gilmour, Gary, 45
Giltinan, J. J., 19
Gleneagles Agreement, 285
gliding, 249
Gloaming, 227
Gochel, William H., 214–15
Goggin, Billy, 188
Golden Casket lottery, 77
'Golden Girl', *see* Cuthbert, Betty
Golden Slipper, 206
Golden Whip, 49
golf, 86, 249, 299, 312
  British Open winners, 312
  clubs, 163
  media promotion, 179–81
  sexual discrimination, 163, 178
golfers, 171, 179–82, 299
  earnings, 179, 182
  mistakes, 235–6
  South African, 289
  women, 163
Gomez, Gerry, 125
Gonzales, Pancho, 220
Goolagong, Evonne, 4, 103, 131, **142–5**, 156, **168**
Gould, Nat, 189
Gould, Shane, 168, 312
governments,
  funding of sport, 266, 271–5
  income from gambling, 74, 84
Governor, South Australia, 141
Grace, Dr William G., 5, 44, 106
Graham, David, 182, 312
Grahame, Carole, 254
Grand Prix race, 175, 209

Australia, 217, 219
Grand Prix sailing, 208–9
Grant, Rob, 181
grass fights, *see* bare-knuckle fights
grass skiing, 249, 251
Graves, Johny 'Whacker', 36
Gray, Edgar 'Dunc', 302
Great Cricket Hijack, 191, **200–4**
'Great White Shark', *see* Norman, Greg
'green and gold', 296–7
Green, Dick, 292
Green, Jackie, 147
Greensborough Gift, 138
Gregory, Dave, 17
Greig, Tony, 200, **202**
Gretel, 201, 209
greyhound racing, 25, 28, 29, **91–2**
  commentary, 191
  crime and, 80
  venues, 273
Griffiths, Albert 'Young Griffo', 30–2
Grime, Billy, 147
gymnastics, school, 263

Haden, Andy, 5
Hadlee, Richard, 109–10
Hagen, Walter, 299
Hagler, Marvin, 206
Haitana, Haydon, 56
Hall, Dr, 215
Hambly, Brian, 40
Hamilton, Robyn, 175
Hammond, Ernie, 33
handball, 22
hand-to-hand combat, 24
hang-gliding, **47–8**, 251
Hanna, Frank, 44
Hannan, Graham, 179
Hanson, Ian, 127–9
Harada, 'Fighting', 131
Hardy, Jeff, 154
Harmer, Elmer, 18
Harris, George, 116
Harris, Lord, 105, 106, 277
Harrison, Henry, 18
Hasenjager, Daphne, 164
Hassen, Jack, **33–4**, 147
Hawke, R. J., 11, 36, 111, 271, 272, 275, 288, 289, *290*, 291
Hawthorn Football Club, 117, 118
Hayes, Colin, 172
Hayman, William, 133
Head-of-the-River, 127
Hearns, Thomas, 206
Hendry, Hunter 'Stork', 214
Henley Royal Regatta, 14
Henricks, Jon, 306
Henry, Albert 'Alec', 135
Higgins, Roy, 99, 171–2
Hill, Clem, *276*, 278, 279
Hill, Wendell, 136
Hill, William, 268
Hilton, Joseph, 62
Hoad, Lew, 220, 221, 223, 242, 299, *301*, 312
Hobbs, Jack, 199
hockey, **240–1**
  dangers, 48
  school, 263
Hogan, Paul, 200, 201, 291
Hollies, Eric, 233
Holmes, Larry, 206
Holt, Harold, 12
Hooker, Halford, 184
Hookes, David, 200
Hope, Lew, 137

Hopkins, Johnny, 299
Hopman, Harry, 167, *300*
Horder, Harold, 186
horse-racing, **13**, 15, **59–61**, **92–9**, 103, 160, 171-2
  betting, 72–7
  clubs, 97–8
  commentary, 190–1
  crime and, 80
  dangers, 48, 49
  France, 49
  prize-money, 92–3
  radio broadcasts, 190
  sponsorship, 206
  trainers, 172
horse-riding, 160
Horton, Peter, 52
hot air ballooning, *48*, 249
Hotham Handicap, 206
housie-housie, *see* bingo
Howard, Ken 'Magic Eye', 190–1
Howland, Sue, 49
Hudson, Peter, 10
Hughes, Kim, **230**, *231*, 285
Hunt, Bill, 136
Hunt, Geoff, 168, 314
Hunter, Johnny, 36
hunting, **15**, 16, 103
  emus, 26, 27
  fox, 25
  kangaroo, 25, 26
  koala, **26**
  rabbits, 26, 27
  wallaby, 25
  see also shooting
Hutchens, Harry, 137
Huxley, Vic, 299
Hyperion Thoroughbreds, 99

Idison, Roger, 17
Illingworth, Ray, 105, **109**
Impetuous, 314
Indianapolis 500, 195
Innes, Neil, 170
Institute of Sport, *see* Australian Institute of Sport
International Cricket Conference, 204
International Management Group (IMG), 179, 196
International Olympic Committee, 240
international rivalry in sport, 105, 106, 109
interstate football, 123
interstate rivalry in sport, 105, 106
Iredale, Frank, 278
iron man event, 127, 215
Ivanov, Vyacheslav, 304

Jackson, Eddie, 155
Jackson, Marjorie, 'Lithgow Flash', **89–90**, 163, 233, 308
Jackson, Mark, *196*, 197
Jackson, Syd, 155
James, Glenn, 155
James Hardie 1000, 195
James, Thomas, 140
Jardine, Douglas, 44, *107*, 108–9, 279
Jarvis, Pat, 34, 35
javelin throwing, 49
Jazy, Michel, 309
Jeans, Alan, *116*
Jenner, Terry, 109
Jerome, 147
Jim Crow, 135
jockeys, 94, 99–102
  Aboriginal, 156
  professional, 254

Index

training school, 102
women, 171–2
Joe the Basket Maker, *see*
   Hilton, Joseph
Johns, Les, 154
Johnson, Bert, 155
Johnson, Ian, 235
Johnson, Jack, **32–3**
Johnson, Ron, 299
Johnston, Bill, 45
Johnston, Craig, *21*
Johnston, Verna, 165, 233
Johnstone, Billy, 53
Jolson, Al, 157
Jones, Alan, 151, 219, 220, 230
Jones, Ernie 'Jonah', 44
Jones, Fred, 38
Jorrocks, 60
Judkins, William Henry, 69, **74**, 76
Junius, 60

Kable, John, 62
Kadron, 209
Kahanamakou, Duke, 128, 215
kangaroo hunting, 25, 26
Kangaroos, Australian Rugby
   League Team, 39–40
Karasick, Al, 191
Kearney, Clayton, 211, 215
Keenan, Peter 'Crackers', 130
Keino, Kip, 228
Kellerman, Annette, **157**
Kelleway, 279
Kelloggs NutriGrain, 211
Kelly, Jim, 30
Kelly, Ned, 3, *24*, 30
Kemp, Archie, **33**
Kenny, Grant, 127, *182*, 211, 215
Kenny, Hayden, 215
Kensai, 13
King, Billie Jean, 4, 145
King Cole, 135
King, Ian, 135
King, William Francis 'Flying
   Pieman', 62, *63*
King's Prize, 294
Kings School, 127
Kingsmill, Fred, 138
Kinnear, Bobby, 137
Kirkwood, Joe, 299
koalas, shooting, 26, 28
Konrads, Ilsa, 167, 302–4
Konrads, John, 302–4
Kookaburra syndicate, 209, 210
Kooyong, 3
Kosmina, John, **127**
Kostadinova, Stefka, 176
Krakouer brothers, 155
Kramer, Jack, 220, 221, 251
Kuts, Vladimir, 308

La Perouse, 3
La Trobe, Governor, 271
Laker, Jim, 236, 237
Landy, John, 237–8, *239*
Lane, Frederick C. V., 296
Lang, Jack, 91
Lang, John Dunmore, 60, 69
Langlands, Graeme, 42, 154
Larkspur, 49
Larwood, Harold, 5, 44, 45, *107*, 108–9, 297
Lasch, Christopher, 206
Laver, Frank, 278, 279
Laver, Rod, 243, 299, 312
Lavigne, Kid, 32
lawn bowls,
   numbers participating, 246, 247–8

school, 263
Lawrence, Charles, 133, 135
Lawson, Henry, 55
Lazarus, Ted, 137
Le Mans, Australian
   participation, 175
Lee, Dick, 112
Leech, Faith, 306
Leech, Guy, 127, *128*, 215–16, *216*
legalisation of two-up, 65
Lendl, Ivan, 206, 208
Les Edwards Transport, 211
Lesnevitch, Gus, 147
Lewis, Carl, 206
Lewis, Chris, 155
Lewis, Johnny, 35
Lewis, Wally, *42*, 105, **123–4**, 150, 197
Lexcen, Ben, 111
Liberty, 1, 315
Liddiard, David, 154
lifesaving, *see* surf lifesaving
Light Car Clubs, 217
Lillee, Dennis, 5, 14, 23, **45–7**, 200, 202, 230
Lillywhite, James, 17, 105, 294
Lindrum, Fred, 252
Lindrum, Walter, **252–4**, 297
Lindsay, Norman, 68, 69
Lindwall, Ray, 45
Lithgow, 164
'Lithgow Flash'/'Lithgow Flyer',
   see Jackson, Marjorie
'Little Master', *see* Churchill, Clive
Little Willie, 138
Langham, Nat, 30, *31*
losers,
   Australians' attitude to, **224–43**
   legendary, 3
lotteries, 66–7, 78
lotto, 78
Louis, Spyros, 211
Lovett, Wally, 155
Lucky Seven, 49
Lukin, Dean, *225*
Lyndon, Marie, 171
Lyons, Cliff, 153, 154
Lyons, Joe, 279

Macartney, 278
MacCallum, Mungo 264–5
Macdougall, Stuart, 52
Mackenzie, Stuart, 14, 302–3
MacKinlay, Louise, 173
Mackintosh, Donald, 211
Macky, Dill, 75
Macquarie, Lachlan, 60
Madigan, Tony, **240**, *241*
'Magic Eye', *see* Howard, Ken
Magic Million, 206
'Magpies' (Australian Rules),
   see Collingwood Football Club
'Magpies' (Rugby League), *see*
   Western Suburbs Rugby
   League Club
Makaha International, 216
male dominated sports, 173
Malone, Tom, 137
managers, sportspeople, 196–7, 200
Manly-Warringah Rugby League
   club 'silver tails', 121, 122, **186**
Mann, Professor Leon, 50
'Manuello', 137
marathon, 13, **62–3**, 195, 256–8
   swimming, 254

women's participation, 176
Marble Bar, 67
Marchant, Tony, 308
Marconi, 190
Maroubra Seals Club, 256
'Marrickville Mauler', *see*
   Fenech, Jeff
Marsden, Samuel, 57
Marsh, Jack, **135–6**, 138
Marsh, Larry, 138
Marsh, Rod, 14, *46*, 200, 230
Marshall (cricketer), 106
Marshall, Fran, 167
martial arts, 16
Martin, Lisa, 176
Martin, 'Plugger' Bill, 213
Martinez, Juan, 229
Marylebone Cricket Club, 163, 279
Masters, Roy, 41, 51, 122, 186
Mathews, Marlene, *166*, 167, 281, 308
'Matilda', 319
Matthews (cricketer), 278
Matthews, Ken, 91
Matthews, Leigh, 51
Maynard, Michael, 135
McAlister, Peter, **276–7**, 278
McAuliffe, Jack, 31, 32
MCC, *see* Marylebone Cricket
   Club
McCance, Norman, **191**
McCarthy, Bob, 38
McCarthy, Richard Laurence
   (Darby), 99–102, 103, **156**
McCormack, Mark, 196
McCosker, Rick, 44
McDermott, Lloyd, 153
McDonald, Bobby, 137, 138
McDonald, F. A., 270
McDonald, Ian, 256
McDonald, Norm, 155
McEnroe, John, 221
McGilvray, Alan, 136, 182–4, *185*, 236
McGowan, J. S. T., 279
McGregor, Ken, 299
McGrowdie, Noel, 49
McIntosh, Hugh D., 33, **189–90**
McKay, Heather, **167–8**, 227, 314
McKechnie, Brian, 5
McKell, William, 267–8
McLaren's boxing saloon, *25*
McLeod, Ian, 216
McLeod, Tom, 137
McMahon, William, 282
McNulty, Andrew, 87
McQuillan, Ernie, 33
Meade, Nathan, 48–9
Meads, Colin 'Pinetree', 52
Meckiff, Ian, 233, 235
media,
   cricket in, 182, 184
   effect on sport, 163
   golf in, 182
   promotion of sportspeople, **179–99**
Melbourne Cricket Club, 111, 114, 271
Melbourne Cricket Ground, 3, 17
Melbourne Cup, 6, **13**, 49, **56**, 66, 72, **93–4**, 191, 206, 209
Melbourne Football Club, 111, 112, 114
Melbourne, importance of sport
   in, 2–3
Mellor, Fleur, 308
Melrose, Tony, 150
Melvile, Lachie, 190
Meninga, Mal, 153, 154

Menzies, Sir Robert, 11, 271, *272*
Mercedes III, 312
Mercer, Darren, 215
Merriman, Bob, 230
Messenger, Dally, 19
Miandad, Javed, 14, 47
Michael Edgley International, 209
Mighty Keys, 98
mile, four minutes broken, 237
Miles, Tom, 138
Miller, Keith, 45
Miller, Tony, 36
Miller, Walter, 191
Mills, Billy, 228
Minnett, *278*, 279
Mize, Larry, 316
Mockridge, Russell, 241, *242*
Moffitt Royal Commission, 78
Monaghan, Jim, 164
Monash University, 10
Monckton, John, 306
Montane, Pierre, 33
Moore, Archie, 147
Moore, George, 49
Moore, Maxie, 31
Moran, Cardinal, 75
Mordey, Bill, 36
Morgan, Lionel, 154
Morgan, Sandra 306
Moriarty, John, 141
Moses, Charles, 184
'Mosquito', 135
Moss, Stirling, 217
Mossop, Rex, **186**, 199
motor cycle racing, 297–9
motor racing, 219, 304
   Grand Prix, 273
   professional, 254
   women's participation, 175
motorboat racing, 249
Mottley, Peter, 117
Mould, Geoff, 150
Mount Panorama, racing circuit, 217
Mouraouskas, 240
Moyes, Bill, 47, 251
Moyes, Johnnie, 279
Mugford, Dr Stephen, 49–50
Muir, Barry, **40**, 123
Mullagh, 133, **135**
Mullins, Barney, 129
Mundine, Tony, 148
municipal councils, 271
Murdoch, Billy, 277
Murdoch (cricketer), 106
Murdoch, Rupert, 192
Murphy, Alex, 40
Murphy, Billy 'Torpedo', 31
Murphy, Chris, 81
Murray, Iain, *313*
Myocard, 97

Nagle, Kel, 182, 235–6, 304, 312
Nappy's Two-Up Game, 64–5
Narke, Phil, 155
Nathan's Cow Paddock, 186
National Aborigines Week, 154
National Basketball League, **125**
National Fitness Council, 271
national identity in sport, 291–319
National Soccer League, 50, 125
National Tennis Centre, 3, 273
native animals, hunted for sport, 25, 26, 27
Navratilova, Martina, 145
Nelson, Peter, 165
netball, 15, **176–8**
   numbers participating, 244
   school, 263

323

New South Wales Amateur Athletic Association, 160
New South Wales government, 272
New South Wales Rugby League, 19
New South Wales, state lottery, 77
New Zealand, as sporting nation, 55
Newcombe, John, 196, 242, 299, 312
Newtown Police Boys' Club, 35
Nicholls, Dowie (Herbert), 138
Nicholls, Sir Douglas, 103, 132, **138–41**, 155
Nicholls, Wally, 138
night surfing, 216
Nike, 209
Nile, Rev. Fred, 82–3
Noble, M. A., 184
'Norm', 224
Norman, Decima, 163
Norman, Greg, **179–81**, 196, 208, 224, 288, 291, 316
Norman, Laura, 181
Norman, Morgan-Leigh, 181
North Melbourne Football Club, 116
Northcote Football Club, 140
Northumberland, 59
Norton, Hughes, 181
Norton, John, 68, 74
NutriGrain, 215
Nyah Gift, 140

Oakes, Frank, 145, 146
Oakes, Jenny, 146
ocean-racing, 103
O'Connell, Maurice, 59
O'Connor, Christy, 236
O'Connor, Michael, 150
off-course betting, **72–7**
off-road four-wheel-driving, 249, 251
O'Hagan, Jack, 213
O'Halloran, Kevin, 306
O'Hara, John, 57–8, 82
Old Trafford Test (1956), 236
Oldfield, Bert, 44, 108
Oller, Pierre, 75
Ollington, 'Nappy', 64–5
Olsen, Larry, 13
Olson, Carl (Bobo), 148
Olympic Games, ancient, 24
  Australian gold medallists, 296
  Australian participation, 22, 268–70, 296–7, 301–4, 305, 312
  boycotts, 170, 276–7, 281
  competitors, amateur status, 213
  competitors, payment, 213
  effect of politics, 266, 275–7
  funding, 270
  medals won, 312
  sponsorship, 221
  swimming events, 158
Olympic Games, Athens, 1896, 22, 296
  Berlin, 1936, 275
  Helsinki, 1952, 164, 233
  London, 1908, 213
  Los Angeles, 1932, 302
  Los Angeles, 1984, 192
  Melbourne, 1956, 191, 238, **277**, **303–9**
  Mexico City, 1968, 238, **277**
  Montreal, 1976, 233, 271
  Moscow, 1980, 170–1, 214, 265, 272, **275–7**
  Munich, 1972, 168–70, **275**
  Paris, 1900, 296
  Rome, 1960, 309
  Seoul, 1988, 192, 213, 221
  Stockholm, 1912, 158, 213, 297
'one-armed bandit', see poker machines
O'Neill, Pam, *172*
Opperman, Sir Hubert, 7
O'Reilly, Bill, 191
organised crime, **78–81**
orienteering, 249
Osaka International Women's Marathon, 176
overarm bowling, 162–3
Oxford, Aub, 52

Packer, Jamie, 87
Packer, Kerry, 13, 45, *87*, 109, 182, 191, **200–4**, 230
Packer, Sir Frank, 111, 201, 209
Pails, Dinny, 251
pak-a-pu, 75
Palestinian guerillas, 275
Palmer, Bill, 125
pankration, 24
parachuting, 47, 48, 249
parents, attitude to children's sport, 261–3
Parkes, Georgina, 240
Parramatta Rugby League Club, 121, **122**
Parry Corporation, 210
Parton, John, 62
Patrick, Vic, 33
Patterson, Gerald, 299
Payakarun, Samart, *35*, 36
Payne, John, 211
Peake, Brian, 155
Pearce, Henry 'Bobby', 302
Peardon, Derek, 155
Pert, Gary, *9*
'pedestrian' running, see sprinting
pentathlon, 24
Penton, Neville, 59
Perkins, Charles, 132, **141–2**, 156
Perpetual Motion, 122
Peter, 135
Pezzano, Tony, 125
'Phantom Puncher', 52
Phar Lap, **12–13**, 60
Pickworth, Ossie, 182
pigeon-racing, 103
Piper, John, 291
Plumb, J. H., 58
Poidevin, Dr Leslie, 296
Poidevin, Simon, **213–14**
poker machines, **78**
'pokies', see poker machines
Police Car, 314
politicians' sports, 11
politics,
  effect on cricket, 277–9
  on Olympic Games, 275–7
  on sport, 266
polo, **86–9**, 103
polo-crosse, *88*
Ponsinet, Edouard, 37
Pooley, 294
Porta, Hugo, 231
Powerplay, 210
press, promotion of sportspeople, **185–6**
Price, Ben, 122
Price, Chris, 122
Price, Graham, 52
Price, Ray, 20, 52, *53*, 104, 122
prime ministers and sport, 11
Pritchard, Bob, 194
prize-money,
  greyhound racing, 92–3
  horse racing, 92–3
prizefighting, see boxing, fighting, bare-knuckle fighting
professionalism in sport, 251–65
Progress Party, 116
Prokopov, Valentine, 277
promotions,
  and sportspeople, 143, 179, 196, 206–8
  football oriented, 104, 114
Protestants, attitude to gambling, 69, 74
Publishing Broadcasting Ltd, 109, 202
Puckeridge, Richard, 61
punters, 96

Queensland Amateur Athletics Association, 137
Queensland government, 273
Quist, Adrian, 299

'Rabbitohs', see South Sydney Rugby League Club
rabbits,
  as lures, 25
  hunting, 26, *27*
race (horse) callers, see horse racing, commentary
Racecam camera, **195**
racecourses, 59, 96–7, 267–8
race-fixing, 80
racehorse syndication, 98–9
racetracks, 59
racial discrimination, 67–8, 141–2
radio,
  cricket commentary, **182–4**
  sports reporting, **190–1**
Ragamuffin, 314
Rail, Vic, 95, 98
Randwick Racecourse, *93*
Ransford, Vernon, 278
Ransom, Sue, 175
Raper, Caryl, 38
Raper, Johnny, **38–40**, 243
ratting, 15
Raudonikis, Tom 'Tom Terrific', **41–2**
Rawson Stakes, 227
Rayner, Jack, 37
'rebel' cricket tour, 285
'Red Cap', 135
Redfern Oval, 186
Redzepovski, Redzep, 35
Referee, **189–90**
Reilly, Elkin, 155
religions, attitude to gambling, 57, **69**, 74
Renford, Des, **254–6**
Rennie, Jack, 146
Rennie, Shirley, 146
Richards, Lou, **186–7**
Richards, Mark, 215, 217
Richards, Ron, **147–8**
Richardson, Vic, 184
Richmond, Joan, 175, *177*
Richtzenhain, 238
Ricoh cameras, 213
rifle-shooting, 294–5
Rioli, Maurice, 155
Ritchie brothers, 148
rivalry in sport, 105–12
Roach, Michael, *115*

Roberts, Paul, 154
Robertson, Austin, 138, **200–2**
Robertson, Denise, 233
Robinson, Edie, 160
Robinson, Elizabeth, 160
Robinson, Ray, 278
Robinson, 'Sugar Ray', 148
Roche, Chris, 150
Roche, Tony, **242–3**
rock-climbers, 249
Rocks Push, 31
Ron Barassi Memorial Lecture, 10
Rorke, Gordon, 235
Rose, 306, 308
Rose, Lionel, 102, 131, **145–6**, 148, 314
Rose, Murray, 281, 306, *307*
Rosewall, Ken, **220–1**, **241–2**, 299, *301*
Rowan, Lou, 109
rowing, 15, *16*, 103, 127, 291–4, 302–3
Rowland-Smith, Rob, 127
Royal Commissions into crime and corruption, 78, 80–1
Royal Easter Show, 146
Royal Life Saving Society, 271
Rozsavolgyi, Istvan, 309
Ruehl, Peter, 209
Rugby League football, 4, **36–42**, 48, 49, 51, 52, 54, 103, 104, 105, 106
  Aboriginal participants, 150, 153–4
  clubs, rivalry, 121, **122–3**
  coaching, 243
  colours, 296
  effect of media, 186
  Grand Final, 11
  history, 19, 121
  interstate rivalry, 123–4
  rule changes, 205
  television broadcast, 193
  violence, 197
Rugby Union football, 10, 18, 48, 51, 52, 103, 106, 121, 127, 288, 297
  Aboriginal participants, **150–3**
  colours, 296
  South Africans' attitude to results, 4
  sponsorship, 213
  Springbok tour, 282–5
  supporters, 121
running,
  history, 22
  the marathon, 13, 62–3, 176, 195, 254, 256–8
Runyon, Damon, 190
Ryan, Dinny, 140
Ryan, Warren, 122

Saddler, Ron, 154
Sadler, Joseph H., 292
sailboards, 249
sailing,
  school, 263
  sponsorship, 208–9
Samuels, Charlie, **137–8**
Sands, Alfie, 148
Sands, Clem, 148
Sands, Dave, 34, 145, 148, *149*
Sands, George, 148
Sands, Ritchie, 148
Sands, Russell, 148
Sands, Russell Jnr, 148
Sangster, Robert, 13
Sargeant, Anne, 176, *178*
Sattler, John, 38, 53, 186

324

Schlam, Sig, 299
Scholl, Eric, 182
school sport, 127, 263
Scott, Colin, 154
Scott, Lady Margaret, 181
Scott, Michael, 181
scrum, dangers, 48
sculling, 291–4, *see also* rowing
Searle, Henry, 294
'Seaweed Streak', *see* Rose, Murray
Sedgman, Frank, 167, 299
Seed, Mary, 175
Sefton, Charles, 62
selectors, 278–9, 281
Sellers, Basil, 209
Sellwood, Neville, **49**
Seven Network, 210
sexual discrimination in sport, 158–9, 160, 178
Shark Attack: Greg Norman's Guide to Aggressive Golf, 179
Sharman, Jimmy, 33, 34, 140, 146, *148*
Shaw, Jack, 91
Shaw, Paul, 153
Shearer, Dale, 153, **154**
Sheehan, Danny, 65–6
Sheffield Shield, 106, 226
Sheldon, Ken, 244
Shepherd, W., 135
shooting, 16
  kangaroo, 25
  koala, 26, 28
  wallaby, 25
Sibthorpe, Richard, 256–8, *259*
Sieben, Jon, 211
Silchev, 240
Simms, Eric, 154
Sinatra, Frank, 100
Sinclair Hill, **87–8**, 89
Siroccos, 162
Sjoberg, Patrik, 176
Sjolin, 240
skateboarding, 249
skiing, grass, *see* grass skiing
skiing, water, *see* water skiing
Skilton, Bobby, *194*
Sky Channel, 13, 190
sky diving, 249
Slack, Andrew, 153, 214
Slater, 'Long Harry', 79
Small, Ken, 125
Smallhorn, 'Chicken', 140
Smith, Dr L. L., 70
Smith, Jonathon, 30
Smith, Sydney, 278, 279
Smith, Tommie, 229, 275
snooker, 200
Snow, John, **109**
Sobers, Gary, 271
soccer, 16, 20–1, 49–51, *49*, 80, 103, **125–7**, 224
  Aboriginal participation, 141–2
  clubs, **125**
  crowd misbehaviour, 105
  dangers, 48
  history, 20
  South Americans' attitude to results, 4
  spectator behaviour, 125–7
  spectator violence, 49
social class, effect on sport, **85–6**, 103
Songkitrat, Chamrern, 304
Soper, Marshall, 50, 125
Sopwith, Sir Thomas Octave Murdoch, 211
South Africa,
  banned from international sport, 285
  effect of apartheid on sport, 281–9, *286*
South Australia, 210
South Australian government, 272
South Sydney Rugby League Club 'Rabbitohs', 36, 38, 121, **186**
South Sydney Union League Club, 78
SP betting, 78–9
Spanja, Rocco, 34
Sparkes, Bill, 30, *31*
Spear Chief, 227
spear,
  fishing, dangers, 48
  throwing, 134
Spearfelt, 73
spectators,
  behaviour, 105, 109–10, 122, 125–7
  football, 11
  violence, 45, 49–50, 197–9
speedway, 103
Spiers and Pond, 5, 204
Spinks, Charlie, 299
sponsorship of sport, 5, 7, 200–3
  school sports, 263
  see also advertising
sport,
  administration, 261
  agents, 196–7, 200
  amateur participation, 261
  as entertainment, 202–4
  Australian tribalism, 104–12
  Australians' attitude, **1–22**, 224–6
  betting and, 56–63
  bribery in, 214
  broadcasting rights, 192, 200–2, 204, 206
  champions, 224–43
  children's, 261–4
  clothing, 7, 204, 205–6
  clubs, 104–5
  colours, Australian, 275, 296–7
  commentators, 182–91
  commentators, phrases used, 190–1
  dangerous, 47–9
  early Australian, **15–16**, 25
  effect of economic class, **85–6**, 103
  effect of government funding, 315
  effect of politics, 170, 266, 275–7, 277–9, 314
  effect of social class, **85–6**, 103
  equality in, 178
  facilities, 270–3
  for women, 16
  government funding, 266, 271–5
  history in Australia, 15
  importance in Melbourne, 2–3
  international rivalry, 105, 106
  interstate rivalry, 105, 106
  journalism, 187–91
  journals, **189**
  male domination, 173
  national identity, 291–319
  numbers participating, 244
  prime ministerial, 11
  professionals, 251–65
  promoters, earnings, 189
  schools and, 127, 263
  sex discrimination, 263
  sponsorship, 7, **200–23**, 263
  types available, 249
  violence, 193, 197–9
Sportsman, 189
sportspeople,
  attitude of Australian public, 315–19
  becoming politicians, 7
  commercial endorsements, 143, 179, 196, 206–8
  earnings, 14–15, **179**, 206–8
  image, 179–81
sportswomen, **157–78**
Springbok Rugby Union, 282–5
Springbok tour, 283, *297*
sprinting, 24, **228–30**, 233, 237–40
  1500 metres, 238
  Aboriginal participation, 133, 137–8
  history, 22
  losses, 233
  one mile, 237
  professional, 137–8
  starting techniques, 137
  women's participation, **163–5**
  see also athletics
squash, 314
  dangers, 48
  players, 227
  women's participation, 167
St George Rugby League team, 38, 304
St Josephs, 127
St Martin, Yves, 49
Stackpole, Keith, 233
Stars and Stripes, 211
State-of-Origin matches, 53, 123–4, 193, 197, 226
Stawell Gift, **23**, 137, 138
Steak 'n' Kidney, 210
'Steel Cat', *see* Farmer, Graham
steeplechases, 16
Stenhouse, Tommy, 33
Stephen, P. J., 74
Stephenson, H. H., 5, 17, 105, 133, 270
Stephenson, Jan, **171**, *172*
Steve, Ginger, 186
Stevens, Bob, 304
Stewart, Bruce 'Larpa', 150
Stewart Royal Commission, 80
Stoddart, Brian, 85–6
Stokes, Henry, 79
Strickland, Shirley, 163, 164, 233, 308
Stubnick, Christa, 308
sugar industry, 211
Sullivan, Mike, 39
Sun (Sydney), 188
Sundown, 135
Surf Life Saving Associations, 175, 271
surf lifesaving, 173–5, *176, 177*, **214–15**
  clubs, **127–9**
surf sports, 127, **215–17**
  rivalry in, 128
Sviridov, Nikolay, 229
Swan Brewery, sports sponsorship, 206, 208
Swanettes, *118*, **194**
sweepstakes, 66–7, 75
swimmers, 157–60, 165, 168
  South African, 289
  women, 157–60
swimming, 15, 22, 157–60, 249, 281, 297, 302–4
  long distance, **157**
  marathon, 254
officials, 158
Olympics, 240
school, 263
surf, 215–17
women's participation, 175
Swindell, Frederick, 91
Sydney City soccer club, 50
Sydney Cricket Ground, 3, 202, *203*, 270–1, 273
Sydney Olympic soccer club, 50
Sydney Opera House, 77
Sydney Rifle Club, 294
Sydney Swans Football Club, 118, 194
Sydney to Hobart, 111
Sydney Turf Club, **267–8**

TAB, *see* Totalisator Agency Board
tackle (football),
  dangers, 48
  spear, 49
Tamati, Kevin, 52
Tattersall's lottery, 66–7, 74
Tattslotto, 67, 78
Tatz, Colin, 132, 184, 283
taxes on betting, 96
Taylor, Joe, 80
Taylor, Lynton, 184
Taylor, 'Squizzy', 79
television,
  advertising, 193, 206
  and violence, 49
  Channel Nine, **184**, 191, 201
  Channel Seven, 195, 206
  Channel Ten, 186
  cricket broadcasts, **184–5**
  effect on attendances, 6
  effect on spectators' attitudes, 6
  effect on sport, 200–2, 221
  golf broadcasts, 182
  sport broadcasts, **184–5**, **191–7**, 200–2, 204, 205–6
Temu, Naftali, 228, 229
tennis, 20, 160, 220–1, 249, 304, **312**
  Aboriginal participation, 131–2, **142–5**
  Australian Open, 206
  Australians' attitude to results, 4
  Grand Slam, 167
  losses, 241
  players, 227, 299
    earnings, 220–1
    South African, 289
  professional, 220–1, 251
  sponsorship, 220–1
  television broadcasts, 205–6
  venues, 3, 273
  Wimbledon champions, 312
Test and County Cricket Board, 204
Theile, David, 306, 308
Thomas, Joe, 64
Thommo's Two-Up school, 64, *65*, 74
Thompson, Duncan, 40
Thompson, Eddie, 125
Thompson, Hector, **34**, 148
Thomson, Jeff, 5, *45*, *46*, 47
Thomson, Peter, 182, 299, 304, 312
Thornett, Dick, *287*
Thornett, John, *287*
Thornett, Ken, 154
thoroughbred racing, *see* horse racing
Thorpe, Jimmy, 213
Tiger, 135

325

tobacco industry, sports sponsorship, 208, 214
Todman, 49
Tollis, Mickey, 34
'Tom Terrific', see Raudonikis, Tom
Tom Wills, 17
Toogood, Peter, 304
Tooheys, sports sponsorship, 206, 213
Toparoa, 49
totalisator, 75
Totalisator Agency Board (TAB), 77, 96
touch football, 173
Toweel, Vic, 304
track and field, see athletics
trail bikes, 249
Traill, Ken, 52
trainers, horse, 94
trampolining, school, 263
triathlon, women's participation, 172–3
tribalism, in Australian sport, 104–12
Trickett, Edward, 292
Trimbole, Robert, 80
trotting, 75
  crime in, 80
Trumper, Victor, 135, 278
Truth, 189
Tuck, Michael, 118, *130*
Tulloch, 49, *96*
Turnbull, Wendy, 254
Turner, Ian, 10
Turpin, Dick (Randolph), 148
Tutty, Dennis, 121
Twopenny, 135
two-up, **63–6**, 75

Ulyett, 103
Underwood, Derek, 202
'Up there Cazaly!', 112–13

Van Praag, Lionel, 299
Vanderbilt, Harold, 211
Varley, Henry, 72
vice and gambling, **78–81**
Victoria Golf Club, 304
Victorian Football Association, 140
  history, 111–12
Victorian Football League (VFL), **8–11**, 43–4, 106, 193, 208
  clubs, 104
  Grand Final, 10, 11, 43, 244
  history, 111–19
  players' earnings, 254
  rule changes, 205
Victorian government, 273
Victorian Racing Club, sponsorship, 206
Victorian Rules, 18
Vinnicombe, Martin, 211, *212*
vintage motor racing, 103
violence in sport, 47, 49–50, 193, 197–9
Vo Rogue, *95*, 98
Voce, Bill, 5, 44, 297
volleyball, 103
Von Halmay, Zoltan, 296
Von Nida, Norman, 182

Waern, Dan, 309
Walasiewicz, Stanislawa, 164–5
Walker, Max, 45
Wallabies (football team), 150
wallaby hunting, 25
Wallis, Joe, 33
Walsh, Terry, 241
Walters, Doug, *202*
Ward, Russel, 56
Warracknabeal Gift, 138, 140
Warren, Mark, 127
water polo, 174, 238
water skiing, 249
Waterman, 136

Weeks, Martin, 261
Weir, Ike, 31
Wells, Debbie, 233
Wells, Harry, 40, 52
West Indies, 271
West, Yvonne, 167
Western Australian Cricket Association, 273
Western Australian government, 273
Western Suburbs Rugby League Club, 6, 41, **122**
Whitehead, Max, 186
Whitehead, Peter, 220
Whitney, Michael, 150
Whitty, 278
Wickham, Tracey, **170**, *171*, 214
Widerberg, Bill, 209
Wilburn, Chuck, 34
Wilding, Anthony, 299
Willesee, Mike, 13
Williams, Esther, 157
Williams, Harry, 141, 182
Williamson, Lionel, 154
Willis, Bob, 44
Wills, Christina, 163
Wills, Thomas Wentworth, 133
Wilmot, R. W. E., 188–9
Wilson, Barbara, 233
Wimbledon, 4, 131, 142, 144, 145, 206
Winfield Cup, 154, 214
Winmar, Nicky, 155
winning, Australians' attitude to, 1, 3, 14, **224–43**
Wintle, George, 78
Without Fear or Favour, 80–1
Wolde, Mamo, 229
women in Olympic events, **158**, 160
women in sport, **157–78**
Women's Cricket Association, 162

Woodcock, Tommy, 13
Woodfull, Bill, 44, 297
Woodward, Jack, 91–2
Woolworths, 210
World Cup (golf), 304
World Cup (soccer), 20
World Masters Snooker, 200
'World of Sport', 187
World Series Cricket, 15, 45, 109, **184**, **191–2**, **200–4**, 230
  clothing, 7
'wowser', 68, 74–5
Wran, Neville, 79
Wren, John, 69, 72, **74–5**, 112
Wrest Point, 80
wrestling, 16, 22, 25, 103
Wright, Ken, 150
Wright, 'Wild', 30
W. S. Cox Plate, 228
WSC, see World Series Cricket
Wylie, Wilhelmina 'Mina', 158–9

'Yabba', see Gascoine, Stephen Harold
yachting, 16, 103, **111**, 225, 312, 315–16
  Admiral's Cup winners, 312
  sponsorship, 209–11
  see also America's Cup
Yamanaka, Tsuyoshi, 306
Young, Cliff, 13, 14
Young, Craig, 51
'Young Griffo', see Griffiths, Albert

Zador, Ervin, 277
Zatopek, Emil, **228**